Sound Communities in the Asia Pacific

Sound Communities in the Asia Pacific

Music, Media, and Technology

Edited by
Lonán Ó Briain and Min Yen Ong

BLOOMSBURY ACADEMIC
NEW YORK • LONDON • OXFORD • NEW DELHI • SYDNEY

BLOOMSBURY ACADEMIC
Bloomsbury Publishing Inc
1385 Broadway, New York, NY 10018, USA
50 Bedford Square, London, WC1B 3DP, UK
29 Earlsfort Terrace, Dublin 2, Ireland

BLOOMSBURY, BLOOMSBURY ACADEMIC and the Diana logo are
trademarks of Bloomsbury Publishing Plc

First published in the United States of America 2021
This paperback edition published in 2022

Copyright © Lonán Ó Briain and Min Yen Ong, 2021

Each chapter © of Contributor

For legal purposes the Acknowledgments on p. x constitute an extension
of this copyright page.

Cover design: Louise Dugdale
Cover image © Min Yen Ong

All rights reserved. No part of this publication may be reproduced
or transmitted in any form or by any means, electronic or mechanical,
including photocopying, recording, or any information storage or retrieval
system, without prior permission in writing from the publishers.

Bloomsbury Publishing Inc does not have any control over, or responsibility for,
any third-party websites referred to or in this book. All internet addresses given
in this book were correct at the time of going to press. The author and publisher
regret any inconvenience caused if addresses have changed or sites have ceased
to exist, but can accept no responsibility for any such changes.

Whilst every effort has been made to locate copyright holders the publishers
would be grateful to hear from any person(s) not here acknowledged.

A catalog record for this book is available from the Library of Congress.

ISBN:	HB:	978-1-5013-6005-3
	PB:	978-1-5013-7574-3
	ePDF:	978-1-5013-6007-7
	ePUB:	978-1-5013-6006-0

Typeset by Integra Software Services Pvt. Ltd.

To find out more about our authors and books visit www.bloomsbury.com
and sign up for our newsletters.

Contents

List of Figures	vii
Acknowledgments	x
Notes on Contributors	xi

Introduction: Musical Media in the Asia Pacific
Lonán Ó Briain and Min Yen Ong — 1

Part 1 Vocalizing Community

1 Getting Our Voices Heard: Radio Broadcasting and Secrecy in Vanuatu *Monika Stern* — 15

2 Sounding an Indigenous Domain: Radio, Voice, and Lisu Media Evangelism *Ying Diao* — 33

3 Narrowcasting into the Infinite Margins: Internet Sonorities of Transient Indonesian Domestic Workers in Singapore *Shzr Ee Tan* — 49

Part 2 Transforming Tradition

4 Harmonies for the Homeland: Traditional Music and the Politics of Intangible Cultural Heritage on Vietnamese Radio *Lonán Ó Briain* — 73

5 Mediation of Tradition: Television and Studio Productions of Khmer Music in Cambodia *Francesca Billeri* — 91

6 Going with the Flow: Livestreaming and Korean Wave Narratives in *P'ansori* *Anna Yates-Lu* — 111

Part 3 Sounding Authority

7 North Korea: Controlling the Airwaves and Harmonizing the People *Keith Howard* — 131

8 The Party and the People: Shifting Sonic Politics in Post-1949
   Tiananmen Square *Joseph Lovell*   151

9 Broadcasting Infrastructures and Electromagnetic Fatality:
   Listening to Enemy Radio in Socialist China *Hang Wu*   171

Part 4 Performing Activism

10 "Change the World Gently with Singing": Queer Audibility and Soft
    Activism in China *Hongwei Bao*   193

11 Sounds of Political Reform: Indie Rock in Late New Order Indonesia
    M. Rizky Sasono   211

12 Finding Agency in Hawaiian Online Collaborative Music Videos:
    Reclaiming "*Kaulana Nā Pua*" in a Contemporary Context
    Min Bee and Jordan Anthony Kapono Bee   227

Index   246

Figures

3.1a	Meikhan Sri Bandar sings live karaoke on Facebook via Smule (accessed December 31, 2019)	54
3.1b	Neng (real name) livestreams a karaoke session in Singapore on Facebook (accessed December 31, 2019)	54
3.1c	Turiyah Mansur (real name) sings karaoke on Facebook via Smule (accessed December 31, 2019)	55
3.2a	Screenshot of Nur Assyifa rehearsing at Newton Mosque captured on video on Neng's Facebook page with Neng as soloist (accessed December 31, 2019)	56
3.2b	Screenshot of public performance by Nur Assyifa featured on Neng's Facebook page (accessed December 31, 2019)	57
3.2c	Screenshot of the Facebook pages of Nur Assyifa rehearsals and performances (accessed December 31, 2019)	57
3.3	Members of Nur Assifya learn songs from YouTube and MP3 files on their mobile phones at Newton Mosque, Singapore, on January 14, 2018. Photo: Shzr Ee Tan	59
3.4a/b	Screenshot of Neng's WhatsApp log for the submission and reward of MP4 recordings by her *sholuwat* group members (accessed September 27, 2019)	60
3.5	*Adhan* apps for mobile phones (accessed September 27, 2019)	64
4.1	VOV traditional music ensemble in the recording studio, July 15, 2016. Photo: Lonán Ó Briain	81
5.1	*lkhaon bassac* performance in Tany district, Kampot province, November 5, 2014. Photo: Francesca Billeri	96
5.2	Introduction of the protagonist from the *lkhaon bassac* story "*Preah Cinwuəŋ*" as featured on the Bayon TV program *Khmer Cultural Heritage*, December 9, 2014. Photo: Francesca Billeri	98
5.3	The big drum (*skɔɔ bassac thom*), wooden-box (*taadok*), and idiophone (*caaŋ*), Kampong Cham province, March 15, 2015. Photo: Francesca Billeri	99
5.4	A participant in the music competition sings during a recording for *Khmer Cultural Heritage* on Bayon TV, April 18, 2015. Photo: Francesca Billeri	101

5.5	*Rɔbam yiike* dancers and musicians in Chuuk district, Kampot province, January 8, 2015. Photo: Francesca Billeri	102
5.6	*Rɔbam yiike* dance on the stage before the start of a *lkhaon yiike* performance, Kampot town, Kampot province, January 7, 2015. Photo: Francesca Billeri	103
6.1	Screenshot of a Facebook livestream of GugakFM's *p'ansori*-themed radio show "*Pat'u-ŭi Sangsadiya*" (a play of words referring to the hosts' performance team name, which also means "up close" and is a common folk song phrase equivalent to fa-la-la; accessed October 3, 2018)	117
6.2	Screenshot of a GugakFM Facebook livestream of a concert introducing music from Chindo Island (accessed October 1, 2018)	118
6.3	Screenshot from a Jeongdong Theater promotional video shared on Facebook on March 30, 2018. The use of subtitles (in this case, saying "I won't get it wrong from tomorrow…") is characteristically used in Korean TV shows (accessed April 30, 2019)	119
6.4	Real-time responses to a concert by Seoul Philharmonic Orchestra of Beethoven's Symphony No. 9, livestreamed on V Live December 8, 2016 (cited in Cho Hŭisŏn 2017)—note the clapping emojis. The comments read: "I am jealous of the four people clapping at the front," and "amazing amazing *tchak tchak tchak* (sound of clapping)"	123
6.5	Real-time responses to the opening ceremony of the Jeonju International Sori Festival 2018, livestreamed on Facebook by GugakFM on October 3, 2018. The comments read "*ŏlsshigu*" (a common *ch'uimsae* phrase), "this is the true definition of a moving performance (smiley face)," "Hyesŭng PD must have gone through a lot, hang on in there (heart emojis)," and "*ŏlsshigu chot'a*" (both common *ch'uimsae* phrases; accessed October 6, 2018)	124
6.6	YouTube video teaching basic *p'ansori* vocalization on the "Bonjour Pansori" channel (accessed April 30, 2019)	125
8.1	Tiananmen Square during the late Qing dynasty from a map of Beijing published in 1908. Tiananmen stands in front of the T-shaped space that still existed in 1949. Source: Wu Hung	152
8.2	Tiananmen Square in 1959: 1. Tiananmen; 2. Monument to the People's Heroes; 3. Great Hall of the People; 4. Museum of Chinese History. Mao's Mausoleum now stands south of the Monument to the People's Heroes. Source: Wu Hung	153

Figures   ix

9.1	"Chairman Mao Gives Us a Happy Life." Xin Liliang, March 1954; IISH collection, BG E16/269. Source: chineseposters.net	179
9.2	"The Grasslands Are Connected with Beijing." Wang Zhiping and Guo Chongguang, October 1977; Landsberger collection, BG E13/334. Source: chineseposters.net	180
9.3	Diagram illustrating how to build a radio receiver. Source: Ai Wu	183
9.4a	Screenshot of film made during the Battle of Iwo Jima between the US Navy and the Imperial Japanese Army in 1945, showing the US soldiers using a similar loudspeaker. Source: Archive Films Editorial 1945	186
9.4b	Wu Shize holding "the nine-headed bird" loudspeaker. Source: Yan Lifeng	186
10.1	Screenshot of the Beijing Queer Chorus on Weibo (accessed February 10, 2019)	197
10.2	Beijing Queer Chorus at the *So Far So Long* concert, Beijing, January 2018. Source: Beijing Queer Chorus	199
10.3	Beijing Queer Chorus in Japan, April 2019. Source: Beijing Queer Chorus	203
11.1	Cover of *Jurnal G-Indie* issue from August/September 1997. Source: Mohamad Aman Ridhlo	216
11.2	Cassette cover for the compilation album *United Underground* (1998). Source: Athonk Sapto Raharjo	218
11.3	Blackboots performing at UGM in 1997. Source: Athonk Sapto Raharjo	222
12.1	YouTube screenshot of Glen Smith in Puʻuloa singing "*Kaulana Nā Pua*" (accessed June 9, 2020)	235
12.2	YouTube screenshot of a tourist walking in front of ʻIolani Palace while Ernie Cruz sings "*Kaulana Nā Pua*" (accessed June 9, 2020)	237

Acknowledgments

As we write, the coronavirus (COVID-19) pandemic rages on. We are grateful for the utmost dedication that our contributors have shown despite the intense pressures felt throughout this pandemic. A project of this magnitude only reaches publication with the most patient and generous of support networks in the field, in our academic circles, and at home. The research here attests to long hours spent discussing and debating music, media, and technology with our collocutors in the Asia Pacific. We are immensely grateful to the people who gave up their valuable time to educate us about how music and sound broadcasting are reshaping their social lives. While many are cited by name, we acknowledge that not every contribution will be made explicit in these pages. To those we have not mentioned, thank you. At Bloomsbury, Leah Babb-Rosenfeld, Jessica Anderson, Amy Martin, and Rachel Moore have encouraged us throughout the developmental and production processes, while Karthiga Sithanandam and her colleagues at Integra did a fantastic job of shepherding the project through production. For their input on earlier iterations of this project, we are grateful to Bart Barendregt, Ruth Finnegan, Keith Howard, Barley Norton, and Gavin Williams. The project was made possible through the financial support of the UK Arts and Humanities Research Council. Finally, we would like to express thanks to our fiercest supporters, Emily, Jordan, and Maeve.

Contributors

Hongwei Bao is an associate professor of media studies at the University of Nottingham, UK, where he also directs the Centre for Contemporary East Asian Cultural Studies. He holds a PhD in gender and cultural studies from the University of Sydney. His research primarily focuses on queer media and culture in contemporary China. He has published articles in journals such as *Continuum*, *Cultural Studies*, *Culture Unbound*, *Feminist Media Studies*, and *Interventions*. He is the author of *Queer Comrades: Gay Identity and Tongzhi Activism in Postsocialist China* (2018) and *Queer China: Lesbian and Gay Literature and Visual Culture Under Postsocialism* (2020).

Jordan Anthony Kapono Bee is a native Hawaiian musician, educator, and researcher. He is also a theological scholar at the London School of Theology. Born and raised in Hawai'i and hailing from an illustrious line of musicians and singers, Jordan has taught at various public and charter schools, played a key role in sustainability projects in Hawai'i, as well as worked with the cultural organization Mana Maoli, producing collaborative music videos and events organizing. As a public speaker and professional musician, he has performed and given talks internationally in the United States, the UK, Germany, and Singapore.

Francesca Billeri received her PhD in ethnomusicology from SOAS, University of London. At SOAS, she organized international workshops on Khmer music (2013) and the impact of new media technologies on Southeast Asian performing arts (2017). Her research interests include Khmer wedding music and the impact of music revival movements on Khmer traditional performing arts. Billeri is currently a doctoral tutor in ethnomusicology at the Brilliant Club, a UK nonprofit organization that aims to widen access to university for students from underrepresented groups, and, with funding from Sapienza University of Rome, she is researching digital sound archives as a tool for community research and restoration.

Ying Diao is a postdoctoral research fellow at the Max Planck Institute for the Study of Religious and Ethnic Diversity in Germany. Ying holds a PhD in ethnomusicology (University of Maryland, 2016). She researches religion, sound, and media, and her specialist area is the musical and religious traditions on China-Myanmar border. Her dissertation investigates contemporary gospel singing of the Lisu in Nujiang and the cultural politics of ethnic and religious expression. Her current dissertation-derived book explores how over the last three decades in the Lisu communities, the devotional practices of faith have been intertwined with media technologies and material culture.

Keith Howard is Professor Emeritus and Leverhulme Fellow at SOAS, University of London, UK, and was formerly professor and associate dean at the University of Sydney. He has held visiting professorships and fellowships at Monash University, Ewha Women's University, University of Sydney, Hankuk University of Foreign Studies, Texas Tech University, Academy of Korean Studies, and the National Humanities Center. Author or editor of 22 books, 170 articles, and 197 book/music reviews, he served as SOAS Musicology Series (Ashgate/Routledge) editorial chair from 2008 to 2017 and founded and managed the SOASIS CD and DVD series as well as OpenAir Radio.

Joseph Lovell is a PhD candidate in the Department of East Asian Languages and Cultural Studies at the University of California, Santa Barbara, USA. His research engages with the fields of sound studies, media studies, and modern Chinese history. He is currently writing a doctoral thesis on the usage and reception of amplified sound, especially loudspeakers and radios, in communist propaganda during the Mao era (i.e., from the foundation of People's Republic of China in 1949 to the death of Mao in 1976).

Lonán Ó Briain is an associate professor of music at the University of Nottingham, UK. His monograph, *Musical Minorities: The Sounds of Hmong Ethnicity in Northern Vietnam* (Oxford University Press, 2018), won the inaugural book prize of the International Council for Traditional Music. He is co-editor of *Made in Ireland: Studies in Popular Music* (Routledge, 2021) and is currently completing another monograph, *Voices of Vietnam: A Century of Radio, Red Music, and Revolution* (Oxford University Press). He has served as reviews editor of *Ethnomusicology Forum*, guest editor of *the world of music*, and multimedia reviews editor of the *Yearbook for Traditional Music*.

Min Yen Ong is an ethnomusicologist in the Faculty of Music, University of Cambridge, UK. She is also a Bye-Fellow at Homerton College and Murray Edwards College, and a research associate at Darwin College, University of Cambridge. Specializing in Pacific island cultures and musical cultures of China, her research focuses on notions of belonging, sustainability, agency, and resilience. She is also interested in practice-based research to empower and privilege people and communities confronted by global structures of inequality. She holds a PhD from SOAS, University of London, and was previously a research fellow in ethnomusicology at the University of Nottingham.

M. Rizky Sasono is a PhD candidate in ethnomusicology at the University of Pittsburgh, USA, where his research is focused on indie music scenes in Indonesia from the 1990s to the present day. He holds two masters degrees, one from Universitas Gadjah Mada on a study of Indonesian contemporary theater and another from the University of Pittsburgh with a thesis on the soundscapes of political protest in Indonesia. His additional research interests are music and sound studies, performance studies, and politics.

Monika Stern is an ethnomusicologist at the CNRS, France, and member of CREDO: Center for Research and Documentation in Oceania (Aix-Marseille University, CNRS, EHESS), specializing in the archipelago of Vanuatu (South Pacific). She has undertaken numerous long-term fieldwork projects since 1998. Her research first focused on traditional and rural music, its interactions with society, music exchanges, and their musicological analysis. In recent years, she expanded her research to music and urban issues, especially focusing on music circulations, the social uses of music, local cultural politics, digital medias, and musical property.

Shzr Ee Tan is a senior lecturer in music at Royal Holloway, University of London, UK. She is interested in impact-based issues of music and decolonization, aspirational cosmopolitanism, and race discourses in music scenes around the world, with a view towards understanding marginality through the lenses of intersectionality. Her publications include the monograph *"Beyond Innocence": Amis Aboriginal Song in Taiwan as an Ecosystem* (Ashgate, 2012) and co-edited volumes *Music, Indigeneity and Digital Media* (University of Rochester Press, 2017) and *Gender in Chinese Music* (University of Rochester Press, 2013).

Hang Wu is a PhD candidate in East Asian Studies at McGill University, Canada. Her research interests include media history and theory, infrastructure studies, animation, and techniques of sovereignty and governance, with a focus on their genealogies in the context of modern East Asia. Her articles on animation and cinema have appeared in journals such as *Animation: an interdisciplinary journal* and *Dangdai dianying (Contemporary Cinema)*. She is currently completing her dissertation, which examines the history of visual effects from the perspective of animation and the nonhuman experience in Chinese and Japanese media from the Cold War to the contemporary era.

Anna Yates-Lu is an assistant professor of Korean music at Seoul National University. She completed her PhD on the traditional Korean sung storytelling art form *pansori* at SOAS, University of London. Her recent research examines the use of social networking services as a promotional tool by traditional musicians in Korea and China. She is also active as a *p'ansori* teacher and performer in Europe and Korea, having been trained by National Intangible Cultural Property No. 5 (*P'ansori Hŭngboga*) disciple Min Hye Sung. She has performed at the Gyeongbokgung Palace (Seoul), Cadogan Hall (London), and Élysée Palace (Paris).

Min Bee: see **Min Yen Ong**

Introduction: Musical Media in the Asia Pacific

Lonán Ó Briain and Min Yen Ong

This book investigates the circulation of musical culture via radio, television, and digital broadcasting in eastern Asia and the Pacific Ocean. Contributors are motivated by two related questions: How do broadcasters shape performing arts practice, and how do these broadcasts shape the cultural, social, and political landscapes of the region? We first gathered to debate these questions at a two-day Arts and Humanities Research Council-funded conference held in the Department of Music at the University of Nottingham on October 19–20, 2018. The theme of that conference was "Cultural Broadcasting in the Asia Pacific Region," and the majority of the delegates focused their attention on music, sound reproduction technology, and the media industries—here we use the term "musical media" as shorthand for the intersection of these industries. At the conference we were treated to two keynote presentations: one by Ruth Finnegan, who spoke about her experiences with Fiji radio musicians (see Finnegan 2016), and another by Bart Barendregt, who revisited his research on the sonic history of Malay world (see Barendregt 2014). Several delegates from that conference have revised and expanded their research for inclusion in this collection, which examines historical and contemporary perspectives on musical media in the Asia Pacific.

Recently published edited collections have considered music and sound production (Bennett and Bates 2018), sound and empire (Radano and Olaniyan 2016), music broadcasting in conflict situations (Grant and Stone-Davis 2013), and digital technology as it pertains to contemporary indigenous music-making (Hilder, Stobart and Tan 2017). Others address intangible cultural heritage in the Asia Pacific or closely related areas (Howard 2016; Norton and Matsumoto 2018). One recent collection on music in the Asia Pacific contains nine chapters largely written from the perspective of Hawai'i (Lau and Yano 2018), while another examines Austronesian music cultures of Oceania and Southeast Asia (Abels 2011). Within this growing body of literature, no comprehensive collection has studied the interface of broadcasting technology and musical culture across the Asia Pacific with a relatively balanced number of studies from across the region. *Sound Communities* addresses this gap by presenting a series of localized case studies linked by their investigation of the relationship between music, media, and technology in this corner of the world. As with the aforementioned collections, however, this volume has an implicit geographic center—in this case, East and Southeast Asia (see also Lockard 1998)—and the case studies tend to coalesce around nearby nation-states. In place of case studies on South Asia, which has been covered extensively in other publications (e.g., Banaji 2010; Fiol 2017; Manuel 1993), we include case studies from several less studied places such as North Korea and Vanuatu.

Many of us are accustomed to seeing maps of the world drawn with Europe at the center, the Americas to the left (West) and Asia to the right (East). While the problematic descriptor "Oriental" is less common these days, those of us at European and North American institutions are used to having our research labeled as the study of Eastern music or music in the "Far East." We use the term "Asia Pacific" as a mechanism for decoupling this subconscious Eurocentric understanding of the world from our studies.[1] The Asia Pacific, or "APAC" in economic and political parlance, is not a fixed geopolitical entity. The United Nations provides one definition via their Economic and Social Commission for Asia and the Pacific. This commission comprises fifty-three member states and nine associate members. With a "geographical scope that stretches from Turkey in the west to the Pacific island nation of Kiribati in the east, and from the Russian Federation in the north to New Zealand in the south," this version of the Asia Pacific includes over 60 percent of the global population.[2] The chapters in this book focus more narrowly on East Asia, Southeast Asia, and the Pacific nations to encourage the reader to hear translocal connections and dissonances between our case studies.

The invention and popularization of several new media technologies, including radio, television, and the internet, were transformative moments in the history of the twentieth century. As these media filtered unevenly across the Asia Pacific, they facilitated the restructuring of social groups and emergence of new communities through sound (Kahn 2016; Sterne 2012). These media rapidly adapted from offering exciting new social, cultural, and political opportunities to settling into the inconspicuous mundanity of the everyday. As the region tackles the COVID-19 pandemic in 2020, people are finding new ways to use these broadcasting mechanisms to establish, direct, and challenge translocal networks of communication. Within this context, imagined communities are being converted into audible social networks (after Anderson 1983). In turn, these networks facilitate the widespread dissemination and transformation of local musical cultures. They also permit the influx of international styles and trends along distinct cultural, social, and economic corridors. Each of the chapters in this volume explores the inherent tensions between the emancipatory potential of broadcasting musical media and the limits and constraints on broadcasters and the listening public in the Asia Pacific.

The diverse topography of the Asia Pacific, from diffuse island nations spread across the Pacific Ocean to densely populated megacities on the mainland of eastern Asia, presents a fruitful geographic locale for researching the dissemination and impact of musical media. By expanding the reach of live performance, these media continue to encourage multiculturalism and inclusivity, raise awareness of indigenous or minority rights, garner action and resilience toward climate change or other pressing geopolitical challenges, connect and unite communities postdisaster, help to sustain musical traditions, or serve as a bridge toward reconciliatory processes. Musicians and media personnel also use forms of cultural broadcasting to promote political ideologies; construct or reshape regional, national, and transnational identities (e.g., Association of Southeast Asian Nations); buttress or challenge geopolitical boundaries; and foment political or social discontent across borders.

The twelve essays in this book take specific musical media as case studies for investigating and unpacking these issues as they relate to local politics, social movements, and economic development. In looking beyond our individual, localized "sonic niches" (Tausig 2019), we grouped these essays into four parts: Voicing Community, Transforming Tradition, Performing Authority, and Sounding Activism. These headings do not provide a comprehensive overview of key themes concerning musical media. For instance, the focus of Part Three on authority and authoritarianism is by no means reflective of trends across the varied political geographies of the Asia Pacific. Instead, this structure draws attention to a series of thematic clusters that percolated during our fieldwork, archival research, and scholarly exchanges. We arranged the themes by contrasting community formation (Part One) with tradition and change (Part Two) and restrictive top-down approaches such as those of authoritarian governments (Part Three) with more radical, emancipatory grassroots initiatives (Part Four). In this way, we hope the volume will contribute to a greater understanding of the depth and diversity of engagements with musical media across the Asia Pacific.

Part One: Voicing Community

Ethnomusicologists, popular music scholars, and others have devoted substantial efforts to examining musical communities as social and cultural formations. As Shelemay writes, musical transmission and performance "help[s] generate, shape, and sustain new collectivities" (2011: 350). With the exception of South Asia (see previously cited literature on that region), the balance of these studies on music in the Asia Pacific has tended to emphasize music performance over transmission, even though mediated performance is now regarded as the originating source for our experience of the vast majority of new music (Lysloff 1997: 208).[3] Part One attempts to redress this balance by examining the processes involved in the production, distribution, and consumption of musical media. The following chapters investigate how musical media are used to vocalize connections between communities that are separated by oceans, mountain ranges, and the need to migrate for employment respectively.

In her chapter, "Getting Our Voices Heard: Radio Broadcasting and Secrecy in Vanuatu," Monika Stern examines how musical media helped to facilitate connections between marginalized island communities and sow the seeds of a shared national cultural identity in the Melanesian archipelago of Vanuatu. Stern illustrates how radio and other media were used to valorize *kastom*—from the English word "custom" in the local lingua franca—around the time of independence in 1980. Alongside this push for cultural unity, the islands' inhabitants also differentiated themselves through local practices over which they claimed ownership. In the 1970s, radio employees helped to popularize a new local musical style, the string band. The Vanuatu Broadcasting and Television Corporation was established in 1994, which shifted policy to more commercial recordings and foreign productions. More recently, as radio and television were becoming less interactive, the internet introduced new possibilities for user participation, and home recording studios have supported the development of the local music industry, with local bands recording styles such as reggae, pop music, and remixes. In surveying the recent history of musical media in Vanuatu—which resembles that of many other island nations in the Pacific Ocean—this chapter outlines the evolution of discourse concerning musical identity, ownership, and secrecy in this postcolonial state.

In Chapter 2, "Sounding an Indigenous Domain: Radio, Voice, and Lisu Media Evangelism," Ying Diao considers the musical media used by Lisu Christian evangelists in mainland Southeast Asia and southwest China. Christian minorities in this region are now equipped with a variety of media technologies that facilitate their sounded religious practices in multiethnic and multireligious societies. Building on recent studies of media-driven religious change, this chapter recognizes the agency of ethnic minorities by comparing two examples of post-1990 media evangelism among the Lisu: a Lisu-run radio ministry in Chiang Mai supported by the US-based Asia Christian Services and Gospel Broadcasting Mission; and the music ministry of the Yangon-based Myanmar Agape Christian Mission, an indigenous mission organization also associated with American missionary networks. Both of these ministries draw on new musical media to propagate a Christian Lisu message. Their denominational affiliations, relationships with missionaries, and funding sources are similar; however, the ways in which they have employed new media technologies in the studio and beyond and the resulting religious changes in the indigenous communities are very different. The analysis distinguishes between different modalities of indigenous media domestication, thereby providing a more nuanced understanding of the degrees of socioreligious transformation even within the same religious tradition of a single ethnic group.

Shzr Ee Tan's chapter, "Narrowcasting into the Infinite Margins: Internet Sonorities of Transient Indonesian Domestic Workers in Singapore," attests to the creative ways in which marginalized communities attempt to get themselves heard through private virtual networks. Transient workers in Singapore make up an invisibilized underclass of low-paid manual laborers traveling to the prosperous city-state largely from the territories of Bangladesh, Indonesia, the Philippines, and Myanmar. Over the internet, however, this invisibility is unveiled through the ability to ride on the fast connections provided—in the case of domestic helpers—within the family homes of Singaporean employers. Based on fieldwork conducted in Singapore between 2017 and 2018, this chapter considers four case studies of mediated musical articulations by Indonesian domestic worker communities: (1) "imagined listening" Campos Valverde (2019) to multiple, publicly circulated "selfie" video recordings of Islamic chant; (2) private channels of communication on platforms such as WhatsApp; (3) online live-jamming karaoke sessions; (4) the silenced—but consciously and audibly vibrated—broadcasts of the Islamic call to prayer emanating from mobile phones. These examples bring together overarching themes of the perceived unlimited "narrowcasting" afforded by online musical media, in private virtual spaces reclaimed from the hegemonic everyday existence of these workers' lives on the island. The chapter reevaluates these articulations as broadcasts targeting specialist and niche audiences in Singapore who serve as imagined listeners as much as they are imagined communities.

Part Two: Transforming Tradition

Recording industry executives from Europe and North America began exploratory tours of the Asia Pacific in the early 1900s (Gronow 1981).[4] The growth of this industry was gradual in the first half of the century, with progress hampered by two world wars and the 1930s Great Depression. The impact of recording and broadcasting on local musical traditions was also limited by the industry's targeting of higher earning workers, often comprising colonial administrators and entrepreneurs who could afford the expensive playback technologies. As the century wore on, independence movements across the region garnered support through their repurposing of traditional melodies with political texts and the composition of national anthems drawing on a fusion of local and international styles. These movements garnered widespread support through print and broadcast media, on which they disseminated their messages often via new musical texts. But the emergence of postindependence national music industries occurred unevenly across the region as certain nations liberalized their economies faster than others, while some were held back by environmental disasters, political upheaval, and war. By the time of the popularization of the cassette tape in the 1970s and 1980s, most of the major independence, civil, and Cold War conflicts in eastern Asia and the Pacific Islands had subsided, and local musicians were ready to embrace the potential of the technology. Part Two of this book presents three ethnographic studies on the transformation of musical traditions through their technological (re)production in three nation-states formerly consumed by war and now occupied by varying degrees of national reconciliation and economic renovation: contemporary Vietnam, Cambodia, and South Korea. These chapters draw attention to "aspects of the original that can be accessed only by the lens" (Benjamin [1935] 2008: 6), which is controlled and manipulated by performers, media producers, and social media users.

Lonán Ó Briain's chapter, "Harmonies for the Homeland: Traditional Music and the Politics of Intangible Cultural Heritage on Vietnamese Radio," examines music production processes at Voice of Vietnam Radio (VOV), the national broadcaster of the Socialist Republic of Vietnam. Drawing on fieldwork at the VOV studios in Hanoi between 2016 and 2017, when he interviewed current members of the broadcaster's national or ethnic music ensemble; observed rehearsals, production sessions, and administrative meetings; and took instrumental lessons from one group member, this chapter provides an ethnographic account of a typical working week for the ensemble. Ó Briain examines how the ensemble represents and reifies the three major cultural regions of Vietnam in their musical recordings. Rather than dismiss these musicians as political puppets devoted to the production of pro-communist music, he investigates their creative, pragmatic approaches to the constraints and contradictions of life in a postsocialist state. Meanwhile, he illustrates how culture brokers within the state media are more directly involved in the politicization of intangible cultural heritage, a process which is justified using the language of cultural sustainability. These brokers commission song texts to be rewritten with pro-communist themes that are supposedly more relevant to contemporary audiences, and the recordings of those songs are disseminated within propagandistic sonic and visual frames that politicize the music in ways that support to continuation of the single party-state system.

Chapter 5, "Mediation of Tradition: Television and Studio Productions of Khmer Music in Cambodia," takes us across the border to Cambodia, where Francesca Billeri examines the framing of musical traditions on national television and by the local music industry. Using case studies of wedding rituals and two traditional theater styles—*lkhon yiike* and *lkhon bassac*—produced for television and commercial recording releases, she illustrates how musicians and media practitioners seek to preserve these traditions by appealing to younger audiences. As they adapt to new media contexts, however, the traditions themselves are undergoing major changes. The music is becoming standardized, and hybrid forms are developing through alterations to performing practices, instrumentation, musical texture, and the extra-musical functions. This process of transformation is considered by some Khmer musicians to be a feature of modernization, as well as a means to rebuild and renovate Cambodian musical and theatrical styles after the massive disruption, discontinuity, and upheaval of the Khmer Rouge regime. These modernized television and studio performances also foster exciting new forms of making music: artists have opportunities to perform for new audiences, and they are developing new compositions inspired by traditional genres. As with the previous chapter, Billeri shows how political control is exerted over cultural programs and how the plots of theater stories are being made to conform to contemporary sociocultural values and political ideology.

Anna Yates-Lu's chapter, "Going with the Flow: Livestreaming and Korean Wave Narratives in *P'ansori*," explores the effects of livestreaming via social networking services on the Korean traditional sung storytelling genre *p'ansori*. Like many other traditional art forms, *p'ansori* has often struggled to stay relevant to contemporary audiences. Various media strategies have been employed by its artists (called *sorikkun*) to help the genre survive, often driven by a desire to emulate the success of K-Pop. Just as K-Pop stars use apps such as V Live, Instagram, or Twitter to engage with their fans, the last few years have seen a steady rise of *sorikkun* attempting to replicate this success by turning to livestreaming. Radio and television broadcasts, recitals, concerts, and theater performances, as well as short rehearsal and promotional clips, are all featured on their online media. These new musical media enable audiences to watch and comment on performances in real time. But does this strategy actually widen the audience pool, or is it simply the same people engaging with *p'ansori* content online and offline? How does online consumption of *p'ansori* change the relationship with the audience, generally considered a key element of *p'ansori* performance? Employing a mixture of online and offline fieldwork and interviews, this chapter sheds light on how intangible cultural heritage and musical traditions in particular are being re-produced in an increasingly digital world.

Part Three: Sounding Authority

Both China's and North Korea's socialist parties came to power at similar times (1949 and 1948 respectively). Part Three explores the themes of political control and state regulation and censorship on cultural production in China and North Korea. Using broadcasting technology (such as radio, loudspeakers, and hidden speakers), each chapter in this part examines the application and efficacy of such technology by the state in its administration of power to mobilize and control the mass populace. To build a nation-state made up of "docile bodies" (Foucault [1977] 1995: 138), creative strategies were employed and these include: building broadcasting structures to facilitate the dissemination of state ideology; establishing, maintaining, and reinforcing an imagined community (Anderson 1983) through a sonic monopolization of space; and embodying power not just within structural relations but in the constant social interaction and everyday practice through cultivating conscious and unconscious acts of listening. The chapters in this section explore these various strategies.

Keith Howard's chapter, "North Korea: Controlling the Airwaves and Harmonizing the People," examines the power of song in narrating and controlling people's lives in the Democratic People's Republic of Korea (North Korea). Songs are promoted by the state broadcaster (the only broadcaster in North Korea), issued by the state media company (the only recording company in North Korea), and distributed worldwide online by the Shenyang-based Uriminzokkiri. Layers of censorship monitor how songs are created and presented, as the state attempts to ensure citizens are kept faithful to the ongoing revolution. Howard focuses on song as a "totalizing" art form with its ability to pervade private and public spaces in everyday life while generating participation when required. In North Korea, the same songs are everywhere at any given time, and Howard writes that "songs provide the relentless soundtrack for the theater that is Pyongyang." Songs carry ideological "seeds"; they act like newspaper editorials and render the everyday extraordinary. In recordings, broadcasts, and online, they are carefully calibrated, cast within formulaic topoi, made portable through detachable melodies that are rearrangeable in myriad forms from the mundane to the spectacular, with or without lyrics, and with or without video/film backings. Songs, as a totalizing art form, become participatory as Foucault's panopticons replace Benjamin's arcades; the people continuously hear, continuously perform, and are continuously observed performing songs.

While Howard focuses on the political messages conveyed through song in North Korea, Joseph Lovell draws our intention to the dynamics of sound and space in the People's Republic of China. In his chapter "The Party and the People: Shifting Sonic Politics in Post-1949 Tiananmen Square," Lovell studies the effects of the installation of loudspeaker equipment and the transformative power of broadcasting technology in the construction of national identity at Tiananmen Square. Reflecting on "earwitness" accounts (Schafer 1993), memoirs, and British foreign office records, he focuses on the sonic aspects of these politically charged parades and rallies in politicizing people's existences. In describing some of the earlier events between 1949 and 1976, he explains how the circulation of sound with the combination of carefully choreographed slogans emanating from speakers and "the voice of the people," which was technologically fed back into a loop, conferred a sense of power on the crowd, thus creating a "sonorous envelope" (Anzieu 1976). This sonorous envelope gave a sense of protection and belonging for those in support of the slogans and the party, but it gave feelings of intimidation to those in opposition—feelings of vulnerability and replaceability. Lovell also touches on the sonic politics of the Tiananmen Square protests in 1989, in which he argues that despite the Chinese Communist Party's efforts to depoliticize public spaces since the late 1970s, the protestors were able to use the power of their voices together with their own amplification equipment to orchestrate their own revolutionary aims.

In "Broadcasting Infrastructures and Electromagnetic Fatality: Listening to Enemy Radio in Socialist China," Hang Wu shifts focus to the construction of broadcasting networks and the nurturing of listening practices, which she divides into ideal listening versus illicit listening. Her chapter begins by laying out China's building of nationwide radio broadcasting networks and the important role that these networks played for the party in disseminating information to far-reaching areas, regulating the national environment, and revolutionizing people's everyday practices. Despite strict regulations and attempts to block broadcasts from "enemy radio" stations and program—Mandarin-based foreign radio stations controlled by the United States, the UK the Soviet Union, Taiwan, and Vietnam—by the state during the Cultural Revolution, clandestine listening practices still took place, particularly along the border. Through her analysis of archival records and oral histories on listening to cross-border radio in socialist China, Wu's chapter examines this cross-border circulation of sounds in the context of Chinese socialism and investigates how multiple listening positions problematized national borders and Chinese imagined listening communities. She argues that the uneven distribution of national radio broadcast infrastructures in the Chinese border areas allowed for the re-engineering of radio frequencies, clandestine rearrangement of sounds, and multiple lines of listening.

Part Four: Performing Activism

From taking a top-down approach that prioritized state control and regulation in the previous section, Part Four adopts a bottom-up approach to activism and agency. The three chapters in this section assess the thoughts and actions of people who express their individual power through music as they resist structures (both social forces and institutions). Due to the sensitive nature of the establishments they challenge, these chapters explore artful expressions and exertions of collective agency using music videos, social media, and radio, as they seek to engender change within their communities and across the region.

Hongwei Bao's chapter, "'Change the World Gently with Singing': Queer Audibility and Soft Activism in China," focuses on Lesbian, Gay, Bisexual, Transgender, and Queer (LGBTQ) choirs in China. With a case study of the Beijing Queer Chorus—the first major LGBTQ choir to perform publicly in China—he articulates how queer activists have had to adopt "culturally sensitive" and "soft" activism strategies in order to circumvent state censorship. This type of queer activism departs from a conventional activist emphasis on visibility, confrontation, and direct intervention into politics. In developing his analytical framework of "queer audibility," Bao interrogates the cultural specificity of queer activism in the Chinese context and argues for a soft type of activism through the production and dissemination of performing arts, culture, and media broadcasting. Through live performances, music video recordings, and interactive social media posts, Bao discusses how these outlets are cleverly used to engage with transforming the minds of a resistant public as well as to build solidarity with other LGBTQ members. Social media savvy members have adopted platform-specific strategies with personalized taglines to target specific user groups. Through these strategies of broadcasting their social and musical activities, the Beijing Queer Chorus have managed to carve out their own independent space that is separate from yet also in dialogue with mainstream Chinese popular culture.

In Chapter 11, "Sounds of Political Reform: Indie Rock in Late New Order Indonesia," M. Rizky Sasono uses the example of student protests in Yogyakarta, which he experienced firsthand as a student at Universitas Gadjah Mada and musician in the band DRS.HIM, to tackle a louder and more visible political movement in Indonesia, the indie rock scene in the mid-1990s. Sasono argues that broadcasting played a key role in the early development of Indonesia's indie scenes, which emerged amid rising political activism among students toward the end of President Suharto's reign and an influx of international styles via radio and television. As an affordable form of entertainment and news, student campus radio stations played an active role in this movement, giving both performance opportunities to emerging indie groups and airtime to discussions of sensitive political issues. The program "G-Indie" on Geronimo FM, a private radio station in Yogyakarta, also encouraged students to record and perform their own music rather than simply cover international popular hits. While many students from this era were political activists, they were also cultural activists as they contributed to the creation of a radical new music scene in Yogyakarta and other parts of Indonesia. As Sasono argues, indie in Indonesia during the late New Order was distinct because it grew not only alongside but as part of a wider movement toward social liberation and political change.

Finally, Min Bee and Jordan Anthony Kapono Bee's chapter, "Finding Agency in Hawaiian Online Collaborative Music Videos: Reclaiming 'Kaulana Nā Pua' in a Contemporary Context," explores the use of music video and social media in cultivating self-determination. The Hawaiian Kingdom, once a sovereign kingdom in the Pacific—recognized as an independent nation within the international community as can be seen through historical treatises with other nations—had its monarchy overthrown in 1893, was subsequently forcibly annexed in 1898, and became a US state in 1959. It is seen by native Hawaiian activists to be illegally occupied by the United States. Bee and Bee's chapter revisits the well-known protest song *"Kaulana Nā Pua"* (Famous Are the Children/Flowers) and investigates the production of a collaborative online music video of the song made by grassroots organization Project *Kuleana* and its role in the revitalization of Hawaiian culture and indigenous identity. At the core of this project lies the concept of *aloha 'aina* (love of the land), and their script features how beneath the soothing melodies and beautiful scenery, the performance of this song carries a potent message of protecting and promoting indigenous rights and the sovereignty of the Hawaiian Kingdom. They explore techniques that lie within the creation of Project *Kuleana*'s "Kaulana Nā Pua" collaborative music video, such as intertextuality, signs, and the reclamation of space, as well as the effectiveness of social media platforms.

Concluding Remarks

With a particular emphasis on East Asia, Southeast Asia, and the Pacific Islands, this book examines four themes in the musical media of the Asia Pacific: community and society, tradition and change, authority and authoritarianism, and activism and agency. We focus on national and regional broadcasters, pirate stations, state-society relations mediated through broadcasting, mobile listening, transnationalism, regional alliances, and cross-border noise, local music industries, broadcasting social activism, contested places, and iconic voices in contemporary and historical perspective. Our research reveals local particularities and regional patterns that are influenced by and can shape the global cultural industries with their associated histories of imperialism and (post)colonialism. We also illustrate the extra-musical impact of performing arts broadcasts by interrogating the ways that authoritarian regimes deploy musical propaganda, amateur fans harness makeshift technologies and sounds to subvert established hegemonies, and local communities use music broadcasts to promote positive social change. Using these rich examples, we seek to establish how a series of technological revolutions transformed and continue to impact cultural life through the study of local, translocal, and transnational cultural currents within the Asia Pacific and beyond.

Notes

1 Another option might have been the more recent formulation "transpacific" (e.g., Hoskins and Nguyen 2014). However, that term consciously omits China from the equation, whereas China is a central influence on the culture- and media-scapes tackled in this book.
2 https://www.un.org/en/sections/where-we-work/asia-and-pacific/index.html, accessed May 20, 2020.
3 For instance, although the landmark 1046-page *The Garland Encyclopedia of World Music: Southeast Asia* (Miller and Williams 1998) is underpinned by an impressive array of accompanying recordings, none of the chapters in the volume is explicitly focused on either the recording or the broadcasting industries.
4 For a rich collection of annotated recordings from this era in Southeast Asia, see Murray (2013).

Bibliography

Abels, Birgit, ed. 2011. *Austronesian Soundscapes: Performing Arts in Oceania and Southeast Asia*. Amsterdam: Amsterdam University Press.

Anderson, Benedict. 1983. *Imagined Communities: Reflections on the Growth and Spread of Nationalism*. New York and London: Verso.

Anzieu, Didier. 1976. "L'enveloppe Sonore du Soi." *Nouvelle Revue de Psychanalyse* 13: 173–9.

Banaji, Shakuntala, ed. 2010. *South Asian Media Cultures: Audiences, Representations, Contexts*. London: Anthem Press.

Barendregt, Bart, ed. 2014. *Sonic Modernities in the Malay World: A History of Popular Music, Social Distinction and Novel Lifestyles (1930s–2000s)*. Leiden: Brill.

Benjamin, Walter. (1935) 2008. *The Work of Art in the Age of Mechanical Reproduction*. Translated by James A. Underwood. London: Penguin.

Bennett, Samantha, and Eliot Bates, eds. 2018. *Critical Approaches to the Production of Music and Sound*. New York: Bloomsbury.

Finnegan, Ruth. 2016. *The Travels and Travails of Music*. Bletchley: Callender Press.

Fiol, Stefan. 2017. *Recasting Folk in the Himalayas: Indian Music, Media, and Social Mobility*. Urbana: University of Illinois Press.

Foucault, Michel. (1977) 1995. *Discipline and Punish: The Birth of the Prison*. Translated by Alan Sheridan. New York: Vintage Books.

Grant, Morag J., and Férdia Stone-Davis, eds. 2013. *The Soundtrack of Conflict: The Role of Music in Radio Broadcasting in Wartime and in Conflict Situations*. Hildesheim: Georg Olms Verlag.

Gronow, Pekka. 1981. "The Record Industry Comes to the Orient." *Ethnomusicology* 25 (2): 251–84.

Hilder, Thomas R., Henry Stobart, and Shzr Ee Tan, eds. 2017. *Music, Indigeneity, Digital Media*. Rochester, NY: University of Rochester Press.

Hoskins, Janet, and Viet Thanh Nguyen, eds. 2014. *Transpacific Studies: Framing an Emerging Field*. Honolulu: University of Hawai'i Press.

Howard, Keith, ed. 2016. *Music as Intangible Cultural Heritage: Policy, Ideology and Practice in the Preservation of East Asian Traditions*. Abingdon: Routledge.

Kahn, Douglas. 2016. "Sound Leads Elsewhere." In *The Routledge Companion to Sounding Art*, edited by Marcel Cobussen, Vincent Meelberg, and Barry Truax, 41–50. New York and London: Routledge.

Lau, Frederick, and Christine R. Yano, eds. 2018. *Making Waves: Traveling Musics in Hawai'i, Asia, and the Pacific*. Honolulu: University of Hawai'i Press.

Lockard, Craig A. 1998. *Dance of Life: Popular Music and Politics in Southeast Asia*. Honolulu: University of Hawai'i Press.

Lysloff, René T. A. 1997. "Mozart in Mirrorshades: Music, Technology, and Ethnomusicological Anxiety." *Ethnomusicology* 41 (2): 206–19.

Manuel, Peter. 1993. *Cassette Culture: Popular Music and Technology in North India*. Chicago, IL: University of Chicago Press.

Miller, Terry E., and Sean Williams, eds. 1998. *The Garland Encyclopedia of World Music: Southeast Asia*. New York: Routledge.

Murray, David, ed. 2013. *Longing for the Past: The 78 RPM Era in Southeast Asia*. Atlanta: Dust-To-Digital.

Norton, Barley, and Naomi Matsumoto, eds. 2018. *Music as Heritage: Historical and Ethnographic Perspectives*. Abingdon: Taylor and Francis.

Radano, Ronald, and Tejumola Olaniyan, eds. 2016. *Audible Empire: Music, Global Politics, Critique*. Durham, NC: Duke University Press.

Schafer, R. Murray. 1993. *The Soundscape: Our Sonic Environment and the Tuning of the World*. Rochester, VT: Destiny Books.

Shelemay, Kay Kaufman. 2011. "Musical Communities: Rethinking the Collective in Music." *Journal of the American Musicological Society* 64 (2): 349–90.

Sterne, Jonathan. 2012. "Sonic Imaginations." In *The Sound Studies Reader*, edited by Jonathan Sterne, 1–17. London and New York: Routledge.

Tausig, Benjamin. 2019. *Bangkok Is Ringing: Sound, Protest, and Constraint*. New York: Oxford University Press.

Valverde, Raquel. 2019. "Understanding Musicking on Social Media: Music Sharing, Sociality and Citizenship." PhD thesis, London South Bank University.

Part One

Vocalizing Community

1

Getting Our Voices Heard: Radio Broadcasting and Secrecy in Vanuatu

Monika Stern

When I returned to Mota Lava in the northern Banks Islands of the Vanuatu archipelago in May 2018 after being away for more than ten years, I was struck that several musicians and groups wanted to be recorded and told me of their dreams of making their own albums.[1] The local journalist Edgar Howard Woleg also asked me to record a few musical examples for his radio programs. All I could offer was to record a few songs on my Zoom H4 and upload the recordings to Secure Digital (SD) cards on their phones so that they could exchange, distribute, and broadcast the recordings as they saw fit.

Vanuatu is a Melanesian archipelago made up of more than eighty islands, whose inhabitants, called ni-Vanuatu since independence in 1980, speak more than 130 vernacular languages, thus holding the world record for linguistic density. As well as these Austronesian languages, there are three official ones (French, English, and the lingua franca pidgin English known locally as Bislama). These three languages stem from the islands' Anglo-French colonial history, known as the Condominium of the New Hebrides from 1906 to 1980. Mirroring this linguistic diversity, traditional (*kastom*) forms of music are many and various according to the different islands, regions, and even villages. Other music genres also exist: string band music, Christian religious music, and popular music (essentially, reggae and hip-hop).

Apart from the islands on which Vanuatu's two towns (Port-Vila and Luganville) are to be found, the other islands are isolated, with poor transport services and often limited or no consistent access to electricity. For these reasons, inhabitants do not always find it easy to be part of national and international news networks or to make their voices heard. National radio and television stations do not consistently reach most of the islands; their main audiences are based in the two urban centers. Since the opening up of the telecommunications market to competition in 2007, mobile phone services have developed considerably, with 3G services now reaching most of the archipelago's islands. However, these new means of communication are expensive and inconsistent. On some islands the network seldom works, while on others the network is only accessible at certain times or locations. Consequently, although its infrastructure does not always sufficiently meet its demand, radio remains as an essential public service for most of the population.[2]

The state-sponsored media broadcasts traditional music from the archipelago's islands and many other genres. But how are choices made in the treatment of these repertoires? How do media practitioners make distinctions between the islands? Is all traditional music accessible to everyone? These questions are connected to an understanding of culture, democracy, and the possibility for everyone to access knowledge and information. Here we will not go into the debates on cultural democratization and democracy specific to notions of class in the West; instead, I deploy the vocabulary used by Harrison (1995) concerning openness and "freedom of access" to knowledge. Melanesia is known for its secrets—in the form of secret societies, secret spirit voices, secret instruments, and secret songs described in many classic anthropological works on the region.[3] A great deal of specific knowledge and practices are reserved for one group, whether that be hierarchical or residential, or a secret society, and only the initiated or people belonging to these groups have access to this shared knowledge. Moreover, publicly showing one's knowledge outside these groups (in the form of public dances for example) brings prestige. Thus in some cases: "knowledge increases in value by being shared. In the other approach... it decreases in value by being shared. There seem to be two contradictory models here for managing knowledge, and two incompatible theories of its value" (Harrison 1995: 12).

This chapter draws on Harrison's (1995) and Lindstrom's (1990) works, which argue it is not a question of simple dichotomy (secrets/open knowledge) but of strategies and political stakes put in place to conceal or reveal knowledge. This knowledge has been observed in Melanesia since the time of anthropologist Bronisław Malinowski. However, what appears to be a regional particularity can be found in many forms, less explicit perhaps, in other parts of the world. Foucault questions this opposition between the secret knowledge of certain cultures and the supposedly free circulation of knowledge in the West as "one of the great myths of European culture":

> To the monopolistic, secret knowledge of oriental tyranny, Europe opposed the universal communication of knowledge and the infinitely free exchange of discourse. This notion does not, in fact, stand up to close examination. Exchange and communication are positive forces at play within complex, but restrictive systems; it is probable that they cannot operate independently of these.
> (Foucault 1971: 17–18)

Foucault demonstrates that these forms of "secret-appropriation and non-interchangeability" exist in numerous contexts in European societies. We shall therefore follow Lindstrom, who has suggested that Foucault's theories have "considerable relevance for making sense of systems of knowledge and power in Melanesia" (Lindstrom 1990: ix).

Radio, which provides a key technological means of cultural broadcasting in the region, is connected to these questions of secrecy, disclosure, and power strategies for these communities. This chapter examines how the ni-Vanuatu use radio and recording technologies as a means of listening to, broadcasting, and producing music. Rather than analyze the media as transformative cultural elements (Bull 2005),

I follow the example of studies that consider how specific historical, social, and cultural contexts deploy the technology (Miller and Horst 2012; Wall and Webber 2014). I begin with a historical overview of national radio and the role it played at the time of independence. The second section considers the constraints in uses of *kastom* music. The third section describes the emergence of the music industry, which favored the development of music for entertainment and its link to radio broadcasting. A final part will then return to the attempts to restructure the national media, based again on local knowledge.

Radio, *Kastom*, and National Identity

Let us first put the notion of *kastom* (in Bislama), which is at times hastily translated as "custom," into context. In Vanuatu, *kastom* has a more complex meaning, particularly because of the political role it played during the push for independence. Jolly explains the double meaning of *kastom* and its revival: on a national level, it represents a means of distinguishing the indigenous ni-Vanuatu as a whole from their former European colonizers. On a local level, the particular practices of *kastom* (marriage, birth or rank-taking ceremonies, myths, dance, and music) are claimed by distinct communities and sometimes passed down in the form of secret or restricted knowledge with explicit ownership rules. This does not preclude the possibility of loaning or exchanging *kastom* (Jolly 1992: 341–4; Stern 2013).

Lissant Bolton (1999) has retraced the history of Vanuatu national radio and the role it played in the 1970s leading up to independence. She demonstrates how radio contributed to the valorization of the archipelago's different oral traditions, especially traditional stories and music. According to Bolton, the history of radio in the New Hebrides began in the 1960s. Its interactive programs (e.g., personal messages, feedbacks, sending of recordings) were inward-looking and focused on national issues: "Rather than seeing the radio as a way of gaining access to the 'world-out-there', the ni-Vanuatu response was concerned mainly with programs that engaged with their own world, the knowledge and practice that arose out of the place itself, and with their own concerns" (Bolton 1999: 346).

Contrary to the fears mentioned in many studies on the introduction of radio in industrialized countries—that the technology would discourage people from talking to each other (Johnson [1988] 2017: 172)—in this island context it was quite the opposite: radio enabled the inhabitants of different islands to communicate. The technology was used—and still is to a certain extent—to send not only collective messages such as information on the circulation of copra boats, which also transport other goods and passengers, but also personal messages. Examples of these personal messages include information on deaths and births, parcels due for collection at the boat, letters carried by someone to be collected at the airport, or the announcement of a forthcoming arrival on the island—as Bolton notes: "Service messages have always been the most listened-to program" (1999: 345). In addition, as we shall see in this chapter, the early years of radio in Vanuatu present an example of a highly participative technology.

When the journalists Godwin Ligo (ni-Vanuatu) and Paul Gardissat (French) launched their respective programs broadcasting local music and oral histories in the early 1970s, people reacted positively across the entire archipelago and these journalists received a great deal of encouraging listener correspondence. Gardissat supposedly received fifty or so letters a day. He even set up a system of "traveling cassettes" by sending a Dictaphone with blank cassette tapes to people on remote islands, which enabled them to make recordings and send them into the station (Bolton 1999: 347). Ligo concentrated on the competitiveness of his listeners' reactions:

> People would hear a story from another island, or another village on their island, or even from another clan in their own area, that was similar to one they also told themselves, and would write to the radio requesting that their version be broadcast. Sometimes, Ligo said, they would write to say that the version first broadcast had been stolen from them. Or they might write to say that they had the same story in their own island, but that it went further than the story that had been broadcast.
>
> (Bolton 1999: 346)

This bears witness to the way in which the inhabitants took advantage of the technical means radio offered in order to extend their possibilities for using the power and prestige surrounding their knowledge into the realm of broadcasting. Ligo clarified, "[t]his did not happen so frequently with songs, which were sung in local languages, and therefore not accessible to the majority of listeners" (Bolton 1999: 347). For, in Vanuatu, knowledge circulates in different ways: "[S]ome knowledge circulates secretly, narrowcast along lineal roads that snake through the forest, or in the private conversations between a knower and his heir. Other knowledge circulates publicly, broadcast from open clearings to surrounding audience" (Lindstrom 1990: 130).

In certain situations such as land disputes, secret knowledge can be divulged in order to testify to the legitimacy of one's claim to this property (Lindstrom 1990: 130). Secret songs containing genealogies and geographical names can also be revealed in this context. Therefore, the creation or performance of songs and dances can protect or hide particular secret content. For example, some songs are sung in idiosyncratic vernacular languages that are difficult to understand even for native speakers (François and Stern 2013); this makes retransmission beyond the original performance difficult. In other cases, as for instance the *newēt* dances of the Torres Islands, the songs are performed by a soloist encircled by other singers and musicians who "cover" his song with a vocal and instrumental ostinato:

> While stamping the board, the musicians sing a hocket *"O ho, Ohé o—O ho, Ohéo"*... Once this setting is created, the soloist can finally begin to sing the *newēt* song proper. Its melody and rhythm seem independent from the main rhythm, and is largely drowned out by the latter. This is in fact deliberate: most *newēt* poems are secret (*toq*; lit. "sacred"), and must remain inaudible to the non-initiated crowd— for fear that the song, which belongs to the singer and his family, be stolen from him. In the Lo-Toga language, the verb *gupe* "hide" designates the way in which

the choristers, with their loud panting ("O ho, Ohé-o"), conceal the voice of the soloist.

(François and Stern 2013: 123)

In a language incomprehensible to the uninitiated, certain secret songs can be broadcast on the radio without divulging the secrets. In this way, *kastom* dances, instrumental music, and songs are known to be part of reserved or restricted repertoires belonging to a family, an island, a village community, or another form of hierarchical group; payment in traditional money is expected for their transmission (Leach and Stern 2020; Stern 2013). These special repertoires, even on a very local scale, regularly give rise to property and ownership claims when performed publicly. At times the inhabitants of neighboring communities accuse each other in ceremonial or festival contexts of stealing a particular song, dance, musical instrument, element of a dance, or even a whole genre, like water or bamboo band music. When this competitiveness and these "arguments" are broadcast on the radio, they are simply an extension and augmentation of the typical local strategies used to control the circulation of knowledge (Bolton 1999: 346).

Although listeners were especially drawn to programs on *kastom* during the early years of radio, other forms of music were also regularly broadcast at this time. Styles included string band music, popular music from other Pacific islands, and Anglophone and Francophone popular styles. We could therefore describe these early days of radio as a time of "cultural democracy," in the classic sense of being open to all cultural forms, opinions, and criticisms: This participation is the democratic ideal par excellence: a society which does not make available to its members the resources necessary for their fulfillment as distinctive individuals and as fully participative members can be neither just nor democratic (Zask 2016: 44). For those who could pick up the signal, radio broadcasting created a space where all members of society could express themselves, share knowledge, discuss cultural matters, criticize, and reply to criticisms. Let us remember Foucault's words about the "ambiguous interplay of secrecy and disclosure" (1971: 18). Through self-controlled disclosure and restriction of information, radio broadcasting enabled individuals on dispersed island communities to make their voices heard across the water.

Between Public Broadcasting and Private Secrets

The first known recordings of the archipelago's music were made by John Layard in 1914 and soon followed by a handful of other researchers and travelers. Most of these early sound documents long remained in the obscurity of archives, scattered all over the world. A select few examples from former colonial archives were recently returned to the archives of the Vanuatu Cultural Centre (*Vanuatu Kaljoral Senta* [VKS]: formerly, New Hebrides Cultural Centre). The Cultural Centre expanded the earlier work by Ligo and Gardissat, by recording and disseminating local knowledge through a multiyear program, *The Vanuatu Oral Traditions Project*. The VKS aspires to digitalize their entire collection and has begun this process. However, it is often other institutions that are making these recordings publicly accessible online.[4] Alongside radio broadcasts of traditional oral culture, the VKS is playing an important part in the future of this local knowledge through its project.

The New Hebrides Cultural Centre was founded in Port Vila in the late 1950s by the two colonial governments, and the center had difficulty attracting local inhabitants at first. In 1976, with financial support from the United Nations Educational, Scientific and Cultural Organization (UNESCO) and the South Pacific Commission, ethnomusicologist Peter Crowe and linguist Jean-Michel Charpentier launched an initiative to record local oral traditions. Their aim was to train locals in recording and archiving techniques so that they could be involved in the production of material that would be conserved at the center. Crowe trained several ni-Vanuatu living in rural areas who were involved in *kastom* practices to make their own recordings for broadcast on local radio (Crowe 1981, 1997). This training project became a focal point of activities at the VKS and helped to develop the skills of local fieldworkers (Bolton 2006). With a view to involving ni-Vanuatu inhabitants in the preservation and valorization of their traditions, researchers like Crowe and Charpentier, and, later, Darrell Tryon, Kirk Huffman, and Lissant Bolton, developed this project by training a network of fieldworkers on most of the archipelago's islands. These local fieldworkers are volunteers who live in their village of origin and come once a year to take part in workshops at the VKS. During the year, they aim to raise awareness about cultural preservation and transmission work among their community, often building on a theme chosen at a VKS workshop. A hundred or so men and women living on different islands in the archipelago are now part of the VKS network of fieldworkers. When Gardissat decided to stop his popular radio program, employees of the VKS and some of the associated fieldworkers began to produce their own. These programs drew on the newly created material at the VKS sound archives, including recordings by local fieldworkers and foreign researchers. In this way, a lasting link was established between radio programs on *kastom* and the VKS.

In 1994, the Vanuatu Broadcasting and Television Corporation (VBTC) was created, including two national radio stations (Radio Vanuatu and Nambawan FM 98). The VBTC adopted a more commercial policy to its precursors, with both stations assuming a "hearing rather than listening model in radio, a development that [was] far from welcome in the islands, as rural Ni-Vanuatu depend[ed] on the radio as the source of all kinds of information" (Bolton 1999: 354). Payments were required for all content broadcast. This reduced broadcasting opportunities for many small-scale organizations and associations including the VKS. The broadcasting of local programs decreased dramatically and was replaced by replays of foreign productions (Bolton 2010: 8). Today, however, the VKS is once again producing cultural programs for broadcast on Vanuatu's radio and television. The legitimacy of the VKS as an official government body and the guarantor of respect for the broadcasting of traditional repertoires is widely recognized by the ni-Vanuatu. Other institutions perhaps feel they have less right to venture into this field. Moses Cakau, a television producer born in the capital, explained to me that broadcasting *kastom* repertoires is not always easy:

Another problem is the secret aspect of *kastom* music. Many people from elsewhere like this music, tourists adore it, but for us ... the definition is different, so to go and record music like that; the VKS does it, but we are aware that these are *kastom* practices ... You know, the reactions of our ancestors' spirits might be feared if we broadcast it. People might not sufficiently respect this music ... There are ways of paying[5] for these *kastom* songs. Also, because if we play these *kastom* songs on the air, the value of these songs decreases; ... if you listen to them at a certain time, in an appropriate situation you will feel a power ... but if you listen to them on the air, some young people might lack respect, because they would be more exposed to mockery.
(Interview, May 29, 2018)

Melanesians often mention precautions needed in the use of this singular repertoire, which exemplifies their desire to protect the repertoire from disrespect or inappropriate use. A similar situation was observed by Lawrence Kalinoe in Papua New Guinea, where a former chief ombudsman cautioned: "our traditional music and dances are unique. They must be recognised and accepted as such, encouraged and promoted, and above all must be protected... I must admit that introducing traditional music and dances into modern music using modern instruments can become mockery" (Kalinoe 2004: 41). The spiritual nature and the connections of this music with its places of origin and kinship make it sacred, intimate, and precious.

The bulk of Vanuatu's indigenous musical repertoire is closely linked with the ancestors. Songs and dances are not considered to be original compositions by living individuals; these art forms were communicated to humans by spirits of the ancestors through dreams. Moreover, certain songs containing geographical and historical knowledge capable of bearing witness to land ownership are strictly secret (Ammann 2012: 44; Lindstrom 1990: 109–10) and they may also possess magic powers. Therefore, those who possess this knowledge constantly waver between secrecy and disclosure: "[a] person is empowered by his public revelation of knowledge" (Lindstrom 1990: 113). Deep knowledge of local rules is necessary to know if and how this music can be broadcast. Some elements are strictly secret, taboo, and dangerous, while others are public and need to be revealed in order to confirm one's social prestige. Thus, Peter Crowe explains that among the secret forms of knowledge, some parts of the repertoire can be heard by all; this public listening brings prestige to those who possess the right to perform these songs:

Secret knowledge is repeated and transmitted during the *Qat Baruqu* rites. The material performed and recorded from the final and 10th night was, however, largely public and suitable for broadcast. Indeed, it is customary for women and children and non-initiated men to listen at this time outside the *ghamali* "men's house" and to be spectators for the dances and audience for the music.
(Crowe 1981: 171–2)

I often encountered words of caution regarding the broadcasting of *kastom* music and dance in Vanuatu and experienced it firsthand with my colleague Alexandre

François on the release of our collection *Music of Vanuatu: Celebrations and Mysteries* (François and Stern 2013). The necessary ethical steps and discussions with the VKS and local communities for that recording took several years. While some repertoires, particularly those for children or forms recreated recently, like water or bamboo band music, pose no major problems except when they are sold for commercial gain,[6] for others, sensitive conflicts over ownership, spiritual aspects, and presupposed origins make their reproduction difficult even for non-commercial recordings. At the same time, this spirituality gives *kastom* music a kind of "aura" which could be compared to that evoked by Benjamin for the "authentic" art work or Adorno for the live performance of "serious" music.[7] For the ni-Vanuatu, spiritual associations with music can make performance outside of a traditional context or subsequent media broadcasting (as for Moses) inappropriate. Until now, *kastom* music has not been mass-produced for commercial distribution by the Vanuatu recording industry.

The Recording Industry and Radio Broadcasting

The development of national radio had substantial implications for local musical practices. Alongside the broadcasting of *kastom* during the 1960s and 1970s, the radio helped to popularize another style, string band music, which later became a nationwide musical phenomenon, largely thanks to the work of French journalist Gardissat, who built the archipelago's first recording studio (Vanuata Productions) and made approximately 150 albums on cassettes, mostly by string band groups, in the 1970s and the 1980s. String band music is played by mostly male groups, sung in falsetto in responsorial form, and accompanied by acoustic string instruments (guitars, ukuleles, and a string bush bass) with light percussion backing on a selection of bamboos, congas, and bongos. Initially inspired by American country music and other popular styles, which were largely introduced by American soldiers based in the archipelago during the Second World War, and pan-Pacific pop, which is influenced by Polynesian music, Vanuatu string band music was created under the influence of the owners of the first tourist hotels in the 1970s around the capital Port Vila (Ammann 2013). For Ammann, string band music was the first real music for entertainment because traditional and Christian music had more important spiritual functions (Ammann 2013). It was also the first local music that was widely recorded and distributed on cassettes. However, according to Bolton, a French producer of one of the first radio programs recorded in the New Hebrides around 1960 is said to have approached local employees of the Vila Town Council, who formed a string band broadcast during the program. This program, which tended to play mostly ni-Vanuatu productions (*kastom* music, stories, and string band music), is said to have left a strong mark on the memory of the local population (Bolton 1999: 339).

As the recording studios were almost exclusively based in Port Vila, it was mostly groups from the islands nearest the capital that made recordings and became known on a national level. That is why during my fieldwork on the relatively remote island of Mota Lava in September 2019, a leader of a local string band that was active during the

1970s and the 1980s told me they were never able to gather enough money to go to city and record an album. Despite these limitations, string band music rapidly spread to all the archipelago's islands. In an informal conversation with Ralph Regenvanu, a former director of the VKS and currently a member of parliament (leader of Opposition), he suggested that while *kastom* music reflected the local identities of particular islands and villages, string band music might better represent the nation because it was present on all the islands and used Bislama, among other languages. The community aspect of string band music is usually consistent because the groups are often made up of musicians from the same islands, interpreting their original songs in the lingua franca, Bislama, and sometimes reusing their community's traditional but public (*kastom*) songs.

The commercialization of string band music, which does not typically contain secret characteristics or hold the spiritual associations of the *kastom* repertoires,[8] peaked in the 1980s when cassette technology spread across the archipelago. While radio could not always be picked up in remote parts, people on the islands could afford the luxury of listening to music on battery-powered tape recorders. As with radio, people usually listened to cassettes in groups. Like elsewhere in the world (Manuel 1993: 3), cassettes also gave rise to a parallel distribution circuit, whether through certain shops that copied albums and sold them with no scruples or through exchanges between private individuals (Stern 2014). At the time, most of the population was not overly concerned by or even aware of international copyright laws. A Copyright Act was written in 2002 but remained unpublished for nearly a decade. It was only in 2011, in preparation for joining the World Trade Organization, that the Act was ratified and the country joined the World Intellectual Property Organization.[9]

After Vanuata Productions, a growing number of recording studios enabled the development of a music industry with local string bands and imported musical styles, especially island reggae, foreign popular music, and remixes. These commercial recordings were first released on cassettes and then CD. With the development of these studios, radio employees no longer needed to continue making a large amount of recordings themselves, especially as the studios left them copies of their creations to broadcast on the radio as this was the only means of getting known. Even copies of music albums imported from abroad for commercialization were left at the radio station for publicity purposes. As former programming director at Radio Vanuatu and current head of the audiovisual section of the VKS Ambong Thompson explained, the first recording studios had contracts with national radio so that neither the radio nor the studios would have to pay and both would reap advantages: for the radio, material to broadcast, and for the studios, publicity (interview, May 29, 2018).

As in many other relatively small countries, recording industries and broadcasting are closely linked (Wallis and Malm 1984: 241). In theory, the former provide the latter with material and the latter publicize the material and boost sales. However, the broadcast media in Vanuatu does not pay royalties to artists, and, due to the limited size of the market, the sale of albums does not bring in substantial revenue. Yet, having an album and getting it broadcast on the media brings renown and prestige, as was the case when in the early days of radio, *kastom* oral traditions were broadcast.

This relationship between the local music and media industries has not always been positive. When payment was introduced for airtime, Georges Cumbo (director of the local branch of Alliance Française) explained how new forms of competition made matters complicated for musicians, producers, and including those at VKS:

> It must be remembered that only two or three years ago, when a group wanted its clip to be on TV, it had to pay, as if it were an advertising space, that's it, so that, that has changed, precisely thanks to, to the pressure group in fact musicians, this has changed, so clips are broadcast without paying rights, let's say, but on the other hand, there is no remuneration.
>
> (Interview, November 8, 2012)

Since then it has become relatively possible to be broadcast on the radio when you have made a single or an album. Political and cultural discourses valorize the broadcasting of local musicians, and this lack of payment (on both sides) enables a fairly easy exchange between the musicians who offer their recordings and the radio that plays them. However, if the majority of this music is broadcast when an album is released, not very many continue to be played repetitively for any longer than a few days, and several musicians complained to me in 2019 that broadcasters tended to play more foreign recordings than local. Nonetheless, the official media do not have a monopoly on broadcasting. In relatively small markets, music can become better known at concerts and festivals where announcements are made and albums can be sold directly to fans (Wallis and Malm 1984: 255–6). Moreover, with digital technology, broadcasts on social media channels like YouTube, Vimeo, Daily Motion, or Facebook are also widespread.

Although the number of studios and recordings is on the increase, apart from a small number of performers playing in the capital's bars and restaurants, few musicians can make a living from their musical activities in Vanuatu. Yet, in towns and rural areas, many aspiring musicians still dream of producing albums. One musician in the capital told me how, after years of practice, approaches to agents, independent fundraising, and other promotional work, by the time the album was released, they completely messed up the advertising and marketing. When finally the CDs were distributed to friends and family, he realized that they had just wanted to fulfill this old collective dream of making an album even if it was not sold. Having an album is a way of speaking out, a possibility to express oneself and to be heard. For musicians, it legitimizes their status. As in the early days of radio, when having one's story or song broadcast helped to assert one's existence or proclaim one's island belonging, nowadays having an album creates the possibility of being heard outside one's own island and gaining prestige (Stern 2017). However, despite this prestige and plenty of activities among local music producers, radio and television programs today play mostly foreign music (Hayward 2009: 63, 2012: 65). The few programs still broadcasting *kastom* music are prepared beforehand by the VKS, which may also agree to broadcast recordings made by inhabitants of the islands but these are rare cases. The interactive programs in which inhabitants of the remotest islands send their own recordings directly to the station are no longer possible. To be heard on the broadcast media today, people need to network intensively with local journalists and broadcasters.

New Cultural Policies: *Kastom* on Air

According to Ambong Thompson, listeners' demand for *kastom* programs is tremendous and the feedback after broadcasts is always very positive (interview, May 29, 2018). Some programs are even rerun due to public demand. However, the VKS does not have sufficient staff to devote themselves exclusively to the production of such programs. For his part, Moses Cakau underlines the necessity for the VBTC to work in closer collaboration with VKS, but he mentions too the lack of staff for such topics on national radio and television, who are also restricted by marketing considerations. In 2007, the first private radio station was created (FM 107); yet according to Thompson, the FM stations do not sufficiently valorize *kastom* music. Cakau stresses the fact that the national stations, Radio Vanuatu and Paradise FM 98—which replaced Nambawan FM98 in 2009—have a particular responsibility, more so than the private radio stations, to broadcast local music. Indeed, as Moses Cakau explained, for the new management in place since 2017:

> The focus is on *man Vanuatu* [the people of Vanuatu], the focus is on promoting the development of Vanuatu culture. So you're going to see that every day you can hear at least an hour of local music... Radio Vanuatu and Paradise FM are Vanuatu stations, they're run by the government and intended for "people from Vanuatu," so we want to broadcast stories about people from Vanuatu, the music of the Vanuatu people, so the OC [Organization Committee] has given more advice about this point.
>
> (Interview, May 29, 2018)

Indeed, the VBTC has been the subject of various restructuring operations, not only on a national scale but also with regional aid for the Pacific islands. The VBTC has been on several occasions linked to corrupt politicians and involved in scandals concerning unpaid salaries, frequent dismissals, and the misappropriation of funds. Furthermore, for a long time radio could not be picked up on the islands far from the capital. To solve these problems, reforms were implemented with considerable international support. This support included input from the Australian public agency AUSAID, which organized an aid program from 2007 to 2013.[10]

Entitled *Vois Blong Yumi* ("Our voices"), one of the goals of the AUSAID-funded project was to give voice to those who could not make themselves heard, especially women, children, and inhabitants of the most remote islands. As stated in one of the reports on the project, it was about "[b]uilding the nation by linking its past to its future and connecting people to knowledge and to each other" (VBY Review 2012: 7). In this way, its initiators wanted to introduce educational aspects by valorizing both local knowledge and development. Following government policies aimed at reducing the lack of local knowledge among urban youth, television programs such as *Art Kalja* (Art Culture) encouraged young people to turn to traditional knowledge for creativity, cultural inspiration, and to generate income.

The importance of radio on the most remote islands was particularly underlined following Cyclone Pam, a category 5 storm that devastated the archipelago in 2015. In its aftermath, people became aware of the importance of a public service that brings radio coverage to all of the islands. Therefore, the valorization of local broadcasts must be understood within the broader context of regional media policies. Around this time the staffing changed substantially. Francis Herman, who has considerable experience in the region's media, especially in Fiji and Australia, took over as general manager: "For Herman, the power of the media rests in its ability to 'look beyond today's news and look at tomorrow's news'. This quality is essential to address key issues in the Pacific such as poverty, climate change and gender inequality.… The media can and should play a very pivotal role in development" (Anderson 2015). Following the arrival of Herman, broadcasting policies were aligned more closely with those found elsewhere in the Pacific.

Moses Cakau emphasized the importance of local music broadcasts, "even if it is true that many international stars (including African ones) are very well-known in Vanuatu, and this is inevitable particularly because of easy access to YouTube and the Internet… our position is that of also playing Vanuatu music so that though the young listen to all this foreign music, they also have to be rooted" (interview, May 29, 2018). Talk shows and programs produced in rural areas were created to generate an interactive spirit. Again in this context, a series of programs was started to train journalists in the archipelago's six provinces and make *Vois Blong Provins* heard, a weekly half-hour program including provincial news, interviews, and public comments (VBY Review 2012: 19). The aim is for production to be in the hands of local people such as journalists from the provinces who know, or are close to those who know, what can and cannot be divulged. This, in a way, has certain similarities with Peter Crowe's idea in the 1970s when he trained fieldworkers.

According to my respondents, among the programs of the *Vois blong Provins* project, the ones from the Banks Islands made by Edgar Howard Woleg were those that met with the most success. The fact that Edgar has considerable experience of working on *kastom* through his collaboration with his brother, a VKS fieldworker, is relevant here. Edgar Woleg is a local journalist from Torba Province, the northernmost in the archipelago, and his province had long been forgotten. People there had no access to news, and even by 2018, the national radio could only be picked up on a weak signal during the day and a slightly better one at night. As Edgar explained:

> It is important to be able to transmit news from the remote islands to government officials in the urban centers. Thus, even if our islands are far away, this service enables news to reach Vila where government departments, NGOs and the representatives of other countries are, and perhaps draw their attention to our problems so they come to help us here.

(Interview, May 18, 2018)

With these words, Edgar makes the point that in an island context, being able to make oneself heard in the national media makes it possible to be part of the nation and provides the opportunity to seek development aid. Unlike in the 1970s and 1980s, the broadcasters (here, island journalists) and the local people interviewed are not necessarily the same as the listeners, who tend to be town dwellers. In order to make the voices of his province (Torba) heard, Edgar uses a form of identification in the content he broadcasts: "When I interview people… I only play music with the unique sound of Torba… Throughout the 30-minute program I only use music from the island talked about, I never use music from elsewhere, not just elsewhere outside Vanuatu but even elsewhere outside Torba, like Santo, Vila, Efate" (interview, May 18, 2018). In his determination to broadcast music from Torba, Edgar is giving a strong identity to the cultural forms of expression of certain regions in the archipelago. However when there are *kastom* forms among this local music, these are repertoires that are partly accessible, with no notion of secrecy, interpreted by legitimate people, the owners of the music. The interplay between what must be kept secret and what can be disclosed, in order to gain recognition and prestige, is thus once again on the air.

Conclusion

Using examples of broadcasting oral knowledge, particularly *kastom* music on Vanuatu radio, this chapter shows how island dwellers in Vanuatu manipulate what can be shared and what must remain secret. This research confirms Harrison's and Lindstrom's theories on the strategies used to maintain a balance between restriction and circulation of knowledge: "The 'management' of knowledge seems therefore to consist in a sort of balancing act, in an attempt to function with some combination of two equally credible, but contradictory, models of the value of knowledge at the same time" (Harrison 1995: 13–14).

The competitiveness that developed around radio broadcasts in Vanuatu bears witness to the way in which the population appropriated this technology upon its introduction. Revealing part or all of a piece of knowledge, making it known that one possesses a more complete version of a musical example, or proclaiming exclusive ownership of cultural property, all demonstrate the importance accorded to this knowledge and to the manner in which it is disseminated. Free radio broadcasting enabled everyone with radio access to become part of this dual system on the air. At first, the classic borders between presenters and audiences were less distinct because radio was structured as a relatively democratic format in which most people in Vanuatu could make their voices heard. However, this participative format of radio *kastom* programs has gradually disappeared, and for several years a media marketing policy has impeded the broadcasting of local knowledge.

Over the past four decades, the VKS's network of fieldworkers legitimized the spread of *kastom* knowledge and, in a sense, institutionalized this dissemination of knowledge as a unique form of broadcasting. In the same way that formal training of local fieldworkers enabled remote villagers to become actively involved in the VKS's cultural activities, the training (and resourcing) of island-based journalists amplified the voices of inhabitants of the remotest provinces. These journalists are being trained to connect local knowledge with current development problems across the Pacific region. What is happening here amounts to an institutionalization of the broadcast word. A second layer of decision-making power in the form of institutions is establishing itself alongside the power stakes "traditionally" in the hands of customary representatives.

Whether via a direct system (individuals-radio) or through these new intermediaries, the strategies concerning the circulation of knowledge are not peculiar to Melanesia alone, even if particular cases are characteristic of this region. Foucault also observes these models in European society:

> None may enter into discourse on a specific subject unless he has satisfied certain conditions or if he is not, from the outset, qualified to do so. More exactly, not all areas of discourse are equally open and penetrable; some are forbidden territory (differentiated and differentiating) while others are virtually open to the winds and stand, without any prior restrictions, open to all.
>
> (Foucault 1971: 17)

However, limiting one of the means available inevitably causes other means to emerge. The institutionalization of broadcasting in Vanuatu has reduced individual control of the circulation of *kastom* knowledge, and, although forms of interactivity remain, the level of interactivity present on early radio is no longer accessible to listeners. These listeners are now finding their voice elsewhere by appropriating other technological means, especially via social media platforms,[11] to discuss this knowledge, the way it circulates, and the legitimacy and manner of broadcasting it.

Acknowledgments

This chapter was translated into English by Deborah Pope. Funding was provided by the Australian Research Council under the project "Music, Mobile Phones and Community Justice in Melanesia" (LP150100973) led by Denis Crowdy and also by the Centre for Research and Documentation on Oceania. Lamont Lindstrom provided valuable feedback on an earlier draft of the text and Thomas Dick did a final rereading. I am also grateful to Ambong Thompson, Moses Cakau, and Edgar Howard Woleg for the time they devoted to answering my questions.

Notes

1. Lamont Lindstrom also noted that during his first fieldwork in Vanuatu in 1978–80, the village string bands all dreamed of traveling to the capital, Port-Vila, to record cassettes albums (personal communication, September 5, 2019).
2. For a consideration of music on digital technologies, see Stern (2014).

3   For texts that look more specifically at the secret aspects of music, see Ammann (2012), François and Stern (2013), Gourlay (1975), Kalinoe (2004: 47–9), Leach and Stern (2020), and McLean (1990).
4   Two notable examples of digitalization and online release come from the archives of the Pitt Rivers Museum (https://pittrivers-sound.blogspot.com/2013/03/field-recordings-from-vanuatu-collected.html, accessed May 20, 2020) and the Research Centre for Ethnomusicology (https://archives.crem-cnrs.fr/search/?q=Vanuatu, accessed May 20, 2020).
5   This is not payment in the commercial sense but a traditional form related to ceremonial exchanges, which can include items such as shells, mats, food, or pigs.
6   For issues concerning conflicting notions of musical value due to commoditization and the imposition of international copyrights, see Leach and Stern (2020).
7   Borrowing from Benjamin's idea that deplores the disappearance of the "aura" in art when reproduced ([1936] 1969), Adorno considers that music produced by mechanical device is not "authentic" and loses its "aura" and "spirituality" ([2006] 2009). He also criticizes in his several works music as commodity and distinguishes "light" and "serious" music (Adorno [1938] 2001).
8   Because of its links with the spiritual world and its secretive features, *kastom* music was generally seen as unsuitable for commercial recordings. Despite these restrictions regarding the music, certain forms of *kastom* dances can be staged for tourist audiences. This situation is similar to that of the Hmong *qeej* (mouthorgan) in Vietnam, which can be either performed using a secretive language in private community gatherings or staged using mundane musical examples for tourist performances (see Ó Briain 2018).
9   For more information on copyright laws in Vanuatu, see Forsyth (2013) and Forsyth and Haggart (2014).
10 Another example is the Pacific Media Assistance Scheme, run by the Australian Broadcasting Corporation International Development (2008–19).
11 I experienced this firsthand after the Melanesian Festival of Arts in Honiara in 2018, where the performances presented by the Vanuatu delegation gave rise to a great deal of online discussion on Facebook about the proper manner to present *kastom*, and the authenticity and legitimacy concerning its presentation.

Bibliography

Adorno, Theodor W. (1938) 2001. "On the Fetish-Character in Music and the Regression of Listening." In *The Culture Industry: Selected Essays on Mass Culture*, edited by Jay M. Bernstein, 26–52. London: Routledge.

Adorno, Theodor W. (2006) 2009. *Current of Music: Elements of a Radio Theory*. Malden, MA: Polity Press.

Ammann, Raymond. 2012. *Sounds of Secrets, Field Notes on Ritual Music and Musical Instrument on the Islands of Vanuatu*. Zürich and Berlin: LIT Verlag.

Ammann, Raymond. 2013. "String Bands in Vanuatu: Pop or Ethno?" *Ethnomusicology and Popular Music Studies* 25: 39–52.

Anderson, Megan. 2015. "Vanuatu's Radio's Active Decay." *The Saturday Paper*, July 18. Available online: https://www.thesaturdaypaper.com.au/news/media/2015/07/18/vanuatus-radios-active-decay/14371416002137, accessed September 17, 2017.

Benjamin, Walter. (1936) 1969. "The Work of Art in the Age of Mechanical Reproduction." In *Illuminations: Essays and Reflections*, edited by Hannah Arendt and translated by Harry Zohn, 217–42. New York: Schocken Books.

Bolton, Lissant. 1999. "Radio and the Redefinition of *Kastom* in Vanuatu." *The Contemporary Pacific* 11 (2): 335–60.

Bolton, Lissant. 2006. "The Museum as Cultural Agent: The Vanuatu Cultural Centre Extension Worker Program." In *South Pacific Museums: Experiments in Culture*, edited by Chris Healy and Andrea Witcomb. Clayton, Victoria: Monash University ePress. Available online: http://books.publishing.monash.edu/apps/bookworm/view/South+Pacific+Museums%3A+Experiments+in+Culture/139/xhtml/chapter13.html, accessed February 11, 2015.

Bolton, Lissant. 2010. "Radio and National Transformation in Vanuatu: A Kind of History." Paper presented at the Melanesian Research Seminar, London, UK, June 25.

Bull, Michael. 2005. "No Dead Air! The iPod and the Culture of Mobile Listening." *Leisure Studies* 24 (4): 343–55.

Crowe, Peter. 1981. "After the Ethnomusicological Salvage Operation—What?" *The Journal of the Polynesian Society* 90 (2): 171–82.

Crowe, Peter. 1997. "The Vanuatu Oral Traditions Project." *Pacific Arts* 15/16: 34–6.

Forsyth, Miranda. 2013. "The Developmental Ramifications of Vanuatu's Intellectual Property Commitments on Joining the World Trade Organization." *Pacific Studies* 36 (1/2): 157–72.

Forsyth, Miranda, and Blayne Haggart. 2014. "The False Friends Problem for Foreign Norm Transplantation in Developing Countries." *Hague Journal on the Rule of Law* 6 (2): 202–29. Available online: https://doi.org/10.1017/S1876404514001092, accessed October 17, 2016.

Foucault, Michel. 1971. "Order of Discourse. Inaugural Lecture Delivered at the Collège de France." Translated by Rupert Swyer. *Social Science Information* 10 (2): 7–30.

François, Alexandre, and Monika Stern. 2013. *Musiques du Vanuatu: Fêtes et Mystères/ Music of Vanuatu: Celebrations and Mysteries*. Paris: CD Inédit/Maison des Cultures du Monde. Available online: http://www.maisondesculturesdumonde.org/vanuatu-musiques-du-vanuatu, accessed December 25, 2013.

Gourlay, Ken A. 1975. *Sound-Producing Instruments in Traditional Society: A Study of Esoteric Instruments and Their Role in Male-Female Relations*. Port Moresby: New Guinea Research Unit, Australian National University.

Harrison, Simon. 1995. "Anthropological Perspectives: On the Management of Knowledge." *Anthropology Today* 11 (5): 10–14.

Hayward, Philip R. 2009. "Local Interpretation: Music Video, Heritage and Community in Contemporary Vanuatu." *Perfect Beat* 10 (1). Available online: http://www.equinoxjournals.com/ojs/index.php/PB/article/view/6110, accessed January 9, 2014.

Hayward, Philip R. 2012. "A Place in the World: Globalization, Music, and Cultural Identity in Contemporary Vanuatu." In *Music and Globalization: Critical Encounters*, edited by Bob W. White, 52–74. Bloomington, IN: Indiana University Press.

Johnson, Lesley. (1988) 2017. *The Unseen Voice: A Cultural Study of Early Australian Radio*. London and New York: Routledge.

Jolly, Margaret. 1992. "Custom and the Way of the Land: Past and Present in Vanuatu and Fiji." *Oceania* 62 (4): 330–54.

Kalinoe, Lawrence. 2004. "Legal Options for the Regulation of Intellectual and Cultural Property in Papua New Guinea." In *Transactions and Creations: Property Debates and the Stimulus of Melanesia*, edited by Eric Hirsch and Marilyn Strathern, 40–59. New York and Oxford: Berghahn Books.

Leach, James, and Monika Stern. 2020. "The Value of Music in Melanesia: Creation, Circulation, and Transmission under Changing Economic and Intellectual Property Conditions." In *The Oxford Handbook of Economic Ethnomusicology*, edited by Anna Morcom and Timothy D. Taylor. New York: Oxford University Press. Available online: https://www.oxfordhandbooks.com/view/10.1093/oxfordhb/9780190859633.001.0001/oxfordhb-9780190859633-e-33, accessed May 20, 2020.

Lindstrom, Lamont. 1990. *Knowledge and Power in a South Pacific Society*. Washington, DC and London: Smithsonian Institution.

Manuel, Peter. 1993. *Cassette Culture: Popular Music and Technology in North India*. Chicago: University of Chicago Press.

McLean, Mervyn. 1990. "Dance and Music Learning in Oceania." *The World of Music* 32 (1): 5–28.

Miller, Daniel, and Heather A. Horst. 2012. "The Digital and the Human: A Prospectus for Digital Anthropology." In *Digital Anthropology*, edited by Heather A. Horst and Daniel Miller, 3–36. London: Berg.

Ó Briain, Lonán. 2018. *Musical Minorities: The Sounds of Hmong Ethnicity in Northern Vietnam*. New York: Oxford University Press.

Stern, Monika. 2013. "Music in Traditional Exchanges in North Vanuatu." *Pacific Studies* 36 (1/2): 59–76.

Stern, Monika. 2014. "'*Mi wantem musik blong mi hemi blong evriwan*' (I Want My Music to Be for Everyone): Digital Developments, Copyright and Music Circulation in Port-Vila, Vanuatu." *First Monday* 19 (10). Available online: https://firstmonday.org/ojs/index.php/fm/article/view/5551/4130, accessed October 7, 2014.

Stern, Monika. 2017. "Is Music a 'Safe Place'? The Creative and Reactive Construction of Urban Youth Through Reggae Music (Port-Vila, Vanuatu)." *Journal de la Société des Océanistes* 144–5: 117–30. Available online: https://www.cairn.info/revue-journal-de-la-societe-des-oceanistes-2017-1-page-117a.htm?contenu=resume, accessed September 14, 2018.

VBY Review. 2012. "Mid-Term Review." Available online: https://dfat.gov.au/about-us/publications/Pages/vois-blong-yumi-mid-term-review-2012.aspx, accessed October 3, 2018.

Wall, Tim, and Nick Webber. 2014. "Changing Cultural Coordinates: The Transistor Radio and Space, Time, and Identity." In *The Oxford Handbook of Mobile Music Studies, Volume 1*, edited by Sumanth Gopinath and Jason Stanyek, 118–31. New York and Oxford: Oxford University Press.

Wallis, Roger, and Krister Malm. 1984. *Big Sounds from Small Peoples: The Music Industry in Small Countries*. London: Constable.

Zask, Joëlle. 2016. "De la démocratisation à la démocratie Culturelle." *Nectart* 3: 40–7.

2

Sounding an Indigenous Domain: Radio, Voice, and Lisu Media Evangelism

Ying Diao

Across southwestern China and Southeast Asia, Lisu people can now tune in to a mix of Lisu language sermon-and-music broadcast from Chiang Mai, Thailand.[1] These independent Lisu radio programs are broadcast via the Manila station of the Far East Broadcasting Company (FEBC), a nondenominational Christian radio network that has been operating since 1948 and now broadcasts in 124 languages from their globally distributed transmitters.[2] The Lisu channel was started in 1966 by American missionary LaVerne Morse, the youngest son of J. Russell Morse, who founded the North Burma Christian Mission (NBCM). The initiative was one of his key strategies to reconnect with indigenous communities in Yunnan province and northern Myanmar after a break following the end of British colonial rule of Myanmar in 1948 and the founding of the People's Republic of China (hereafter referred to as China) in 1949. Present-day Lisu radio broadcasts continue to be produced for the purposes of reaching the unconverted and strengthening the spiritual life of converted communities living in remote locations. Teacher and evangelist SaMoeYi, a native Lisu of Burmese origin, serves as the host addressing Lisu listeners across the region from the remote settlements in northern India (Arunachal Pradesh) to the city-dwelling Lisu in Yangon and Chiang Mai.

Over the past century, most of the Lisu on the China-Myanmar border have converted from animism to Christianity. The Lisu in China have a larger Christian population than any other Chinese ethnic minorities: about 80,000 in Nujiang Lisu Nationality Autonomous Prefecture (henceforth, Nujiang Prefecture)—the largest Chinese Lisu settlement—alone by 2012 (Feng 2012). By December 2017, over 90 percent of the 0.5 million Burmese Lisu self-identified as Christians affiliated with five denominations.[3] In recent years, the personal electronic media of these Lisu Christians have become visible and audible throughout the border region and are now readily accessible via mobile devices. Although these media now include radio broadcasts, cassette tapes, video compact discs (VCDs), digital video discs (DVDs), and cell phones with internet access to social media sites access, the Lisu were first introduced to sound recording technologies on a large scale via American missionaries' radio evangelism in the late 1960s. This radio evangelism aimed to make immediate connections between spatially dispersed communities and sustain the spiritual life of the nascent Lisu church. As Bolter and Grusin have argued in their discussion of remediation, "[n]ewer media do not necessarily supersede older media because the process of reform and refashioning is mutual" (1999: 59). For the Lisu, their current media habits and trends are influenced by historical radio broadcasting. Missionary radio programs first introduced the technologies, which transmitted mediated voices guiding Lisu worship and religious participation. In recent years, these voices from outside the community have been replaced by new indigenous voices on the radio, sounding a more relatable indigenous domain for the Lisu.

The "technologically-mediated voice" of speech and music is an effective entry point for studying the agency of media evangelists. Amanda Weidman argues that "culturally constructed ideas about the voice … determine how and where we locate subjectivity and agency; they are the conditions that give sung or spoken utterances their power or constrain their potential effects" (2014: 45). In this chapter, Lisu-mediated religious voices correspond with conceptualizations of the voice as disassociated from individual agency and subsumed by social ideology (see also Feld et al. 2004). While much scholarship has focused on how the physical body shapes certain sonic features of the voice, thus creating specific values and subjectivities with which people come to identify (Eidsheim 2019; Harkness 2014; Inoue 2006),[4] this research examines the reproduction and circulation of human voices through media technology. Data is drawn from oral histories, missionary newsletters,[5] and the archives of Lisu radio broadcasters. I collected ethnographic data on trips to Kachin State, Yangon, and Chiang Mai between December 2017 and February 2018, and this data is informed by my doctoral research on Lisu gospel singing in Yunnan (Diao 2015). In this chapter, I compare and contrast two Lisu-run media ministries formed since the 1990s: the Lisu radio ministry in Chiang Mai, which is supported by the Asia Christian Services and Gospel Broadcasting Mission (ACS-GBM),[6] and the media ministry of Yangon-based Myanmar Agape Christian Mission (MACM). Both of these indigenous Christian missions are situated in postcolonial mainland Southeast Asia, but the ways in which Lisu evangelists engaged with sound technologies to produce their mediated gospel voices and the resulting socioreligious changes in their respective communities are very different.

There are two main threads in the account that follows. First, inspired by the writings of several recent radio ethnographies on the immanent power of broadcast media and the ideologies of immediacy and directness they can enable (Blanton 2015; Englund 2018; Fisher 2009, 2016; Kunreuther 2010, 2014),[7] this chapter describes how the material form of radio brought into being a sense of directness and intimacy for the Lisu. The mediated voice, historically facilitated through the work of previous missionaries, connects and links geographically dispersed religious communities. The second thread follows a recent cross-disciplinary interest in the capacity of new media technologies to curate religious traditions and institutions. In particular, drawing on perspectives from a recent "media turn" in the anthropology of religion that underlines the intrinsic inseparability of religion and media (De Vries 2002; Engelke 2010; Meyer 2008)—as opposed to the view of the mediatization of religion insisting on the succumbing of religious practices under the logic of media (Hjarvard 2016)—I trace how the radio and other media technologies are localized by the Lisu socioreligious world and how they enhance interactions between these believers and the divine. I also explore how the circulation of mediated gospel voices interacts with other aspects of the public sphere such as secular entertainment and other forms of popular culture.

A Short History of Lisu Christian Radio

The story of radio in the Lisu transnational community begins with the American radio evangelists who produced programs on religious themes for remote, largely unconverted communities. In the highlands of southwest China and mainland Southeast Asia, radio ministry became a necessity in the mid-twentieth century, where the scope for traditional face-to-face mission work was limited in recently independent countries—for instance, in China, all missionaries were expelled upon the founding of the new Communist government in 1949. Lisu language radio production began with the collaboration of two Western mission efforts in the late 1960s: the FEBC, which pioneered the broadcast of shortwave programs to many hard-to-reach ethnic groups through their transmitters based in the Philippines,[8] and the Morse family, who eventually settled in Chiang Mai in 1972. The Morse family hailed from the American Church of Christ and had first started to work among the Lisu in the 1920s. They left China for northern Myanmar in 1950 and continued their mission there in 1965 until they were ousted by the military government (Morse family n.d.). In 1966, LaVerne Morse established the South East Asia Evangelizing Mission (renamed as ACS from 1983; hereafter collectively referred to as ACS) under the direction of the First Christian Church and Maple Lawn Church of Joliet in the United States. The ACS mission began their outreach program through sending letters and distributing printed literature, such as Christian hymnbooks and teaching materials in indigenous languages, before turning to gospel radio broadcasts from 1968.[9] Between 1968 and 1991, their Lisu gospel program was produced primarily under the supervision of LaVerne Morse and broadcast daily through FEBC's broadcasting network.

Several of ACS's evangelistic strategies had ramifications for the public airing of socioreligious bonds within Lisu communities. First, from the very beginning LaVerne Morse coordinated both American and indigenous leaders to engage in multisited production. Before the first recording studio was completed in the Chiang Mai Bible Institute (a subdivision of ACS) in 1979, radio materials recorded in Thailand were mostly edited and combined into high-quality cassette-recorded programs in Cincinnati (USA) and then delivered by post to FEBC. Such modality of cooperation embodies an incipient overlapping of Lisu transnational religious networks and those undergirding the work of this Christian media ministry. Second, the training of an indigenous leadership was a top priority for the ACS founders; they wanted to prepare indigenous evangelists to produce their own radio programs. For first-generation indigenous evangelists, this training provided an opportunity to learn skills in media production and facility management. Third, radio evangelism formed a perfect marriage between uses of sound technologies and the affective preaching voice; radio was an ideal carrier of the voice of esteemed *malpha dama*[10] (senior church pastoral staff), delivering words of exhortation and encouragement to the people. The Lisu referred to their radios as "sound-of-wind," "puller-of-sound-of-wind," and "paths-of-the-wind."[11] In addition to the textual dimensions of the Bible and hymnbook, the Lisu could now engage with the Christian faith through radio-mediated voices, with which they more easily identified.

In the early radio programs, LaVerne Morse was one of the main preachers addressing Lisu Christian listeners and potential converts. The mission distributed leaflets telling villagers when to tune in to hear LaVerne, and listeners responded to him with their letters. One listener living close to the Tibetan border wrote: "To Preacher Joseph [LaVerne]: Beloved teacher, even though we are not able to meet with you face-to-face, our beloved and much-missed teacher, because we hear your voice speaking to us on the radio, we thank you very much" (reprinted in *ACS* Newsletter, July 1975). This is just one example of many letters detailing Lisu Christians' early responses to the radio-mediated gospel voice. The powerful sound of this renowned preacher's voice became an alternative form of religious mediation, an embodiment Christian belief that was essential to sustaining and building the transnational Lisu Christian community.

Directness, Liveness, and Shortwave Radio

In her research on the history of FM radio and ideologies of the voice in Nepal, Laura Kunreuther describes the nature of spontaneity in live broadcasts, especially in call-ins and live dialogue between the host and listeners. This "ideology of directness is clearly tied to several technological and material features of FM broadcasting" (Kunreuther 2010: 336). In contrast, Lisu radio programs have always been prerecorded. They achieve a sense of directness through alternative modes of programming, distribution, and liveness. First, liveness and intimacy are realized through the addition of indigenous modes of expression that index kinship relations and religious affiliation between the host and listeners. For example, during my fieldwork in Nujiang Prefecture between 2012 and 2014, the host often started the program with the markedly Lisu pronominal terms such as *alyir nissat be alzi nima* (brothers and sisters), *qotbaiq* (friends), and *atrritsu* (everyone) to communicate fellowship and friendship to the listeners. These were often followed by the phrase *Hwa hwa* (How are you?), the most popular Lisu colloquial greeting used to begin a conversation between friends and acquaintances. Throughout the program, the studio preacher talks into the microphone and makes contact to his imagined listeners by addressing them all as "brothers and sisters."

This cultivation of a direct voice in Lisu broadcasting is not restricted to the production process but also through the stage of distribution that involves how listeners congregate around radio receivers. For instance, when there were few radio receivers in the China-Myanmar border region, large numbers of Lisu Christians gathered around one or two transistorized radio receivers to hear broadcasts[12]—here, radio became the first of what Brian Larkin calls a "public technology" (2008: 48) among the Lisu. In Nujiang, several times prior to the worship services I heard recorded radio programs played over an outdoor loudspeaker bolted to an external wall or an electricity pole so that the whole village could hear—this resonates with the ACS missionary report in their 2000 newsletter. Furthermore, due to the critical lack of indigenous *malmit jiasu* (preachers) in China, some local churches used radio broadcasts as a substitute for the preaching sections of their services, which created an illusion of temporal copresence that brought the congregation into an immediate connection with the preacher despite their physical distance.[13] Radio has been supplemented by more recent technologies in Lisu Christian communities. When tape players became common in the 1980s and the 1990s, copies of taped radio broadcasts were circulated between friends and neighbors. In the last two decades, with financial support from American Christians, more battery-operated shortwave radios, MP3 players, and other portable playback devices have been sent to these Lisu villages, providing locals with the kind of technological spaces where they can continue to advance their knowledge of Christianity. Nowadays Lisu broadcasts are also streamed via online platforms, thus expanding the radio-based technological spaces further.

Music brings particular value to the cultivation of directness over the radio. In the 1970s, ACS missionaries—among whom Paul Fuller was a key figure—sought to develop unique "ethnic" broadcasts to help indigenous people use their musical and cultural idioms in praise of God.[14] LaVerne Morse referenced Virgil Warren—known as "Preacher Paul" on air—because he composed music for guitar using a pentatonic scale for broadcasts in Lisu and Rawang languages.[15] In 1973, Lisu radio broadcast a series of lyrical ballads from a cassette album titled *Siljje Niqchit Mutgguat* (Songs of Deep Yearning, henceforth referred to as *Siljje*). Generally considered the first Lisu-language music recording, the album comprises thirty-four lyrical ballads featuring two-part singing with acoustic guitar accompaniment written and performed by Joni Morse (singer) and Bobby Morse (guitarist), the third generation of the Morse family. Thematically, their repertoire includes Christian songs expressing love of God and secular ballads speaking to the nostalgic themes of family, friendship, loss, and longing for the homeland in the far north of Myanmar (see Morse 1974). For example, the popular song "*Mileix matdda a'ma Mulashiddei*" (Unforgettable Mulashidi) expresses the two singers' longing for their former home in Myanmar's northernmost town of Putao. Musically, the distinct vocal style of *Siljje* songs differs from that of congregational singing of the translated missionary hymnody. For the Lisu listener, the rough, loud, and emotionally neutral voice of congregational singing contrasts with a soft, lyrical, and sentimental voice sung in the first person on *Siljje*.

The broadcasting of *Siljje* songs popularized not only a new vocal style but also new ideas of vocalizing one's own religious beliefs. Through those first broadcasts of songs from the album *Siljje*, the Burmese Lisu were inspired to start writing and recording Lisu music themselves from the early 1980s onwards. In the sections that follow, I compare and contrast two relatively new Lisu media ministries to understand how Lisu media practitioners and musicians subsequently developed their own media-centered evangelistic work. Through their initiative, the media has become one of the central dimensions of Lisu Christian religious practice, and these indigenous ministries now serve as powerful vehicles for voicing an emergent Lisu ethno-religious domain.

Ahdi Mark-GBM: Religious Mediation on the Radio

In 1991, Chiang Mai-based Lisu evangelist Ahdi Mark became the chief editor of Lisu radio broadcasts. His radio ministry continued to be supported by funding under the ACS-GBM cooperation.[16] There were five full-time staff members—including two young male musicians Jay Yo and Jay Tsi—by January 2018, when I visited GBM's Chiang Mai studio, where Lisu programs were produced. Ahdi Mark and his team members also engaged in the production of broadcasts in four other ethnic languages: Rawang, Wa, Achang (Ngochang), and Jinghpaw.[17] Prerecorded broadcasts were loaded onto a compact disc one month in advance and sent to FEBC for daily broadcasting at a price of 1,800 USD per month. The components of their regular Lisu radio program have not changed much over the years, except that the duration was extended from fifteen to thirty minutes in October 2000.[18] A standard thirty-minute program starts with the host's warm greetings framed with Lisu traditional instrumental music that invites all to join in and study God's words on air. After this musically framed calling of familial and spiritual bonds and one Lisu Christian praise song of mostly Burmese origin, the majority of time (around twenty minutes) is allocated to a prerecorded sermon by an esteemed preacher—preachers would often record dozens of short sermons in one studio visit—followed by several gospel music tracks with optional requested songs at the end. This is not a live radio program, so audiences cannot call in to request specific songs live on air.[19]

Radio-mediated gospel music serves as a powerful signifier for what two editors, Ahdi Mark and SaMoeYi, referred to as the Lisu church's unique "voice," which they believe stands out from the voices of other ethnic churches within FEBC's transnational broadcasting networks. According to Ahdi Mark, his predecessor used to incorporate a bell sound to announce the start of the program. They stopped doing this when they realized that bell-ringing could also signify death and funerals among some ethnic groups. So, instead, they started to frame the radio greetings with Lisu traditional instrumental music. Ahdi Mark and SaMoeYi explained to me that this was because "the sound of *qibbe* [Lisu four-stringed plucked lute] has been widely considered as a signifier of Lisu culture—we [Christians] do not play the traditional *qibbe* anymore, but we still recognize the sound. So anyone would know that it is a Lisu program upon hearing it" (interview, February 19, 2014). In addition to making recordings of ethnic sounds that derive from traditional *qibbe* tunes and imitated on the acoustic and electronic guitars, they recorded Lisu traditional music played by rural folk musician Ngwa Pha. Both types of recordings were recycled as their opening thematic music.

Christian pop songs written by the Burmese Lisu were another source of mediated gospel voices on air. Lisu Christians in Myanmar were so inspired by the Morse brothers' album *Siljje* that they started to compose and record their own songs in the early 1980s, albeit with limited resources. Evolving from those early lyrical ballads sung to an acoustic guitar accompaniment, the styles of the present-day repertoire are more diverse. Nevertheless, the majority of Lisu Christian pop is in verse-chorus form and accompanied by a typical rock band instrumentation of electric guitars, drum kit, and keyboard. In recent years, Myanmar has become the center of Lisu media and music production. During their frequent trips back and forth between Myanmar and Thailand, Ahdi Mark and his crew purchased Lisu music recordings produced in Myanmar or received them as gifts. In some cases, they even got the master copies before the completed and packaged albums were released for commercial circulation through church networks, private connections, and the unwelcomed pirated market. Once back in the studio, those newly acquired recordings were copied onto the editing computer as MP3 or WAV files. The nomenclature of their digital music folders was based on the names of singers, language (Lisu or English), purpose or use (e.g., opening or closing songs, seasonal songs), genres (e.g., choir songs, praise songs, traditional tunes), and a separate folder for the special anthology compiled by SaMoeYi. Thanks to their many years of archiving, Ahdi Mark's GBM studio now has the most extensive collection of Lisu modern Christian songs,[20] from which the editors are able to choose freely for their broadcasts and remixes.

While continuing to focus on the production of radio broadcasts, since the early 2000s Ahdi Mark has been making Lisu music recordings for other purposes in his spare time, and his studio as of now has the capacity to draw on the latest audiovisual technologies as part of the production process.[21] Two main kinds of Lisu music videos have been produced at the GBM studios over the past two decades. The first kind is karaoke DVDs that include singing, visuals of the rural landscape, and acting plots; featured singers contribute the prerecorded audio segments to accompany these videos. The second audiovisual production at GBM is the master copies of Burmese-produced Lisu music albums, which they reproduced for local Christian communities. In fact, many Burmese Lisu singers and musicians would happily ask Ahdi Mark for a favor to sell and distribute homemade copies of their own recordings. With his rudimentary video equipment and editing software, Ahdi Mark started to make drama films with the help of Lisu friends and relatives in 2011. They used GBM's studio space and equipment to do the editing work, and by 2017, four movies had been produced. These producers were largely self-taught in the craft of filmmaking. Such self-teaching went along with their high degree of self-motivation. The main aim of filmmaking, according to Ahdi Mark, was to educate those Lisu youths in trouble—social issues in the community include drug abuse, prostitution, and physical violence—or promote the importance of school education and legitimate work for their future. He believed that today's commercial films were about becoming rich, which in the long term was not good motivation for Lisu youths. For him, it was important to counter these popular media with his teachings about the right path of life through film, and he was excited to tell me about his next movie and aspirations:

> Sometimes we had to use our own money for film productions. But we wanted to do it. We have recording equipment here in GBM's radio studio and we have free time. We do not want to stay home. Why not make more Lisu music and films that

voice aloud our Lisu needs? Our next film is based on a true story about fourteen teenagers singing, dancing, drinking, and doing bad things in the jungle thirty years ago, for which they were eventually killed by a tiger. People who escaped from that incident recounted the story and said it was a punishment. Now I need to learn animation for the tiger part.

(Interview, January 11, 2018)

Recording projects in Ahdi Mark's media ministry aimed to facilitate the radio transmission of Christian preaching. Their interpretations of the scripture were used to sustain Christian communities by engaging members of Lisu church across this borderland region. The radio-mediated voice of senior male church leaders continues to dominate the scene in this Chiang-Mai-based Lisu radio ministry. But Ahdi Mark's focus on production in the studio contrasts with the music and media ministry of Lazarus Fish, who runs the MACM mission in Yangon.

Lazarus Fish-MACM: Performing an Emerging Indigenous Domain

Lazarus Fish's popularity is derived as much from participation in other aspects of the public sphere and in non-Christian environments. Compared with Ahdi Mark's radio ministry, Lazarus's studio production was complemented by frequent off-air gospel trips, where he produced programs of "live broadcasting." These programs appeal to his listening public through the broadcast of live singing and informal, spontaneous interactions between singers and audiences. While radio serves as a platform for an intra-indigenous circulation of mediated gospel sounds, Lazarus' media ministry sends messages and speaks to those outside the Lisu faith communities in the public domain. By implementing a series of initiatives over nearly two decades, Lazarus has risen to fame as a self-made religious and cultural leader in the community. He is renowned for his substantial investment in updating the multimedia equipment of his recording studio, which he uses to train a small group of young enthusiasts with musical talent to become musicians, singers, and songwriters. These performers have established the institutions of Lisu music and media production in sacred and secular settings, and several of them have acquired a special position as "big names" for their ability to mobilize indigenous communities through music.

Lazarus was born into a Lisu preacher family in Putao, Myanmar. His father was one of the first converts among the Burmese Lisu and was converted by the founder of NBCM, J. Russel Morse. With a Master of Divinity from Lincoln Christian University in Illinois (1998) and Doctor of Missiology from Asbury Theological Seminary in Kentucky (2002), Lazarus is now fluent in Lisu, Burmese, and English. His US training in leadership, evangelism, and church planting prepared him for becoming a traditional church leader. In December 2002, he established Myanmar Agape Christian Mission (MACM) and formed a missionary family of his own—with his wife Acha Fish and four children—with financial support from American Christian donors. This multifaceted mission includes the Yangon Christian College and Seminary (YCCS: a college-level degree program established in January 2003), the China Border Training Center (a nondegree program founded in June 2003), and a media-and-music ministry for evangelization.

They began the radio ministry early in November 2002 and launched a sound recording center in January 2003 to produce radio broadcasts and gospel music recordings. In their first decade, the studio made eighty-five albums primarily in Lisu language.[22] Similar to Ahdi Mark's radio broadcasts, the MACM radio programs were prerecorded in the studio. In addition to preaching, singing, and song requests, their programs included teaching, messages in the form of proverb, and Christian dramas. MACM's radio broadcasting only existed in the initial years;[23] however, the extensive training that young evangelists received in the process of producing these radio programs equipped them with the essential skills for launching their own media projects in the future.

Lazarus' media evangelism was popular because he created a new format that not only served evangelism but also became an essential part of Lisu Christians' social life. He introduced an alternative evangelistic vehicle that combined open-air preaching with live gospel music concerts. In most cases, there were no seats and the audience had to stand throughout the performance. These gospel concerts include preaching, musical performances, and other entertainment in styles commonly found at a standard pop concert. This form of media evangelism brought musicians out of the recording studio to interact with the listening public, who had previously only heard these musicians' voices over the radio or through other forms of sound reproduction technologies. The concerts often began with an introductory speech and passionate preaching by Lazarus. MACM's own Net Music Band served as an accompanying ensemble, playing for a group of singers who came onto stage one by one—sometimes in pairs or small groups—to sing one or two songs each. A short introduction and words of encouragement before each song were also an integral part of these gospel concerts in the Lisu church. In contrast with typical pop concerts in Myanmar, most Lisu gospel concerts were rather long, with the singers performing from dusk until close to midnight with no formal intermission.

The earliest video recordings of MACM's gospel concerts can be traced back to 2004, when Lazarus and his team were invited by the local government authorities in China to perform at the celebration of the fiftieth anniversary of the founding of Nujiang Prefecture. In the official promotional material, the group was introduced as "Burmese Lisu Folk Art Troupe." The troupe prepared a secular Lisu-and-unity-centered music program for this "gospel trip"[24] that included ethnic songs of encouragement, Lisu versions of romantic Chinese love songs, and modern street dances. Unlike MACM's other gospel concerts where singing was accompanied by a live band, for this series of performances in Nujiang Prefecture all the accompanying soundtracks were prerecorded on a taped cassette. Ahdi sang his signature song, "Lisu"; the so-called "Lisu Song King" WaNyi Ahwu performed a cover version of "More Than I Can Say"; and a group street dance was choreographed to "*Gudan Balei*" (Lonely Ballet), a 2002 hit by Taiwanese singer Xu Huixin. The highlight of each concert was an ensemble performance of the encouragement song "*Titnit Titwa*" (One Mind, Same Root). The lyrics repeat major Lisu clan names (today used as common surnames); emphasize how the Lisu people have been good-hearted, diligent, and intelligent; and suggest that intra-ethnic and intra-community unity should be the primary goal of the Lisu. The wide range of vocal styles was unusual on the official stage in Nujiang Prefecture. These included WaNyi Ahwu's soft, low voice in a sentimental manner, the female singer Jeveny's powerful mezzo-soprano voice, and male guitarist Marteeyet's rhythmic rap improvisation. The 2004 tour was also the first time most Nujiang Christian Lisu met second-generation Lisu singers from Myanmar. Thus Lazarus' outreach performances caused quite a sensation.[25]

This gospel concert format laid the foundation for the evening concert as an essential part of day-long activities at Lisu cultural festivals. These festivals were initiated by the Christian Lisu elites in Myanmar and have gained popularity throughout the international Lisu community since 2011. In this context, the technologically mediated voice migrated from religious ritual or evangelistic contexts into public, secular settings often associated with youth popular culture, entertainment, and even business. After the establishment of MACM, Lazarus insisted that contemporary Christian gospel music not be produced and performed to entertain but to move and touch the hearts of people. Yet in 2011 at the first Lisu international New Year celebration held in Myitkyina, Kachin State, Lazarus volunteered to lead a so-called "music entertainment" committee in charge of providing the sound system and music programs for four consecutive nights of the festival; as he writes in the MACM newsletter, "forty-five Lisu popular singers which included twelve singers from China participated in the evening cultural/entertainment performances."[26] This was the first time Lazarus used the term "popular singer" instead of "gospel singers" in the monthly field report written for his generous American donors.

Another hallmark of Lazarus' media evangelism was his emphasis on the use of media practices to attract Lisu youths, who tended to be more interested in the latest technological innovations and entertainment forms. Lazarus mobilized them through his open-air preaching, music ministry, and eventual leadership of the community. YCCS students were given many opportunities to engage in weekly evangelistic programs, practice contemporary gospel singing and modern dance, and learn media production in the Fish Studio on the YCCS campus. Students were also trained in the construction of stages—including the installation of the platform, lighting systems, cables, and wires—as well as in the transportation of musical equipment and stage decoration. Lazarus frequently included photos of YCCS students constructing the stage for their open-air preaching and concerts in the MACM newsletters, showing his pride in this initiative for the training of music-centered evangelism and church planting.

Among current Lisu media practitioners, only a handful actually established separate studios. Instead, most operate from home with rudimentary recording equipment in place of professional facilities. For example, guitarist Marteeyet explained that he improved his guitar-playing skills and recording techniques during his work at MACM. After that, he worked full time as a professional pop musician in Yangon and eventually opened his Omega Studio in a small flat in Sanchaung Township near the Myaynigone intersection, where his wife and three children live. By contrast, given the primacy of uses of sound technologies in MACM's various ministries, Lazarus was able to invest heavily in improving his standalone recording studio. He renamed it the "Fish Studio" and reopened for recordings on August 22, 2015, with top-class digital Pro Tools HD recording equipment, all purchased and brought back from the United States, to replace the old analog system. In addition to making their own gospel albums in both Lisu and Burmese languages, the studio also provides external recording services. During my visit to the studio on January 26, 2018, I met Rebecca Win, one of Myanmar's most famous female pop singer, who was recording a single for a gospel album sponsored by a Chinese Christian businessman.

Lazarus was able to pick and choose from a pool of gifted YCCS students and train them to become leading figures in Lisu music and media production. The first batch of these students became the core members of the first-generation Net Music Band, which makes popular gospel albums and regularly performs in MACM's gospel trips. Their ongoing studio production and live performances in the preaching-and-concert programs foreground the activities of second- and third-generation Lisu musicians, and they have now become well known in the Lisu transnational religious community. Since the late 2000s, upon becoming capable of doing a combination work of live performance and music recordings, these well-trained and experienced Lisu gospel musicians and singers have come to play an essential role in the standardization of Lisu Christian pop, in terms of both singing and performance styles. The electronically mediated voices of these popular gospel singers are now widely appreciated, and they have become privileged members of Lisu Christian communities.

Among the second generation of Lisu musicians, the voices of three female singers (Jenevy, Seiseipi, and Aivei) stand out. Their non-high-pitched, lyrical, and gentle voices—Jenevy's deep, rich sound was particularly unique at the time—were distinct from what had been expected from a conventional Lisu female singer performing "ethnic folk." The Nujiang congregation learned to match their voices with recordings of these singers that they found in the local farmers' markets. Burmese Lisu singers' vocal quality was a frequent topic of conversation with my Nujiang Lisu informants, who cited the impact of the Burmese-produced music recordings on their Christian experiences and media practices. They insisted that the Burmese Lisu have "better" voices and play the guitar more beautifully using the commonly used Lisu term for "good sound" (*nasa ssair*)—when "*nasa*" is used to compare different sonic qualities, it can be translated as "polished" or "refined." The combination of *nasa* and *gaqchit* (literally, "cheerful") in their descriptions of Burmese Lisu singers' vocal styles differentiates the affective power of the technologically mediated voice of contemporary Christian pop from that of the congregational hymn.

In recent years, Lazarus has promoted a Lisu young singers' competition in Myanmar, with the final often being held at one of the Lisu transnational cultural festivals. Young contestants are required to sing preselected signature songs of the most renowned first- and second-generation Lisu musicians. Singing is judged on the qualities of their voices (including timbre, intonation, vocal register, and musical interpretation), together with criteria such as articulation (including during the introductory speech before singing), timing control, stage etiquette, dress code, and bodily gestures. A two-round contest concludes with an award ceremony in which honors are ceremonially presented to the winner and finalists. Participants prepare for this competition by studying the original recordings of competition songs, now viewed as the classical repertoire of Lisu Christian pop. In this way, the singing contest standardizes the ways that Lisu youths should sing and promotes development of solo singing in the public domain as a valued form of socioreligious interaction.

Conclusion

Technologically mediated voices over the radio and in live performance have become the audible heart of an emerging indigenous domain. After emerging as part of an outside missionary evangelical enterprise, in recent decades these voices have come to represent indigenous Lisu media production. This chapter examined two Lisu indigenous media ministries to explore the work these evangelists put into the production of technologically mediated voices. This work contributes to the creation of an indigenous domain beyond the sacramental and ritualistic life of the church. My analyses have unearthed the unevenness of media-driven transformations of religious experiences and practices beyond the Christian North Atlantic and Islamic contexts by attending to the internal differences in how religious minorities make the best use of the possibilities of particular media technologies to produce their mediated gospel voices. Both media ministries are situated in minority Christian contexts of postcolonial Southeast Asia; however, the two examples here present contrasting models for connecting dispersed indigenous socioreligious communities across the region.

Unlike Lazarus Fish, who proactively absorbed globally popular evangelistic formats, Ahdi Mark and his GBM-supported media ministry continued to produce radio-mediated gospel voices through the adoption of sound technologies and editing software, and through the incorporation of Lisu modes of address and musical idioms, as the indices of Lisu-ness. Although he made great efforts to engage with the local community in producing more music recordings and gospel dramas for non-radio use, the focus of Ahdi Mark's work was on achieving GBM's original goal: reaching remote indigenous communities to strengthen their spiritual life. The mediated voice shaped by his radio broadcasting was mostly confined to religious contexts and produced based on tightly structured religious institutions, networks, and funding sources. Nevertheless, his collection and archiving of Lisu music recordings for radio production created a link between the Lisu evangelistic media ministry and transnational music industries.

By contrast, Lazarus Fish switched his focus from radio and gospel album production to the evangelistic outreach outside of the studio through well-organized gospel trips to remote indigenous communities. Therefore, his transmission of the mediated voice migrated from traditional Christian ritual contexts into other aspects of the public sphere. In doing so, he became known as a Lisu religious and cultural activist. The rise of new voices of religious authority such as Lazarus, and the second and third generations of Lisu singers and musicians whom he trained in MACM, was made possible by his intensive adoption of the latest recording equipment and media technologies—all of this was, of course, made possible by the financial support of his North American Christian donors. The work of consolidating and expanding Lisu transnational socioreligious links was shaped by live music performance, creating an alternative sense of directness and intimacy and permitting new forms of listening and performing the gospel beyond the medium of radio and sound recording. Overall, Lazarus' MACM media ministry showed greater media-driven religious changes; however, his media evangelism still served to provide support for religious and youth mobilization rather than functioning merely as a popular media outlet.

This comparative study of the materiality and historicity of indigenous media broadcasting suggests the necessity of understanding the Lisu religious use of new media technologies from three perspectives. First, the concept of the direct voice in religious mediation is a historically and culturally specific construction in accordance with radio's material and technical affordance; such ideologies of voice determine how the gospel voice is heard, shared, and felt among the dispersed members of Lisu church. Second, outside the realm of radio mediation, singing directly about Christian aspirations in a public performance setting is also central to the process of forming a normative model of media practice for indigenous communication. Lastly, the agency of indigenous media practitioners should not be ignored; through their creative work of absorbing the poetics of indigenous modes of speech and musical traditions, these media programs acquired a distinctly indigenous voice for Lisu Christians.

Acknowledgments

I would like to thank the Chiang Ching-kuo Foundation for International Scholarly Exchange and the Max Planck Institute for the Study of Religious and Ethnic Diversity for supporting the research for this chapter.

Notes

1 The Lisu are a Tibeto-Burman-speaking, highland-dwelling, egalitarian ethnic group living in these areas. In China, the Lisu are one of the fifty-five state-recognized nationalities. In India, they are a scheduled tribe of Arunachal Pradesh, and in Thailand, a tribal people. The status of the Burmese Lisu presents a more complex picture. The Lisu are recognized as one of 135 official ethnic groups in post-socialist Myanmar; being part of the "Kachin," however, has long been essential to the making of the Burmese Lisu identity in the Kachin region.
2 https://www.febc.org/learn-about-us, accessed May 25, 2020.
3 This information was obtained in conversations with a number of church leaders in Myanmar. However, according to Michele Zack only 75–80 percent of the Burmese Lisu were Christian by 2015 (2017: 217).

4   These scholars draw attention to the ascription of cultural meanings to particular vocal qualities or speech styles further associated with a particular socio-racial-religious identity—respectively, the middle-class Japanese women (Inoue), aspiring Christian Koreans (Harkness), and "acousmatic blackness" (Eidsheim).
5   The mission's newsletter was established in 1966 as *South East Asia Evangelizing Mission* and renamed *Asia Christian Service* from 1983. Hereafter the mission's newsletters are collectively referred to as *ACS Newsletter*.
6   GBM was later renamed as GBM-TCH (The Christian Hour).
7   In particular, Anderson Blanton articulates the phenomenon of what he calls "radio tactility" as an effective point of contact for the communication of healing prayer in the charismatic Christian worship of southern Appalachia.
8   Ngo (2009) studies why the conversion of thousands of Hmong in Vietnam was made possible by the FEBC's gospel programs. She examines the history and strategies of FEBC and the Hmong's response to the gospel programs. For a brief consideration of the religious music of Christian Hmong, see Ó Briain (2018: 152–5).
9   *ACS Newsletter*, June 1974.
10 Romanization of Lisu terms (Lisu Pinyin) follows the phonetic system adopted in Xu Lin et al. (1985).
11 *ACS Newsletter*, July 1972.
12 *ACS Newsletter*, July 1972.
13 Similar reports can be found in *MACM Newsletter*, September 2004.
14 After graduation from Columbia University's PhD program in ethnomusicology, Paul Fuller traveled to Thailand in 1975 hoping to produce gospel music based on his own musical training and drawing on cultural idioms of the indigenous communities with whom he was working (*ACS Newsletter*, December 1973).
15 *ACS Newsletter*, September 1969. The Rawang are an ethnic group residing in Kachin State, Myanmar.
16 The broadcasts are produced by the ACS team and production expenses paid by Bill McClure, director of GBM.
17 The Achang language is a Tibeto-Burman language spoken by the Achang in Yunnan, China. The Wa are an ethnic group that live mainly in northern Myanmar, in the northern part of Shan State and the eastern part of Kachin State, near and along Burma's border with China, as well as in Yunnan, China.
18 *ACS Newsletter*, November, December 2000.
19 My informants in Putao recalled an earlier form of song requests: pastors would collect the song titles and send them to a designated mailbox in Chiang Mai; this information accords with Ahdi Mark's recollections that he would receive letters from Myanmar and China, requesting specific Lisu songs, making suggestions, and expressing appreciation for the program.
20 Most Lisu musicians and media practitioners I interviewed in Myanmar did not have a habit of archiving albums they were involved in during production. In many cases, when I asked if I could listen to songs recorded a few years earlier, they often suggested I go to Ahdi Mark's GBM studio in Chiang Mai.
21 In addition to Lisu music recording, in August 1998 he also made recordings in four other languages (Saw Karen, Pao Karen, Lahu, and Akha) to educate people who did not understand the risks of HIV.
22 *MACM Newsletter*, March 2012.

23 Lazarus was hesitant to discuss the reasons for the discontinuation of radio production at his studio.
24 During their stay in Nujiang, evangelistic outreach activities were conducted more discretely away from the main stage after each performance.
25 This account is based on informal discussions with Lisu Christian musicians, studio producers, and sidewalk vendors of pirated recordings.
26 *MACM Newsletter*, March 2011.

Bibliography

Blanton, Anderson. 2015. *Hittin' the Prayer Bones: Materiality of Spirit in the Pentecostal South*. Chapel Hill, NC: The University of North Carolina Press.

Bolter, Jay David, and Richard Grusin. 1999. *Remediation: Understanding New Media*. Cambridge, MA: MIT Press.

De Vries, Hent. 2002. "In Media Res: Global Religion, Public Spheres, and the Task of Contemporary Comparative Religious Studies." In *Religion and Media*, edited by Hent De Vries and Samuel Weber, 3–42. Stanford, CA: Stanford University Press.

Diao, Ying. 2015. "Gospel Singing in the Valley: An Investigation into the Hymnody and Choral Singing of the Lisu on the China-Burma/Myanmar Border." PhD thesis, University of Maryland.

Eidsheim, Nina. 2019. *The Race of Sound: Listening, Timbre, and Vocality in African American Music*. Durham, NC: Duke University Press.

Engelke, Matthew. 2010. "Religion and the Media Turn: A Review Essay." *American Ethnologist* 37 (2): 371–9.

Englund, Harri. 2018. *Gogo Breeze: Zambia's Radio Elder and the Voices of Free Speech*. Chicago, IL: Chicago University Press.

Feld, Steven, Aaron A. Fox, Thomas Porcello, and David Samuels. 2004. "Vocal Anthropology: From the Music of Language to the Language of Song." In *A Companion to Linguistic Anthropology*, edited by Alessandro Duranti, 321–45. Oxford: Blackwell.

Feng, Rongxin. 2012. "Nujiangzhou Jidujiao qingkuang huibao tigang." Unpublished manuscript. Nujiang Committee of the Three-Self Patriotic Movement of the Protestant Church.

Fisher, Danial. 2009. "Mediating Kinship: Country, Family, and Radio in Northern Australia." *Cultural Anthropology* 24 (2): 280–312.

Fisher, Danial. 2016. *The Voice and Its Doubles: Media and Music in Northern Australia*. Durham, NC: Duke University Press.

Harkness, Nicholas. 2014. *Songs of Seoul: An Ethnography of Voice and Voicing in Christian South Korea*. Berkeley, CA: University of California Press.

Hjarvard, Stig. 2016. "Mediatization and the Changing Authority of Religion." *Media, Culture & Society* 38 (1): 8–17.

Inoue, Miyako. 2006. *Vicarious Language: Gender and Linguistic Modernity in Japan*. Berkeley, CA: University of California Press.

Kunreuther, Laura. 2010. "Transparent Media Radio, Voice, and Ideologies of Directness in Postdemocratic Nepal." *Journal of Linguistic Anthropology* 20: 334–51.

Kunreuther, Laura. 2014. *Voicing Subjects: Public Intimacy and Mediation in Kathmandu*. Berkeley, CA: University of California Press.

Larkin, Brian. 2008. *Signal and Noise: Media, Infrastructure, and Urban Culture in Nigeria*. Durham, NC: Duke University Press.

Meyer, Birgit. 2008. "Sensational Forms: Why Media, Aesthetics, and Power Matter in the Study of Contemporary Religion." In *Religion: Beyond a Concept*, edited by Hent De Vries, 704–23. New York: Fordham University Press.

Morse, Eugene. 1974. *Exodus to a Hidden Valley*. New York: Reader's Digest Press.

Morse family. n.d. "A Brief History of Our Mission." Unpublished manuscript. North Burma Christian Mission.

Ngo, Thi Thanh Tam. 2009. "The 'Short-Waved Faith': Christian Broadcasting and Protestant Conversion of the Hmong in Vietnam." In *Mediating Piety: Technology and Religion in Contemporary Asia*, edited by Francis Khek Gee Lim, 139–58. Leiden: Brill.

Ó Briain, Lonán. 2018. *Musical Minorities: The Sounds of Hmong Ethnicity in Northern Vietnam*. New York: Oxford University Press.

Weidman, Amanda. 2014. "Anthropology and Voice." *Annual Review of Anthropology* 43: 38–51.

Xu, Lin, Mu Yuzhang, Shi Lüqian, Ji Jianwen, Zhu Huasheng, Mu Shunjiang, Luo Zhenyue, Ma Jianliang, and Qi Kuoting, eds. 1985. *Li-Han Cidian*. Kunming: Yunnan Minzu Chubanshe.

Zack, Michele. 2017. *The Lisu: Far from the Ruler*. Boulder, CO: University Press of Colorado.

3

Narrowcasting into the Infinite Margins: Internet Sonorities of Transient Indonesian Domestic Workers in Singapore

Shzr Ee Tan

Transient workers in the Chinese-dominant city-state of Singapore make up an invisibilized underclass of low-paid manual laborers traveling to the prosperous Southeast Asian territory largely from the countries of Bangladesh, Indonesia, the Philippines, and Myanmar. Numbering some 540,100 in 2019, they make up more than 10 percent of Singapore's total population, while mostly working and living twenty-four hours a day in the private family homes of their employers.[1] In these residences, most workers continue their labor in separation from each other, performing housekeeping or caregiving duties in a relatively quiet and invisible way. On the internet, however, this invisibility becomes quickly unveiled through the ability of such communities—in the case of this study, Indonesian female workers—to regroup in their spare, liminal moments and stake their identities and spaces online while riding on the fast connections provided in their workplaces. On various social media platforms, different expressions of identity and alternative claims of cultural, religious, and political spaces are made. Often presented as podcasts and selfie videos, many of these articulations are aimed at an intersecting range of audiences and overlapping viewerships within different groups of transnational migrants in Singapore. Parallel to this audience, these expressions also draw upon networks in many workers' specific villages of origin as well as expanding "sisterhood" networks of migrant and ex-migrant workers in Indonesia itself. Based on fieldwork conducted in Singapore between 2017 and 2019, this chapter focuses on sound-based expressions and considers four case studies of mediated articulations by Indonesian domestic worker communities.

First, I examine how imagined listening Campos Valverde (2019) takes place in multiple, publicly circulated "selfie" video recordings of mushrooming Islamic chant groups populated by these workers. Here, their rehearsals and official performances are widely shared and reposted (though not necessarily listened to) on social media in demonstrations of identity staking and capacity building. Second, I investigate voyeured interactivity in the related arena of internet-enabled live-jamming karaoke sessions, livestreamed on apps such as Smule via Facebook, by Indonesian workers based in Singapore and their friends on the island of Singapore as well as overseas. Third, I look at more private channels of communication on groupchat platforms such as WhatsApp and Facebook Messenger, where self-recorded MP4 files are exchanged and re-recorded by the same members of these ensembles in the name of "distance-learning" repertoire at night, in the workers' small pockets of free time. Finally, I consider the silenced—but consciously and audibly vibrated—broadcasts of the Islamic call to prayer, emanated five times a day from the mobile phones of Indonesian workers.

Through their alternative modes of transmission, these technological articulations collectively encourage Indonesian worker communities in Singapore to participate in new ways of private as well as public listening, the latter acts of which are in themselves variously directed and variously intended. More importantly, these acts of listening are also active performances of identity utterance. The several examples I examine in this chapter bring together overarching themes of perceived unlimited "narrowcasting" afforded by internet technologies, in private virtual spaces reclaimed from the regimented everyday existence of these workers' lives on the island. Collectively, I reevaluate them as intersecting assemblages that provide inroads to interrogating shifting sonic agencies and positionalities in the Indonesian migrant diaspora in Singapore.

Sonic Selfies and Life-Journaling: Private Journeys as Public Narrowcasting

The term "narrowcasting" has been used since the 1960s' radio and television era to refer to a directional and niche-marketed—as opposed to mass-marketed—approach toward broadcasting in a commercial context (Chae and Flores 1998; Smith-Shomade 2004; Utley 1997). Here, I reinterpret its original definition to examine how production, delivery, and distribution of music and lived sonorities via mobile and internet technology manifest themselves in different aspects of the lives of transient workers in Singapore, on the increasingly interactive world of social media. In these examples I analyze below, the by-now familiar tropes of the end-user as creator of content (Davis and Moar 2005; Fiore 2008; Humphreys and Grayson 2008) appear again. Here, they exist in context to the shifting audiences of not only fellow members of the Indonesian diaspora in Singapore but also distance-removed family members in Indonesia itself and members of other migrant diaspora (Filipina, Bangladeshi) in Singapore. Together, these rhizomic and integrated communities connected through shared musical identities form the wider group of transient but densely networked conscious listeners and sounders.

The emerging genre of sonic/musical selfies and life-journaling videos as well as their wider accompanying range of secondary audio-signaling material can be considered first as one of the more ubiquitous cases for discussion. Where most domestic workers are confined to laboring and living exclusively in the family homes of their employers, the de facto conflation of private and work space-time as a matter of tailoring one's labor to the life routines and care needs of Singaporean families has led to the opening up of new spaces on the internet as protected and zoned-off arenas where control of self-narratives can be independently exercised. As Xinyuan Wang

(2016: 58) and Venkatraman (2017: 29) write of parallel spaces in social media worlds inhabited by transient workers and citizens of China and South India, online sites such as Facebook provide an even more meaningful sense of reality (as opposed to the material reality of their actual lives in Singapore) for many Indonesian workers in spite of their virtual construction. However, unlike the fantasy-as-life depictions shown by users in China putting up soft-focused and fanciful images of romantic castles and exotic holiday destinations, the self-narrative broadcasts of many Indonesian workers are performative testimonies of the way they live their actual lives—and sometimes, work—in Singapore, curated for public viewing.

Almost always made via the recording functions of mobile phones, one popular manifestation of these short videos includes first-person-player-style logs of Sunday (alternate off-day) trips to local and free-access public tourist destinations in Singapore, such as the airport, Gardens by the Bay, the Merlion statue, or the extended grounds of the casino-hotel complex Marina Bay Sands. Sometimes, audio commentary describing the journeys to such places or casual laughter can be heard on these videos for the specific purpose of bringing the viewer into the experience of walking alongside or in the shoes of the video recorder. Some of these videos are perspectively re-angled such that they turn to face the videographer herself in a moving selfie; other videos pan to feature sister characters in the story being told—often, of fellow workers socializing in the same group or space. In addition to the above selfie-journeys or vlogs, another subgenre of these selfie videos features workers who make recordings of themselves in a would-be YouTube tutorial format, putting on makeup, for example, after-hours or just before they leave their homes on their days off or cooking complicated meals in the home-kitchens where they work. Inspired by many beauty product showcases found across a global range of communities on YouTube, or in imitation of the wide range of recipe-realization videos populating the internet via channels such as Tastemade, the Indonesian migrants' vlogs reflect a certain cosmopolitanism in their internet consumption, represented by the breadth of content they have clearly been exposed to and have been influenced by in their own attempts at the same DIY vlogging genres.

In most of these videos, the element of sound is usually a performative marker of acknowledgment or engagement with the videographer to an imagined audience and expressed in a direct greeting—either from a character to the videographer or from the videographer in a selfie to her eventual audience. Sometimes, footage shown does not necessarily involve direct exchanges with the videographer. Instead, characters are shown engaging in a particular activity—eating at a food court, chatting in shopping center hallway, dancing or singing in a park. While the visual dimensions of such videos depict the activities in question with a seemingly "objective" eye, it is the sonic element that brings them to the viewer in an active presence and performance of the moment.

And yet, herein lies the sonic paradox of Facebook, or the primary platform through which these videos are shared: with the technology's current default settings, many of these videos that appear on the scrolling newsfeed of viewers run as screens-within-screens of silent moving images unless they are specifically clicked on, whether or not they are actively "liked" on the app's menu of button-option responses at the foot of each broadcast. Here, the issue of narrowcasting can be invoked as a means of explaining how these videos are created and how they reach and affectively impact their targeted and/or eventual readers. The fact that these videos are posted mostly on Facebook as opposed to public video-sharing and keyword-searchable sites such as YouTube or Vimeo means that not only does one have to *know* about the existence of them in order to know how to find them; one also usually has to be a personal friend of the videographer in order to view content. These intra- and insider-group functional flows have also been tracked to media sharing in marginalized communities, such as the indigenous world of Taiwan (Tan 2017: 28–52), and also in subsegmented news media groups (Barasch and Berger 2014: 286–99). While one might argue that this is par for the course for any kind of viewer-uploaded video on Facebook, the nature and content of these Indonesian migrants' videos, and the way they are viewed and interacted with, is specific to the daily lives of Singapore's transient workers.

As mentioned already, these (for the most part, time-unlimited and freely hosted) videos function as important virtual territories claimed by workers whose private existence, and staking of personal (much less public) space, in Singapore is severely limited, regimentalized and marginalized on social and political levels. Specifically curated and strategically lensed as these selfie videos come, they are also self-narrated testimonies of happy and successful lives in Singapore the workers want to exhibit to families and friends in Indonesia, with whom they now remain in contact with largely via the internet. Collectively, they are archives of the self and provide documentation of lives led away from home. Tini, a young mother from a village near Surabaya,[2] who has been working in Singapore for three years, puts it this way:

> I make these recordings to show my daughter and my mother back in Surabaya that I am alive and well. I am talking to them, and this is the way I share my life with them, day by day. I also WhatsApp call them if I can but with these videos I can just make them whenever I am working, and upload them whenever I want, no need for appointment.
>
> (Interview, January 4, 2018)

Family and friends back in Indonesia, however, are not the only audiences—proxy-listeners or otherwise—of these videos. A casual survey of frequent commentators and "likers" of these videos shows that many of the viewers are also fellow transient workers in the Indonesian domestic worker diaspora—largely based in Singapore but also in Hong Kong, Taiwan, and the Gulf, and also sometimes hailing from the Filipino or Burmese community. Here, it is in the numerous, expanding, and long lists of comments around the videos—in Bahasa Indonesia, as well as English—which show the broadcasts as serving the equally important purpose of fostering crucial community and capacity-building among migrant worker communities, that working conditions and logistics otherwise make for particularly dislocated experiences in physical group-bonding.

Narrowcast as they come in these privately produced videos' restricted and niche viewerships, which are often protected by privacy settings away from employers' eyes in versions of safe spaces, the expressions can, however, also be understood as broadly cast: this is through their functioning as community announcements in exchanges of conversations, news updates, gossip, and views of local current or Indonesian affairs. As to whether these videos are individually and actively *listened* to (as opposed to simply "liked"), or watched to the full length of their duration, this is a separate story.

A young Indonesian worker Yati, in her early twenties, who has been working in Singapore for seven years, relates:

> Sometimes I just "like"; other times I watch the videos until the end—maybe I am in some of them. Sometimes I just *kaypoh* [act like a busybody] want to find out what my friends are up to and how they behave or what they look like, what they are wearing or singing in a video. It's not the same as other kinds of videos you find on YouTube, or TV dramas for entertainment. Because you *know* these people personally in the video, they become my family and *mba* [sisters] in Singapore. If I'm bored, I just click fast forward or move the time-slider. But it's important that I write some comments to let them know I have watched their videos. And they also do the same for me in return. I'm sure not all of them watch all my videos to the end. But maybe they watch or listen a little bit.
>
> (Interview, January 7, 2018)

Yati's story echoes the observations of Raquel Campos Valverde (2019), who writes of imagined listening on the internet and on social media, where the act of "liking" a music video is performative in itself—whether in the show of solidarity or friendship with fellow Facebook contacts, or a semi-public expression of taste, or, simply virtue-signaling. Such imagined listening may well be the case for many of these workers' videos. But the high volume of commentary in addition to "favorite" or "like" clicks shows that even if partially engaged with, many of the target viewers actually do take time to consciously click on—and hence sonically activate—and pay attention to the broadcasts. Where the listening or viewing may be imaginary, the meanings and affective results are not.

Interactive Musicianship on the Internet: From Smule to WhatsApp Chains

Two off-shoots of the sonic selfie genre can be given further examination in this chapter in light of its focus on music and sound. The first is that of interactive and live-captured karaoke streaming, enabled by the popular online-live backing-track and live-duet app, Smule.[3] In further extrapolation of self-expression and community bonding, a few musically oriented Indonesian workers have taken to making stylized livestreamed recordings of themselves, in work clothes or in performance garb and stage makeup, rehearsing, jamming, or performing Indonesian pop songs on Smule's database of backing tracks, as has become a hobby of Meikhan Sri Bandar,[4] who prides herself as cheerfully working for imagined "Kingdom of Dangdut Unity" on Facebook (see Figures 3.1a–3.1c). Many of these articulations often incorporate coperformances of either fellow workers in the diaspora in Singapore or friends and

Figure 3.1a Meikhan Sri Bandar sings live karaoke on Facebook via Smule (accessed December 31, 2019).

Figure 3.1b Neng (real name) livestreams a karaoke session in Singapore on Facebook (accessed December 31, 2019).

Figure 3.1c Turiyah Mansur (real name) sings karaoke on Facebook via Smule (accessed December 31, 2019).

family back in Indonesia. In both of these cases, the interactivity is expressly facilitated through musicking as a capacity-building and bonding activity but also knowingly and deliberately performed to designated niche publics. The effect is akin to enjoying the kick and novelty of a distance-separated Skype conversation with a friend or acquaintance via a fixed and relatively safe and predictable musical script in public, with viewers and listeners of the narrowcast-as-broadcast engaging in live time or afterwards in sought-after comments and "likes."

A second kind of example of the musical selfie involves the specific subgenre of Islamic *sholuwat*, *zikir* (devotional prayer), or *qasidah* (Islamic chanting in groups) mediated online—but not necessarily always for social media broadcasting. Here, I examine how audio-only MP3 recordings circulated via WhatsApp, and video recordings sent via WhatsApp and other social media platforms, are produced by devotional chanting groups comprising Indonesian workers rehearsing live in Singaporean mosques on their days off.

The mosque-based live activities are in themselves a phenomenon beyond this edited volume's theme of cultural broadcasting. Between 1980 and 2019, the figures of foreign workers in Singapore—of which Indonesian domestic workers make a key demographic—have grown from around 168,000 to 550,000 with a substantial surge during the 1980s, which saw the local population almost double between 1990 and the 2010s (Yang, Yang, and Zhan 2017: 10).[5] In 2012, it was estimated that one in six households in Singapore employed a domestic worker (Freire 2013: 2). For many such workers, attached to and living away from the public eye in the private family homes of their employers, leisure hours when available on alternate or once-a-month Sundays are usually spent in public and semi-public spaces such as an Indonesian-friendly shopping center (e.g., City Square Mall), a public garden (East Coast Park being a favorite), or the community-in reach skills-upgrade center of the Sekolah Indonesia Singapura, run by the Indonesian government. However, in recent years,

Singaporean-run mosques have come to be spaces of intimate sanctuary for smaller Indonesian worker groups who wish to convene socially in a more private setting. Offering air-conditioned indoor facilities with comfortable carpeting and accessible washroom options, these spaces provide a club-like atmosphere in which the workers can socialize quietly, "away from the din of the street or the heat of the sun, where we don't have to spend money to buy a drink or meal just to be there" (Neng [real name], interview, January 7, 2018).

Still, a catch here is that the mosques are places of worship and learning, where social exchange is unofficially understood to be taking place under the auspices of Islamic ministration. To this end, many Indonesian groups have banded together for the educational or spiritual purpose of learning and practicing devotional songs if only to find active and legitimate reason for the use and claim of this sacred—and personal, intimate—space in Singapore: the sounded activity literally becomes a place-staking activity. The rise of *qasidah*, such as Nur Assifya in Singapore's 500-person-capacity Masjid Abdul Hamid Mosque in the Newton area, has been the result of such developments. Many of these groups recruit first-time *zikir* singers who have only begun undertaking this activity in Singapore; indeed, many of them—feeling the need to defend or hold on to their Indonesian identities in Singaporean diaspora—have also admitted to only becoming religious upon leaving Indonesia and finding a comforting sense of "home" in the relatively familiar Islamic space of a Singaporean mosque. The irony is that some of these groups, formed ostensibly for space-claiming purposes, have come to be so well-rehearsed and musically accomplished that they have become model-foreign worker societies in their own right. Nur Assyifa, alongside sister groups such as Nasyid An-Nida, have been invited to perform at events organized by the Indonesian embassy, as well as public showcases for Singaporeans run by quasi-governmental Singapore groups at community centers and shopping arcades.

The capturing of musical activities for online dissemination in these groups makes for useful analysis. The video performances themselves range from long clips of recordings of start-stop and semi-improvisatory rehearsals in mosques to full-length items and costumed concerts in public performances (see Figures 3.2a–3.2c).[6] In

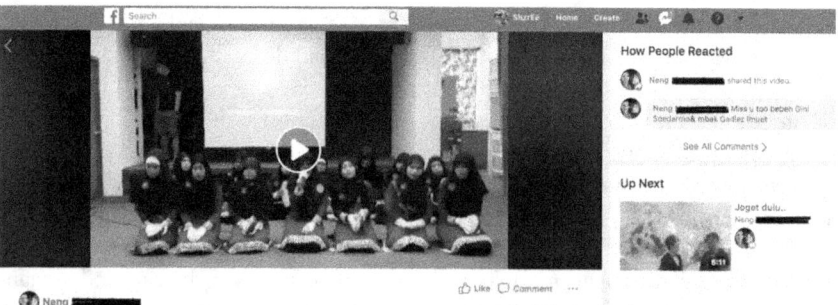

Figure 3.2a Screenshot of Nur Assyifa rehearsing at Newton Mosque captured on video on Neng's Facebook page with Neng as soloist (accessed December 31, 2019).

Narrowcasting into the Infinite Margins 57

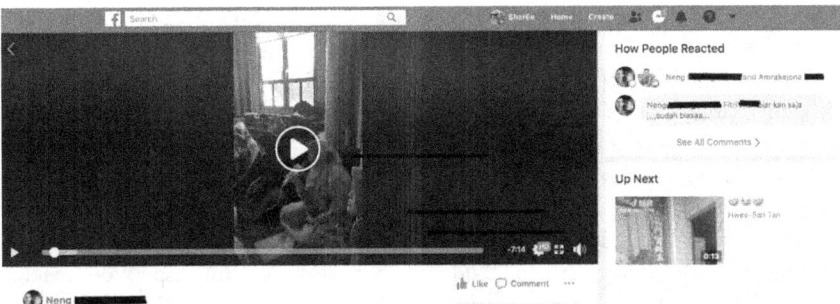

Figure 3.2b Screenshot of public performance by Nur Assyifa featured on Neng's Facebook page (accessed December 31, 2019).

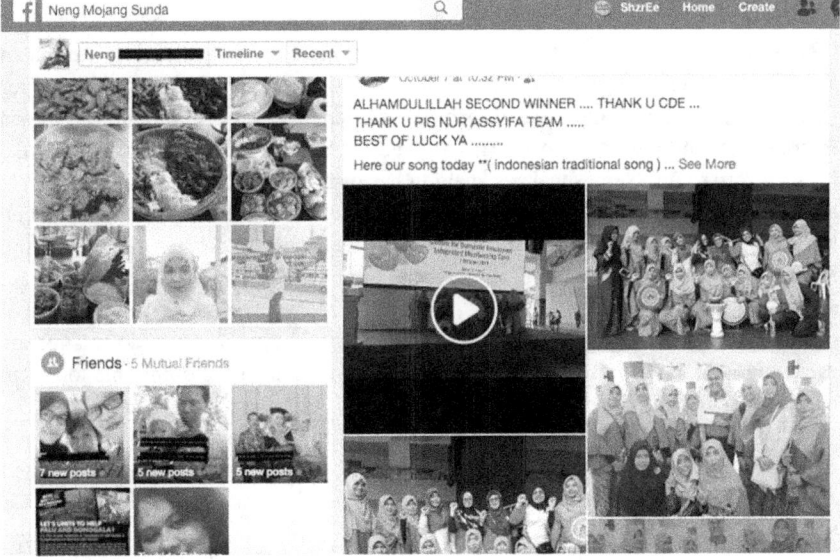

Figure 3.2c Screenshot of the Facebook pages of Nur Assyifa rehearsals and performances (accessed December 31, 2019).

comparison to the sonic selfies or video journals mentioned earlier, these are conscious performances, featuring an attempt at creating artistic value, and almost always longer in duration—sometimes taking up as much as half an hour of broadcast time. Most of these videos are shared on Facebook alongside or as part of albums of group photos of singers and chant ensembles, and they invite the same kinds of interaction from niche publics.

A spin-off activity to the narrowcast manifests in the form of audio-only MP3 files, shared interactively as educational material exclusively on WhatsApp and Facebook

Messenger groupchats. In the case of Nur Assyifa, run until 2019 by lead solo singer and teacher Neng, the recordings function as "model exercises" and pieces of homework from which members of the group and other interested parties can learn "how to sing properly" (interview, January 21, 2018). Neng (who has been working in Singapore for almost two decades with her employer's family that she calls "her second family") has, herself, been largely taught via the internet, downloading devotional songs by the Lebanese-Swedish singer Maher Zain and Malaysian singer Hafiz Hamidun for her own study and adaptation for the ensemble she leads. In addition, Neng also surfs other Indonesian pop, Bollywood, and Arabic music videos for inspiration, making tongue-in-cheek conversions of "famous Shah Rukh Khan songs or Siti Nurhaliza songs I found on YouTube" into sacred *zikir* songs. As she explains: "the tune is very good and easy to remember and catchy, people recognise it. We just change the lyrics sometimes into Bahasa to praise Allah, and it becomes *sholuwat* … you can find anything on YouTube!" (interview, January 21, 2018; see Figure 3.3).

Where the internet (largely via Facebook) has served as an archive for the life-journal video and sonic selfies of migrant workers in the case studies examined above, it now serves as a different kind of archive—a resource and musical bank for inspiration, education, and research—for these *qasidah* singers. More importantly, via internet chat and messaging platforms, the online platform has also become a virtual musical classroom. Neng speaks of making her own model solo recordings of pieces she has scoured and adapted. These are in turn sent as audio files, with accompanying lyrics, to Nur Assyifa's chat groups followed by instructions to listen repeatedly and memorize. Every singer in her group is then commanded to record the same excerpt and send it back to her as evidence of study, and also, "for feedback and correcting of singing mistakes… I tell them also how to improve. They all have to do this for me every night, after they finish work. It is also good to make time doing this for *Allah* every day as well" (interview, January 21, 2018).

Thus, this time-lapsed iterative approach to distance learning music via chain messaging here takes advantage of the affordances of the internet in the limited operative logistics of these workers' lives, work schedules, and distanced locations. At the same time, the mediated structuring of the learning process, single-voice-by-single-voice, taps into a different level of individuated intimacy in which notions of hierarchy are also evident in the community-bonding and capacity-building process. As Neng's ability to "boss my singers around" shows, there is clearly a chain of command in terms of who is generating new musical material and controlling or guiding the process in which it is developed (interview, January 21, 2018).

Neng herself talks candidly of awarding internet stickers and emojis as prizes for those who adhere to the musical learning schedule she has set up. She relates: "Every day I give them a reward, if any member doesn't send a voice recording without informing me so I will let them send double voice recording the next day" (personal communication via groupchat, September 27, 2019; see Figures 3.4a–3.4b). At the same time, Neng also speaks of the need to regroup these articulations in a live and ensemble-based context, when the singers gather once a week to rehearse (on the back of socializing, eating, and worshipping) together at Newton Mosque.

Figure 3.3 Members of Nur Assifya learn songs from YouTube and MP3 files on their mobile phones at Newton Mosque, Singapore, on January 14, 2018. Photo: Shzr Ee Tan.

Figure 3.4a/b Screenshot of Neng's WhatsApp log for the submission and reward of MP4 recordings by her *sholuwat* group members (accessed September 27, 2019).

A note can be made here about the polymediality, multimediated, and remediated aspects of these performances, which have also been observed of internet-enabled and social media communities in Turkey, Trinidad, and Chile (Costa 2016: 43; Haynes 2016: 54; Sinanan 2017: 108). Of interest is that while most of the *sholuwat* singers rehearse and perform in acoustic sets with basic percussion instrumental backing, soloists in the group also carry and use their own portable microphones and amplifiers—both in rehearsals and performances. These may in turn be further picked up for reamplification in some public concert venues. The resulting distortion—when such performances are then recaptured on mobile phones and uploaded yet again, a third time—is sometimes part of the aesthetic and expected sound quality of the semi-amateur *qasidah* scene, where notions of acoustic norms, standards, and tastes are gleaned from small-amplifier-disseminated broadcasts of pop music on regional transport systems (such as buses) and village and town shops in Indonesia itself.

Such sonic aesthetics have come to be remediated in newer, internet manifestations alongside the cleanly produced tracks of singers like Maher Zain otherwise downloaded directly into smartphone storage and played back via earphones. But the smartphones are not always connected to earphones in playback. Indeed, very often they are enjoyed in semi-public without earphones and sometimes used as speaker devices for small group-oriented sharing and playback, such as in the case of a group of *qasidah* singers crowding around a single friend's phone to peer at and pore over a video or MP4 file. Crucially, the remediation is polymedial in its crossing of several different platforms—from microphone to amplifier to mobile phone speaker, and within mobile phones themselves across app platforms from Facebook to Messenger and WhatsApp. One might comment that the sprawling aspect of such cross- and inter-mediated sonic disseminations is a product of what Jenkins has termed "convergence culture" (Jenkins 2006), where utterances continue to exist in old as well as newer formats in additive and parallel simultaneity.

Musical Havens and Secret Signals: Sonic Envelopes and the Vibrated Call to Prayer

A final strand of analysis of internet sonorities as narrowcasting among Singapore's Indonesian worker diaspora can be found in approaches toward understanding how sounded worlds operate as private and safe spaces. Often, these spaces are highly textured and multimediated acoustic experiences of time, space, and place. By this, I refer to aural codes hidden via sonic wraparound effects (Bull 2001) in newly engendered ways of listening from the margins.

Some background can be given through discussion of the phenomenon of the Sony Walkman effect: this has long been documented since the debut of the technology in the 1980s, in the writings of Michael Bull, who has theorized on how "public space is increasingly turned into a utilitarian space of private mediated activity. Time is reclaimed in terms of its 'usefulness' and multi-tasked in relation to the possibilities embodied in users' smartphones" (Bull 2013: 248). Four decades since its invention, the portability of hermetically sealed, private, and experiential worlds created through the personalization of a sonic bubble or sonic enveloping has become an accepted postdigital state of modern existence.

For many Indonesian workers in Singapore, the functional aspects of the sonic bubble-turned-safe space provided by MP3 players streaming from the internet, or the playing of albums of downloaded tracks, prevail in strategic ways that reflect their negotiations within marginalized existences that have crucial invisibilized aural dimensions. An example can be given of Medan-born Sri, in her mid-twenties, who talks about how she has learned to pick up scratches of basic Mandarin and Hokkien after seven years of working in a Singaporean household with the elderly parent of her employer. Every morning, she accompanies "granny" to the local park to practice tai chi, followed by a trip to a local hawker center, where her elderly ward eats and socializes with friends.

Preferring to sit in a corner by herself away from the central activity of the hawker center, she then puts on her earphones to listen to devotional Islamic music. Sri says it is not a question of her feeling excluded from her ward's social space,

> Because I can speak Chinese a little bit, or at least understand a little… I'm not like some of the newer workers who don't know what people are saying about them or other things. Rather than half-listening in Chinese, better to block everything and listen to my own songs, be a good Muslim at the same time.
>
> (Interview, December 27, 2017)

The problem, she points out, is that she needs to "tune out" and avoid focusing on the conversations, which she can be unwittingly drawn into. The hawker center "has too much noise, too many people talking. I need to listen to my MP3s and bring myself inside my head" (interview, December 27, 2017). To this end, she chooses to listen to devotional Islamic chants by the Swedish-Lebanese singer Maher Zain and the Malaysian *sholuwat* singer Hafiz Hamidun, the albums of which she downloads from the internet connection provided by her employer or a relatively cheap mobile phone plan. Many other workers, like Sri, have also come into religious chant and taken on newer religious identities only as a recent phenomenon of seeking sonic solace and spaces of musical interiority via Islam upon migrating to Singapore. Sri explains, "Anytime I want to escape from the worries of life, or the hard work and sad stories, or if I'm missing my daughter, I just put on my earphones" (interview, December 27, 2017).

Devotional songs, however, are not the only mainstay of listening lists used by Indonesian workers. Apart from Sri, many home-based domestic helpers assemble separate and multiple playlists for the purpose of energizing themselves while conducting different types of labor at home. Many capitalize on the availability of free streaming services, such as Spotify or YouTube channels, focusing on particular genres, which are then tailored into soundtracks for particular household activities. Suminda N, from Semarang, who is in her thirties and works in a large condominium in Singapore, says for example: "Dangdut sometimes I listen to for mopping the floor, although it's very old fashioned, Siti Nurhaliza for cooking and K-pop or Lady Gaga for washing the toilet! Must have energy for housework!" (personal communication via Facebook chat, July 4, 2018).

In the mornings on a typical weekday schedule, these labor-oriented musical soundtracks are frequently played back using the workers' mobile phone speakers without the aid of earphones—workers are left alone in their employers' homes to conduct their chores while their employers and their children head for work or schools; the immediate aural proxemical space is temporarily under their control. In the case of elderly wards of workers who stay as live-in parents with Singaporean employers and are present at home in the mornings, or in the case of afternoons when the children of employers return from school, many domestic workers opt to use earphones for the dual purpose of "not disturbing the family" or "to just focus on my music when they watch their TV program or Taiwanese or K-dramas" (Suminda N, personal communication via Facebook chat, July 4, 2018). In occasional instances, when Indonesian workers form close bonds with their wards, afternoons can sometimes be spent watching children's television programs or potboiler soap operas together. In the evenings, after household work has officially concluded, many Indonesian workers withdraw to their tiny bedrooms (often doubled up from the designated pantry or bomb shelter[7]), where they are absorbed into their private virtual worlds and engage in online social media activities, viewing videos or continuing to listen to music in sonic bubbles-within-bubbles. Across the course of a single day's schedule, sounded activities—in the form of the reception of purposeful narrowcasts and indirect broadcasts (the latter seen in how workers participate from the side in cowatching K-dramas or children's programs for example)—are co-articulated according to time, space, and person-to-person interactions.

Of note here is how mediated interactions take on different kinds of polymedial intimacies, especially via mobile phones. Where the affordances of a private musical world in sonic bubbles are easy to observe, a more interesting phenomenon is the development among Indonesian workers of a new way of listening to the call for prayer. Previously heard five times a day at changing times in various parts of Indonesia itself as broadcast in public via multidirectional loudspeakers mounted on the minarets of local mosques, these electronically mediated sounds have become technologically muted in Singapore, for reasons of sociopolitical acoustic control within a largely Chinese-dominant population (Lee 1999: 86–100). As such, many Indonesian workers who have become *more* religious after arriving in Singapore for work can have come to rely on a range of downloadable and free (or cheap) mobile phone apps that bring the equivalent of a recorded *adhan* to their immediate sonic vicinities, according to the changing Islamic calendar (see Figure 3.5). While this is in theory a convenient replacement for a mosque's minaret, depending on the time of day or the religious affinities and other relationships workers have with their employers, many workers keep their mobile phones on silent mode when their employers and their families are not in the homes where they work.

Dewi, twenty-two, from Aceh, who has been living in Singapore for six months and works in a government-subsidized Housing Board flat for a family of four, points out:

> Sometimes it's not because I think my employer doesn't tolerate my Muslim faith, but that I just want to play safe a bit. Just in case they get annoyed because they are Christian… I think they are generally ok. But I also don't want them to think my phone is always going off and I am not doing my work properly or I am some extremist. So it's just easier to set the phone to vibrate. And now I can tell what the different vibrations are like on silent mode—whether it's a WhatsApp, Facebook, or text, or *adhan*. They are all different, even some *adhan* apps have different vibration modes, sometimes the vibration is longer or got beat and you can change them! I don't think my employer can hear them or tell the difference, but it doesn't matter because they only vibrate for me. I can hear them because I sometimes expect them and am waiting.
>
> (Interview, July 21, 2019)

Figure 3.5 *Adhan* apps for mobile phones (accessed September 27, 2019).

For many like Dewi, such acoustic self-censorship has led to the emergence of a new, attenuated way of listening—not to the *adhan* itself but to the subtly audible, electronically charged but physical-material signaling of it, when their mobile phones move against the tabletops or pockets on/in which they are placed. This adapted approach to listening for "secret" signals in plain sight—or perhaps plain hearing—is a new phenomenon that has come to develop among specific Indonesian domestic worker communities and reflects both the performative agency and the lack of it in sounded practices within variously sonically disciplined workplaces-as-living and private quarters. While it would be a stretch to classify the behavior of tuning in to vibrated *adhans* as acts of resistance, I argue here that it is possible to understand these motions as a hidden reclamation and control of sonic space as private space.

A final observation can be made of this phenomenon outside the homes and private workplaces of the Indonesian domestic workers, in a different intimate and safe space of the mosques as described previously, where devotionally inclined workers gather to sing *qasidah*. Even in a relative safe space of a mosque, some workers continue to leave their phones on silent mode "because it's easier to do it permanently just in case I forget to switch it off later" (Suminda N, interview, January 4, 2018). Others, however, flip their speaker switches on. When the time for the call to prayer does come around in the course of an afternoon of rehearsals, the sonic presentations of a short but continuous chorus of not-fully-synchronized mobile phone vibrations, mobile phone playbacks of voice-recorded *adhan*, and actual live voice performances of a *muezzin*, amplified within the mosque itself, is a multisensorial experience of complex sonic strands, interwoven through digitality, liveness, site-specificity, and temporality.

In my own participant observation of one such occasion in 2017, I witnessed an ensemble of migrant worker-singers begin preempting the chorus itself by telling one another to wind down their chats and prepare to clean themselves and prostrate in the main area of the mosque for prayer. At the same time, they seemed to take pleasure and acknowledgment in the large variety of vibrations and playback *adhan* recordings going off, unsynchronized but simultaneously. One singer pointed out in jest that the lack of synchrony across the apps meant that the standardized internet-set timings across mobile phone settings was not as accurate as the Singapore government would have intended but that the chorus and messiness in itself was a beautiful moment.

Conclusion: Narrowcasting as Broadcasting

A concluding thought on the description, contextualization, and analysis above of the various examples of internet and poly-mediated sonorities can be made by way of reinterrogating the notion of narrowcasting applied to the Indonesian worker diaspora. One way of tackling this question can be through examining the niche aspect of the (re)creators as well as receivers of content, and the hierarchies and intersections within and without these overlapping communities.

To a certain and obvious extent, intended audiences of the music selfies, life-journal videos, recorded performances, and audio files shared on personal social media pages or on groupchats are by and large members of the same community of the content creators—the Indonesian transient workers themselves, and the variously intersecting fields of their immediate families and friends in Indonesia. Social media and chat groups function as important, semi-private spaces of congregation even for people living so close together on such a small island, and who only meet up physically every other weekend: these spaces become all the more precious, as are the friendships, solidarities, and alliances formed within.

But this is also where the specifically Indonesian and transient aspects of their existence in Singapore (and in relation to different origin-villages or towns in Indonesia) make for different ways of parsing their "narrowcasts" as translocal and transnational interplays. Many of the voicings and comments seen on and around shared videos reflect the use of the standardized Bahasa Indonesia, often a second language for many workers who speak regional dialects as mother tongues. Interestingly, often, English-language comments with random Singlish words also appear frequently.

For many, the use of Bahasa online is a means of unifying and consolidating pan-Indonesian experiences on the internet, as a matter of functional communication but also as a show of broader Indonesian solidarity in the diaspora. For others, the use of English could also be a potential signaling of an Indonesian worker's status in Singapore as a cosmopolite city-dweller with an overseas job, much as how Janet Arnado writes of migrant Filipino workers who learn about different ways of the imagined "West," or about new consumer and Filipino-adapted trends found overseas, which they indulge in and bragged about as a matter of new personal, "overseas-trained" identities (Arnado 2009: 239).

A third interrelated point here is that the audiences of some of these workers are not only fellow Indonesians in the diaspora, or second-level Venn diagrammatic intersections of their families "back home," but new friends and allies made as a result of their migrant experiences. By this, I refer to different hierarchies of an already niche audience produced from the Singapore migration experience: fellow transient workers from the Filipina, Burmese, and Bangladeshi communities also active in Singapore, and—increasingly—local Singaporean allies (including the odd employer).

Here, the ubiquity and reach of Facebook as a global and globalizing platform has encouraged a number of Indonesian workers to see themselves as engaging with internationally, outside Indonesia, as equal citizens of the world, even as they are operating from the perspective of a very niche-bonded community ostensibly interacting with closed and "safe" groups of "Friends" or "Friends of Friends" optional categories on the site. Where the internet can function as an archive of inspiration for many migrant workers, their posts on Facebook, and sometimes on YouTube, create a collective archive of testimonies of their identities, ways of life, and being at work and play. These not only are created for a marginal narrowcast audience but also function as ideological broadcasts—for the sake of history, and to anyone who wants to know about the fact that these workers have existed, continue to exist, and have a voice and want to use it to talk about their experiences overseas. Thus the paradoxically private workplace intimacies that are recorded from the everyday lives of these workers and represented in selfie videos are not only niche-channeled to relatives back home or fellow workers "who get our same jokes," but also deposited for the imaginary internet-as-world-out-there. To be sure, one might argue that home videos and selfie videos are par for the course in Indonesia itself or indeed any society or community around the world. However, the precarity and transience of the Indonesian workers' lives and stints in Singapore make the volume and tone of such productions especially significant.

A final story can be found in the life of Widya, a young mother in her late thirties, who has been working for a three-generation family in Singapore for eight years and is thinking of retiring and returning to her hometown of Medan to start a restaurant with whatever savings gleaned from work after remittance to her family "back home." She puts it this way:

> At first I thought I was going to be here for only 1 year. I was lucky I had a good employer renewed my contract. Because my time here is so precious, I wanted to record it and save it on the internet. I want people to know we are migrant workers. We are the people working so hard to make Singapore what it is, but we are not noticed. On Facebook, I don't just have Filipina and Bangladeshi friends. I also have Singaporean friends. I am very proud that they want to know what we are doing and what our lives are like, and how to make things better. But it is funny that they ask me about all this through Facebook, when sometimes they can just ask the people who work for their relatives, or sometimes even their parents at home.
>
> (Interview, August 6, 2019)

Widya's final perspicacious comment has sparked off a desire to investigate my own positionality in my research with migrant workers over the last two years. As a London-residing Singaporean who two decades ago had grown up in the Southeast Asian city, I was part of a family that, like many in Singapore, had enjoyed and profited from the labor of an Indonesian worker called Sri. Arriving in our home at the age of nineteen, with short hair and without a headscarf, she had spent three years with us before deciding to explore further horizons in Hong Kong. By the time she left, she had reconsidered her initial dress sense and appearance when she had first made her journey to Singapore; no longer wearing her hair short and exposed, her day-off Sunday dress now included fashionable *tudung* of different colors, which covered her head. I have more recently tried to track down Sri over the internet, but to my regret without much success (although I have been more successful with an earlier domestic worker from the Philippines named Maria Gloria, who has since retrained as a nurse and is happily living an affluent life in Canada with her own family).

As I began conducting my research online and offline on transient workers in Singapore, making many new Indonesian friends on Facebook even as I have come to attend a few of their outings, song rehearsals, and public performances while on fieldwork, I have been made ever more aware that my own conduct on social media has taken on an especially reflexive approach in relation to my online interactions with these new friends. How would my Indonesian friends reflect on my own semi-political posts on, for example, going on a University and College Union college strike in the UK in stark contrast with their own grossly unequal job contracts in Singapore? How would my notion of travel—"shown off" through pictures of conference sites around the world, or food shots taken during the odd personal holiday—make them feel about their own migratory pathways and experiences? What do they think of the music videos and sound-studies/ethnomusicology-related news I share regularly, alongside random geek-academic memes and gifs?

Neng, whom I first met in 2017 and is now a friend with whom I remain in regular contact via Facebook messenger, is a frequent "liker" of my posts, although we also share different kinds of life and news stories to each other privately, beyond the semi-public platforms of personal pages. She continues to post a wide range of music and sound-oriented material (from Indonesian ballads to traditional dance) on her page, although culinary and craft-oriented videos reshared from sources other than herself have become important mainstays of her Facebook page. Neng's approach to narrowcasting as broadcasting here is a final reminder that Indonesian workers have just as much recourse as anyone else in an increasingly globalized world to different identities and learning experiences in their internet representations. As a young woman with a teenage daughter, she not only posts "Indonesian" or "migrant worker" content but is also eager to learn about and share everything and anything encountered on her version of the internet, from memes about Tom and Jerry to photos of spectacular sunsets, trailers of Bollywood films, and new egg-farming technologies she has kept an eye on for her private business venture "at home." As to whether or how music and the sounded and mediated worlds play a part in her expression of self, Neng says with humor and wisdom: "Of course it is part of my identity. But I have so many sides to my identity, my life. I am not just a singer, or musician, migrant worker, but do so many other things" (personal communication via Facebook chat, December 3, 2019).

Acknowledgments

I would like to thank Neng, Meikhan Sri Bandar, Turiyah Mansur, members of Nur Assyifa, members of Nasyid An-Nida, organizers of the Migrant Cultural Show, the Migrants Writers of Singapore Group, the Sekolah Indonesia Singapore, and also Tini, Suminda N, Sri, Widya, Yati, and Dewi for their generosity and sharing of insight, time, food, humor, and singing in the course of conducting fieldwork for and writing up this chapter. I would also like to thank Lonán Ó Briain and Min Yen Ong for their editorial suggestions on this chapter.

Notes

1 https://www.mom.gov.sg/documents-and-publications/foreign-workforce-numbers, accessed December 31, 2019.
2 All names have been anonymized in this chapter in safeguard of the consultants' privacy, except where otherwise indicated. All communications are in-person conversations in Singapore unless otherwise stated.
3 Smule is a social media-optimized app developed in the United States in 2008 for collaborative live music making over the internet.
4 Meikhan has allowed the use of her real name in this chapter.
5 http://factsanddetails.com/southeast-asia/Singapore/sub5_7c/entry-3785.html, accessed December 31, 2019.
6 Sholuwat performances on Neng's Facebook Page (restricted) https://www.facebook.com/jihan.suprihatin/videos/2221123887959658/and https://www.facebook.com/jihan.suprihatin/videos/1208516559220401/

UzpfSTEwMDAwMTg2MjA0NzU0NToxMjA4NTE2OTQ1ODg3MDI5/, accessed December 31, 2019.
7   All new apartments built in Singapore since 1996 are fitted with mandatory reinforced walls and blast-proof doors under the country's building code.

Bibliography

Arnado, Janet M. 2009. "Localising the Global and Globalising the Local: The Global Households of Filipina Trans-Migrant Workers and Their Singapore Employers." In *Reframing Singapore: Memory, Identity, Trans-Regionalism*, edited by Derek Heng and Syed Muhd Khairudin Aljunied, 229–48. Amsterdam: Amsterdam University Press.

Barasch, Alixandra, and Jonah Berger. 2014. "Broadcasting and Narrowcasting: How Audience Size Affects What People Share." *Journal of Marketing Research* 51 (3): 286–99.

Bull, Michael. 2001. "The World According to Sound: Investigating the World of Walkman Users." *New Media & Society* 3 (2): 179–97.

Bull, Michael. 2013. "iPod Use: An Urban Aesthetics of Sonic Ubiquity." *Continuum* 27 (4): 495–504.

Chae, Susan, and Daniel Flores. 1998. "Broadcasting Versus Narrowcasting." *Information Economics and Policy* 10 (1): 41–57.

Costa, Elisabetta. 2016. *Social Media in Southeast Turkey: Love, Kinship and Politics*. London: UCL Press.

Davis, Stephen, and Magnus Moar. 2005. "The Amateur Creator." In *Proceedings of the 5th Conference on Creativity & Cognition*, 158–65. Available online: https://dl.acm.org/doi/10.1145/1056224.1056247, accessed May 25, 2020.

Fiore, Anne Marie. 2008. "The Digital Consumer: Valuable Partner for Product Development and Production." *Clothing and Textiles Research Journal* 26 (2): 177–90.

Freire, Tiago. 2013. "How the 1978 Changes to the Foreign Domestic Workers Law in Singapore Increased the Female Labour Supply." *The Singapore Economic Review*. Available online: https://mpra.ub.uni-muenchen.de/44448/1/MPRA_paper_44448.pdf, accessed May 25, 2020.

Haynes, Nell. 2016. *Social Media in Northern Chile*. London: UCL Press.

Humphreys, Ashlee, and Kent Grayson. 2008. "The Intersecting Roles of Consumer and Producer: A Critical Perspective on Co-production, Co-creation and Prosumption." *Sociology Compass* 2 (3): 963–80.

Jenkins, Henry. 2006. *Convergence Culture: Where Old and New Media Collide*. New York: New York University Press.

Lee, Tong Soon. 1999. "Technology and the Production of Islamic Space: The Call to Prayer in Singapore." *Ethnomusicology* 43 (1): 86–100.

Mendelsohn, Matthew, and Richard Nadeau. 1996. "The Magnification and Minimization of Social Cleavages by the Broadcast and Narrowcast News Media." *International Journal of Public Opinion Research* 8 (4): 374–89.

Sinanan, Jolynna. 2017. *Social Media in Trinidad: Values and Visibility*. London: UCL Press.

Smith-Shomade, Beretta. 2004. "Narrowcasting in the New World Information Order: A Space for the Audience?" *Television & New Media* 5 (1): 69–81.

Tan, Shzr Ee. 2017. "Taiwan's Aboriginal Music on the Internet." In *Music, Indigeneity, Digital Media*, edited by Thomas Hilder, Henry Stobart, and Shzr Ee Tan, 28–52. Rochester, NY: University of Rochester Press.

Utley, Garrick. 1997. "The Shrinking of Foreign News: From Broadcast to Narrowcast." *Foreign Affairs*. Available online: https://www.foreignaffairs.com/articles/1997-03-01/shrinking-foreign-news-broadcast-narrowcast, accessed May 26, 2020.

Valverde, Raquel. 2019. "Understanding Musicking on Social Media: Music Sharing, Sociality and Citizenship." PhD thesis, London South Bank University.

Venkatraman, Shriram. 2017. *Social Media in South India*. London: UCL Press.

Wang, Xinyuan. 2016. *Social Media in Industrial China*. London: UCL Press.

Yang, Hui, Peidon Yang, and Shaohua Zhan. 2017. "Immigration, Population, and Foreign Workforce in Singapore: An Overview of Trends, Policies, and Issues." *HSSE Online* 6 (10): 10–21.

Part Two

Transforming Tradition

4

Harmonies for the Homeland: Traditional Music and the Politics of Intangible Cultural Heritage on Vietnamese Radio

Lonán Ó Briain

On state-society relations in Vietnam, Benedict Kerkvliet suggests these seemingly disparate entities should be viewed together as active arenas for debate: "Rather than trying to say that one entity is part of the state and another entity is part of society, a more fruitful approach is to think of arenas in which boundaries, rights, jurisdictions, and power distribution between state and societal agencies are debated, contested, and resolved (at least temporarily)" (Kerkvliet 2001: 240). One example of these political arenas can be observed in the state media apparatus, where Kerkvliet notes "an undercurrent of debate" (Kerkvliet 2001: 253). Studies on media broadcasting elsewhere have noted similar debates where, instead of functioning as a listless vehicle for information, agents within the system take actions that change the course of history. As Bronhman observes for radio in the Caribbean: "wireless and broadcasting proffered new repertoires of contention and participated in, rather than merely reporting on, the events at hand" (Bronfman 2016: 9; see also Couldry 2006). Since the late-colonial era, radio has been a central means of communication between state and society in Vietnam (e.g., Ó Briain 2018). This chapter examines the production process for music recordings broadcast on national radio in the contemporary era. The research focuses on the perspectives of the content producers, studying the workflow within the rehearsal halls and recording studios of state radio in Hanoi, in an attempt to understand how creative practice intersects with political policy and ideology. Even within the confines of persistent regimes of censorship and restrictive regulation overseen by the Communist Party of Vietnam, diverse content on politics, culture, and society are regularly produced for broadcast. By examining production processes and creative practices at the station, we can understand the debates that occur within the state-run media rather than simply between authorities or pro-state parties and anti-state or anti-communist dissidents.

Voice of Vietnam Radio (*Đài Tiếng nói Việt Nam*; henceforth VOV) has been one of the most active producers of music for the most omnipresent form of sound-based broadcast media in Vietnam since the mid-twentieth century. The VOV music ensembles are responsible for producing the largest proportion of new recordings broadcast on air.[1] These musicians also have a legacy to uphold. Older musicians who started out with the station around the beginning of the reform era, when funding increased and new staff joined with limited or no experience of the war, have since taken up senior administrative positions within the ensembles. These individuals are responsible for maintaining a roster of talented musicians and continuing to produce high-quality, pro-party outputs that are also popular among their listeners. They straddle an uncomfortable divide between answering to the administration, maintaining the respect of their fellow musicians, and keeping the attention of their "listening public" (Lacey 2013). Instead of liberating the musicians' creative inclinations during the reform period, this devolution of administrative duties, combined with the precarious financial circumstances of performing artists under Vietnam's socialist-oriented market economy, has pressured the ensembles into reproducing pro-party messages.

This chapter takes the processes of music production by the VOV traditional music ensemble (*nhóm nhạc dân tộc*; lit., national or ethnic music ensemble) as a case study. In stepping into the rehearsal halls and recording studios of the VOV—their relational spaces of creativity (Gibson 2005)—this ethnography investigates how and why VOV musicians are keeping their communist-themed musical outputs relevant in contemporary Vietnam. In this way, the research seeks to understand the "humanity, sociality, and spatiality" (Sterne 2003: 236) behind their ongoing recordings of red music (*nhạc đỏ*).

Here, the hypernym "red music" is more suitable than one of its hyponyms, "modern national music" (*nhạc dân tộc hiện đại*)—described by Arana as a form of neotraditional music revitalized within a communist framework (see Arana 1999)—for at least three reasons: red music refers to the music's social function more so than its abstract sonic properties, the term "red music" is far more common in the vernacular,[2] and music within this umbrella term can be compared and contrasted with styles in other communist states, especially those with close political and economic ties to Vietnam (e.g., Russia and, until the 1990s, Bulgaria) or those with closely related musical cultures (e.g., China). Like red music in these other communist states, Vietnamese red music principally includes nationalist songs and music used to perpetuate the control of the party (see also Ó Briain 2021). Music on traditional instruments or in traditional styles comprise only a minority of the wider corpus of red music, but these styles are among the most powerful sonic icons of cultural nationalism because their places of origin can be more convincingly traced to the villages and hamlets of rural Vietnam. Recordings of red music by the VOV ensembles help to reproduce the idea of an idyllic homeland that remains harmonious under one party.

Drawing on interviews with VOV musicians and participant-observation fieldwork in their rehearsals and recording sessions over an eleven-month period between June 2016 and April 2017, this chapter provides an account of one working week at the rehearsal hall and recording studio of the traditional music ensemble in mid-July 2016. Through an ethnographic study of the workflow of this ensemble, the research investigates how political messages are embedded in musical outputs at the point of realization and later magnified by culture brokers—predominantly, broadcasters, and television producers—through bespoke sonic and visual frames. These culture brokers rationalize their strategic manipulation of musical and lyrical texts under the guise of safeguarding intangible cultural heritage (ICH), while the resulting broadcasts justify the continuation of the party-state system.

The Politics of Intangible Cultural Heritage

In his analysis of heritage discourse promoted by Vietnam's Ministry of Culture and Information concerning the Central Highlands, Oscar Salemink argues that "[culture] is objectified and instrumentalized for ulterior political purposes, which implies that the people embodying cultural practices branded 'heritage'—the 'culture carriers'— are instrumentalized as well" (2013: 173). Culture carriers, or culture bearers, are responsible for living the traditions. They can be contrasted with culture brokers, who operate within the field of cultural heritage management and are often the ones responsible for this "instrumentalization." For Geertz, culture brokers are specialists concerned with the integration of local traditions into a national framework (1960).[3] In working toward a model for cultural sustainability, Titon refers to culture brokers as those who "implement policies meant to protect and preserve outstanding musical (and other cultural) traditions considered to be threatened" (Titon 2009: 120; see also Kurin 1997).

Musicological research on ICH has tended to preference the work of culture bearers because we view them as the primary source of the culture. Brokers, on the other hand, tend to be more active at the intersection of politics and ICH. Their funding or sponsorship often comes from an external source, such as an organ of the state, and their motivations are often divided between supporting the culture bearers and answering to their funders. Consequently, interventions by culture brokers can upend the work of culture bearers when "the bureaucratic and scholarly superstructure acts as a brake, slowing down and reining in processes of diversification, experimentation and innovation" (Bithell 2019: 208). In single-party countries like Vietnam, the prevalence of top-down initiatives by state-sponsored brokers has led to "allegations of an authoritarian edge to safeguarding" (Grant 2012: 41; see also Norton 2014).

While Salemink focuses on the ministry's appropriation and management of ICH, the nationwide audience for that discourse is reached via the broadcast media, where the folklorization of the public sphere shapes "people's attitudes to their own culture and the way they represent it to others" (Hafstein 2018: 14). In the late-reform era, one person stands out as the culture broker *par excellence* at national radio: VOV3 (the music channel) broadcaster, administrator, publicist, and unofficial figurehead of the traditional music ensemble Mai Văn Lạng. Lạng and his colleagues are attuned to international discourse concerning the sustainability of ICH, which argues that traditional music and folk songs must be kept malleable to remain resilient and relevant (e.g., Titon 2015). As Lạng explained in a 2018 interview with party newspaper *The People* (*Nhân Dân*), folksongs will be sustainable if their traditional structures are used to address contemporary issues. We (the VOV and its affiliated composers) must not abandon the fundamental poetic structure of Vietnamese folksong, he argues; the lyrical content is the problem, with too many songs about obsolete rituals and customs that are not relevant to modern life in the reform era. If we write new lyrics that conform to the traditional musical and lyrical styles, we will draw in new listeners.

One example of these new lyrics added to old tunes is published in *New Folksongs (Những Bài hát Dân ca Lời mới)*, a book dedicated to the life and musical outputs Quốc Anh (born 1937). The introduction is written by Mai Văn Lạng and includes a biography of the composer. An appendix is devoted to song texts comprising formerly unattributed folksongs—mostly drawn from northern Vietnamese *chèo* folk theater—with new lyrics written by Quốc Anh, who now claims authorship of the songs. This appendix also includes the melodic style (*làn điệu*) and the soloist(s) who recorded each song with the VOV. The main sections of the book are divided into five categories comprising songs about: the party and Uncle Ho (former Premier Ho Chi Minh), the homeland or motherland, mother, Hanoi, and war veterans and martyrs (Quốc Anh 2015). These themes are reflective of the VOV's restrictive conceptualization of important issues for contemporary Vietnamese society; they are defined in relation to the needs of the party-state, not the people. As the following descriptive account of one working week in the VOV studios illustrates, the VOV ensembles are devoted to "revitalizing" traditional music and folksong using these pro-party themes.

Representing the Nation with Traditional Music

The VOV traditional music ensemble achieves its aspirations to be an ensemble for the people by producing recordings on three regional representative styles—northern (*Bắc Bộ*), central (*Trung Bộ*), and southern (*Nam Bộ*), which happen to correspond with the colonial protectorates of Tonkin, Annam, and Cochinchina respectively. Cát Vận, a composer and former director of the VOV music ensembles during the transition to the reform era, explained how the troupes have evolved to meet these demands of their audiences and employers: "the national or traditional music division includes singers performing folk music of the three regions of Vietnam. For example, *chèo* in the north, *cải lương* in the south and *hát Huế* and *hát bài chòi* in the central region. This means that in folk music the particularities of all regions of Vietnam are represented" (interview, July 11, 2016). *Hát chèo* is a centuries-old form of musical theater from northern Vietnam. The VOV studios are closer to its location of origin than to that of the other styles—100 km south of Hanoi in the Hoa Lư district of Ninh Bình Province—and two senior figures in the ensemble were brought up in this style: one is the director of the traditional music ensemble, renowned *chèo* singer Hồng Ngát, and the other is the primary culture broker for ensemble, Mai Văn Lạng. Under their leadership, *chèo* recordings make up around two-thirds of this ensemble's recorded output. *Cải lương* reformed theater was popularized in southern Vietnam in the early twentieth century and rapidly spread to other parts of the country; staged performances have been hosted in Hanoi since colonial times and an established *cải lương* troupe is now based in the city center. *Ca Huế* or *hát Huế* folksongs are heavily inflected with the central Vietnamese accent and consequently demand that they are performed by singers from that region fluent in the style. The traditional ensemble employs three or four *chèo* singers and one each for *ca Huế* and *cải lương*. On occasions that they record more unusual styles such as *hát xẩm* or *ca trù*—two poetic musical styles of folksong from northern Vietnam traditionally performed with just one or two accompanying instruments—they draft in part-time collaborators.

While most of the VOV singers are specialists in just one or two styles, often related to places where they were raised, the instrumentalists relocate those traditions within a national musical framework. These instrumentalists tend to be more stylistically versatile as they fluently code-switch between musical traditions at the whim of the musical director. Unlike the singers, they also attend nearly all of the recording sessions, which provide stability to the ensemble, as director Hồng Ngát explained:

> The traditional orchestra itself is very stable. When we record in particular styles such as *bài chòi* [playful form of musical theater from central Vietnam] or *cải lương*, we sometimes draft in outside players. Otherwise the orchestra is very comfortable in *chèo*, *quan họ* folksongs, *ca Huế*, *hát văn* [a secular, sanitized form of *chầu văn* mediumship ritual songs (see Norton 2009)], folksongs of the north, folksongs of the south, the orchestra can handle it all.
>
> (Interview, October 13, 2016)

This demands virtuosic technical ability and an encyclopedic stylistic knowledge of Vietnamese music not normally needed in other settings: "Generally speaking, this ensemble can record under pressure with the highest quality of tuning and ready to adjust to the appropriate melodic styles. Each of the respective styles demands particular adjustments to instrument tuning and regionally appropriate forms of ornamentation" (op. cit.).

To gain a better understanding of these stylistic shifts, I took end-blown flute (*sáo tiêu*) lessons with ensemble member Nguyễn Thắng. Thắng had studied with former VOV flautist Ngọc Phan (1938–2017) prior to his formal education at the National Academy of Music with Lê Xuân Phổ. Ngọc Phan, from the first Academy class of 1959, joined the VOV after his studies. Under the leadership of revolutionary-poet-turned-composer Nguyễn Đình Tấn, Ngọc Phan was given a traditional eight-holed flute from Lôi Tiên. This instrument was fine when playing standard diatonic red music, he explained to me, but inadequate for more elaborate compositions. Several versions of the pentatonic scale can be found in Vietnam, and new musicians representing the people of Vietnam through multiple traditional styles have to adjust to those pitches.[4] Ngọc Phan decided to bore two additional holes into his instrument, which expanded the melodic range of the flute and facilitated a greater array of ornamentation styles. Through his iconic performances with the VOV in the 1960s, he became an early exponent of the ten-hole transverse flute (*sáo trúc*) in Vietnam (interview, August 16, 2016).

Following on from the legacy of his teachers, who sought to expand the melodic range of their instruments, Thắng explained how the Vietnamese end-blown flute has only six finger holes, whereas the Chinese version of this instrument has nine holes. He plays the nine-hole Chinese *tiêu* in most of his VOV recordings because that instrument enables him to play in far more keys—the difference is equivalent to a comparison between a six-holed Irish tin whistle and a nine-holed German recorder. When playing in certain regional styles, Thắng has to adjust pitch slightly too. He uses alternative fingering and sometimes a different instrument when changing regional style or aiming for more florid ornamentation (*nốt hoa mỹ*). Thắng most regularly played ten-hole bamboo flute and nine-hole end-blown flute in the traditional music ensemble depending on the requirements of his musical director (interview, December 12, 2016). This is the most cost-effective approach because the ensemble does not need to hire multiple flute players. Without visuals, the radio listener is unable to tell precisely which instrument is being played, and complaints about radio ensemble performers playing Chinese instruments are not a concern. Therefore, unlike traditional musicians in the past who tended to develop expertise in just one style often related to their local or regional affiliation, Thắng and his colleagues have become the experts at switching seamlessly between styles as they seek to represent the people through nationalized forms of traditional music.[5]

In the Rehearsal Hall, July 12, 2016

At 9:00 a.m. in the middle of torrential rain and strong winds, I arrive at the Theater of the VOV Ensembles (Nhà Hát Đài TNVN), which is in a new building around the corner from the former Bạch Mai broadcasting center used to produce the Declaration of Independence in 1945 (lane 128C Đại La). A rehearsal of the traditional music ensemble is scheduled to start at 9:30 a.m., but everyone is given a free pass for being late due to the storm. I wait in the office with Long, an administrator of the ensembles, where we drink green tea and discuss the day ahead. As the musicians and singers filter in, he introduces my project to each of them. We also talk about differences between Ireland and Vietnam and discuss football—Dũng, a two-stringed fiddle (*đàn nhị*) player, jokes that they're still recovering from a late night on Sunday after staying up to watch the final of the 2016 European Football Championship. These informal conversations over tea belie the gradual build-up of intensity concerning the working week. Yesterday, the musicians had discussed repertoire and collected their music for individual practice; today, the ensemble will begin formal rehearsals together; and on Friday afternoon, they will reconvene for a recording session at the VOV headquarters on Quán Sứ street. This workflow, which culminates in a recording session at the end of the week, is a typical production cycle for these radio musicians.

On my first visit to the rehearsal hall that Tuesday, Trần Xuân Hiến, another two-stringed fiddle player, cautiously reminds the others of my recording device—he is younger than several of the musicians but appears to serve as the party representative in the room. Two singers sit at a desk with me while the musicians run through the score. Chu Cường, one of the singers, asks an assistant to refill the hot water flask we're all using to make tea. The singers sit, joke, chat, take selfies of themselves, and check updates on Facebook—this platform is currently one of the primary mediums for performing arts promotions and social networking in Vietnam. The room isn't wide enough for all of the musicians to sit in a circle; some have to sit in rows instead. The conductor stands in front of the ensemble beside a solo singer, who waits for the musicians to finish their rehearsal. The instrumental ensemble today comprises one monochord (*đàn bầu*), one moon lute (*đàn nguyệt*), one short-necked lute (*đàn tứ*), two two-stringed fiddles (*đàn nhị*),[6] one transverse bamboo flute (*sáo trúc*), one end-blown flute (*sáo tiêu*), one four-stringed lute (*đàn tỳ bà*), two zithers (*đàn tranh*), one hammered dulcimer (*đàn tam thập lục*), and a pair of drums (*trống*) and woodblocks (*khối gỗ*)—additional percussion will be added in the recording studio. The rehearsal schedule for the week is on a board in front of the musicians, Marx and Lenin are on the opposite side of the room behind them, and a commemorative banner for the ensemble hangs on the side wall.

Diệu Hương is first up to rehearse an arrangement of folksongs entitled "Love for Our Youthful Country" (*Yêu sao non nước quê mình*). This is a medley of *ca Huế*, classical songs from the central Vietnam, and its complex transitions eat up most of the rehearsal time. While the musicians use staff notation to improvise around a fixed melody in heterophonic texture, Hương reads from a lyrics sheet without musical notation. She interprets the rhythm from the classic Vietnamese poetic couple form of six-eight (*lục bát*) and performs with an iambic tendency in sync with the accompanying ensemble. The absence of a strictly prescribed melodic and rhythmic framework for her permits scope for improvisation and personalization. When performing with an ensemble of this size, however, inconsistencies in timing throw the musicians off, demand additional practice, and restrict the scope for elaboration on her part.

Thiên nhiên, cảnh sắc, con người
Hoà trong câu hát nhịp đời sinh sôi
Niềm vui lan toả đất trời
Quê hương tươi sáng, cuộc đời bình yên
Muôn lòng thêm vững niềm tin
Chung tay để nước non mình đẹp hơn
Từ phố thị đến xóm thôn
Nối liền một dải giang sơn, giang sơn hữu tình.

Nature, scenery, people
Harmony in the reproductive song of life
Joy spreads from sky to earth
Radiant homeland, peaceful earth
Ten thousand hearts in more steadfast belief
Joining hands to make our land more beautiful
From town to village
Connecting this stretch of country, [our] charming country.

Hương sits for the beginning of the rehearsal, possibly expecting this to go on for a while, and then stands up later on. Her silky voice soars above the ensemble as she performs with stage-like charisma, and she theatrically casts her script aside at the conclusion of the piece. The dynamics between her, the conductor, and the musicians are tense. This conductor plays a diminished role in this ensemble compared with the conductor of the VOV's new music ensemble (*nhóm nhạc mới*). His duties are restricted to beating simple duple time and occasionally criticizing Hương when she enters late. Here, the musicians contribute more spoken advice and guidance concerning style, with the percussionist providing most of the input for this particular piece. Overall, the rehearsal is run as a communal effort with no one person standing out as the leader.

Chèo singer Chu Cường is left with just fifteen minutes to rehearse his song, and he stands throughout. He infers the melody from the subheading, which indicates the song should be performed using the pentatonic pitches of a popular *chèo* melody (*luyện năm cung*) adapted to the specific tones of the words of this poem. The lines again follow the six-eight couplet style. The oldest member of the ensemble, fifty-five-year-old moon lute player Trần Luận, is much more involved this time, and his playing is particularly lively. With fewer awkward transitions between parts, the entire ensemble is able to improvise more freely here. The simplicity of the structure and its arrangement, in the most commonly recorded style at the VOV (*chèo*), means that less time is needed to rehearse this piece.

Quê hương biết mấy thân yêu,
Điệu chèo ai hát sớm chiều ngân vang.
Vẳng nghe sau lũy tre làng,
Cùng đàn ai nảy lại càng thêm yêu.

This homeland that knows so much love,
[Where] verses of *chèo* sung throughout the day resound brightly.
On hearing these verses in the traditional village,[7]
Together the people bounce back with even greater love.

At the end of the rehearsal, Hiền passes out administrative updates to all the musicians—they're getting a raise and there will be a major performance on VOV3 on the August 21, another party commemorative event. Everyone disperses by 11:15 a.m. for lunch and, later, to attend to other performance and teaching duties outside of the VOV.

In the Recording Studio, July 15, 2016

On my first visit to the recording studio on Level 2 of the VOV headquarters at 58 Quán Sứ Street, Nguyễn Thị Thu from the International Cooperation Department helps me navigate my way around the building and ensures I get into the recording session on time. Although the official start time was 2:00 p.m., we don't begin recording until after 2:30 p.m., and one of the singers expects that we'll finish by 4:00 p.m. The control room door to the corridor is kept open because smokers and socializers like to go out for breaks when the singers have questions for the sound engineer, and traffic noise filters into the control room, which the musicians pass through to enter the enclosed live room. The studio is much smaller than the one used by the VOV's new music ensemble but still a respectable size for a chamber ensemble. There's no tea like in the rehearsal room, just bottled water, and Hồng Ngát politely ensures that Cường the singer brings me water.

"Silence! Record, recording!" Long, the recording engineer today, shouts from behind the soundboard. He has worked at the VOV for twenty-four years and feels comfortable with barking orders at the musicians. The VOV sound engineers use Nuendo on a standard desktop PC to manipulate the recordings. The editing is quite light while live recording is taking place. Long has to adjust the microphones briefly at the start of the session and then again when the hammered dulcimer is added to the ensemble for the second singer. This instrument consistently causes problems during my visits to the studio. The mallets make microphone placement difficult and the sound spills into other nearby microphones. Yet the dulcimer is also a key instrument for this ensemble because it bridges the gap between the percussion and melodic instruments. Singers also follow the hypnotic bouncing mallets when judging the elasticity of their vibrato or rubato—at another session in October, when recording Mai Văn Lạng's *hát văn* "Sending Spring Love Home" (*Tình Xuân Xin Gửi Nơi Quê*), singer Văn Chương went through several takes attempting to get the accelerating pace and narrowing frequency of his vibrato on the final note perfectly in time and tune with the dulcimer.

The power dynamics are different here than during rehearsal. Hồng Ngát, who sits next to Long in the control room (see Figure 4.1), commands the most respect during

Figure 4.1 VOV traditional music ensemble in the recording studio, July 15, 2016. Photo: Lonán Ó Briain.

this process. A former singer, she is now the official musical director of the traditional music ensemble. She provides frequent guidance to the singers on musical styles. The conductor also commands more respect in this space. His role takes on greater significance because he is the visual link between the control and live rooms. Musically, his focus is on the tempo, which demands attention at the opening and closing of pieces. His visual cues to the musicians and singers are also more important now because he cannot provide vocal cues as he had done in the rehearsal hall.

Few casual discussions take place because the musicians want to get out without delay. Only an occasional off-microphone conversation takes place while the singers, who are now central to the entire process, sort out their parts under the council of Hồng Ngát. Half an hour into the session, Hương interrupts the recording because she began her part early, and we have to restart. Intermittent breaks are needed to let the singers, engineer, and director resolve issues with the vocals, and this allows the musicians take a brief cigarette break and chat. Fiddle player Dũng tells me his father plays flute and mother plays monochord, and, on comparing his background to mine, he uses the phrase "*con nhà nòi*" to explain how we inherited the skills and passion for music from our parents. After an hour and a half of recording, the instrumental ensemble wraps up. Hương wants to cut and paste a couple of vocal bars. Everyone is kicked out of the live room for her to complete these parts before we wrap up the session.

At a recording session later that autumn, another long-serving engineer named Nguyễn Hồng Hải described the process of preparing the equipment and recording while the musicians are in the studio:

> In general, when you record you need to understand the characteristics of the musical instruments, where the sounds come from, what the typical sound of each instrument is… It's hard to say which is the most difficult to record because every instrument has its own feature, but for the musicians or for the recording technicians, we have to record the truest sounds. That's the most important thing. And we have to record in a way that we can feel the sounds of each instrument.

His goal was to record the raw sounds of the instruments without adding any artificial textures or veils: "The sounds in the recording studio and the concert hall are completely different. When you record it has to be of good quality, the sound has to be clear, the sound has to be beautifully played. In short, the recording studio presents unique demands" (interview, October 6, 2016).

One challenge for the traditional music ensemble was their use of a variety of Vietnamese traditional and world percussion instruments. The drum kit at the back of the studio was especially difficult to record alone and then balance with lighter Vietnamese percussion. As Hải explained:

> The percussion instruments need the most attention when recording, the traditional percussion instruments, because our traditional percussion is pretty similar to that of Western music. Like Western jazz percussion, our traditional percussion has many instruments that support each other, like this large drum,

the small drum, the cymbal, and many others. A whole set may include five or six instruments. We need the percussion; it's very important in our traditional orchestra just as in the Western cannon.

In fact, the basic drum kit used by this ensemble was no different to a standard international kit, although the percussionists added a few Vietnamese instruments to localize their sound palette. Under pressure to produce substantial quantities of red music in a variety of traditional styles within a short timeframe, they chose the pragmatic option of a versatile international instrument better suited to the studio context over traditional instruments suggested by the Vietnamese Institute for Musicology in their UNESCO ICH submissions.

Postproduction and Dissemination

After all of these recordings are complete, the musicians let the recording engineer deal with postproduction edits and the transfer of the recording to the VOV Sound Center. Hải outlined this postproduction process from his perspective:

> I am going to listen to everything again, mix all the parts so that it creates good harmony, and then I will make a master... I will send that to the central office where a board of well-known composers will see if they can approve the recording. After they have unanimously approved it, the master will be sent to the archives and the music content editor [at VOV3] will take it from the archives for broadcast.

In fact, the recordings were always approved by this board because compositions recorded by the VOV musicians were mostly written by party members or senior VOV officials. The process of selecting pieces for recording involved a team of senior administrators, directors, and editors who made cautious decisions based on their knowledge of the contemporary political landscape. Once the sound engineer is finished manipulating the audio file, the dataset is passed over to the VOV Sound Center, where an archivist adds the recording and its accompanying information to the digital database. From there, VOV music editors select them from drop-down menus for inclusion in their broadcasts.

In certain cases, VTV takes over at this stage to produce music videos based on the audio files, which can recontextualize the soundtrack and transform its meaning. VTV and its affiliates produce music videos for both VOV music ensembles as part of major staged shows, communist commemorations, and cultural festivals and as part of VTV musical features prerecorded in their studios with performers lip-syncing to the soundtrack. The traditional music ensemble also records music videos staged in picturesque rural settings, the perceived homeland of traditional music and folksong (see also Meeker 2013). Typically featuring only the soloists, these folkloric reconstructions depict traditional music as a place-bound, age-old cultural product. Although the music was recorded inside an invisible "black box" studio located in the middle of a bustling metropolis, television viewers experience the spectacle of a singer in a quaint village recalling his or her love of the nation through the heightened medium of song. By shrouding freshly authored nationalist texts in the sonic veil of traditional musical forms and then portraying these sounds within the visual frame of a timeless bucolic landscape, these folkloric music videos transform the performance into a powerful tool for communist propaganda. From the perspective of musical sustainability, these spectacles portray traditional music and folksong as inherently linked with the rural past, an essentialized stereotype of Vietnam that is at odds with the fast-paced reality of life in this dynamic country.

Over the past two decades, VOV broadcasters and other culture brokers have been uploading MP3 files of these programs and making them publicly available online via the VOV website. This trend is similar to that of many other national radio station employees who engage their listeners online to supplement live radio broadcasts. In the case of the VOV, only recently produced programs are uploaded within a few weeks of broadcast. As of 2020, the back catalog of dormant recordings online is largely unattended, and many older recordings are either corrupted or dysfunctional. Yet even in partial form, this online resource provides an important means for listeners to catch up on broadcasts they may have missed or allows them to listen back to earlier episodes of a program they have just encountered, thereby fulfilling the public service duties of the station.

Although the VOV has no official YouTube page of its own, several editors now share their latest recordings via ad hoc channels. In most of these YouTube channels the channel name is closely related to the program. No individual is celebrated as the sole creator, aside from an acknowledgment of the featured announcers for each episode, and the production is a collective effort on behalf of the VOV. A minority of VOV employees skirt this trend by curating their own independent media presence online, and perhaps the most prolific of these is the aforementioned VOV3 editor Mai Văn Lạng.[8]

Lạng curates his own public profile via an eponymous website,[9] Facebook page, and YouTube channel (named "author Mai Văn Lạng" [soạn giả Mai Văn Lạng] followed by the tagline "Official Channel" written in English). In contrast with the YouTube pages dedicated to particular programs that omit even the name of the curator, Lạng's biography features prominently in his online media. Lạng describes himself as an author, editor, and figurehead of traditional music programming on VOV3. Aside from the financial benefits of this online visibility,[10] he and a handful of other powerful individuals at the VOV dictate what gets recorded in the studio and what people get to hear on their public service broadcasts. Lạng uses his position with VOV3 to distribute and comment on the latest recordings from the traditional ensemble. By March 2020, he had uploaded over 7,000 blog posts to his website, his YouTube site had over 900,000 subscribers, and over a dozen of his YouTube videos had more than 1 million views. As he explained, the internet is a key vehicle for delivering new recordings to potential listeners. Intellectual Property Rights are not an obstacle to publishing these recordings online because, as the director of the ensembles, he believes he is responsible for circulating these recordings by whatever means possible (interview, March 28, 2017).

Conclusion: Harmonies for the Homeland in the Late-Reform Era

Although culture brokers at national broadcasting institutions frequently operate as central nodes in local musical networks (e.g., Gubbins and Ó Briain 2021), brokers in the media networks of countries that lean toward authoritarianism or those with relatively restrictive limitations on press freedom can have an even greater impact on the cultural landscape. The brokerage system in Vietnam is compounded by nepotistic employment practices and the slow turnover of staff at public institutions. As the composer of hundreds of new red songs based on traditional musical forms, a senior director at VOV3, and an advisor to the VOV's traditional music ensemble, Mai Văn Lạng controls the flow of information between the VOV traditional music ensemble, the station, and the public. Although brokers like Lạng may be acting with the best of intentions, this concentration of power is at odds with the recommendations of studies on musical sustainability that express concerns about "professionalization, commercialization, and a media-driven revival of music" (Titon 2009: 22) because these processes promote fixed presentational performances within tightly controlled heritage spaces (see also Grant 2012; Turino 2009). While these studies highlight the impact of commercialization on cultural diversity—an issue I have highlighted elsewhere for Vietnamese minority music cultures (Ó Briain 2014)—Vietnam's musical ecology is also constrained by excessive politicization and restrictive administration. One musical consequence of these centralized roadblocks is that *chèo* continues to be the dominant form of music recorded by the station's traditional music ensemble. The origins of *chèo* can be traced to Ninh Bình province during the Lý dynasty (tenth to thirteenth century), which is hailed as the legitimate precursor political entity to the contemporary Vietnamese state. The VOV's devotion to this music since the station began producing recordings of traditional music in the mid-twentieth century limits the airtime for many other musical traditions and stifles the diversity of the country's musical ecology.

In addition to musical stasis, these culture brokers are promoting political stasis which suits the CPV and the brokers themselves. While new broadcasting technologies are helping to facilitate a more collective approach to musical distribution and diverse political commentary online (see Kerkvliet 2019), the party ensures that power at the VOV remains with only a handful of people who are tasked with distilling the plural micro-cultures of millions into one unifying macro-culture, that of the party-state. The potential for political manipulation is rife. For instance, the pages of Lạng's blog are colorfully illustrated with stories, interviews, and recordings of influential musicians, but a strong pro-party undercurrent is evident—this is particularly transparent in the dozens of pages dedicated to the Spratly Islands, including one photo-essay recounting his personal 2015 trip to this contested archipelago in the South China Sea.[11] The presentation of this music within a political framework supports the ruling elite, promotes political stagnancy, stifles creativity, and limits the natural ebb and flow of cultural traditions.

As Kerkvliet suggests, there is scope for debate within the rehearsal hall, in the recording studio, and elsewhere in the production line, where micro-acts of resistance and retaliation can creep in to the broadcasts. In reality, most musicians and broadcasters are more passionate about the competence of their artistic outputs than the promotion of particular political ideologies. The musicians at the VOV are first and foremost engaged in creative practice. In the studio, these musicians "empower themselves by means of the loopholes that poetic ambiguity and play produce" (Meintjes 2003: 260). Some are aware of the wider implications of their politically charged recordings, especially those responsible for song compositions, and all know of the influential historical recordings produced at the station during times of major conflict. As Cát Vận explained, "the sense of nationalism has always been there, securely, even with the new music" (interview, July 11, 2016). Yet the current crop of musicians at the VOV rarely meet most of their audience, and they are largely unconscious of the ways their recordings are used once they are finished in the studio. Similarly, the administrators of the traditional ensemble are focused on rotating their pool of folk singers and songs and maintaining a group of versatile instrumentalists who can adjust their playing styles to adequately appeal to their diverse body of listeners throughout Vietnam.

The production process in the reform era is far more elaborate than in times past, and creative artists are losing agency over representations of their work to culture brokers, who rationalize politicized alterations to intangible cultural heritage in the guise of making musical traditions relevant for contemporary audiences. Each recording now demands several weeks of planning and preparation. The number of teams involved means that the musicians, engineers, and producers have to relinquish control over their creative outputs at several stages. At the outset, the text is selected for its suitability to adhere to the needs of the ministry and the party. In many cases those texts have been authored or suggested by party officials, such as lyrics by Mai Văn Lạng written to old *chèo* melodies or musical arrangements of provocative poetry by VOV CEO Nguyễn Thế Kỷ. In postproduction the programs are subjected to vetting by the ministry for suitability in the contemporary climate. Recordings approved by the board are then passed on to culture brokers such as Mai Văn Lạng for distribution within a pro-party framework. The political potency of the music is often combined with provocative images and text to create powerful cultural propaganda. These videos are posted to sites such as YouTube, while the other side of the debate is silenced by "Notice and Take Down" requests from government lawyers.

Professional musicians in contemporary Vietnam are mostly low-income performing artists living in precarious economic circumstances. The absence of any notable music industry framework, limited enforcement of Intellectual Property Rights, and competing concepts of ownership mean that musicians are not able to benefit from the sale of recordings beyond a flat fee for production. Those who are fortunate to be employed by the ministry in one of its musical troupes, such as the Music Theater of the VOV, are reliant on the regular, albeit humble, salary and its benefits. As Buchanan notes of radio musicians in socialist Bulgaria, these jobs provide "social legitimacy and government sanction for the pursuit of professional music careers" (1995: 387). Beyond financial security and media visibility, long-serving musicians with these ensembles are rewarded with honorific titles by the ministry.[12] In the post-pandemic economic climate, where the vast majority of performing artists find themselves on the wrong side of an increasingly prominent income disparity between the rich and the poor, these musicians are forced into a dependency relationship with their employer, which ensures that these pro-party recordings will continue to be produced whether the audience listens or not.

Radio work provides a steady salary that facilitates independent creative activities by enabling the musicians to experiment in other areas of their musical lives. The VOV musicians participate in rehearsals and recording sessions at the broadcasting center in the morning and then in the afternoon work on individual projects, such as teaching at the National Academy of Music or performing their own-choice repertoire at public venues elsewhere in Hanoi. Thanks to the financial security of his post at the VOV, flautist Nguyễn Thắng was able to experiment and take risks on other performing arts projects. He refined his virtuosic playing techniques in the studio, but his creative potential was unleashed elsewhere in artistic projects that did not have to be financially successful to ensure that he could feed his children. One example was a "world music" ensemble he set up with his wife, a zither player and teacher at National Academy of Music, which included his arrangements of world fusion that combined Vietnamese ethnic minority musical instruments and clothing styles with other Vietnamese traditional music within semi-improvised jazz framework. Using his status as a VOV musician, he was able to gain media exposure for the project and draw a reasonable audience. Opportunities like this for rewarding, independent musical experiences rely on a consistent contribution to the VOV as a recording musician. Unless this state of dependency is separated from the requirement to produce romanticized, nostalgic recordings that yearn for a past that never was, and more pluralistic voices are permitted on air, the final product will inevitably be centered on nuanced political content that legitimizes (and reproduces) the power of the party.

Acknowledgment

Funding for this research was provided by the Arts and Humanities Research Council (UK).

Notes

1. One senior figure at the station estimated that these groups produced 30 percent of all new music on the radio. The remaining 70 percent comprises field recordings, recordings of other state ensembles, and independent productions of popular and other music in home studios—the economic architecture of the Vietnamese music industry has not yet facilitated independent production on a large scale. Foreign productions are not included in this estimate.
2. A cursory search for these terms on Google reveals just over 2,000 mentions of *nhạc dân tộc hiện đại* in contrast to over 500,000 for *nhạc đỏ* (accessed May 28, 2020).

3   Drawing on Geertz's use of the term, Dimick describes how People's Artists (*nghệ nhân*) in Vietnam push back against unnamed culture brokers of the state who wished to politicize musical traditions (2013: 189).
4   For an example of the range of pentatonic tuning styles and pitch names found in Vietnam, see https://www.oxfordmusiconline.com/grovemusic/view/10.1093/gmo/9781561592630.001.0001/omo-9781561592630-e-8000007210?rskey=r6v7i6, accessed March 1, 2020.
5   Lê (1998: 92) and Beebe (2017: 66–7) note similar changes for the zither (*đàn tranh*) and monochord (*đàn bầu*) respectively as professional musicians are now modifying their instruments and developing fluency in several styles of music.
6   Vietnamese two-stringed fiddles tend to have round sound boxes. Hiển's fiddle sound box was hexagonal, perhaps based on the design of the southern Chinese *erhu*, while Lê Quang Dũng's was round.
7   *Lũy tre làng* refers to an idealized view of the traditional village protected by a barrier of bamboo trees (*lũy tre*).
8   See, for example, the YouTube channel "VOV MEDIA" (https://www.youtube.com/channel/UCNeKKKdm8Ayh70yD05-8qpQ/featured, accessed March 10, 2020), which has a playlist of full-length evening stories previously broadcast on the VOV and over 100,000 view counts for its most popular upload. In contrast to Mai Văn Lạng's channel, no individual is named as the host and the channel tag uses an official VOV graphic.
9   www.maivanlang.com, accessed May 27, 2020.
10 Although we did not discuss the income received from advertisement revenue, YouTube pays as much as $2,000 for one video with over 1 million views.
11 http://www.maivanlang.com/2015/08/chum-anh-chuyen-i-truong-sa.html, accessed June 5, 2020.
12 At each round of these awards over the past few years, at least two VOV musicians have been awarded the title of NSUT, which secures the legacy of these musicians in Vietnam. In 2019, VOV fiddle player Lê Quang Dũng and singer Hoàng Tùng were bestowed with this title at the ninth iteration of these awards (https://sankhau.com.vn/website/search.aspx?word=Ngh%E1%BB%87+s%C4%A9+%C6%B0u+t%C3%BA+%C4%91%E1%BB%A3t+3, accessed June 3, 2020).

Bibliography

Arana, Miranda. 1999. *Neotraditional Music in Vietnam*. Kent, OH: Nhạc Việt.
Beebe, Lisa. 2017. "The Vietnamese *Đàn Bầu*: A Cultural History of an Instrument in Diaspora." PhD thesis, University of California, Santa Cruz.
Bithell, Caroline. 2019. "Folklore, the City and a World in Transition: Intangible Cultural Heritage in Georgia (Caucasus)." In *Music as Heritage: Historical and Ethnographic Perspectives*, edited by Barley Norton and Naomi Matsumoto, 193–215. London and New York: Routledge.
Bronfman, Alejandra M. 2016. *Isles of Noise: Sonic Media in the Caribbean*. Chapel Hill, NC: University of North Carolina Press.
Buchanan, Donna A. 1995. "Metaphors of Power, Metaphors of Truth: The Politics of Music Professionalism in Bulgarian Folk Orchestras." *Ethnomusicology* 39 (3): 381–416.

Couldry, Nick. 2006. *Listening Beyond the Echoes: Media, Ethics and Agency in an Uncertain World*. Boulder, CO: Paradigm Press.
Dimick, Bretton F. 2013. "Vietnam's Ca trù: Courtesans' Songs by Any Other Name." PhD thesis, University of Michigan.
Geertz, Clifford. 1960. "The Javanese Kijaji: The Changing Role of a Cultural Broker." *Comparative Studies in Society and History* 2 (2): 228–49.
Gibson, Chris. 2005. "Recording Studios: Relational Spaces of Creativity in the City." *Built Environment* 31 (3): 192–207.
Grant, Catherine. 2012. "Rethinking Safeguarding: Objections and Responses to Protecting and Promoting Endangered Musical Heritage." *Ethnomusicology Forum* 21 (1): 31–51.
Gubbins, Helen, and Lonán Ó Briain. 2021. "Broadcasting Pop: The Fanning Sessions as a Gateway to New Music." In *Made in Ireland: Studies in Popular Music*, edited by Áine Mangaoang, John O'Flynn, and Lonán Ó Briain, 31–41. New York: Routledge.
Hafstein, Valdimar Tr. 2018. *Making Intangible Heritage: El Condor Pasa and Other Stories from UNESCO*. Bloomington, IN: Indiana University Press.
Kerkvliet, Benedict J. Tria. 2001. "An Approach for Analysing State-Society Relations in Vietnam." *Sojourn: Journal of Social Issues in Southeast Asia* 16 (2): 238–78.
Kerkvliet, Benedict J. Tria. 2019. *Speaking Out in Vietnam: Public Political Criticism in a Communist Party-Ruled Nation*. Ithaca, NY: Cornell University Press.
Kurin, Richard. 1997. *Reflections of a Culture Broker*. Washington, DC: Smithsonian Institution.
Lacey, Kate. 2013. *Listening Publics: The Politics and Experience of Listening in the Media Age*. Cambridge: Polity Press.
Latour, Bruno. 2005. *Reassembling the Social: An Introduction to Actor-Network-Theory*. Oxford: Oxford University Press.
Lê Tuấn Hùng. 1998. *Đàn Tranh Music of Vietnam: Traditions and Innovations*. Springvale, Victoria: Australia Asia Foundation.
Meeker, Lauren. 2013. *Sounding Out Heritage: Cultural Politics and the Social Practice of Quan Họ Folk Song in Northern Vietnam*. Honolulu: University of Hawai'i Press.
Meintjes, Louise. 2003. *Sound of Africa! Making Music Zulu in a South African Studio*. Durham, NC: Duke University Press.
Norton, Barley. 2009. *Songs for the Spirits: Music and Mediums in Modern Vietnam*. Urbana and Chicago, IL: University of Illinois Press.
Norton, Barley. 2014. "Music Revival, *Ca Trù* Ontologies, and Intangible Cultural Heritage in Vietnam." In *The Oxford Handbook of Music Revival*, edited by Caroline Bithell and Juniper Hill, 158–79. New York: Oxford University Press.
Norton, Barley, and Naomi Matsumoto. 2019. "Introduction: Historical and Ethnographic Perspectives on Music as Heritage." In *Music as Heritage: Historical and Ethnographic Perspectives*, edited by Barley Norton and Naomi Matsumoto, 1–17. London and New York: Routledge.
Ó Briain, Lonán. 2014. "Minorities Onstage: Cultural Tourism, Cosmopolitanism, and Social Harmony in Northwestern Vietnam." *Asian Music* 45 (2): 32–57.
Ó Briain, Lonán. 2018. "Musical Cosmopolitanism in Late-Colonial Hanoi." *Ethnomusicology Forum* 27 (3): 265–85.
Ó Briain, Lonán. Forthcoming. *Voices of Vietnam: A Century of Radio, Red Music, and Revolution*. New York: Oxford University Press.
Quốc Anh. 2015. *Những Bài hát Dân ca Lời mới*. Hanoi: Nhà Xuất bản Sân khấu.

Salemink, Oscar. 2013. "Appropriating Culture: The Politics of Intangible Cultural Heritage in Vietnam." In *State, Society and the Market in Contemporary Vietnam*, edited by Hue-Tam Ho Tai and Mark Sidel, 158–80. New York and London: Routledge.

Sterne, Jonathan. 2003. *The Audible Past: Cultural Origins of Sound Reproduction*. Durham, NC: Duke University Press.

Titon, Jeff Todd. 2009. "Music and Sustainability: An Ecological Viewpoint." *The World of Music* 51 (1): 119–37.

Titon, Jeff Todd. 2015. "Sustainability, Resilience, and Adaptive Management for Applied Ethnomusicology." In *The Oxford Handbook of Applied Ethnomusicology*, edited by Svanibor Pettan and Jeff Todd Titon, 157–99. New York: Oxford University Press.

Turino, Thomas. 2009. "Four Fields of Music Making and Sustainable Living." *The World of Music* 51 (1): 95–117.

5

Mediation of Tradition: Television and Studio Productions of Khmer Music in Cambodia

Francesca Billeri

In contemporary Cambodia, Khmer ritual music and traditional theater are being transformed by commercial productions for the mass media. Musicians view these productions as features of modernization that can help to make their music more appealing to younger audiences and tourists. They also view these changes as opportunities to preserve and promote Cambodian national identity. In this chapter, I analyze commercial recordings and television broadcasts of traditional wedding rituals and theater music genres to understand the impact of these reproductions on the traditions themselves. On the one hand, the process of recording performances for commercial distribution demands an alteration to performing practices, instrumentation, musical texture, and the extra-musical functions of Khmer traditional music. On the other hand, these processes act as means of preservation, promotion, and revival that foster new ways of making music and sustaining endangered traditional genres.

The research considers two representative forms of traditional ritual music and popular theater genres, *lkhaon yiike* and *lkhaon bassac*, as they are transformed and adapted to new, "modern" performance contexts. Originally *lkhaon yiike* consisted of a dance performance (*rɔbam yiike*) accompanied by large drums called *skɔɔ yiike*, from which the genre's name is derived. Later, a theatrical performance was added to *rɔbam yiike*. Nowadays, this dance is performed by a group of female dancers at the beginning of a theatrical performance. According to Thiounn, *lkhaon yiike* was brought to Cambodia by Muslim merchants from Java or Malaysia, and it has common elements with Malay *Jikey* and Thai *likay* (Thiounn [1930] 1956: 32). The name *lkhaon bassac* derives from the Bassac river in southern Vietnam, from which it originated at the end of the nineteenth century. This theatrical form is characterized by alternating dialogues, recitatives, songs, and acrobatic pantomimes. According to my informants, *lkhaon bassac* was influenced by the Chinese opera and southern Vietnamese *cải lương*.[1]

These two traditional genres are now regularly performed within musical competitions on national television. In addition to the transformation and popularization of traditional practices, the ways in which Khmer traditional music is disseminated and reproduced have changed due to the growing popularity of new media and communications technologies. The widespread availability of these new technologies has also helped to make certain art forms and their performers famous: performers featured on television programs almost invariably maintain Facebook pages, and they upload performances to YouTube to further their popularity, especially among younger audiences, and to advance their professional careers. How do these forms of media affect the presentation of traditional culture? How are these media being used to shape a new Cambodian cultural identity? And how do new ways of disseminating and reproducing traditional music affect listeners' perceptions of traditional genres? To explore these questions, I examine two case studies: a musical competition program, *Khmer Cultural Heritage*, broadcast on the national broadcaster Bayon TV; and a series of recordings produced by a local NGO, Cambodian Living Arts (CLA), in collaboration with local artists. After examining these two relatively new performance contexts, the analysis focuses on two versions of the famous wedding song, *"Haom Rooɲ"* (The Sacred Pavilion), as an example of the process of decontextualization, recontextualization, and cultural change within the traditional performing arts. The first version of this song is a recording from a wedding I attended in 2009, and the second version is extracted from a CD that was recorded outside of the ritual context. With these examples, this study aims to examine the transformation of traditions as they are re-produced for the media, their impact on the dissemination of Cambodian traditional music more broadly, and the ways in which traditions are being reconfigured as part of wider sociocultural changes in contemporary Cambodia.

Reconstruction of Traditional Dance, Music, and Theater after the Khmer Rouge

Before examining recent changes in traditional music and theater, it is necessary to consider the "cultural gap" created by the Khmer Rouge regime during their rule between 1975 and 1979. This gap is currently reflected in the small numbers of elderly master musicians who keep traditional music alive despite the relative economic poverty of the country and limited funding for projects and initiatives relating to cultural development and reconstruction. Reflecting on revival activity around the world during the nineteenth and twentieth centuries, Hill and Bithell (2006) suggest four motivational categories. One of these categories is a practical response to human disasters, which has resulted in the suppression and abandonment of traditional cultural practices and musicians themselves imprisoned, deported, or killed (Hill and Bithell 2006: 12), such as the case of Cambodia following the dark period of the Khmer Rouge regime.

One consequence of the Khmer Rouge period was the loss of the supporting role of traditional music in the ceremonial and communal life of Cambodians (Grant 2016a; Kallio and Westerlund 2016). After the downfall of the Khmer Rouge, Cambodian authorities have attempted to reconstruct classical dance and music. The National Theater troupe was reestablished to influence the process of cultural reconstruction of the principal traditional genres (Giuriati 2003). In fact, many classical and traditional art forms, including *lkhaon bassac*, were performed from the 1980s. The difficulties in reconstructing an "original" version of a music genre—due to the small number of musicians who survived the Khmer Rouge regime and the rapid processes of social and technological change, urbanization, and modernization—suggest that such attempts will lead to a transformation, a reinvention rather than restoration of musical heritage. The Khmer, of course, have experienced centuries of sociocultural transformations, and what is currently considered "traditional" is likely to be a relatively recent invention (see Hobsbawm and Ranger 1983).

One example of an invented tradition in Cambodia is the current version of the choreography to the *Apsara* dance, which is regarded as an icon of the Royal Ballet and a symbol of Khmer cultural identity. The traditional choreography of the *Apsara* dance was re-created, or reinvented, by Queen Mother Sisowath Kossamak Neary Roth for a scene in Marcel Camus' film *L'oiseau de Paradis* (1962).[2] The choreography of the *Apsara* dance created for Camus' film is now considered the traditional version of the *Apsara* dance. Milstein (2014) suggests that the revival of tradition has led to innovation rather than the recycling of practices. However, innovations that directly manipulate historical material are also fundamental components of revival (Conlon 2014).

During the 1980s the rebirth of classical dance via the National Theater was impacted by the spread of television and radio programs that broadcast performances *of lkhaon yiike* and *lkhaon bassac*. In the subsequent decade, the process of cultural reconstruction was strengthened by international collaborations focused on this endeavor such as the collaboration between the University of Bologna, Italy; the University of Technology, Sydney; and the Royal University of Phnom Penh between 1997 and 2003. These collaborative projects launched university courses in the field of tourism (Callari-Galli 1999, 2001). In fact, tourism was considered one of the best strategies to promote and keep alive Khmer traditions at that time.

In the late 1990s, Arn Chorn-pond, a former child soldier for the Khmer Rouge, brought together master artists of traditional musical theater who had survived the genocide to teach and pass on their knowledge to younger generations. With funding from the US embassy in Cambodia and support from NGOs, he founded the CLA in Phnom Penh. However, a lack of longer-term investment from the Cambodian government to restore and maintain traditional arts has resulted in young people choosing other fields of study in order to pursue employment opportunities, thus leading to the precarious situation of traditional performing arts today (Grant 2016b). In rural areas, artists have found it hard to make a living from their performing skills. Consequently, the viability and vitality of traditional genres are threatened. In urban areas, despite a growing middle class with an ability to financially support traditional arts, there is little appreciation of its value. Due to a glut of foreign music and entertainment options pouring into Cambodia via these new media technologies, young people tend to consider traditional genres old-fashioned. As Yourn Young explained to me, "The young are not interested in traditional music but they like modern music like Korean pop songs" (interview, February 9, 2015).

Nowadays, with the widespread accessibility of mass media technologies, cultural tourism, and the "Westernization" of traditional practices, ritual music, such as wedding music (*lkhaon yiike*) and *lkhaon bassac*, is becoming popular in style. This is primarily due to the introduction of Western instruments and performance structures, which appeal to younger generations and tourists. The adaptation of traditional music and theater to new performance contexts such as television reflects new economic and political trends across the region.

In the context of television, producers pay particular attention to the content of dramatic stories, which must respect Khmer cultural, political, and social values. Bayon TV producer Sou Chamraun explained the process as follows: "Each scene is carefully checked; every word is checked to make sure that everything is appropriate to the television context and not criticized by the government" (interview, December 9, 2014). For example, in the story *Preah Chang Korup* (Respect the Moon), there is a scene that the performers titled "Manoria [the protagonist] betrays her husband." Bayon TV decided not to broadcast this title because it was deemed morally inappropriate and could lead to criticism from the government. So they changed the title to *Koh Bandam Kruu* (Do Not Follow the Master's Precept). The presenters of the program read the plot of each scene, which was written by the director, according to Sou Chamraun, "to avoid any mistake, to make sure that people understand the story and to promote Khmer literature as well as theater" (interview, April 9, 2015).

Musicians and theater troupes working for the government, particularly for the Ministry of Culture and Fine Arts, are regularly invited to perform on television. Consequently, they have the opportunity to promote themselves and acquire more popularity and recognition so that clients can easily reach and contact them. But musicians from rural areas who do not have any contact with the government cannot promote their theater companies on television. For example, the *lkhaon bassac* theater troupe, Ol Samang's *Lkhaon Bassac* (OSLB), and other famous Khmer musicians who specialized in wedding music with whom I worked during my fieldwork in 2015 were featured in television programs. Some of these musicians have close connections with the government and collaborate with the CLA. In this way, television, nongovernmental organizations, and the state are interconnected in the process of preserving and promoting Cambodian traditional music and theater. Through a cyclical process, political forces control television, the CLA seeks operational and financial support from the government to promote its projects, and the government encourages the CLA's projects in "exchange" for sharing profits from cultural initiatives such as tourism performances and the sale of "cultural products"—mostly, CDs of traditional music and examples of traditional Khmer handcrafts—such as the *phlae pkaa* (fruitful) show. The *phlae pkaa* show consists of three-day shows in a tourist district of Phnom Penh (situated behind the national Museum) and Siem Reap. This project is an example of the "collaboration" between the government and CLA; the government gives the CLA permission to build a stage at the back of the National Museum by sharing 10 percent of the profits.

In contemporary Cambodia, the situation of traditional music reflects the paradox of maintaining traditional music while, at the same time, transforming it (Grant 2016a;

Winter and Ollier 2006). There is also awareness and fear, especially among the older master musicians, of the potential for "contamination" and "corruption" of traditional Cambodian genres, especially due to the introduction of foreign instruments, which they feel leads to the hybridization of genres and inappropriate transformation of musical features, and the adaptation to new performance contexts such as musical competitions on television and tourist shows. Therefore, performers must constantly seek to balance their artistry between preservation and change.

Televised versus Live Performances: *Lkhaon Bassac*

I rarely watched Cambodian television during my fieldwork, but one evening I thought to test my knowledge of Khmer language by watching a bit. While channel-hopping, I stopped on Bayon TV, one of the most important national channels, because I immediately recognized the *lkhaon bassac* troupe OSLB. This professional troupe was established in 2007. Most of the musicians and actors in OSLB, which usually included up to forty members, were trained at local institutions or by the troupe's leader, Ol Samang. After a ten-minute feature by the OSLB, a musical competition started. Young people selected from representative provinces of Cambodia sang traditional songs for a jury composed of well-known local artists, professors from the Royal University of Fine Arts, and famous musicians.

A few days later, I attended the recording of an *lkhaon bassac* performance at the Bayon TV studios. It was the first time I attended a television studio. Once there, Ol Samang introduced me to the producer and director Sou Chamraun. He was pleased to know that a European researcher was interested in TV performances because this theatrical genre is not famous outside Cambodia. *Lkhaon bassac* and *lkhaon yiike* are broadcast either on their own in prerecorded performances or live within musical competition programs. On that day, Ol Samang's troupe was going to record a *lkhaon bassac* performance based on the story of *Preah Puthy Ciy Komar* (The Understanding of a Child's Victory), which is a modern (*samay*) story written by Ol Samang.[3] The story is combined with ancient (*bouraan*) stories according to the audience's preferences. In fact, according to Nong Chak, a former *lkhaon bassac* singer, "the audience does not like old stories because people already know the plot and the characters. They like something new" (interview, October 13, 2014).

Lkhaon bassac is performed whenever hosts request it, although the most frequently chosen times are following Buddhist festivities such as: *Bon Kathin*, in late October when people bring clothing and gifts to the monks; *Bon Pkaa* (Flower Festival), a fund-raising event for the pagoda celebrated at any time during the year; *Bon Baŋcoh Səymaa*, a ceremony to celebrate the construction of pagoda; *Bon Claeŋ Samethiphal*, held for the inauguration of a building; and *Bon Paccay Buən*, a thanksgiving ceremony for parents. A stage is built by a group of workmen, engaged and supervised by the troupe's leader, in the space surrounding the pagoda where there are traditional food stalls, bumper cars, and other amusements to entertain followers (Figure 5.1).

Figure 5.1 *lkhaon bassac* performance in Tany district, Kampot province, November 5, 2014. Photo: Francesca Billeri.

In the traditional performance context of *lkhaon bassac*, the audience frequently interacts with the characters, particularly the comedians. In addition to having fun and playing an entertaining role, the comedians serve as narrators who outline the plot of the story. They improvise around a minimal plot and are inspired by the audience and its reactions: Samang explained how requests could redirect the performance: "Sometimes, at the end of the performance, the audience asks them to play something else" (personal communication, May 23, 2015). This interaction between audiences and performers is common to other Southeast Asian theatrical performances, such as the Balinese *Derama*, where characters "warm up" the audience before the beginning of the performance: "The problems of performing in television become obvious. You know little of your audience, nor have any means of gauging their receptiveness. Not only is there no script to rely on, or blame; but Balinese audiences require to be wooed into becoming engaged" (Hobart 2000: 187). Just like in Bali, Cambodian audiences need to be engaged and "warmed up" by the characters. If people like the comedians and the story, they will invite their friends and relatives to attend the performance. Consequently, the troupe's leader extends the length of the performance according to the audience's reaction and the number of people who remain until the end of the performance.

Television, as Hobart observed in Bali, "inhibits this dialogue but does not eradicate it: the addressee is still there, but under different discursive conditions" (2000: 202). The *lkhaon bassac* performances I attended in rural areas started at dusk and lasted for up to nine hours.[4] On television, the stories are shortened to fit the shorter time frame, as Sou Chamraun explained:

> Time is very limited. So if the story is very long no one will watch it and also may change channel. So each story has to be divided into eight scenes. Each scene must last no more than twelve minutes. They [i.e., the troupe] have to select the scenes carefully since the audience should be able to understand the entire story. The length of the story is one hour and a half in total. There are eight scenes; each scene is performed on that a different day for two weeks. If the length of each scene is too long the related song is omitted.
> (Interview, December 9, 2014)

For the televised performance, Ol Samang's troupe was reduced to fifteen characters for the eight scenes of the story, *Preah Puthy Ciy Komar*. The director gave detailed instructions to the performers regarding their position on the stage, the structure and length of the scenes, and the order of the songs;[5] sometimes, musicians were even asked to play "quickly" in order to respect the time frame. Ruah Somart, a *lkhaon bassac* player, explained the limitations as follows:

> In TV we [musicians] have to play carefully and perform to get the audience's attention so that we can be invited to play frequently. We have to follow the director's instructions. The songs are chosen by the TV director who has to follow the time frame. For example, one song can be sung by one actor but when we play in the villages the troupe's leader chooses the songs. The actors can sing two or three songs in one scene or even more because we have lots of time.
> (Personal communication, December 15, 2014)

The presenters of the program read the plot of each scene, which is written by the director, as Sou Chamraun explained, "to avoid any mistake, to make sure that people understand, and to promote Khmer literature as well as theater". To simplify things for the viewer, "The title of the scene and the story's name is shown on the TV screen" (interview, April 9, 2015).

A few days later, I attended a live recording for the program *Khmer Cultural Heritage*, which is a music competition between young people who come from different provinces in Cambodia. They perform different kinds of Khmer traditional songs including wedding repertoire, such as *phleng kar*, *camriəŋ yiike* (*yiike* singing) and *camriəŋ bassac* (*bassac* singing). *Camriəŋ yiike* and *camriəŋ bassac* songs are extracted from *lkhaon yiike* and *lkhaon bassac* repertoire but are performed for entertainment outside of the context of the theater. Minor distinctions between the *lkhaon bassac* and *camriəŋ bassac* repertoires as well as *lkhaon yiike* and *camriəŋ yiike* repertoires are only relevant to the formal Khmer classificatory system because, in practice, the songs share the same musical features and repertoire.

Between the two sections of the competition, there are also short performances of *lkhaon yiike* and *lkhaon bassac*, which function as entertainment and "advertisements" for the theater troupes. During an episode of *Khmer Cultural Heritage* on April 28, 2015, a *lakhon bassac* troupe performed a short scene, "*Psong Snae Kbae Chongkom Yeaq*" (Finding Love Near the Giant's Teeth), extracted from a well-known older Khmer story named after the main character, *Preah Cinwuəŋ*. This character introduces himself through song (Figure 5.2). The accompanying *lkhaon bassac* ensemble was composed of the typical traditional melodic instruments—*trɔ quu* (lower-pitched two-stringed fiddle), *trɔ chee* (two-string fiddle), *khloy* (bamboo flute), and *khim* (hammered dulcimer)—but the traditional rhythmic instruments—*skɔɔ bassac* (drum) and *caaŋ* (cylindrical-shaped idiophone)—were replaced by a contemporary drum set and an electric keyboard. Ruah Somart explained the reasoning behind these substitutions to me: "Western instruments can be used for introducing the show by playing modern music while the actors prepare themselves. However, these instruments can also be employed in the story. For example, the special effects of the electric keyboard are used for reproducing the wind or the storm" (interview, December 15, 2014).

Figure 5.2 Introduction of the protagonist from the *lkhaon bassac* story "*Preah Cinwuəŋ*" as featured on the Bayon TV program *Khmer Cultural Heritage*, December 9, 2014. Photo: Francesca Billeri.

The inclusion of a drum (*skɔɔ bassac*)⁶ is one of the defining characteristics of traditional *lkhaon bassac*; the replacement of its sound with that of a drum set and keyboard, therefore, transforms the music in a fundamental way. In traditional performances of *lkhaon bassac*, the drum, *caaŋ* (cylindrical-shaped idiophone), and *taadok* (wooden-box) accompany the entrance and exit of characters as well as the opening and closing of the curtain (Figure 5.3). These percussion instruments symbolize real sounds to help the narration of the story, to create an atmosphere, and to highlight emotions, gestures, or sound effects. They also signal the transition from one scene to another and attract the spectators' attention at the beginning of the performance. For example, in a battle scene the idiophone *caaŋ* reproduces the sounds of the swords; when it accompanies the giants' entrance onto the stage, it reproduces the sounds of their footsteps or movements called *huən*.

The use of nontraditional instruments is also due to financial limitations. Although nontraditional instruments could possibly be used for performances in rural areas,

Figure 5.3 The big drum (*skɔɔ bassac thom*), wooden-box (*taadok*), and idiophone (*caaŋ*), Kampong Cham province, March 15, 2015. Photo: Francesca Billeri.

I never observed their use in village performances during my fieldwork. According to Ol Samang, they can be added to Khmer instruments according to the leader's preference:

> If they sound good, I use them. The number of the instruments employed depends on the economic availability of the group. Sometimes the western instruments can replace the Khmer ones. For example, the electric keyboard can replace the sound of the *skɔɔ bassac* and *caaŋ* [which are played by two different people] and other instruments so that one person can replace three by playing only a single instrument.
>
> (Personal communication, May 23, 2015)

The use of nontraditional instruments is also considered by the musicians as a form of "modernization" of the *lkhaon bassac* music, which can appeal to the audience, especially younger viewers. Bayon producer Sou Chamraun justified their inclusion as follows: "The aim of performing these kinds of popular theater as part of the competition is to preserve these art forms and remind people of the disappearing theater. So that the next generations will be aware of these performances and the audience love the Khmer popular theater" (interview, April 9, 2015).

These genres have adapted in response to the expectations of new audiences and requirements of new performance contexts through use of atypical musical instruments and introduction of new characters and storylines. This modernization of traditional genres was viewed by Khmer musicians and TV producers I interviewed as a means of promoting and preserving these art forms especially among younger Cambodian audiences.

Televised Performances of Wedding Songs (*Phleng kar*) and New Compositions of Yiike Songs (*Camriəŋ Yiike*)

Another episode of *Khmer Cultural Heritage* that I attended included the performance of some famous wedding songs (*phleng kar*).[7] The musical ensemble included both Khmer traditional instruments (*phleng kar samay kandaal*) and Western instruments, including an electric bass, a guitar, a mandolin, a drum set, and a keyboard (Figure 5.4). In Cambodia, this kind of ensemble that combines traditional and Western instruments is called *samay* (modern).[8] One of the wedding songs presented at the competition was "*Haom Rooŋ*" (The Sacred Pavilion). This song is played for the ritual offering of music to the masters, *Pithi Haom Rooŋ*, which is performed before the beginning of a wedding ceremony to evoke their protector Preah Pisnukaa to ensure a good performance.

By comparing the televised version of *Haom Rooŋ* with the live one performed during a wedding ceremony, one can identify some changes. In the wedding ceremony the song is played on traditional (*bouraan*) or semi-traditional (*samay*) instruments. In the television performance, the heterophonic texture of Khmer traditional music,

Figure 5.4 A participant in the music competition sings during a recording for *Khmer Cultural Heritage* on Bayon TV, April 18, 2015. Photo: Francesca Billeri.

expressed through the simultaneous improvisation of the melodic instruments on a rhythmic pattern, is reproduced through the use of Western instruments. Another important factor is the decontextualization of the song. In its original wedding context, it is infused with a sacred aura since it is offered to the god of the musicians and the spirits of the masters. The sacred function of this specific song and the intimate character of wedding music, in general, are lost in the competition performance context.

Television performances foster different forms of creativity and new ways of making music. Young artists have the opportunity to showcase their talent and create new compositions while being inspired by traditional genres. Within the same program, other musical genres were performed, including songs extracted from another kind of popular theater, the *lkhaon yiike*, called *camriəŋ yiike* (*yiike* singing). Some of the young performers participating in the competition composed new songs based on traditional genres. The process of composing new songs inspired by traditional songs allows for a crossover of genres; melodies from traditional songs are adapted to new lyrics and set within new performance styles. For example, Yourn Young, a famous performer who won the competition in 2012, was invited to sing at the recording I attended.[9] For this, he wrote the lyrics to a famous *yiike* melody known as "*Noang Pisaraa*."[10] The title of Yourn's song set to this melody was "*Samrah Preah Pnom*" (The Mountain Beauty). The text describes the poetical beauty of Khmer nature. Yourn Young explained his sources of inspiration to me briefly: "I am mostly inspired by *bouraan* stories. I sit down and think about the story first and how to adapt the story to the music" (interview, February 9, 2015).

Traditionally this melody is used to accompany *yiike* dancing (*rɔbam yiike*). After an interview with members of a *lkhaon yiike* group in Kampot province, they performed *Noang Pisaraa* for me at the front of the troupe's leader Maan Prum's house (Figure 5.5). However, nowadays, *yiike* dance is performed on the stage before the start of the *yiike* theater performance (Figure 5.6). From watching this performance, one can see the prominent musical role played by the drums (*skɔɔ yiike*). Their rhythm accompanies the movement of the dancers' hands and their timbre identifies the genre as *lkhaon yiike*. The text expresses nationalistic and patriotic images of Khmer people who proudly evoke the cultural heritage of the "Kingdom of Wonder"—a slogan used to promote tourism in Cambodia. A chorus includes foreign words, perhaps in Malay or Thai, with the meaning of that section unknown even to the singers themselves. Although the melody of *Noang Pisaraa* and the vocal style are maintained in Young's version, the choir is omitted and the heterophonic texture of the music is mixed with hints of functional harmony, mirroring the instrumental changes instigated within recontextualized *lkhaon yiike*. On another occasion, I observed the performance of a wedding song on Ol Samang's Facebook page.[11] The function of that song—to invite the ancestors' spirits to join the wedding banquet— was lost in the televised performance. The rhythm of wedding music was changed due to the use of drum kit and bass, and the original wedding vocal style was adapted to the *bassac* vocal style.

Figure 5.5 *Rɔbam yiike* dancers and musicians in Chuuk district, Kampot province, January 8, 2015. Photo: Francesca Billeri.

Figure 5.6 *Rɔbam yiike* dance on the stage before the start of a *lkhaon yiike* performance, Kampot town, Kampot province, January 7, 2015. Photo: Francesca Billeri.

New Ways of Disseminating Khmer Traditional Music and Theater

Walking through the narrow aisles of tourist markets in Phnom Penh or even in local markets of provincial towns, one can find many music stalls selling a variety of recordings of Khmer popular music, Korean and Chinese-influenced popular music, and "popularized" traditional music for both locals and tourists. Nowadays, Khmer traditional wedding music, as well as popular theater performances and songs, is marketed and produced by the CLA and commercial record companies through the large-scale production of recordings produced on CD and DVD for local and international consumers.

Tuchman-Rosta (2018) shows how the slow transition of the Cambodian classical dance from ritual to secular global commodity has facilitated a resurgence of classical dance in the decades after the civil war, thus making its practice a viable, though challenging, option for dancers to attain financial stability and enhance their social standing. Although commoditizing the traditional performing arts, such as music, may be an appropriate strategy toward cultural sustainability, and it helps support the artists who perform them in the short term, this approach can affect important musical and extramusical features of traditional music. These changes are evident in two areas: the introduction of nontraditional instruments from abroad has changed the performance practices of traditional genres, and the performers' adaptation to new performance contexts has decontextualized ritual songs and theater performances.

To highlight changes in performance practices and the decontextualization of performances, I examine two versions of one of the most popular wedding songs here, "*Haom Rooŋ*" (Consecrate the Pavillion), as an example of music performed on television and on CD recordings. The first version of the song is performed during a wedding ceremony by a renowned *phleng kar* ensemble led by Yun Theara, a former professor at the Royal University of Fine Arts and a CLA teacher; the second version is performed by renowned singer and CLA teacher Ieng Sithol. The latter version has been extracted from an unlabeled recording made outside of the ritual context, which was uploaded to YouTube. A comparison between these two versions of *Haom Rooŋ* shows the changes that are occurring in instrumentation and performance practice.

Khmer traditional wedding music is based on a process of improvisation that musicians explain through the metaphor of "taking different roads" or "traveling on different routes and meeting at some specific points." Each instrument improvises by "taking a road," consisting of individualized renditions of a melody in heterophonic texture; then all the instruments land on the same note on the damp stroke of the cymbals (*chiŋ*). The succession of these notes constitutes the "inner melody" or "abstract melody" that is not heard by the listeners but is only in the musicians' minds (Giuriati 1988; Sam 1988). In commercial recordings and televised performances, wedding and theater genres are performed by the modern *phleng samay* ensemble (a combination of traditional and nontraditional instruments). As a result, the process of improvisation, which gives to Khmer music its characteristic heterophonic nature, is adapted to new instruments and performance practices.

A rendition of "*Haom Rooŋ*" (an opening ritual) performed by Ieng Sithol provides one example of this adaptation[12]: simple melodic bass lines are adapted to the melodies of the wedding repertoire to re-create the traditional musical texture. The introduction of foreign instruments to this ensemble is considered as a way of modernizing traditional repertoires, which appeals to younger audiences and enriches the tradition. As Aubert writes, "the nature of tradition is not to preserve intact a heritage from the past, but to enrich it according to present circumstances and transmit the result to future generations" (Aubert 2007: 10).

In addition to the different instrumentation and performance practices, the short duration of "*Haom Rooŋ*" as performed by Ieng Sithol illustrates a further feature of the decontextualization of traditional wedding songs. In fact, in the wedding ceremony context, the length of the songs strictly relates to the ritual scene. For example, *Haom Rooŋ* is played not only during the *Pithii Haom Rooŋ* ritual but also to entertain the guests while the bride and the groom change their ceremonial dress and during the transitional moments of the ceremony. Consequently, the song is played many times throughout the ceremony, and its length, as well as lyrics, varies according to the ritual actions. The duration of Ieng Sithol's commercial version is shortened and consists of repetitions of one section (A), while the traditional wedding version of this song is composed of three sections (A-B-C).

Ieng Sithol's musical style is now considered iconic of Khmer traditional music. In an interview with renowned performer Nong Chak at his current place of residence in Banteay Meanchey province, he described the challenges he faced while working in Phnom Penh, noting especially how he found it difficult to accommodate the new trend of "Westernized" *bassac* and *phleng kar* influenced by Ieng Sithol's style: "people ask for guitar, bass, and loudspeakers during the wedding as Ieng Sithol uses them. Now students prefer studying with Ieng Sithol because he organizes tours in America and Europe; so students are encouraged to learn from him in Phnom Penh" (interview, October 13, 2014).

Music is also commercialized as a cultural product for fundraising. For example, the CLA sells its CDs at cultural shows and other performance venues in Phnom Penh and Siem Reap to support its activities. Between 2012 and 2013 the CLA's team traveled to the music masters' homes to film performances in their communities and then invited them to Phnom Penh to record in a professional studio. They produced five CDs from these sessions, including albums such as *Offering to the Ancestors: Traditional Khmer Songs for Weddings* (2012) and *Offerings to the Masters: Traditional Khmer Songs for Spirit Possessions* (2014). They include in-depth interviews with the musicians and provide links to resources to learn more about their work. The CLA has also recently produced three full-length documentaries about *smot* (poetic chanting), classical wedding music and *kantaoming* (traditional funeral music), which were broadcast on the Cambodian TV channel CTN in 2013 and 2014.[13] Other CDs such as *Sarekakeo* by Ieng Sithol and Ouch Savy (Cambodian Living Arts 2007) are collections of famous wedding songs played on a combination of traditional and Western instruments, although the vocal style of traditional wedding music is maintained. Through these activities, the CLA aims to raise money from tourists to support the work of their master musicians, who they believe will keep the "authentic" nature of Khmer traditional music alive.

The CLA is also aiming to popularize traditional music so that it appeals to their Cambodian market. Nowadays, many CDs and DVDs of traditional ritual and theater genres are disseminated on the internet, largely via YouTube uploads. Famous artists' performances and local television programs are available on social media too, which facilitates the wider in dissemination of traditional art forms less known outside of local communities in Cambodia. Social media is also useful as a means of advertising theater troupes and performers. For example, Ol Samang, the *lkaon bassac*'s troupe leader, has a very active Facebook profile, which has helped him gain popularity and advertise the work of his troupe in Cambodia and abroad.

Conclusions

The patterns of change delineated in this chapter show how the preservation of "authentic styles" by the CLA and the production of popularized versions of these traditions for local consumption on television and commercial recordings coexist in contemporary Cambodia. These changes relate to transformation and adaptation of traditional music and theater to new performance contexts, which are regulated by wider economic and sociocultural trends. Howard (2006: 28) discusses how the process of preserving the performing arts implies a restriction on artists' personal freedom; artists push back against these restrictions as they seek wider distribution for their products by modifying recordings and performances to attract sales. The Cambodian case shows that preserving traditional music can also foster creativity and new ways of making music. The example used here was a song by Yourn Young, which was based on a traditional *yiike* melody and combined traditional musical features with new instrumentation and newly composed lyrics. The popularization of *yiike* songs appeals to new generations and helps to keep the genre alive for local audiences. This is taking place within an environment where foreign popular music, particularly Korean pop, is becoming more commonplace, and this is impacting the community of traditional artists who are struggling to recover their craft and resources (Turnbull 2006). To appeal to new audiences, elements considered "modern" are added to traditional music such as foreign musical instruments. This syncretism is a form of "popularizing" of the tradition to make it more marketable and often involves sacrificing important musical features and performance practices as the product is adapted to the market. However, new genres can help to maintain their identity through contact with other musical traditions. As Ricœur observes, "The problem is not merely to repeat the past, but rather to take root in it to ceaselessly invent" ([1961] 2007: 51). The question remains: Are artists aware of the potential impact of their choices on their own culture?

The traditional artists I worked with are of two minds, and Cohen (2016) has observed a similar division. He notes that, on the one hand, there are recognized experts of tradition who monumentalize heritage through the nomination of living national treasures and the standardization and codification of artistic genres. On the other hand, tradition is considered as a set of new ideas and resources available for local practitioners to resist the homogenization effects of the global capitalism. In between these camps are the traditional artists who continue to perform in the "traditional" way but, at the same time, are keen to learn and appropriate the latest trends to attract contemporary audiences (Cohen 2016: xvi).

Although the adaptation of traditional music and theater to the conventions of television has contributed to the decontextualization of these repertoires, the repurposing of traditional genres also enforces nationalistic views. As Grant observes: "traditional genres also can strengthen social, cultural, and national identity; bring economic gain through performance and tourist activities; and reinforce social fabric by transmitting Cambodian values and ideals" (2016a: 434). Arn Chorn-pond also emphasized this point: "Through traditional music young people learn about their history, their country, and their parents. They learn who they are. They can also make money and have decent jobs in the art sector" (interview, December 12, 2014). The modernization and popularization of traditional music help to keep traditional art and artists alive by adapting traditional music to new contexts after the devastating actions of the Khmer Rouge. This process encourages young artists to create new musical genres and build their careers through fostering creativity, innovation, and entrepreneurship. For them, modernity operates as a means for rewriting and reinventing the past (Cohen 2016: xix).

The process of producing recordings involves a hybridization of traditional musical features and performance practices but also, at the same time, allows for the circulation of songs across different genres (Billeri 2019). One way to describe this process is with the term "genre gap," which involves "reconfiguring the song under a different genre label" (Sparling 2008: 415). The "genre gap" discussed by Sparling is shown in the above example of a wedding song performed by Ol Samang and his troupe for television. Ol Samang adapted the *bassac* nasal vocal style to the melodic line of the song. Although the song's traditional lyrics, which are intended to recall the ancestors' spirits to join the wedding banquet, lose their original ritual meaning and the *bassac* ensemble is replaced by the *phleng samay* modern ensemble, it is still possible to distinguish several key traditional components such as the *bassac* vocal style and heterophonic interplay.

Traditional genres that were once embedded in oral tradition and functioned within ritual ceremonies are nowadays being moved onto modern theatrical stages and screens, into recorded media formats, and into large-scale festival contexts. As part of this process, they are becoming increasingly "presentational" in nature—that is, staged performances prepared by musicians for others to listen to (Turino 2008: 52). The frame for a presentational performance consists of specific cues such as a formal stage with microphones and stage lights that create a clear division between performers and audience. Nowadays, theater performances are becoming more presentational as they move from their traditional context, which consisted of a mat surrounded by the audience in rural villages, onto the stage, using lighting, sound effects, and amplification systems. It is not possible to preserve and promote intangible cultural heritage without change because societies are also changing (Blacking [1978] 1987: 112). The traditional genres described here are transforming and adapting to emerging performance contexts too. There is not only loss, destruction, and impoverishment but also enrichment, adaptation, syncretism, and a demonstration of how the patterns of these transformations reflect people's current perspectives on traditional practices in contemporary Cambodia.

Notes

1 For further information on *lkhaon bassac*, see Pich Tum (1997) and Billeri (2019).
2 For a historical contextualization of *Apsara* dance, see Phim and Thompson (1999).
3 Other TV channels such as TVK precheck the story to ensure that it is written by a known writer, while CTN and Bayon permit the troupe's leader to choose the story. In both cases, the plot is carefully checked for conformance to political and sociocultural requirements.
4 According to my informants, in the past the story frequently lasted one week and sometimes went on for several months.
5 Preexisting melodies are adapted to literary titles related to the scene. Songs are also adapted to the theme of each scene. Other songs are borrowed from different Khmer traditional genres and adapted to the theater context, such as *phleng kar* songs for a wedding scene or *smout*, a chant accompanying the soul of the dead, in a scene of death.
6 Two forms of *skɔɔ bassac* are played in *lkhaon bassac*: the *skɔɔ bassac thom* (big *bassac* drum) is used for battle scenes, wars, and the reproduction of onomatopoeic sounds;

    the *skɔɔ bassac touc* (small *bassac* drum), also called *louk skɔɔ*, is used for the entrance and exit of the characters.
7   For further information on wedding music, see McKinley (2002) and Billeri (2016).
8   Musicians distinguish two different wedding ensembles: the ancient *phleng kar bouraan* and the semi-traditional *phleng kar samay kandaal*. The main differences between the two ensembles concern the instruments and the musical texture. The *bouraan* ensemble is composed of ancient Khmer instruments such as the monochord (*ksaediəw*), the three-string fiddle (*trɔ khmer*), and the long-necked lute (*capey dong weng*), while the semi-traditional ensemble includes a combination of the ancient instruments and instruments of foreign influence, specifically Thai and Chinese traditional instruments, such as the zither (*taakee*), the dulcimer (*khim*), and the two-string fiddle (*trɔ sao*). A related ensemble is the *phleng samay* (modern wedding ensemble) composed of Khmer semi-traditional instruments and nontraditional instruments (guitar, electric bass, mandolin-banjo, and drum set; see Billeri 2019: 139).
9   For Young's rendition of this song, see https://www.youtube.com/watch?v=vJOKQjhbM7M, accessed May 28, 2020.
10 The titles of *yiike* songs usually indicate the movement of the dancers or consist of a mixture of different languages such as Lao, Thai, and Malay, whose meaning is unknown to the singers themselves. The *yiike* titles reflect the foreign origins of the *lkhaon yiike*, but as in this case, they do not translate easily to English.
11 https://www.facebook.com/olsam.ang/videos/546158788880835/, accessed September 10, 2016.
12 For Sithol's rendition of this song, see https://www.youtube.com/watch?v=9lHLM4R9V_w, accessed May 28, 2020.
13 https://www.cambodianlivingarts.org/4-archiving-project/, accessed October 15, 2019.

Bibliography

Aubert, Laurent. 2007. *The Music of the Other: New Challenges for Ethnomusicology in a Global Age*. Translated by Carla Ribeiro. Aldershot: Ashgate.

Billeri, Francesca. 2016. "Traditional Song Lyrics and Ritual Actions in Cambodian Weddings." *Asian Musicology* 26: 11–34.

Billeri, Francesca. 2019. "Interrelations among Genres in Khmer Traditional Music and Theatre: *Phleng Kar*, *Phleng Arak*, *Lkhaon Yiikee* and *Lkhaon Bassac*." PhD thesis, SOAS, University of London.

Blacking, John. (1978) 1987. *A Commonsense View of All Music: Reflections on Percy Grainger's Contribution to Ethnomusicology and Music Education*. Cambridge: Cambridge University Press.

Callari-Galli, Matilde. 1999. "A Project to Introduce Tourist Studies at University Level." In *Seminar on Training of Cultural Experts in Development Programming and Management of Tourism in Cambodia*, 1–4. Phnom Penh: Royal University of Phnom Penh.

Callari-Galli, Matilde. 2001. "Development of Cultural Tourism in Cambodia: The Contribution of the Universities." In *Entrepreneurship and Education in Tourism*, edited by Karin Bras, Heidi Dahles, Myra Gunawan, and Greg Richards, 53–63. Tilburg: Atlas Asia.

Cohen, Matthew Isaac. 2016. *Inventing the Performing Arts: Modernity and Tradition in Colonial Indonesia*. Honolulu: University of Hawai'i Press.
Conlon, Paula J. 2014. "Bending or Breaking the Native American Flute Tradition?" In *The Oxford Handbook of Music Revival*, edited by Caroline Bithell and Juniper Hill, 442–65. Oxford: Oxford University Press.
Giuriati, Giovanni. 1988. "Khmer Traditional Music in Washington D.C." PhD thesis, University of Maryland.
Giuriati, Giovanni. 2003. *Musiche e danze della Cambogia*. Milan: Ricordi.
Grant, Catherine. 2016a. "Finding New Ground. Maintaining and Transforming Traditional Music." In *The Handbook of Contemporary Cambodia*, edited by Katherine Brickell and Simon Springer, 432–41. New York: Routledge.
Grant, Catherine. 2016b. "Socio-Economic Concerns of Young Musicians of Traditional Genres in Cambodia: Implications for Music Sustainability." *Ethnomusicology Forum* 23 (3): 306–25.
Hill, Juniper, and Caroline Bithell. 2006. "An Introduction to Music Revival as Concept, Cultural Process, and Medium Change." In *The Oxford Handbook of Music Revival*, edited by Caroline Bithell and Juniper Hill, 3–42. Oxford: Oxford University Press.
Hobart, Mark. 2000. "Live or Dead? How Dialogic Is Theatre in Bali?" In *To Change Bali: Essays in Honour of I Gusti Ngurah Bagus*, edited by Adrian Vickers, I. Nyoman Darma Putra, Michele Ford, and I. Gusti Ngurah Bagus, 183–99. Denpasar: Institute of Social Change and Critical Inquiry, University of Wollongong.
Hobsbawm, Eric J., and Terence O. Ranger, eds. 1983. *The Invention of Tradition*. Cambridge: Cambridge University Press.
Howard, Keith. 2006. *Preserving Korean Music: Intangible Cultural Properties as Icons of Identity*. Aldershot: Ashgate.
Kallio, Alexis Anja, and Heidi Westerlund. 2016. "The Ethics of Survival: Teaching the Traditional Arts to Disadvantaged Children in Post-Conflict Cambodia." *International Journal of Music Education* 34 (1): 90–103.
McKinley, Kathy. 2002. "Ritual, Performativity, and Music: Cambodian Wedding Music in Phnom Penh." PhD thesis, Brown University.
Milstein, Denise. 2014. "Revival Currents and Innovation on the Path from Protest Bossa to Tropicália." In *The Oxford Handbook of Music Revival*, edited by Caroline Bithell and Juniper Hill, 418–41. Oxford: Oxford University Press.
Phim, Toni Samantha, and Ashley Thompson. 1999. *Dance in Cambodia*. Kuala Lumpur: Oxford University Press.
Pich Tum, Kravel. 1997. *Yiike and Bassac Theaters*. Phnom Penh: Royal University of Fine Arts.
Ricœur, Paul. (1961) 2007. "Universal Civilization and National Cultures." In *Architectural Regionalism: Collected Writings on Place, Identity, Modernity, and Tradition*, edited by Vincent B. Canizaro, 43–53. New York: Princeton Architectural Press.
Sam, Sam-Ang. 1988. "The Pin Piət Ensemble: Its History, Music and Context." PhD thesis, Wesleyan University.
Sparling, Heather. 2008. "Categorically Speaking: Towards a Theory of (Musical) Genre in Cape Breton Gaelic Culture." *Ethnomusicology* 52 (3): 401–25.
Thiounn, Samdac Chaufea. (1930) 1956. *Danses Cambodgiennes*. Phnom Penh: Institut Bouddhique.

Tuchman-Rosta, Celia Johanna. 2018. "Performance, Practice, and Possibility: How Large Scale Processes Affect the Bodily Economy of Cambodia's Classical Dancers." PhD thesis, University of California, Riverside.

Turino, Thomas. 2008. *Music as Social Life: The Politics of Participation*. Chicago, IL: University of Chicago Press.

Turnbull, Robert. 2006. "A Burned-Out Theater." In *Expressions of Cambodia: The Politics of Tradition, Identity, and Change*, edited by Leakthina Chau-Pech Ollier and Tim Winter, 133–49. London and New York: Routledge.

Winter, Tim, and Leakthina Chau-Pech Ollier. 2006. "Introduction: Cambodia and the Politics of Tradition, Identity and Change." In *Expressions of Cambodia: The Politics of Tradition, Identity, and Change*, edited by Leakthina Chau-Pech Ollier and Tim Winter, 1–19. London and New York: Routledge.

Discography and Filmography

Cambodian Living Arts. 2007. *Sarikakeo Love Songs and Other Favourites with Cambodia's Best Loved Traditional Singer Ieng Sithol and Rising Star Ouch Savy*. Cambodia: Three Sixty Records, CD.

Cambodian Living Arts. 2012. *Offerings to the Ancestors: Traditional Khmer Songs for Weddings*. Produced by Chhuon Sarin and Yun Khean Theara. Cambodia: Three Sixty Records, CD.

Cambodian Living Arts. 2014. *Offerings to the Masters: Traditional Khmer Songs for Spirit Possessions*. Produced by Chhuon Sarin and Yun Khean Theara. Cambodia: Three Sixty Records, CD.

Camus, Marcel, director. 1962. *L'oiseau de Paradis*. France: Cinédis, film.

6

Going with the Flow: Livestreaming and Korean Wave Narratives in *P'ansori*

Anna Yates-Lu

This chapter explores the effects of livestreaming through social networking services (SNS) on the traditional Korean sung storytelling genre *p'ansori*. *P'ansori* consists of a solo singer performing an epic story on a straw mat using song, narration, and gesture to act both as narrator and all the story's characters. Traditionally, they are accompanied by a single drummer playing a barrel-shaped drum, the *puk*, who emits shouts known as *ch'uimsae*. These shouts function as a form of encouragement, affirmation, or commiseration—depending on the singer's state and the content of the song—and are also shouted by members of the audience familiar with the story and its rhythms, who are known as *kwimyŏngch'ang* (lit., "ear master singers"). Being preserved within the government-sponsored Intangible Cultural Property system, which also protects the various Korean court, folk, and literati musical traditions collectively known as *kugak* (lit., national music), *p'ansori*, like many other traditional cultural forms, is used both at home and abroad as an emblem of the Korean nation (see Adams 2013; Aykan 2015; Tsitsishvili 2009; Vail 2014). However, like many other traditional art forms, *p'ansori* has often struggled to stay relevant for contemporary audiences. As Sutton describes it, the linkage between national identity and appreciation for tradition is complicated: "While most would not deny that these forms are indeed part of their cultural heritage as Koreans and are clearly and unambiguously identifiable as 'Korean arts,' they also feel culturally 'estranged' from them" (Sutton 2011: 6). Various strategies have been employed by *p'ansori* artists (called *sorikkun*) to help the genre survive, often tending toward popularization to narrow the gap with audiences more accustomed to popular culture (see Finchum-Sung 2009; Kim 2004; So Inhwa 2015; Yi T'aehwa 2013). This is partially driven by an awareness of and desire to emulate the success of the Korean Wave (*hallyu*), and K-Pop specifically.

The Korean Wave began to spread across the Asia Pacific in the late 1990s with the sudden and unexpected popularity of Korean television dramas, films, and, shortly after, pop music (e.g., Chua and Iwabuchi 2008; Howard 2006). The term *hanliu* (韩流; lit., Korean wave) was coined by the Chinese news media. This term was incorporated into Korean discourse, where it became *hallyu* (한류), and was gradually diversified to also include games, animation, fashion, beauty, food, and design. At least since 2007, the Ministry of Culture, Sports, and Tourism has also been actively promoting Korean traditional culture as part of the Korean Wave, with their "HanStyle Policy" (Ministry of Culture, Sports, and Tourism 2007), which promoted the six "*hans*": Korean writing (*hangŭl*), Korean food (*hanshik*), Korean clothing (*hanbok*), Korean houses (*hanok*), Korean paper (*hanji*), and Korean music (*han'guk ŭmak*). While Korean films and dramas continue to make inroads into the international cultural landscape, as the success of the film *Parasite* (*Kisaengch'ung*; Bong Joon-Ho 2019) attests, it is arguably K-Pop which is currently the most high-profile aspect of the Korean Wave, as idol groups have capitalized on their savvy social media use to help further spread their global popularity.

This trend has been inspiring for Korean traditional musicians as well. In the same way that K-Pop stars use apps such as V Live (an app in which Korean Wave stars share both livestreamed and prerecorded videos), Instagram, or Twitter to engage with their fans, the last two years have seen a steady rise of *sorikkun* attempting to replicate this success by turning to video sharing on social networking platforms as a means of attracting new audiences. Radio and TV broadcasts, recitals, concerts, and theater performances, as well as short rehearsal and promotional clips are all featured on various SNS, which allow people to watch and comment on these performances in real time without having to physically be present at the performance.

But how successful is this strategy? Is the use of SNS able to widen the audience pool, or is it just the same few people who are engaging with *p'ansori* content, both online and offline? How does online consumption of *p'ansori* change the relationship between audience and performers, generally considered a key element of *p'ansori* performance? Park (2003: 235), for example, highlights the "three-way *p'an*"[1] as the ideal in *p'ansori* performance, whereby the *sorikkun*'s song interweaves with and responds to the drummer's accompaniment, as well as shouts of encouragement (*ch'uimsae*) given by both the drummer and the attending audience. But how does this change the performance dynamics when this three-way relationship is interacted via online platforms? As more and more aspects of life are lived out online, traditional artists are forced to face the question of how to carve out a space for themselves within this new context, and negotiations over traditional art via new media are by no means unique to Korea (e.g., Cannon 2016).

This research was inspired by my own practice as a *p'ansori* performer and promoter, a role that emerged as an unexpected consequence of my PhD fieldwork on *p'ansori* in Korea between 2014 and 2015. Through participating in performances, I became aware of how my coperformers were using social media to help promote their activities. Once sensitized to this topic, it soon became clear that Korean *kugak* performers and producers, particularly enabled by the ever-increasing abilities for streaming videos through what is often touted as the fastest internet in the world (Boyland 2019), were increasingly making use of video sharing on SNS as a promotional tool. Through this analysis, then, I aim to shed light on how intangible cultural heritage is being re-produced in an increasingly digital world, as a first step in developing a broadly applicable road map for better engagement between traditional art and digital technology.

Kugak in a K-Pop World

The struggle of *p'ansori* to retain contemporary relevance is by no means new—in his famous text *Chosŏn Ch'anggŭksa* (The History of Chosŏn Singing Theater), Chŏng Noshik exhorts *p'ansori* performers to create more contemporary pieces:

> Esteemed *kwangdae* [another word for *p'ansori* performer], rather than spending energy on classical *ch'anggŭk* [*p'ansori*] tunes, how would it be if we accede to the demands of modernity and take a new direction. *Ch'unhyangjŏn, Hŭngbojŏn*,[2] or other classical pieces are of the past and are pieces which were shaped on the background of that time; should we not be able to produce pieces shaped on the background of today?
>
> (Chŏng 1940: 5)

While waning interest in *p'ansori* can be traced back at least to the onset of modernity in Korea in the late Chosŏn dynasty (1392–1910) and following colonial period (1910–45), the huge popularity of the Korean Wave sets a particularly striking contrast to the struggles *kugak* performers face to bring in audiences. Howard (2016: 462) profiles the practice of *ch'odaekwŏn* (tickets handed out as invitations to an event) as endemic to the *kugak* world, and *sorikkun* have told me that even when they give half the tickets away to family, friends, and sponsors, it is still difficult to fill all the seats at a concert hall (Ch'oe Yongsŏk, interview, March 11, 2015).[3]

Finchum-Sung describes how *kugak* artists attempt to engage audiences geared more toward consuming Korean Wave products, focusing particularly on the use of visual elements to help express *kugak*'s contemporary relevance (2012: 420). She cites an interview with *kagok* (a form of Korean lyrical singing) performer Kim Young-gi, where he stated: "A music culture… follows the culture in which it exists… Audiences are accustomed to seeing more than hearing, so you can see it as a kind of service for audiences, perhaps" (quoted in Finchum-Sung 2012: 405). This does not mean, however, that appropriation of the visual spectacle elements of the Korean Wave is necessarily contrary to tradition. *Sorikkun* Kim Pongyŏng made a passionate defense for letting *p'ansori* develop together with the resources available today:

> Until now, *p'ansori* had to do everything with words alone, because they didn't have any [stage] equipment, plus they were performing in an open square, they didn't have any equipment at all. But now we have all kinds of equipment, so if you have the money, if you've got the production money, you can use all kinds of things. But not using it on purpose, just clinging to that [old performance style] I think is lacking in development. If it's retaining the character of *p'ansori*, then using equipment, not just as eye candy but in a way intimately connected to *p'ansori*… I don't stray far from tradition [in making use of stage equipment]. I want to make a living tradition.
>
> (Interview, April 2, 2015)

This argument can easily be transferred to the use of digital technology—after all, if it is there, why not use it? When a traditional art form is at risk of being sidelined, it is not surprising that performers engage with the strategies and technologies of the dominant narrative (in this case, that of the Korean Wave) in order to retain contemporary relevance. With the development in technology, both in terms of performance production and in sharing content online, we can see the evolving engagement of *kugak* musicians with both the Korean Wave and its visual elements—in this case, the use of video and livestreaming technology.

V Live: The K-Pop Model

What, then, does the dominant narrative consist of, particularly in relation to the use of SNS and livestreaming technology? While YouTube, Twitter, and Instagram are undoubtedly also of great importance (e.g., Oh and Park 2012), Aisyah and Nam (2017) highlight the particular role of the V Live app in furthering the spread of the Korean Wave. This app, which has been active since 2015, is owned by Naver Corporation, which also operates Naver, the main search platform used in Korea. Similar to other SNS platforms, on V Live K-Pop stars can upload both prerecorded and livestreamed videos, of music videos, performances, backstage footage, dance rehearsals, or just going about their daily lives while answering questions their fans submit through the messaging section. What has made V Live particularly helpful to the spread of the Korean Wave is the subtitling feature, which allows fans to provide subtitles for the videos, hence enabling the wider reach of the video content to those not fluent in Korean.

This provision of access to various parts of the artists' lives, as well as active engagement with fans through digital platforms, is undoubtedly successful: K-Pop mega boyband BTS, for example, had 13 million followers on their channel as of April 29, 2019, with a video uploaded by BTS leader RM on April 23 telling the behind story of their newest album *Map of the Soul: Persona* having been viewed 6 million times and liked 300 million times.[4] BTS are similarly active on other SNS platforms, such as Twitter and Instagram, and this has undoubtedly been a key element of their current international success: they won the Top Social Artist Award at the Billboard Music Awards in 2017, 2018, and 2019. While not expecting the same scale of engagement, it is nevertheless this image of success through savvy SNS usage that *kugak* artists hope to emulate with their turn to livestreaming.

Schultz, in his description of using social media in clothing retail, gives the following basic outline for how SNS functions as a marketing tool:

> Firstly, individuals directly create value by engaging in transactions with the brand. Secondly, incentives may initiate recommendations from existing consumers that lead to the acquisition of new consumers. Thirdly, intrinsic motivation may result in recommendations and thus in converting prospects, retaining consumers, and increasing shopping value. Many consumers find information provided by other consumers, such as comments and recommendations, to be more valuable than

corporate information. Thus, these consumer interactions may increase trust in a company and consequently increase consumption intention and revenue. Fourthly, consumer interactions on social media platforms provide a data source for market research, for example for product improvements and innovations.

(Schultz 2016: 1)

There is a chain effect in this model, then, whereby an individual first engages with a particular form of content (say, a new music video by a K-Pop band). They share this content on their personal SNS pages, providing a recommendation to their friends or followers, which these consider more reliable than if the same information were provided by a corporate entity. Simply put, someone not familiar with K-Pop is more likely to click on a K-Pop music video shared by a friend than if they happened across it on YouTube, where it is promoted by an entertainment company. The engagement with the initial content via social media (through comments, likes, etc.) then becomes a source of feedback for the content producer to take into account the production of new content.

Of particular importance, then, is the interpersonal element of sharing content (also discussed in Oh and Park 2012: 374), as the main drive for the spread of content comes from being inspired to engage with something after seeing one's acquaintances share their engagement. The obvious issue with this model is that the spread of content will be limited to those who are part of the same social circle. This is an extension of the "echo chamber" principle, defined as "A mainstreaming ideological effect in which a group worldview is reinforced through continual circulation amongst like-minded people (such as an online or social media echo chamber)… The feedback loop is amplified by algorithmic recommendation engines, so that individuals dwell within filter bubbles."[5] While this term is most often applied to political debate, it is easy to see how the spread of other content is also likely to follow similar algorithmic pathways to be concentrated within similar interest groups.

Extension of V Live Model to Other Genres

Kugak is not the only music genre trying to ride on the wave of V Live's popularity. In fact, since 2016, V Live has had an entire section dedicated to classical music. Yang Chinha (2017) describes the reasoning for this classical channel in the first instance as a means to distance the music from only being for "mania" fans by making it more accessible to a wider public, when few media provide exposure for classical music otherwise. V Live is also a means of spreading awareness of young local talent overseas and encouraging audiences to actually attend concerts, with the livestreaming providing a "taster session" that might draw audiences to the live performances. This strategy seems to have been effective at least in some ways—a replay of the V Salon Concert featuring Julius Kim (Kim Chŏngwŏn) and friends, uploaded on October 15, 2018, had 26,038 views and 1,829,478 likes as of September 15, 2020. However, the majority of videos on the V Classic channel had no more than 1,000 views, demonstrating that livestreaming is not always a sure-fire method of drawing and retaining attention and online views do not necessarily translate into real-life audiences.

Nevertheless, when livestreaming works, it can be extremely effective. Cho (2017) reports that at the beginning of 2017, the Arts Council Korea (ARKO; *Han'guk munhwa yesul wiwŏnhoe*) selected six productions to be livestreamed on both Naver TV Cast and V Live. The first of these productions, the musical "Red Book" (*Redŭbuk*), despite not featuring any star performers, was watched by around 13,000 people during the livestream, and the next morning it had risen to second place in the rankings of the musical section of ticket reservation site Interpark, with the remaining shows being completely sold out. While broadcasting an entire performance in order to encourage people to pay may seem counterintuitive, Shin Sangmi, head of Performance Support of ARKO, argues for its value: "We received feedback from some people asking whether livestreaming wouldn't further reduce ticket sales, but we have rather found that verified reviews had the effect of drawing people to the performance venue" (cited in Cho 2017).

As with Schultz's model above, it seems that here also it is the interpersonal connections that sharing via SNS allows that were instrumental in encouraging people to attend these performances, and this continues to be the draw for performers and producers in a wide range of genres to apply this method, particularly if these genres are not usually associated with the younger demographic that commonly uses SNS. Within the traditional music scene, Cho reports that in January 2017, the *madangnori* (a form of musical that fuses traditional music with popular music and comedic elements) "Here Comes Nolbo" *(Nolbo ka onda)* by the National Changgeuk Company of Korea (*Kungnip ch'anggŭkdan*) was the first traditional-style piece to be shown by livestream, with the hope of combating perceptions of *madangnori* as being only for old people and attracting a younger demographic. In attempting to promote such performances, then, both performers and producers increasingly turn to online spaces, to provide younger audiences with exposure to genres they are unlikely to seek out in real life, and thus try to convince them of the value of these other art forms.

Institutional Use of Video Material on SNS

Aside from the National Gugak Center (*Kungnip kugakwŏn*), probably the most established and well-known institution promoting *kugak* since 2001 is GugakFM, a radio broadcasting station devoted to *kugak*, with an associated online TV station that broadcasts concerts, documentaries, lectures, and classic performance clips.[6] In addition to its traditional broadcasting activities, GugakFM has been active on Twitter since 2010, YouTube since 2011, and Facebook since 2012.[7] Most of GugakFM's SNS activity focuses on promoting cultural events or upcoming special broadcasts, usually with a photo attached. Separate from the videos uploaded on YouTube, which mainly feature performances, documentaries, and radio broadcast highlights, GugakFM also employs livestreaming on SNS as a promotional tool. Pak Inhyŏk of the GugakFM Culture Video Contents Department explained that GugakFM mainly uses livestreaming to broaden their audience base, with most livestreaming activity concentrated on Facebook. He further stated that the content that is chosen for livestreaming includes radio broadcasts and live performances (see Figures 6.1 and 6.2), whereby GugakFM only selects content for livestreaming that already has an established audience base (within a demographic that is able to use SNS) to a certain extent. The reason why GugakFM has turned to livestreaming on SNS is that they have observed a rising trend of viewing content through SNS rather than alternative sources—their choices for promotion are hence driven to a certain extent by the development of technology and audience viewing habits (personal communication, September 20, 2018).

Jeongdong Theater (*Chŏngdong kŭkchang*) is a venue that has become known for its hosting *kugak*-inspired performances. It was established in 1995 as a restored version of the Wŏngaksa Theater (1908–14), birthplace of the *p'ansori*-inspired musical theater form *ch'anggŭk*, and rebranded in 2010 as a venue for tourist outreach projects promoting Korean traditional culture. In February 2017, one of its performances

Figure 6.1 Screenshot of a Facebook livestream of GugakFM's *p'ansori*-themed radio show "*Pat'u-ŭi Sangsadiya*" (a play of words referring to the hosts' performance team name, which also means "up close," and is a common folk song phrase equivalent to fa-la-la; accessed October 3, 2018).

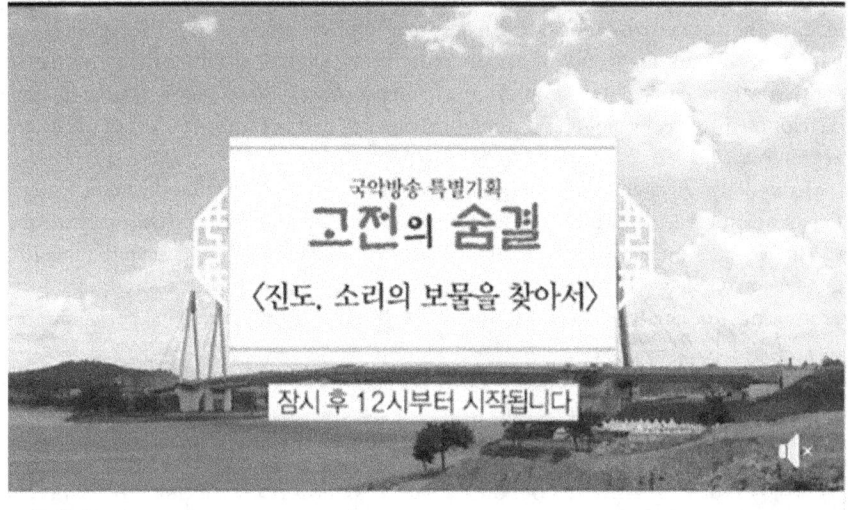

Figure 6.2 Screenshot of a GugakFM Facebook livestream of a concert introducing music from Chindo Island (accessed October 1, 2018).

titled "*Chŏkpyŏk*" (Red Cliff), which combined elements from the *p'ansori* story of the same name with vigorous dance performances and more musical-style numbers, was selected to be streamed live on Naver's main search page. This performance was hugely successful, with all performances sold out, inspiring reruns (also completely sold out) in 2018 and again in 2019, and helped cement Jeongdong Theater's reputation as a venue for *kugak* fusion performances. Kim Chunwŏn of the Jeongdong Theater Performance Planning Team revealed their motivation for employing video content for their promotional material:

> Videos are the most direct method to show viewers a real "performance." For example, rather than writing the words "a meeting between *p'ansori* and contemporary dance," I'm sure everyone will agree that even if you show just a short scene to viewers it will be more effective. Not just performance videos, but also rehearsal videos, seeing the process of production for oneself, we aim to show the various charms of a performance by revealing the processes that aren't usually shared… With the development of the internet and related media the trends in

popular contents have changed a lot, particularly now is the age when anyone can become a content creator themselves. It is the age when information is shared not via text but via videos. That is why since last year (2017) we have focused particularly on video production.

(Personal communication, October 22, 2018)

Jeongdong Theater's promotion strategy hence usually follows the basic formula of first, a thirty-second spot for promotion; second, a thirty-second video of rehearsals; and third, a thirty-second highlight video. Since 2018, they also share moving posters (similar to gifs) of the main performers. After "*Chŏkpyŏk*," Jeongdong Theater has also shared one further performance as a full livestream, as well as sharing a highlight reel of another. In addition, Kim explained that they will make sure to share particularly entertaining videos on SNS, to further target the young demographic most active there. For the 2018 performance cycle of "*Chŏkpyŏk*," for example, one of the promotional videos shared was a "surprise attack changing room interview" with some of the performers, employing on-screen text and graphics that emulate the style of many Korean TV shows (see Figure 6.3).

This style of sharing short clips, particularly of performance highlights or humorous episodes backstage, is a common promotional strategy used by venues hosting *kugak-*

Figure 6.3 Screenshot from a Jeongdong Theater promotional video shared on Facebook on March 30, 2018. The use of subtitles (in this case, saying "I won't get it wrong from tomorrow…") is characteristically used in Korean TV shows (accessed April 30, 2019).

related performances. I would argue that, rather in line with the motivations for livestreaming the *madangnori* "Here Comes Nolbo" described above, this use of video clips becomes a means to demonstrate *kugak*'s connectedness to contemporary trends by emulating the style of media sharing found in other genres. This motivation is, of course, by no means limited to institutions: many *sorikkun* and other *kugak* performers employ the same strategies for personal promotion. Thus what becomes important is that, not only are *kugak* performers, producers, and institutions using video sharing on SNS as a promotional tool but they also demonstrate their close awareness to trends in contemporary society by their choices of how they frame their content.

Personal Use of SNS

An online survey on SNS usage among *kugak* (predominantly *p'ansori*) performers I conducted in autumn 2018 revealed the following trends: the most common SNS platforms used were Facebook (60.9 percent) and Instagram (39.1 percent). Focusing specifically on *kugak*-related content, the videos these *kugak* performers watched were mostly performances or performance promotion videos, of their own performances, or of their friends or teachers. Many mentioned watching livestream or rerun broadcasts such as from GugakFM, with some highlighting this as a means to catch up on performances they wanted to attend but couldn't. Interestingly, many of them mentioned fusion, crossover, or collaborative videos, which would indicate that the newness of the sharing medium may well also bias the available content toward more "new" performance styles. This has wide-reaching consequences for the potential of social media to work as an effective promotional tool for traditional music. Fusion as a genre of redeveloped *kugak* often focuses heavily on pop influences and is often critiqued for being undertaken by artists who aren't competent enough in the traditional repertoire (Yates-Lu 2019: 60–1). Finchum-Sung (2009: 52) and Chan Park (2011: 35) both critique the potential hollowing out of tradition that might occur from too strong a focus on fusion, and the potential bias toward fusion content online may further exacerbate this problem.

The videos being shared were also mostly performances, predominantly by the performers themselves, although many also shared performances by friends, clips of master performers of the past, lectures by master singers, or content from GugakFM. Reasons given by survey respondents for sharing these videos included: allowing people not attending to still take part, hoping to develop and promote *kugak*, wanting to promote oneself, sharing news and letting acquaintances hear Korean traditional music, making it possible to watch and learn later, and wanting to share good content widely. The engagement with video content hence has both educational and promotional aspects: performers want to educate themselves and the people around them, particularly those who have not encountered *kugak* before. At the same time, they hope that sharing these videos will help raise the profile of both performers themselves and *kugak* in general, providing extra stimulus to their careers and the art to which they have dedicated their lives.

This becomes further apparent when exploring responses by survey participants as to why there seemed to be a rise in *kugak* performers doing livestreaming or uploading short videos. Responses can be grouped into four groups: the first group focused on how promotional strategies have changed, stating for example that "This is the era of self-PR" (survey response, October 18, 2018).[8] Another respondent argued: "Amongst young *kugak* performers, their perception of promoting content through the internet has changed, I think they are also actively changing it. Also because there are a lot of *kugak* performers so they consider this the best method for promoting themselves or their team" (survey response, October 19, 2018). In the cut-throat competitive environment that is the current *kugak* world, in which many artists compete for what is already a small audience base, young artists especially are continually watching trends in order to maximize any opportunity to be more widely recognized, thus hopefully securing more gigs in the future.

The second group of respondents focused on changes in how audiences consume content, with one respondent stating bluntly, "Lately people don't read or watch long content" (survey response, October 19, 2018). This point of view was also regularly mentioned in my PhD fieldwork: *sorikkun* Ch'oe Hani, for example, told me of her desire to create five-minute hook songs based on the five core *p'ansori* stories, to attract listeners who stumble on the material by chance (interview, September 23, 2014; see also Yates-Lu 2019: 59). As we saw with the example of Jeongdong Theater's promotional formula above, in streaming and sharing short video clips, performers streamline their content to suit their target audiences' perceived consumption habits, thus hoping to maximize impact and hopefully draw in interest for deeper engagement with their performances.

The third group of respondents focused on their desire to promote *kugak*, or, as one respondent put it, "help the development of *kugak*" (survey response, October 19, 2018). One respondent argued that the modernization of the genre increases its potential to be shared in alternative ways:

> Although *kugak* may not be as popular as before, it does seem like lately interest in *kugak* has increased, also as *kugak* is gradually moving away from its image as stuffy and old-fashioned and taking on contemporary colours, so I think it has potential for use as [online] content. That's why there are more "tradition + contemporary" contents which match the palate of contemporary people, and compared to before there is now an invigoration of the sharing of short videos or livestreaming.
> (Survey response, October 21, 2018)

As we saw above, a desire to make *kugak* palatable to contemporary audiences has gone hand in hand with a rise in fusion performances, and this newness of content is hence considered more suited to being shared on new platforms.

Finally, some respondents focused on the personal desires of the users themselves, stating that the rise in video sharing comes from "the wish of sharing one's own art world widely" (survey response, October 19, 2018), or "for the fun of [doing] promotion and [reading/writing] comments" (survey response, November 3, 2018).

This ties in more with changing trends in social media use more generally, as *kugak* performers, as active participants in contemporary society, also engage with and enjoy social media as a personal platform from which to express themselves as an individual. I should also state that one respondent did not feel that there had been an increase in *kugak* performers sharing video content, although the overwhelming majority of respondents did feel there had been an increase.

We can see, then, that contrary to accusations of *kugak* performers as being out of touch with contemporary trends (as addressed in So Inhwa 2015: 31–2), members of the traditional music scene are very aware of the developments in technology, as well as what format of content is most popular among general audiences, and they actively make use of this knowledge in order to promote both themselves and *kugak* as a whole.

New Development of *Ch'uimsae*?

A specific element of online consumption of *kugak* content not addressed so far is that of audience responses, which are played out online in the comment section of the shared videos. As we saw in the introduction, audience participation is a key part of a *p'ansori* performance, without which it is not considered complete. Chan Park (2003: 234–6), for example, laments the loss of authentic audience responses, as modern-day audiences are no longer familiar enough with the songs and performance style to comfortably shout *ch'uimsae* and are more likely to sit quietly and only applaud when a performance is finished. Pak Pŏmhun (2008), however, argues for a broadening of the concept of *ch'uimsae* into daily life, to include any means of giving positive feedback or signaling approval, which could also include online interactions, such as posting comments (see Figure 6.4). Indeed, it can be observed that comments on *kugak* performance videos by viewers, apart from comments complimenting the performance or expressing gratitude for sharing a video, often include *ch'uimsae* responses (see Figure 6.5).

In this employment of a traditional response to a new performance format, *p'ansori ch'uimsae* being typed out on SNS become a means of reengaging audiences in a way that is familiar to them. This encourages a new form of immediacy and closeness that is otherwise undermined by the spatial distance between performer and online audience. However, this immediacy is mainly built with those who already understand the rules of engagement and would be just as comfortable employing *ch'uimsae* if physically present at the performance venue. As Figure 6.5 illustrates, online audiences do not exclusively revolve around the *ch'uimsae* that would be used in an offline performance, as there are plenty of other ways to express their appreciation of the performance online. Conversely, these online interactions are unlikely to convert into more use of *ch'uimsae* in an offline performance setting, as the timing for typing a comment and it becoming visible to viewers is unlikely to match up to the music in the way directly spoken *ch'uimsae* would when the audience is physically present. Hence the possibilities for broadening the base of engagement to others less familiar with the

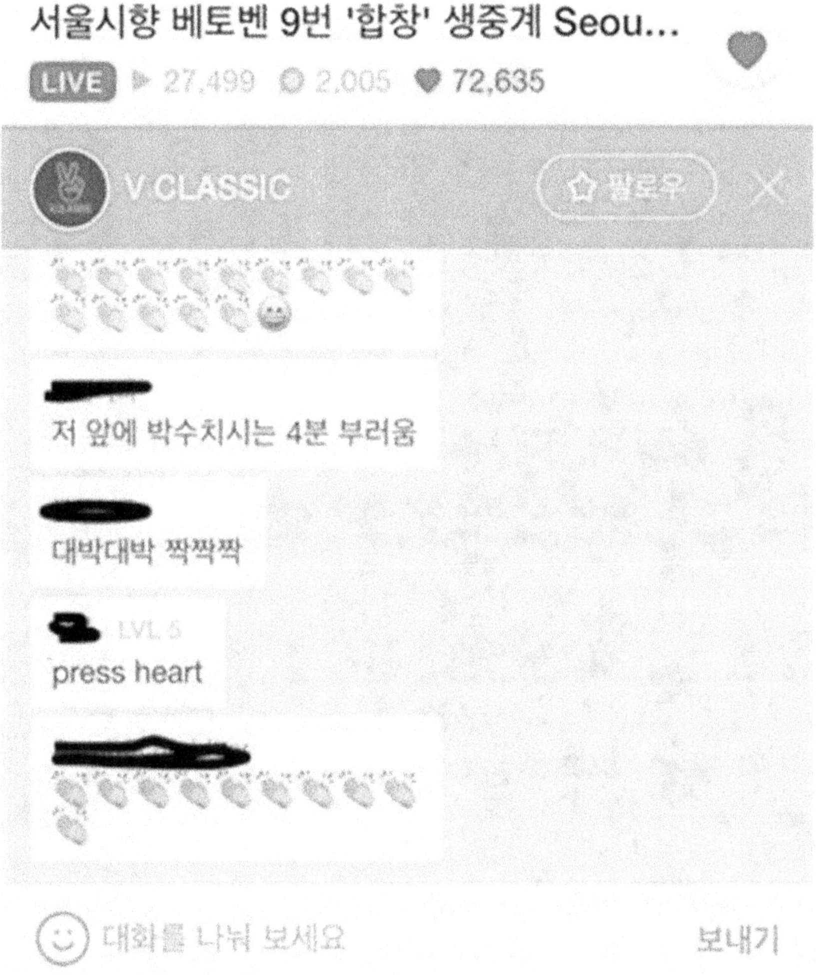

서울시향 베토벤 9번 '합창' 생중계 Seou...

LIVE ▶ 27,499 ◎ 2,005 ♥ 72,635

V CLASSIC   ☆ 팔로우

저 앞에 박수치시는 4분 부러움

대박대박 짝짝짝

LVL 5
press heart

⊙ 대화를 나눠 보세요   보내기

Figure 6.4 Real-time responses to a concert by Seoul Philharmonic Orchestra of Beethoven's Symphony No. 9, livestreamed on V Live December 8, 2016 (cited in Cho Hŭisŏn 2017)—note the clapping emojis. The comments read: "I am jealous of the four people clapping at the front," and "amazing amazing *tchak tchak tchak* (sound of clapping)."

conventions of *kugak* performance are limited. Lee Eungchel (2016: 118) highlights the power of SNS to allow people to seek out their own interests and create their own communities based around these interests. However, he also cautions that this ability to form concentrated groups also limits the potential for content to spread beyond these established groups—the "echo chamber" effect addressed above. Still, hope remains for the potential of video sharing as a promotional tool for *kugak* if we focus, returning

Figure 6.5 Real-time responses to the opening ceremony of the Jeonju International Sori Festival 2018, livestreamed on Facebook by GugakFM on October 3, 2018. The comments read "*ŏlsshigu*" (a common *ch'uimsae* phrase), "this is the true definition of a moving performance (smiley face)," "Hyesŭng PD must have gone through a lot, hang on in there (heart emojis)," and "*ŏlsshigu chot'a*" (both common *ch'uimsae* phrases; accessed October 6, 2018).

to Schultz's argument on using SNS as a marketing tool, on the increased trust people place in the word of mouth by friends as opposed to external branding. There is after all never a perfect overlap between interest groups, so the potential remains for those previously unaware of a form of content to be exposed to it through the sharing by a friend. In this way, knowledge and enjoyment of *kugak* may still be gradually spread to a larger audience.

Extending the Reach of *P'ansori*

Clearly, the strategies for expanding audiences are continuing to develop and diversify. In February 2019, my *p'ansori* teacher Min Hyesŏng began a YouTube channel called "Bonjour Pansori" dedicated to teaching *p'ansori* to a French-speaking audience, based on the demand of students from the two-week workshops she holds in France and Belgium once a year to be able to continue to learn outside the workshop as well (see Figure 6.6). Featuring both French and Korean students, and with a mixture of on-the-spot interpretation and French subtitles added later, this channel teaches basic *p'ansori* vocalization and how to read the *chŏngganbo* box notation that Min usually uses when teaching overseas, as well as teaching "*Sarangga*" (The Song of Love), an extract from the *p'ansori* story *Ch'unhyangga* (The Song of Ch'unhyang), which is split over five videos. The channel also shares promotional material for Min's *p'ansori* performance group, Soeul Soripan (*Soŭl sorip'an*), as well as performance clips that heavily feature Min's French students who are currently active in Korea, especially Cameroon-born Laure Mafo, who has been featured on numerous Korean TV programs and news reports since becoming known for her appearance on KBS' *Iutchip Ch'alsŭ* (My Neighbor Charles).

While this project is currently very much in its beginning stages, the potential for SNS to be employed as a further means for promoting *kugak*, not just within Korea but abroad as well, demonstrates the linkage between the international features of the Korean Wave and its promotional strategy and carries potentially interesting

Figure 6.6 YouTube video teaching basic *p'ansori* vocalization on the "Bonjour Pansori" channel (accessed April 30, 2019).

ramifications for a style of music considered intimately related to Koreans' sense of nationhood. As traditional music is spread by means outside the old lines of transmission, widening access also begins to raise questions of who is qualified to share and receive such knowledge. Although I know many *sorikkun* who would be very excited to hear about French people learning *p'ansori* through YouTube, I doubt anyone would classify them as *p'ansori* learners in the same sense as someone who is learning from their teacher directly. The use of SNS for spreading of awareness of *p'ansori* and *kugak* shows great potential, but the use of this technology is also complicating matters by raising new questions as to what can be considered legitimate practice of the art.

Conclusion

To conclude, then, we can observe a rising trend in the use of video for self-promotion and as a means of exchange with friends. Both on the institutional and personal levels, *p'ansori*, and by extension the *kugak* scene as a whole, is following this trend as performers and presenters try to combat perception of *kugak* as old and out of touch with contemporary reality. The pertinent question, of course, is whether this strategy is effective. Clearly, the scale of interest in *kugak* is nowhere near that of content shared by Korean Wave stars like BTS. The most successful *kugak* content tends to be more fusion-oriented than purely traditional. On a personal level, outreach by *kugak* performers beyond their own circle of friends is limited. Sharing video content on SNS is another complementary means to interact with the same group of *kugak* aficionados, acting according to offline rules. Still, as my teacher Min Hyesŏng put it, if opening new communication pathways attracts at least one new fan, it must be counted as a success (personal communication, June 21, 2018). *Kugak* artists' online activities hence demonstrate their diversification of strategies to keep traditional art forms relevant to contemporary life.

Notes

1. This is a very flexible term meaning either an open space or an event. It is also part of the etymology of the name *p'ansori*, whereby *p'an* refers to the fact that the genre was traditionally performed in open spaces, such as the marketplace, and *sori* refers to both song and sound, as *sorikkun* not only sing but also emulate various sounds of nature in the process of telling a particular story.
2. These refer to two of the five core texts of the *p'ansori* repertoire, the *Tale of Ch'unhyang* and the *Tale of Hŭngbo* respectively.
3. Harkness (2014: 179) highlights a similar issue in the Western classical singing scene in Korea.
4. Contrary to other video-sharing platforms, V Live allows its users to like a video more than once.
5. https://www.oxfordreference.com/view/10.1093/acref/9780191803093.001.0001/acref-9780191803093-e-424?rskey=SYTaht&result=2, accessed May 28, 2020.

6   For a more in-depth introduction to this institution, see Kwon Hyun Seok (2014: 231).
7   Separate radio shows also have Instagram accounts, but there is no account for GugakFM as a whole. This may be because the radio hosts also use these accounts to communicate directly with their listeners. As GugakFM is going to open a TV channel at the end of December 2019, it will be interesting to see whether this causes a shift in their SNS promotion strategies.
8   In order to allow the respondents to feel more comfortable in expressing their opinions in this survey, all responses were anonymous.

Bibliography

Adams, Laura L. 2013. "Ethnicity and the Politics of Heritage in Uzbekistan." *Central Asian Survey* 32 (2): 115–33.

Aisyah, Aznur, and Yun Jin Nam. 2017. "K-Pop V Fansubs, V LIVE and NAVER Dictionary: Fansubbers' Synergy in Minimising Language Barriers." *The Southeast Asian Journal of English Language Studies* 23 (4): 112–27.

Aykan, Bahar. 2015. "'Patenting' Karagöz: UNESCO, Nationalism and Multinational Intangible Cultural Heritage." *International Journal of Heritage Studies* 21 (10): 949–61.

Boyland, Peter. 2019. "The State of Mobile Network Experience: Benchmarking Mobile on the Eve of the 5G Revolution." *Opensignal*. Available online: https://www.opensignal.com/sites/opensignal-com/files/data/reports/global/data-2019-05/the_state_of_mobile_experience_may_2019_0.pdf, accessed December 13, 2019.

Cannon, Alexander M. 2016. "Tradition, Still Remains: Sustainability through Ruin in Vietnamese Music for Diversion." *Ethnomusicology Forum* 25 (2): 146–71.

Cho Hŭisŏn. 2017. "Nae sonan e dŭrŏon kongyŏnjang… shilshigan chunggye ŭ chinhwa." *Sŏul shinmun*, March 31. Available online: http://www.seoul.co.kr/news/newsView.php?id=20170401016001, accessed October 18, 2018.

Chŏng, Noshik. 1940. *Chosŏn ch'anggŭksa*. Seoul: Chosŏn ilbosa.

Chua Beng Huat, and Koichi Iwabuchi, eds. 2008. *East Asian Pop Culture: Analysing the Korean Wave*. Hong Kong: Hong Kong University Press; London: Eurospan.

Finchum-Sung, Hilary. 2009. "Image Is Everything: Re-Imaging Traditional Music in the Era of the Korean Wave." *Southeast Review of Asian Studies* 31: 39–55.

Finchum-Sung, Hilary. 2012. "Visual Excess: The Visuality of Traditional Music Performance in South Korea." *Ethnomusicology* 56 (3): 396–425.

Harkness, Nicholas. 2014. *Songs of Seoul: An Ethnography of Voice and Voicing in Christian South Korea*. Berkeley: University of California Press.

Howard, Keith, ed. 2006. *Korean Pop Music: Riding the Wave*. Folkestone, Kent: Global Oriental.

Howard, Keith. 2016. "The Institutionalization of Korean Traditional Music: Problematic Business Ethics in the Construction of Genre and Place." *Asia Pacific Business Review* 22 (3): 452–67.

Kim, Kee Hyung. 2004. "Ch'angjak p'ansori ŭi sajŏk chŏn'gae wa yochŏngjŏk gwaje." *Kubimunhak yŏngu* 18: 1–27.

Kwon, Hyun Seok. 2014. "Cultural Globalization and the Korean Promotion Policy for Music Based on Tradition: A Study of the Activation Plan and Its Background." PhD thesis, SOAS, University of London.

Lee, Eungchel. 2016. "Uri-nŭn hangsang muŏsin'ga-ŭi p'aen-ida: P'aendŏm-ŭi hwaksan, tŏkjil-ŭi ilsanghwa, ch'uihyang-ŭi ŭnpye." *Han'guk munhwa illyuhak* 49 (3): 95–135.
Ministry of Culture, Sports, and Tourism. 2007. "Hansŭt'ail yuksŏng chonghap kyehoek." Available online: https://www.mcst.go.kr/web/s_notice/press/pressView.jsp?pSeq=8462, accessed December 31, 2018.
Oh, Ingyu, and Park Gil-Sung. 2012. "From B2C to B2B: Selling Korean Pop Music in the Age of New Social Media." *Korea Observer* 43 (3): 365–97.
Pak, Pŏmhun. 2008. *Pak Pŏmhun-ŭi ch'uimsae*. Seoul: Kyŏnghyang Sinmunsa.
Park, Chan E. 2003. *Voices from the Straw Mat: Toward an Ethnography of Korean Story-Singing*. Honolulu: University of Hawai'i Press.
Park, Chan E. 2011. "Reclaiming Korea from 'Korean Performance Tradition': A Critique of the Contemporization of *Kugak*." *Korean Studies* 35: 25–43.
Schultz, Carsten D. 2016. "Driving Likes, Comments, and Shares on Social Networking Sites—How Post Characteristics Affect Brand Interactions in Apparel Retailing." Available online: https://dl.acm.org/doi/10.1145/2971603.2971612, accessed May 27, 2020.
So, Inhwa. 2015. "The Popularization of Gugak: A Case Study of the MIJI Project, a Gugak Girl Group." *Journal of the International Association for the Study of Popular Music* 5 (2): 22–40.
Sutton, R. Anderson. 2011. "'Fusion' and Questions of Korean Cultural Identity in Music." *Korean Studies* 35: 4–24.
Tsitsishvili, Nino. 2009. "National Ideologies in the Era of Global Fusions: Georgian Polyphonic Song as a UNESCO-Sanctioned Masterpiece of Intangible Heritage." *Music and Politics* 3 (1): 1–17.
Vail, Peter. 2014. "Muay Thai: Inventing Tradition for a National Symbol." *Sojourn: Journal of Social Issues in Southeast Asia* 29 (3): 509–53.
Yang, Chinha. 2017. "Sŭmat'ŭp'on sok raibŭ kongyŏn... taese ro ttŭn shilhwangjunggye." *Han'guk ilbo*. January 25. Available online: http://www.hankookilbo.com/News/Read/201701251537061451, accessed October 18, 2018.
Yates-Lu, Anna. 2019. "When K-Pop and *Kugak* Meet: Popularising *P'ansori* in Modern Korea." *Yearbook for Traditional Music* 51: 49–71.
Yi, T'aehwa. 2013. "P'ansori e taehan ŏtkallin inshik kwa taejunghwa ŭi hyangbang." *P'ansori yŏn'gu* 35: 153–82.

Filmography

Bong Joon-Ho, director. 2019. *Kisaengch'ung*. South Korea: Barunson E&A, feature film.

Part Three

Sounding Authority

7

North Korea: Controlling the Airwaves and Harmonizing the People

Keith Howard

Totalitarian states attempt to control literature and art. State apparatuses, as Louis Althusser (1971) put it, are repressive, reinforcing the class state, collectivizing and institutionalizing nationhood, elevating paramount leaders, and claiming authority through the judicious promotion of historical facts, myths, and legends. Today, much of this is a given, and is hardly novel. However, control impacts writers and artists, imposing requirements to embed ideology in all cultural production. Nostalgia may be allowed, but it will both celebrate and erase memories, constructing a selective view of the past to reinforce both the present reality as promoted officially and the promise of a utopian future. Securing that future requires, it will be argued, state organs to be supported in the present, requiring the population to remain faithful to the shared cause. Music is given prominence in the broadcasting of this constructed reality because, as Jacques Attali notes, "since noise is the source of power, power has always listened to it with fascination" (1977: 6). Songs routinely become the vehicles for musical messaging, because lyrics project meaning with clarity. Lenin once riled against selfish artists who made use of vagueness (Lunacharsky 1967: 259–60), and Arnold Perris, summing up the situation that pertained in both Stalin's Soviet Union and Mao's China, writes that "apolitical artists are useless" (1985: 71). In this same vein, Dmitri Shostakovich, after criticism in the 1930s, remarked that Soviet "music... [had become] a vital weapon in the struggle" (cited in Schwarz 1983: 130). Not surprisingly, then, to North Korea's second leader, Kim Jong Il (1942–2011),[1] the son of the first leader, Kim Il Sung (1912–94), "music without politics is like a flower without scent" (cited in Yi 2006: 167).

This chapter explores how music's political messages are conveyed to the North Korean populace through state-controlled and state-censored recordings and broadcasting, focusing on how songs, as the favored medium of communication, are experienced in everyday life.[2]

The Aural Soundtrack of Pyongyang

For music to have political impact, and in order for primacy to be given to its messaging, the inherent ephemerality of sound needs to be overcome. Music has a plasticity that requires interpretation; hence, Robert Adlington (2013: 5) notes that appealing to the aesthetics of sound tends to blur the intended messages. It is because of this, he argues, that composers in socialist systems attract criticism. Indeed, Richard Taruskin has pointed out that policing music in the Soviet Union "always implied a body count" (2010: xii). This was most famously seen in Andrei Zhdanov's January 1948 speech to the meeting of Soviet music workers[3] and the subsequent resolution of the Central Committee of the Communist Party carried in *Pravda* two weeks later (on February 11, 1948).[4] Zhdanov, after Stalin's criticism of Muradeli's opera *Velikaya Druzhba* (*The Great Friendship*), set out to control artistic production (Fairclough 2016: 201–13), and six leading composers were denounced, among them Shostakovich. Again, Barbara Mittler (1997: 59) comments that under Mao in China, the more complicated and intricate a piece of music was, the more it was regarded with suspicion by bodies that policed cultural production. Some argue that music, as sound, is a form of language, but this still preserves some ambiguity, since linguistic paradigms do not match musical structures and the correlation of its symbols to the assigned meanings of words is not exact.[5] But, where messages are given by lyrics, ambiguity subsides. Songs, then, are bounded objects, their lyrics giving them meaning. Kim Jong Il remarked, in a speech delivered on May 6, 1975:

> Before good songs can be produced prettily-worded texts are necessary. The words should be poetic. But many [lyrics] are turned into prose… [so] no good songs can be produced… Our creators of music do not accept Party policy with sensitivity. I gave them the task of composing powerful songs capable of inspiring the masses… but as yet they have failed to produce a good song about grand construction.
> ("For the further development of our Juche art," 1975)

In North Korea, songs reign paramount. Songs have, ever since the monochromatic ideology of juche (an ideology that will briefly be discussed below), was embedded into cultural production during the 1960s, provided the relentless soundtrack for the theater that is Pyongyang. This pervasiveness challenges the claim of the guitarist Jason Carter, in musings on the Copenhagen-based Freemuse website[6] and in the world music journal *Songlines* (2007), that after a few days in Pyongyang, a visitor stops noticing the aural barrage. Rather, as the former Python Michael Palin discovered in a 2018 television documentary,[7] recorded songs are played from the crack of dawn onwards, emanating from hidden speakers across and above Pyongyang, reaching the top rooms of high-rise hotels, to where workers toil in the fields and on construction sites, and to students rehearsing on pavements and in squares and parks for the next state-sanctioned celebration. Wherever one goes in North Korea, songs are impossible to ignore.

Songs are monitored by layers of censorship to ensure that they carry the correct messages. Although the first decades of the Soviet Union saw high art championed, to "intellectualize the working classes and class-ize the intellectuals" (Armstrong 2003: 166–7, after Fitzpatrick 1979), by March 1947, barely two years after Korea's liberation from Japanese rule, the Central Committee in Pyongyang had begun to impose control over cultural production, stating that art should not be about aesthetics but should "educate the people in socialism and serve the nation and people" (Kwŏn 1991: 59). The mechanisms of control have changed over time but broadly work within a strict hierarchy: a ministry under the Korean Workers' Party at the top, a Korean Literature and Arts Union acting as a confederation of separate unions for writers, artists, and musicians, then institutions that employ artists, then collectives of artists, then individuals.[8] This system can somewhat surprisingly be turned on its head, since production is censored from the bottom upwards: an individual artist takes steps to ensure that they have complied with all requirements before presenting their creation to the collective of artists they are assigned to work with.[9] The result is that artists in Pyongyang today endlessly revert to stereotypes that channel duty, dedication, and selfless sacrifice, to the authorized history and accounts of foreign aggression, and which conform to the ideology demanded by the state. But, the layers of control are kept deliberately opaque. This is starkly seen in the 2016 documentary *Liberation Day*, in which the Slovakian anti-fascist band Laibach fails to negotiate the different layers of censorship prior to a concert in Pyongyang.[10] Opacity enforces conformity through a discursive rhetoric, and this adds additional control, because violence is reserved by the state to punish infringements of even unannounced shifts to that rhetoric (after Coronil and Skurski 2006: 3–6; Debord 2010: 64). Taruskin's "body count" is the inevitable, but to the state desirable, result. Still, Kim Jong Il maintained in his 1975 speech, "We are making a revolution, and we should inspire the people to the revolutionary struggle by means of songs."

Control extends to recordings and broadcasts. Songs are issued on one of a number of labels by the state media company, Meari (Echo)—the only recording company in North Korea. Its labels include the unfortunate acronym "PEE" for the 180+ albums released that feature the Pochonbo Electronic Ensemble, "WJS" for the 50+ releases of Wangjaesan Light Music Band, and "KM" or "KMC" for the long-running *Chosŏn ŭi norae* (*Songs of Korea*) series. Recordings are distributed abroad online by the Shenyang-based Uriminzokkiri (which over the last decade has largely replaced the clunky North Korea- and Japan-based websites of the state-run Korean Central News Agency). The state maintains its monopoly over broadcasting. Televisions and radios are factory-set to receive only state channels, and speakers are built into many apartments that are fixed to "on," usually without volume controls, ensuring that all receive all broadcasts. All signals beamed from beyond North Korea's borders are blocked. Unannounced inspections of radios and televisions as well as recording and playback equipment are a routine part of life, policed in Pyongyang through the secretive "Group 109."[11] Although toward the end of the last millennium, three state television channels functioned, recent visitors report that only one or two channels exist at any given time, broadcasting for around five hours each evening. The internet is controlled and monitored, requiring special authorization to access; there is no free access to the world outside. Again, the rapidly multiplying number of smartphone users must accept tight government screening and regular checks.[12]

Maintaining control over the airwaves stems from history. The Korean peninsula was a Japanese colony from 1910 until 1945, and in 1927 Japan established the first radio station in Seoul (then known as Keijō [J.] or Kyŏngsŏng [K.]). Initially, its towers limited the range over which broadcasts could be received, but soon subsidiary stations were set up, including in Pyongyang. Broadcasts were subject to strict control. For the first few years, Korean programs were separated from Japanese, but from 1932 some bilingual broadcasting was introduced (Fuchs, Kasahara, and Saaler 2018: 292–3; see also Robinson 1999). Taking its lead from Tokyo, music for group callisthenics (J. *rajio taiso*) was broadcast at set times, and this was used by workers in factories and by students in schools. This suggests a root for the hidden speakers in Pyongyang's public spaces, but we should not forget that public speakers remained part of everyday South Korea into the 1980s, notably under the rule of Park Chung Hee (1961–79), where they were a channel through which "healthy songs" (*kŏnjŏn kayo*) could be promoted, and as a means to encourage group construction projects allied to the New Village Movement (*Saemaŭl undong*) (Maliangkay 2006a: 53–8). Radio broadcasting was an easy tool for propaganda, and during the Korean War (1950–53), radio was part of what Frances Saunders (1999) calls the "Cultural Cold War": broadcasts from South Korea but also from China and Russia left a legacy of distrust in North Korea, and a desire to overcome its relative paucity of resources to create absolute control over what people could listen to. During the war, VUNC (Voice of the United Nations' Command) and AFN (American Forces Network) dominated the airwaves. While AFN (AFKN in its Korean incarnation) received new-fangled vinyl discs of current popular music from the Los Angeles-based AFRTS (American Forces Radio and Television Service) and primarily served American troops, VUNC focused on propaganda.[13] Maliangkay cites Bob Richards, a veteran sent to work at the station:

> VUNC Radio was broadcast in the Korean language. It was set up to give the Korean people the true news of the day. They used well-known Koreans, such as movie stars. I, in fact, one day was sent to pick up a Korean movie star. When I arrived, a very beautiful young lady came to the jeep with her escort and I took them to our unit and she went into the broadcasting trailer and made some statements and then I returned her to her home. I was not allowed to talk to her. The radio station was used to broadcast to North Korea and I am sure it also broadcast propaganda. VUNC Radio also had loudspeakers at the DMZ and broadcast over them to farmers working in fields on other side.
>
> (2006b: 23)

Control through "Self-Reliance:" Juche Ideology

From September 1998 until April 2019, every television news broadcast in North Korea superimposed a small image at the top left of the screen. It can be seen on the many news clips uploaded to YouTube and Youku. Back in 1998, the initial image was of a rocket. It first appeared days after North Korea claimed to have launched its first satellite, Kwangmyŏngsŏng (Bright Star). International observers warned that the technology required to get a satellite into orbit was much the same as that required to launch missiles; hence the television reporter announced, and the superimposed image reinforced the message, that the satellite had a peaceful purpose: it was broadcasting North Korean songs 24-7 around the world. Nobody outside North Korea has reported picking up any such broadcasts, but then the claim—much as the songs—was intended for domestic consumption. Before long, the image changed to a torch, similar in size and color. This was the juche torch, reminding citizens of the state's fundamental ideology.

Juche provides a key for understanding cultural production and broadcasting within the hermetically sealed northern state. What, though, is juche? The official account states it is an ideology with roots in the 1930s and in the guerrilla activities of Kim Il Sung against Japan's colonial expansion.[14] Kim subsequently emerged as the northern state's first leader. If juche does come from the colonial period (and notwithstanding parallels in other, earlier, Korean nationalist thought[15]), then it may well have begun as a reflection on the bloody Minsaengdan incident, when between 1932 and 1935 up to 2,000 Korean communists were killed by their Chinese brethren who feared bases had been infiltrated by spies (Han 2013). However, the first mention of "juche" comes much later, in a speech delivered by Kim on December 28, 1955, "On eliminating dogmatism and formalism and establishing juche in ideological work."[16] To give a context, the speech needs to be juxtaposed with a campaign, the "flying horse movement" (*Chŏllima*), which harnessed the image of a mythical horse (*ma*) able to gallop a thousand (*chŏn/chŏl-*) miles (*ri/li*) in a day. The campaign began a year later with a further speech by Kim at the Kangsŏn steel mill, which exhorted managers to mobilize workers to greater production. In its efforts to boost production, Pyongyang had already championed a Korean, Kim Hoeil, a train engineer, as the equivalent to the Soviet miner Stakhanov who had reputedly moved 102 tons of coal in a single shift.[17] Both speech and movement made Kim sole arbiter, rendering his actions and statements identical to the wishes and desires of the people. The hegemony of his leadership was treated as the most ordinary thing, and monochromatic repetition rendered, for workers, "the mundaneness of everyday life... extraordinary" (Kim 2018: 102). For artists, imposing mechanisms to control all production ensured what Kofi Agawu has characterized, though in another context, as the "embrace of sameness" (2003: 169).

Essentially, both speech and campaign delinked Korea from international influence and reinforced a nationalistic binary worldview of Korea-and-the-rest (Suh 2013: 8–15). In this, they fit squarely with the post Korean war period, and real or perceived challenges of that time. The speech demanded that cultural production should, henceforth, be nationalist in form, while the campaign demanded that industry be developed through the efforts of workers. Both retained Stalin's autarkic economic model of socialism in one country.[18] The campaign fashioned a Korean approach to socialist state-building (David-West 2007: 130–41; Gittings 1993; Suh 1988), responding to threats to Kim's authority. Such challenges were nothing new, but with recovery from the destructive Korean war well underway, Kim turned on those who had returned to Pyongyang after the liberation of the peninsula at the end of the Pacific War. Among those in the political arena, some had been with Mao in Yan'an, while others had links to the

Soviet Union. The latter became emboldened when after the death of Stalin, the Soviets signaled an intention to reform. Again, some had moved northwards from Seoul, as had many influential artists and writers—the targets of the juche speech. It has been argued that when the Pacific War ended in 1945, there was no established communist intellectual tradition among Korean artists and writers (Gabroussenko 2010: 167), so those who settled in Pyongyang did so as part of a bourgeois compromise: it is not unusual for artists and writers with bourgeois backgrounds to take up socialist causes, since to train as an artist or a writer requires money or, at the least, the ability to spend time honing creative and performing skills rather than toiling long and hard in fields or factories to provide food for one's family. As the writers and artists in Pyongyang set cultural policy, partly through practice, they occupied, to cite Katherine Verdery in respect to Romania, a "space of legitimation" (1991: 17). But, the everyday extraordinary celebrated proletarianism, promoting artists from among the masses who lacked formal training (or, at least, those who had only trained locally, since the colonial period had seen many travel to Japan or North America to study). Artists with bourgeois backgrounds found their positions challenged, and many were purged.

In promoting proletarian cultural production, Kim took his lead from Mao, who in turn echoed Stalin—who unwittingly channeled Plato (Armstrong 2003: 170): "the genuine creator of great art is always the people. No excellent work of art fails to command the people's love, and if a work of art does not enjoy the people's understanding and appreciation, it cannot be an excellent one" (Kim Il Sung, "On some questions arising in our literature and art," June 30, 1951). Where juche preached that art and literature represented the people, it also required it to be supported by the people. Therefore, the creators of art and literature must learn from the people but, since the people were perfectly understood by the leadership, they must work to promote the messages—the ideology—of the Party (Yi and Sŏ 2013: 25–34).

Juche ideology can appear somewhat chimerical, and as a consequence it has been described as little more than "a farrago of Marxist and humanist banalities" (Myers 2006, cited in Lankov 2015: 70). It is more, though. "Juche" literally means "subject," and Alzo David-West cites three volumes of Kim Il Sung's biography that sequentially define it as "independent stand," "spirit of self-reliance," and "principle of self-reliance," the three being consistent with Stalinism since they invoke party spirit (*partiinost*), national character (*narodnost*), and ideology (*ideinost*), and with Mao's notion of man as the decisive factor (2007: 138–40). John Jorgenson pithily sums up the whole complex as "culturally specific ethnic nationalism" (1996: 282), while Victor Cha states that juche makes people masters of the revolution (2012: 37–43). However, Kim Il Sung nailed himself to juche ideology, exhorting people to "inherit the tradition of single-hearted unity and be unfailingly loyal to the Party,"[19] and this is reflected in many commentaries, such as this, from his son and heir Kim Jong Il: "The juche idea is the Party's unshakeable ideology that guides our revolution to victory… [It] is a fully scientific revolutionary doctrine for man's emancipation… Kim Il Sung has established a man-centred philosophical outlook on the world for the first time in history."[20]

Juche championed sameness. The ideology took time to mature, but by the early 1960s, its impact on the production of music was clear, as an edited collection published in 1963 by the Korean Literature and Arts Federation, *Hyŏndaesŏnggwa uri ŭmak* (The present day and our music), stands witness to (e.g., Wŏn 1963). Vocal style had begun to be reformed, replacing high art's coloratura and the distinctiveness of local folksong styles (the nasal vibrato of northwestern folksongs, the hoarseness of *p'ansori* [epic storytelling through song], the vibrato, "falling tone" [*kkŏngnŭn mok*], and "sad voice" [*aewan chŏng*] of southwestern folksongs) with a plainer delivery. The new style was said to derive from folksongs, but in reality it was modeled on the 1930s and 1940s recordings and broadcasts of folksongs by professional, urban singers—some of whom had migrated to Pyongyang. The style used a consistent, silky smooth vocalization given in a relatively high tessitura— the "juche voice" (*chuch'e ch'angbŏp*)—together with a standardized deportment (rigid holds, militaristic steps and salutes, heads held high, open bodies with hands stretched out). Instruments had begun to be reformed, removing ornamentation and distinctive timbral features, much as in the smoothing out of local folksong dialects. Solo instruments were matched in ensembles, and their ranges expanded, introducing keywork and other mechanisms to enable higher and lower pitches to be produced and to replace the pentatonicism of old with Western diatonicism. The favored term *kaeryang*—Chinese *gailiang*—means "improved," but in respect to instrument development, influence came not just from China but also from the Soviet Union, where Andreyev's Russian orchestra had been established in the 1890s and the State Russian Folk Orchestra, commonly associated with its later leader, Osipov, in 1919. And, because instrumental and orchestral compositions must be popular and populist, classical but nonprogrammatic forms such as symphonies, concertos, and quartets inherited from Western art music were discarded. New compositions were to be songs, or to be based on songs, but they should utilize national elements: folkloric melodic forms, phrases, and rhythmic cycles—though with local distinctiveness removed. In fact, the structures that composers were expected to use—departing from the Soviet textbook for budding composers that had first been published at the Moscow Conservatoire in 1939—were derived from colonial-era popular songs (Rim 2014: 197–230, 269–340).[21]

Songs as Everyday Extraordinary

Juche required songs to be carefully calibrated. They were henceforth cast within formulaic *topoi*—melodic forms given particular expression by motivic arrangements, and through rhythmic and the contours of phrases.[22] *Topoi* allowed songs to recast preexisting marches and well-known songs. Songs were made portable through detachable melodies that could be rearranged in myriad forms to service the mundane and the spectacular, with or without lyrics, and with or without film or video imaging to reinforced messages. The messages, initially given by lyrics, complied with what became known as "seed theory" (*chongjaron*)—a term that seems to have first appeared in print in 1972.[23] Seeds distilled fact and fiction, reinforcing ideology through allegory, supporting an unchallengeable account of North Korean life and history, and looking forward to the utopia-to-come. And, seeds rendered creativity less important than Party policy since, as one text puts it, "The seed constitutes the core of art and determines its essential value. Only when the creator of an artwork properly determines the core is he or she able to convey appropriately the ideological and aesthetic intentions and secure the philosophical ground of the work" (Korean Association of Literary Criticism 1990: 20–1).

Songs, because lyrics gave clarity to ideology, became foundations not only for compositions but also for mass games and spectacles. Essentially, North Korea regards songs much as Lenin and Stalin did film, but where audiences can only watch films and reflect on them in subsequent group ideology sessions, so songs have become a totalizing art form, both because they can be endlessly broadcast across the country to fill public and private spaces and because they can be made participatory. In this, North Korea shifts the very concept of popular culture, going beyond how pop has been harnessed by socialist regimes across the world, whether it be the former Soviet Union (MacFadyen 2001, 2002), Uzbekistan (Klenke 2019), or East Germany (Rauhut 1998; Wicke 1992). Broadcasting, like film, readily extends from Walter Benjamin's discussion of the nineteenth-century's 360-degree panoramas or the arcades of Paris (Kang 2014: 150–201): it is able to remove the audience from the everyday world and transport them into a super-reality, reinforcing the utopic vision and rendering the extraordinary ordinary. When broadcast, then, songs are not a background soundtrack but part of control: they must be heard, and no competing broadcasts are permitted to vie for attention.

Equally importantly, North Korean songs break the "fourth curtain" as people continuously hear and continuously perform them, whether watching and listening or singing, dancing, and marching. The theater of daily life in Pyongyang is, therefore, not just a culture of observation but conforms to Michel Foucault's notion of the panopticon in *Discipline and Punish* (1977). Indeed, this has become a familiar trope in futurology, illustrated by the all-seeing Big Brother of Orwell's *1984* and in films such as *The Truman Show*.[24] North Korea has made fiction real, making observation less important than taking part, perfecting a legacy inherited across time and space from the collective unity of the German Friedrich Jahn's (1778–1852) *Turnverein* ("Turners") gymnastics movement and the Czech Miroslav Tyrs' (1832–1884) *Sokols* (Falcons), through the carnivalesque Gorky Park celebrations in the mid- and late-1930s and the nationalistic Red Square processions and parades that long outlived Stalin. Hence, North Korea's "*Arirang*" festival—held from 2002 to 2015, resuscitated with a new name in 2018, and abruptly curtailed in 2019 after the current, third-generation leader Kim Jong Un (b.1983[25]) criticized it—was performed by a claimed 100,000. "*Arirang*" featured backdrops created by children holding books of cards to form gigantic mosaics that projected around three of the four sides of the auditorium, limiting the size of the physical audience. Again, in 2000, I attended the annual mass dance of "*chŏngsonyŏn*," where 50,000 young workers and students danced for an audience of 200 or less in Kim Il Sung Square, the site of processions and parades that are North Korea's equivalent to those of Red Square under Stalin. Notwithstanding that mass spectacles are filmed, distributed, and broadcast, Kim Jong Il regarded them as enabling: participants become "fully developed communist people... firmly equipped with our Party's juche idea and the validity and great vitality of our Party's lines and policies" ("On further developing mass gymnastics," 1987: 1-2). The individual, then, surrenders to the group and, through participation, becomes harmonized with the unified collective—the populace—under their dynastic leaders. People compete, and it is a great honor to be chosen to be part of a mass spectacle (after Merkel 2013: 1254).

One of the first songs created to serve the regime and its authorized take on the everyday extraordinary was "*Kim Ilsŏng changgun ŭi norae*" (Song of General Kim Il Sung). Composed in June 1946 by Kim Wŏn'gyun (1917–2002) and setting lyrics by Ri Ch'an to celebrate the first anniversary of liberation from Japanese colonialism, this was a simple, four-square ternary march featuring dotted rhythms, pairing two-bar phrases to give four sets of four bars, all supported by clearly articulated functional harmony. It was a socialist paean, similar to Chinese *geming guqu* or Soviet *massovaya persnya* mass songs. But, it was also similar to Japanese Meiji-era *shōka*, school songs that had been popularized across the Korean peninsula (as K. *ch'angga*) during the colonial period. Written nine months after Kim Il Sung gave his first speech as he returned to Korea a month after Japan had surrendered (in September 1945), at a time when factional infighting was rife and two years before the Democratic People's Republic of Korea was declared a separate state (in September 1948), it was one of the first works to set out Kim's credentials as leader. Its lyrics conform to what became the authorized history, with Kim situated at the center of 1930s' guerrilla activities. Ever since, it has been printed as the first song in song collections, confirming its importance to the regime.

"Song of General Kim Il Sung" was soon joined by a set of "revolutionary" (*hyŏngmyŏng*) songs supposedly written during the guerrilla years. Typically, the composers are not named—the mask of anonymity maintaining Kim's preeminent position in the liberation struggle.[26] One of the most celebrated was "*Choguk ŭi p'um*" (Embrace of the Motherland), cast as a Viennese waltz, its sixteen bars dividing into four phrases giving a ternary arch. The lyrics of its two initial verses were Kim's reminiscences, describing his home and family, and reminding citizens that he fled with his mother to Manchuria in his childhood but was unable to return while Japan controlled Pyongyang:

The red glow in Moran hill,
The beautiful rainbow on Taedong river...
The new spring when azaleas are in full bloom,
The sky where the skylarks sing merrily,
The embrace of the motherland as warm as spring days
Is my mother who brought me up.

Moran (Peony) hill was where the towers of the broadcasting station stood, beneath which Kim gave his first speech in 1945, while the Taedong River passes Kim's birthplace at Man'gyŏngdae. A third verse, however, situated the song in a different time:

The morning sun rising on the sea,
The stars twinkling in the night sky,
The embrace of the motherland as bright as sunrays
In the bosom of the fatherly General.

Here, "morning sun" refers to Kim, who, as the "fatherly General," oversaw national rebuilding *after* the 1953 armistice that brought the Korean War to an end. That this third verse cannot possibly refer to Kim's guerrilla years has been explained somewhat fancifully in official organs: it was added by Kim's prodigious ten-year-old son, Kim Jong Il, in 1952.²⁷ Though, 1952 would be before reconstruction, and before the roll-out of juche and the Flying Horse campaign made Kim Il Sung's leadership immutable.

Broadcasting News through Songs

In North Korea, as elsewhere in the socialist world, the arrival of pop groups was engineered by the state. The first, Wangjaesan Light Music Band (Wangjaesan kyŏng ŭmaktan), debuted in 1983, and the second, Pochonbo Electronic Ensemble (Poch'ŏnbo chŏnja aktan), followed in 1985. Both were, according to official statements, established by North Korea's second leader, Kim Jong Il. The name of the first came from Mount Wangjae in North Hamgyŏng province, where official history has it that Kim Il Sung presided over a meeting of guerrillas. The "light music" tag allied the band to popular songs descending from colonial times that featured a persistent foxtrot rhythm (*ryuhaengga*, more commonly rendered as *taejung kayo* or, in South Korea, as *ppongtchak*) and the frequent use of nightclub instruments including saxophones—to Kim Jong Il in his treatise *On the Art of Music/Ŭmak yesullon* (published in English in 1991), saxophones had no place in Korean music except in light music. The name of the second group memorialized the site of a 1937 battle where, according to official history, Kim Il Sung fired the first bullet to signal his guerrillas to launch what proved to be a successful but short-lived attack on a police station; "electronic" indicated the use of synthesizers and electric guitars, although their manufacturer labels were carefully covered or removed to hide the capitalist companies that supplied them. The two groups generated the beginnings of a commercial music market; they toured Japan and beyond, and on a visit to Pyongyang in 1992, I witnessed long queues waiting to buy tickets for Wangjaesan performances.²⁸

If pop signaled an attempt to modernize, then song styles needed to change, without, though, challenging the primacy of seeds and keeping Party messages intact. Both Wangjaesan and Pochonbo were part of North Korea's mass-media catch-up, and as their songs tackled topical issues, songs were transformed into stories on the broadcast news and newspaper editorials explaining ideological shifts. In 1992, Wangjaesan's fourth album contained a particularly important song: "*Sahoe chuŭinŭn uri kŏya*" (Socialism Is Ours), with words and music by Ryu Yongnam. It told citizens— somewhat belatedly—that East Germany was no more and that Eastern European allies were moving away from the socialist fold. North Korea knew it faced daunting challenges: a rapprochement between China and South Korea had begun with the 1988 Seoul Olympics and the 1990 Beijing Asian Games, and formal diplomatic relations were established in 1992, two years after the Soviet Union and South Korea signed formal agreements. North Korea had long relied on an unequal barter trade, not least for imports of Soviet oil and advanced technology, but by 1992, both major former allies were demanding hard currency for goods. With the Kim family so tied to North Korean ideology, Pyongyang had little flexibility in what it could do; hence, "Socialism Is Ours" ran:

We go straight along the path we have chosen,
Though others forsake, we remain faithful.
Socialism is ours, socialism is ours,
Socialism defended by our Party's red flag is ours.
We'll never follow others' styles and fashions
We'll be firm even though the wind blows.

Jumping forward, Kim Jong Il, who succeeded Kim Il Sung after the latter's death in 1994, disappeared from public view in 2008. He had suffered what commentators concluded were one or more strokes.[29] Resolving who would be his successor became unexpectedly urgent, and it was songs that announced the succession. Kim Jong Il had three sons, but the eldest two were compromised: Kim Chŏngnam (1971–2017), by his father's first mistress, the film actor Song Hyerim, had in 2001 fallen from grace after being arrested at Narita Airport traveling on a fake passport and was eventually murdered in Kuala Lumpur in 2017, most likely on the order of his youngest half-brother, Kim Jong Un. The second son, Kim Chŏngch'ŏl (b.1981), by Kim Jong Il's consort Ko Yŏnghŭi, was considered "unmanly." This left the youngest son, Kim Jong Un, the second with Ko Yŏnghŭi. He began to emerge from obscurity in March 2009, when he was named on the ballot for elections to the Supreme People's Assembly.[30] At the same time a new song premiered, "*Palkŏrŭm*" (Footsteps), which did not name the younger son but announced the achievements of the "general" (*taejang*), eighteen months before Kim was elevated to such a rank. Growing up in a cloistered environment, he had never served in the military, but "Footsteps" squared the circle, portraying an unstoppable forward trajectory in which the youthful, vigorous successor walked in Kim Jong Il's footsteps and would bring no sharp policy shifts—this is the message given by the mention of February, the month of Kim Jong Il's birth:

Tramp, tramp, tramp,
The footsteps of our *taejang*,
Spreading the spirit of February,
Tramp, tramp, tramping upwards.
Footsteps, Footsteps,
Stepping with vigorous energy,
Strongly throughout the land,
March with the convoys,
Tramp, tramp, tramp.

The song was broadcast everywhere. In September, a radio report from Tokyo by Mark Willacy for Australia's ABC network noted how the song was being hummed on farms and in factories. The "general's" footsteps were said to make mountains and rivers murmur with joy. The national soccer team had just qualified for the 2010 World Cup, and one of its number reported to ABC how the team "sang the song with deep emotion; it inspired us to win!" It was used as the backing track for synchronized swimming and gymnastic displays (although such frivolity has subsequently been deemed inappropriate). It was used for parades. Kim Jong Un followed through on a revitalization of cultural production that his father had started, exploring the potentials of new groups, and sidelining Wangjaesan and Pochonbo. This was particularly apparent when the all-girl group Moranbong debuted on June 6, 2012: "The beauty of its members, their fashion-creating hairstyles and make-up, and the jewelry worn with all kinds of outfits, symbolized that life could be good in present North Korea, especially among its middle and higher urban classes enjoying the benefits of the new economy" (Korhonen and Cathcart 2017: 15).

Behind the public face of North Korea, the early 2000s had seen the emergence of a nouveau-riche urban elite, and outlets were needed to satisfy the consumption habits of their offspring. Bored with established song production, these began to secretly consume South Korean pop and, reportedly, to frequent secret nightclubs. Moranbong, flouting modernity, was intended to sate their needs. Its synthesizers now proudly displayed Roland manufacturer labels; skeleton Yamaha violins and cellos provided melodic interest. Its instrumentalists acted like stars, moving sinuously, demanding attention. It was North Korea's equivalent to China's 12 Girls' Band: both mixed local and foreign music; both featured cute, consummate instrumentalists; and both mixed tightly rehearsed extended solos with group extemporizations. Complex lighting and lasers made stages sparkle, while video backdrops reminded audiences of the missing lyrics.

Moranbong was designed to be consumed online; it has also been argued that it was meant to counter furtive imports of South Korean bubble-gum pop (Chŏn 2015; Draudt and Lee 2013; Kim 2014).[31] However, Moranbong songs, even in instrumental versions, kept the familiar—songs that linked the three generations of leaders, that told the official history, and that retold the everyday extraordinary. The portable frame was kept, and video backdrops featuring military operations, rocket launches, and on-the-spot guidance by the Kim dynasty reinforced the messages. Certainly, some renditions were meta versions of old songs—new suits of clothes upping the tempo, adding beats and melodic decorations. Still, Korhonen and Cathcart note how Moranbong members were "visibly moved" and played "with emotion and strength" when they celebrated the December 2012 launch of a satellite and how they visited a military base in April 2013 to play for conscripts in the midst of a major security crisis (2017: 16, 18–19). Again, Zeglen writes about their 2012 concert commemorating the 1953 armistice that ended the Korean war (2017: 145), while Kim and Han (2013) explore their 2013 New Year celebration of the Party.

Conclusion

Has anything really changed? State control was never far away, and it reasserted itself in October 2013, when Moranbong's lead violinist Sŏnu Hyanghŭi vanished. She reappeared briefly in March 2014 only to disappear again two months later. The whole band briefly vanished in July 2015. Rumors spread about executions, and more. When they resurfaced in September 2015 (Sŏnu returned only in December), the members were chastened. Their outfits were less sexy. They wore less makeup. Musical arrangements had been simplified, and singers were added to the line-up who returned to the juche voice. Soon, Moranbong had the opportunity to prove loyalty: having arrived in China for a high-profile tour, they returned to Pyongyang before their first concert, responding to Chinese government criticism of North Korean nuclear tests. Censorship, control, and violence: the state mechanisms of old were still in place. And control had been deemed necessary, removing the vagueness of message in instrumental renditions of songs, and returning to songs with lyrics that restated the everyday extraordinary, songs that would—or were intended to—harmonize the people.

When the Winter Olympic Games were held in PyeongChang, South Korea, in 2018, late in the day, North Korea decided it would participate. In January 2018 a delegation was dispatched to negotiate terms. One of its members was Hyŏn Songwŏl, who had come to prominence as a singer with Pochonbo, who had been appointed a merit artist, and who had once directed Moranbong: she was received as a pop star by the southern media. In February a large troupe with 137 members—Samjiyŏn—was sent to give two concerts, one near the Olympic site and one in Seoul. Samjiyŏn, taking its name from an area where guerrillas had been supposedly based in the 1930s, began as an all-female ensemble spun out from the veritable Mansudae Art Troupe in 2009. For some years, it had languished as Moranbong hogged the spotlight, but now, enlarged and mixed, it began its two performances with the Pochonbo song, "We Are Glad," and made its way through a medley from *Phantom of the Opera* and the "Derry Air"-based "You Raise Me Up." There were North and South Korean songs, but while Samjiyŏn kept away from ideological songs about the northern leadership and its military, its repertoire remained, doggedly, songs. Songs, the everyday extraordinary, remained, but now songs were sung to unify a divided people.

Notes

1 Commentators consider Kim Jong Il was born in 1941, but a 1942 birthdate is given in official accounts, most likely to align more auspiciously with his father's birthdate.
2 This chapter reports part of my ongoing research on North Korean music. My research has been conducted as Kent R. Mullikin Fellow at the National Humanities Center, North Carolina (2017–18), and with the support of a Leverhulme Trust

Emeritus Fellowship (2018–20). A fuller consideration of my topic here is in Howard (2020).

3   Published in *Sovetskaya muzika* 1 (1948: 14–26), and reprinted in Zhdanov (1950, chapter 3) and at http://www.marxists.org/subject/art/lit_crit/zhdanov/lit-music-philosophy.htm, accessed May 26, 2020.

4   See, "The Zhdanov Decree 1948," http://dschjournal.com/wordpress/onlinearticles/dsch09_zhdanov.pdf, accessed May 26, 2020. The decree details are beyond my scope here, and even Frolova-Walker sensibly prefaces her discussion (2016: 222–57) with the comment "the story is long and complex."

5   John Blacking, after for a while attempting to apply Chomskian linguistics to music, backtracked in works subsequent to *How Musical Is Man?* (1973), as he accepted that analogies between musical grammar and speech grammar were inexact and partial.

6   http://freemuse.org/freemuseArchives/freerip/freemuse.org/sw18963.html, accessed May 26, 2020.

7   http://www.channel5.com/show/michael-palin-in-north-korea/, accessed May 26, 2020.

8   The upper components of this hierarchical structure, as it operated in 1980, are discussed by Seekins (1981: 97ff), who notes a double screening of all cultural production by a committee within the union and then by Party censors is (or was, in 1981) standard. A more comprehensive South Korean account of the structure, detailing changes from the 1960s through to the 1980s, is by No and Song (1990: 116–28).

9   Parallels can be drawn to other totalitarian states. Frolova-Walker and Walker (2012: 310–13) translate an account by Davidenko about how he composed a song, note by note, trying out many versions until satisfied with a version to put before his colleagues in the Soviet Union.

10 http://www.liberationday.film/film/, accessed May 26, 2020.

11 In recent years, policing has involved searching for thumb drives and DVD players (for which, see Hassig and Oh [2015: 111–15], Boynton's 2011 report in *The Atlantic*, "North Korea's Digital Underground," http://www.theatlantic.com/magazine/archive/2011/04/north-koreas-digital-underground/308414/, accessed May 26, 2020, and http://www.vice.com/en_us/article/7x9x8d/north-koreas-secret-weapon-is-terrible-synth-pop), accessed May 26, 2020. Note that one persistent rumor is that televisions in Pyongyang hotels are bugged, adding to the expectation that visitors to North Korea will be monitored day and night.

12 Recent years have seen increases in the smuggling of phones, chips, and thumb drives into North Korea, and as a result some defectors in China and South Korea have been able to contact family members remaining in the North. Pyongyang, not surprisingly, attempts to crack down on such contacts from time to time and introduces ever more sophisticated technology to counteract potential threats to its monopoly on information. See, e.g., http://thediplomat.com/2018/08/whats-behind-north-koreas-new-internet-opening/, accessed May 26, 2020; http://www.38north.org/2018/08/mwilliams080118/, accessed May 26, 2020; https://nknetobserver.github.io; http://www.bbc.co.uk/news/world-asia-37426725, accessed May 26, 2020. A recent crackdown has involved the confiscation of karaoke equipment—including machines manufactured in North Korea—searching for illicit South Korean pop hidden within playlists (see Leonzini 2020).

13 Discs were of larger diameter than the twelve-inch LPs, which became standard in the mid-1950s. A valuable collection of recordings made during the period is Theodore

(Ted) Conant's collection, now housed at the Starr East Asian Library at Columbia University, New York. Conant worked as a recording engineer for the UN command but stayed behind after the war until the early 1960s.

14 Tertitski and Tertitskiy (2019) give a critique of the guerrilla activities claimed by the state, focusing on his newly discovered 1941 Soviet personal file.
15 Particularly among the so-called "cultural nationalist" (*munhwa undong*) loose grouping of writers, folklorists, and entrepreneurs; see further Robinson (1988).
16 In Kim Il Sung *Selected Works* 1 (1971: 582–606).
17 For the parallel Soviet movement, see Siegelbaum (1990).
18 Stalin's dictum, socialist in content and national in form, is discussed in respect to the Soviet cultural commissar and playwright Lunacharsky by Frolova-Walker (1998: 331–71).
19 "Young people must accomplish the revolutionary cause of Juche, upholding the leadership of the Party," a letter addressed to the Eighth Congress of the League of Socialist Working Youth, January 22, 1993 (1993: 5).
20 "On some problems of education in the Juche idea," a talk to senior officials of the Central Committee of the Korean Workers Party, July 15, 1986 (English version, published as a booklet in 1987, cited here, with Romanization adjusted). Also available at http://purl.library.uoregon.edu/e-asia/ebooks/read/3020.pdf, accessed May 26, 2020.
21 Boris Krasin's 1918 report on the Music Section of the Moscow Proletkult, and both earlier and later collections of folksong in Russia and the Soviet Union attest to the same ideas, while in China, folksong anthologies by the likes of the composer Xian Xinghai gave way to folksong adaptations with new ideological texts (see Mittler 1997: 30–1; Taruskin 1997).
22 This idea is applied to North Korean revolutionary operas by Lisa Burnett (2016: 23–4), citing Carl Dalhaus (1985) and others in respect to the *topoi* concept in Wagner, but also Richard Taruskin's (2008) analysis of Prokofiev and Isabel Wong's (1984) consideration of Mao's China.
23 The year 1972 marked the beginnings of a concerted effort to create a theory around "revolutionary operas" (*hyŏngmyŏng kagŭk*), seen in the pages of two monthly journals, *Chosŏn ŭmak (Korean Music)* and *Chosŏn yesul (Korean Arts)*. The first revolutionary opera, "*P'i pada*" (Sea of Blood), premiered in 1971.
24 As cited in Fischer (2015: 211). Ryang (2012: 50ff) explores the all-pervasive presence of Kim Il Sung, permanently observing, even in death, from his portraits in every household and public building.
25 Or 1984. North Korea has never formally announced when he was born.
26 While "revolutionary" is used elsewhere in the socialist world, the term *pulmyŏl* ("immortal") has become a standard marker for cultural products that celebrate the leadership cult. This is discussed in respect to literature by Meredith Shaw, in "Inside North Korea's literary fiction factory" (http://thewire.in/218228/inside-north-koreas-literary-fiction-factory/, accessed May 26, 2020).
27 *Chosŏn ŭi onŭl (Korea Today)*, April 4, 2016 (http://www.dprktoday.com/index.php?type=2&no=11692, accessed May 26, 2020).
28 I was told by my guide that a ticket cost 3 *wŏn*, about 10 percent of the average monthly wage at the time.
29 Kim was beset by illness; although since state media only showed him in still photographs, his words spoken by others, determining much about his health was

never easy. He disappeared from view in August 2008, but it was only when he failed to attend a military parade to mark sixty years of the state's existence a month later that rumors began to multiply.
30 http://news.bbc.co.uk/1/hi/world/asia-pacific/7930775.stm, accessed May 26, 2020.
31 See also "North Korean Celebrities Are Struggling Because of the Hallyu Wave." http://www.allkpop.com/article/2011/11/north-korean-celebrities-are-struggling-because-of-the-hallyu-wave, accessed May 26, 2020.

Bibliography

Adams, Laura. 2010. *The Spectacular State: Culture and National Identity in Uzbekistan*. Durham, NC: Duke University Press.
Adlington, Robert. 2013. "Communisms, Communist Music." In *Red Strains: Music and Communism Outside the Communist Bloc*, edited by Robert Adlington, 1–19. Oxford: Oxford University Press.
Agawu, Kofi. 2003. *Representing African Music: Postcolonial Notes, Queries, Positions*. New York: Routledge.
Althusser, Louis. 1971. "Ideology and Ideological State Apparatus (Notes towards an Investigation)." In *Lenin and Philosophy and Other Essays*. Translated by Andy Blunden. New York: Monthly Review Press. Available online: http://www.marxists.org/reference/archive/althusser/1970/ideology.htm, accessed June 1, 2020.
Armstrong, Charles K. 2003. *The North Korean Revolution, 1945–1950*. Ithaca, NY: Cornell University Press.
Attali, Jacques. 1977. *Noise: The Political Economy of Music*. Translated by Brian Massumi. Minneapolis: University of Minnesota Press.
Blacking, John. 1973. *How Musical Is Man?* Seattle: University of Washington Press.
Burnett, Lisa. 2016. "The Artwork of the People: A History of the Gesamtkunstwerk from Richard Wagner to Kim Jong Il." PhD thesis, Stanford University.
Carter, Jason. 2007. "Guitar Diplomacy." *Songlines* 46: 17.
Cha, Victor. 2012. *The Impossible State: North Korea, Past and Future*. New York: HarperCollins.
Chŏn Hyŏnshik. 2015. "Moranbong aktan ŭi ŭmak chŏngch'i." *Shinjin yŏn'gu nonmunjip* 7: 514–614.
Coronil, Fernando, and Julie Skurski, eds. 2006. *States of Violence*. Ann Arbor, MI: University of Michigan Press.
Dalhaus, Carl. 1985. *Richard Wagner's Musikdramen*. Stuttgart: Reclam.
David-West, Alzo. 2007. "Marxism, Stalinism, and the *Juche* Speech of 1955: On the Theoretical De-Stalinization of North Korea." *The Review of Korean Studies* 10 (3): 127–52.
Debord, Guy. 2010. *The Society of the Spectacle*. Detroit: Black and Red.
Draudt, Darcie, and Jimin Lee. 2013. "Packaged and Controlled by the Masculine State: Moranbong Band and Gender in New Choson-Style Performance." *Sino–NK*, May 3. Available online: http://sinonk.com/2013/05/03/packaged-and-controlled-by-the-masculine-state-moranbong-band-and-gender-in-new-choson-style-performance/ accessed June 5, 2020.
Fairclough, Pauline. 2016. *Classics for the Masses: Shaping Soviet Musical Identity under Lenin and Stalin*. New Haven, CT: Yale University Press.

Fischer, Paul. 2015. *A Kim Jong-Il Production: Kidnap, Torture, Murder… Making Movies North Korean Style*. New York: Viking.

Fitzpatrick, Sheila. 1979. *Education and Social Mobility in the Soviet Union, 1921–1934*. Cambridge: Cambridge University Press.

Foucault, Michel. 1977. *Discipline and Punish: The Birth of the Prison*. Translated by Alan Sheridan. New York: Pantheon.

Frolova-Walker, Marina. 1998. "'National in Form, Socialist in Content': Musical Nation-Building in the Soviet Republics." *Journal of the American Musicological Society* 51 (2): 331–71.

Frolova-Walker, Marina. 2016. *Stalin's Music Prize: Soviet Culture and Politics*. New Haven: Yale University Press.

Frolova-Walker, Marina, and Jonathan Walker. 2012. *Music and Soviet Power, 1917–32*. Woodbridge: Boydell Press.

Fuchs, Eckhardt, Tokushi Kasahara, and Sven Saaler, eds. 2018. *A New Modern History of East Asia*. Göttingen: V&R unipress GmbH.

Gabroussenko, Tatiana. 2010. *Soldiers on the Cultural Front: Developments in the Early History of North Korean Literature and Literary Policy*. Honolulu: University of Hawai'i Press.

Gittings, John. 1993. "The Secret of Kim Il Sung." *Papers of the British Association for Korean Studies* 4: 31–58.

Han, Hongkoo. 2013. "Colonial Origins of Juche: The Minsaengdan Incident of the 1930s and the Birth of the North Korea-China Relationship." In *Origins of North Korea's Juche: Colonialism, War, and Development*, edited by Jae-Jung Suh, 33–62. Lanham: Lexington Books.

Hassig, Ralph, and Kongdan Oh. 2015. *The Hidden People of North Korea: Everyday Life in the Hermit Kingdom*. Lanham: Rowman and Littlefield.

Howard, Keith. 2020. *Songs for "Great Leaders:" Ideology and Creativity in North Korean Music and Dance*. New York: Oxford University Press.

Jorgenson, John. 1996. "Tan'gun and the Legitimization of a Threatened Dynasty: North Korea's Rediscovery of Tan'gun." *Korea Observer* 27 (2): 273–306.

Kang, Jaeho. 2014. *Walter Benjamin and the Media*. Cambridge: Polity.

Kim, Cheehyung Harrison. 2018. *Heroes and Toilers: Work as Life in Postwar North Korea, 1953–1961*. New York: Columbia University Press.

Kim, Suk-Young. 2014. *DMZ Crossing: Performing Emotional Citizenship Along the Korean Border*. New York: Columbia University Press.

Kim, Sumin, and Han Sŭngho. 2013. "2013-nyŏn Moranbong aktan shinnyŏm ŭmakhoe ŭi ŭimiwa chŏngch'ijŏk ŭido." *P'yŏnghwahak yŏn'gu/The Journal of Peace Studies* 14 (4): 247–64.

Klenke, Kirsten. 2019. *The Sound State of Uzbekistan: Popular Music and Politics in the Karimov Era*. Abingdon: Routledge.

Korhonen, Pekka, and Adam Cathcart. 2017. "Tradition and Legitimation in North Korea: The Role of the Moranbong Band." *The Review of Korean Studies* 20 (2): 7–32.

Kwŏn, Yŏngmin. 1991. "Literature and Art in North Korea: Theory and Policy." *Korea Journal* 31 (6): 56–70.

Lankov, Andrei. 2015. *The Real North Korea: Life and Politics in the Failed Stalinist Utopia*. New York: Oxford University Press.

Leonzini, Alexandra. 2020. "More Than Just Simple Fun: North Korean Karaoke in Pyongyang and Beyond." *European Journal of Korean Studies* 19 (2): 109–28.

Lunacharsky, Anatoly. 1967. *V. I. Lenin: On Literature and Art*. Moscow: Progress Publishers.
MacFadyen, David. 2001. *Red Stars: Personality and the Soviet Popular Song, 1955–1991*. Montreal: McGill-Queen's University Press.
MacFadyen, David. 2002. *Songs for Fat People: Affect, Emotion, and Celebrity in the Russian Popular Song, 1900–1955*. Montreal: McGill-Queen's University Press.
Maliangkay, Roald. 2006a. "Pop for Progress: Censorship and South Korea's Propaganda Songs." In *Korean Pop Music: Riding the Wave*, edited by Keith Howard, 48–61. Folkestone: Global Oriental.
Maliangkay, Roald. 2006b. "Supporting Our Boys: American Military Entertainment and Korean Pop Music in the 1950s and Early-1960s." In *Korean Pop Music: Riding the Wave*, edited by Keith Howard, 21–33. Folkestone: Global Oriental.
Merkel, Udo. 2013. "'The Grand Mass Gymnastics and Artistic Performance Arirang' (2002–2012): North Korea's Socialist-Realist Response to Global Sports Spectacles." *The International Journal of the History of Sport* 30 (11): 1247–58.
Mittler, Barbara. 1997. *Dangerous Tunes: The Politics of Chinese Music in Hong Kong, Taiwan, and the Republic of China since 1949*. Wiesbaden: Harrassowitz Verlag.
Myers, Brian. 2006. "The Watershed That Wasn't: Re-evaluating Kim Il Sung's 'Juche Speech' of 1955." *Acta Koreana* 9 (1): 89–115.
No Tongŭn, and Song Pangsong. 1990. "Pukhan ŭi ŭmak." In *Pukhan ŭi yesul*, edited by Kim Munhwan, 91–200. Seoul: Ŭryu munhwasa.
Perris, Arnold. 1985. *Music as Propaganda: Art to Persuade, Art to Control*. Westport: Greenwood Press.
Rauhut, Michael. 1998. "Looking East: The Socialist Rock Alternative in the 1970s." In *Popular Music. Intercultural Interpretations*, edited by Toru Mitsui, 343–8. Kanazawa: Kanazawa University.
Rim Kwangho. 2014. *Urishik kojŏn ŭmak. Chosŏn sahoe kwahak haksulchip* 493: *Munhak p'yŏn*. Pyongyang: Sahoe kwahak ch'ulp'ansa.
Robinson, Michael. 1988. *Cultural Nationalism in Colonial Korea, 1920–1925*. Seattle: University of Washington.
Robinson, Michael. 1999. "Broadcasting, Cultural Hegemony, and Colonial Modernity in Korea, 1924–1945." In *Colonial Modernity in Korea*, edited by Gi-Wook Shin and Michael Robinson, 52–69. Cambridge, MA: Harvard University Asia Center.
Ryang, Sonia. 2012. *Reading North Korea: An Ethnological Inquiry*. Cambridge, MA: Harvard University Asia Center/Harvard University Press.
Saunders, Frances Stonor. 1999. *Who Paid the Piper? The CIA and the Cultural Cold War*. London: Granta Books.
Schwarz, Boris. 1983. *Music and Musical Life in Soviet Russia, 1917–1981*. Bloomington, IN: Indiana University Press.
Seekins, Donald M. 1981. "The Society and Its Environment." In *North Korea: A Country Study*, edited by Frederica M. Bunge, 47–105. Washington: Foreign Area Studies, The American University.
Siegelbaum, Lewis H. 1990. *Stakhanovism and the Politics of Productivity in the USSR, 1935–1941*. Cambridge: Cambridge University Press.
Suh, Dae Sook. 1988. *Kim Il Sung: The North Korean Leader*. New York: Columbia University Press.
Suh, Jae-Jung. 2013. "Making Sense of North Korea: Juche as an Institution." In *Origins of North Korea's Juche: Colonialism, War, and Development*, edited by Jae-Jung Suh, 1–32. Lanham: Lexington Books.

Taruskin, Richard. 1997. *Defining Russia Musically*. Princeton, NY: Princeton University Press.
Taruskin, Richard. 2008. *On Russian Music*. Berkeley, CA: University of California Press.
Taruskin, Richard. 2010. *The Danger of Music and Other Anti-Utopian Essays*. Berkeley, CA: University of California Press.
Tertitski, Konstantin, and Fyodor Tertitskiy. 2019. "The Personal File of Jin Richeng (Kim Il-sung): New Information on the Early Years of the First Ruler of North Korea." *Acta Koreana* 22 (1): 111–28.
Verdery, Katherine. 1991. *National Ideology under Socialism: Identity and Cultural Politics in Ceauşescu's Romania*. Berkeley and Los Angeles, CA: University of California Press.
Wicke, Peter. 1992. "The Times They Are a-Changin': Rock Music and Political Change in East Germany." In *Rockin' the Boat: Mass Music and Mass Movements*, edited by Reebee Garofalo, 81–92. Boston, MA: South End Press.
Wŏn Hŭngnyong. 1963. "Ch'anggŭk 'Hongnumong' ŭi ŭmage taehayŏ." In *Hyŏndaesŏnggwa uri ŭmak*, 114–40. Pyongyang: Chosŏn munhwa yesul ch'ong tongmaeng ch'ulp'ansa.
Wong, Isabel K. F. 1984. "Geming Gequ: Songs for the Education of the Masses." In *Popular Chinese Literature and Performing Arts in the People's Republic of China, 1949–1979*, edited by Bonnie McDougall and Paul Clark, 112–43. Berkeley, CA: University of California Press.
Yi Hyŏnju. 2006. *Pukhan ŭmakkwa chuch'e ch'ŏlhak*. Seoul: Minsogwŏn.
Yi Yongdŭk, and Sŏ Chaegyŏng. 2013. *Chuch'e ŭi ŭmak yesul riron. Chosŏn sahoe kwahak haksulchip* 426. Pyongyang: Sahoe kwahak ch'ulp'ansa.
Zeglen, David. 2017. "Rockin' in the Unfree World: North Korea's Moranbong Band and the Celebrity Dictator." *Celebrity Studies* 8 (1): 142–50.
Zhdanov, Andrei. 1950. *Essays on Literature, Philosophy and Music*. New York: International Publishers.

8

The Party and the People: Shifting Sonic Politics in Post-1949 Tiananmen Square

Joseph Lovell

To most people visiting Beijing's Tiananmen Square today, from the Chinese mainland or elsewhere, it is images from the People's Republic of China (PRC) era (post-1949) that would most likely be called to mind. Tiananmen Square is a public political space, of great national importance and international renown, which evokes memories of the Mao Zedong years, past National and May Day parades, large rallies, and major public protests. Outside of China, the historical event most strongly associated with Tiananmen Square is the protest there that formed part of the wider democracy movement in 1989, which was violently suppressed by the Chinese Communist Party (CCP). Images related to Tiananmen Square, such as Mao with the Red Guards at the beginning of the Cultural Revolution (1966–76), and the "Tank Man" photograph, of the individual who defiantly stood before a column of People's Liberation Army (PLA) tanks in 1989, are regarded as iconic.

As this chapter will argue, however, it is not just the famous images from Tiananmen Square that have an afterlife. The sounds, as well as the sights, at many previous Tiananmen Square events still evoke memories and have a sense of power. This sense of power, which I argue was present in the chanting and singing at Mao era (1949–76) Tiananmen Square parades, rallies, and other public events, is something that was apparent in post-Mao public protests at Tiananmen Square and is something that still needs to be carefully managed by the CCP. It is a sense of power that was developed by the "revolutionary" history of Tiananmen Square, the symbolism of the site and its monuments, and the intense sonic politics of public events in this space during the Mao years.

On October 1, 1949, when Mao Zedong proclaimed the founding of the PRC from the top of Tiananmen (the famous "gate" at the northern end of the plaza, known as the "Gate of Heavenly Peace"), he faced a T-shaped space (see Figure 8.1), rather than the vast quadrangle that now exists. Extensive reconstruction work on this area in central Beijing, which necessitated the demolition and removal of numerous walls, gates, roads, and various other pieces of architecture, began shortly afterwards, and by the time of the tenth anniversary of the PRC's founding, Tiananmen Square looked more or less as it does today.

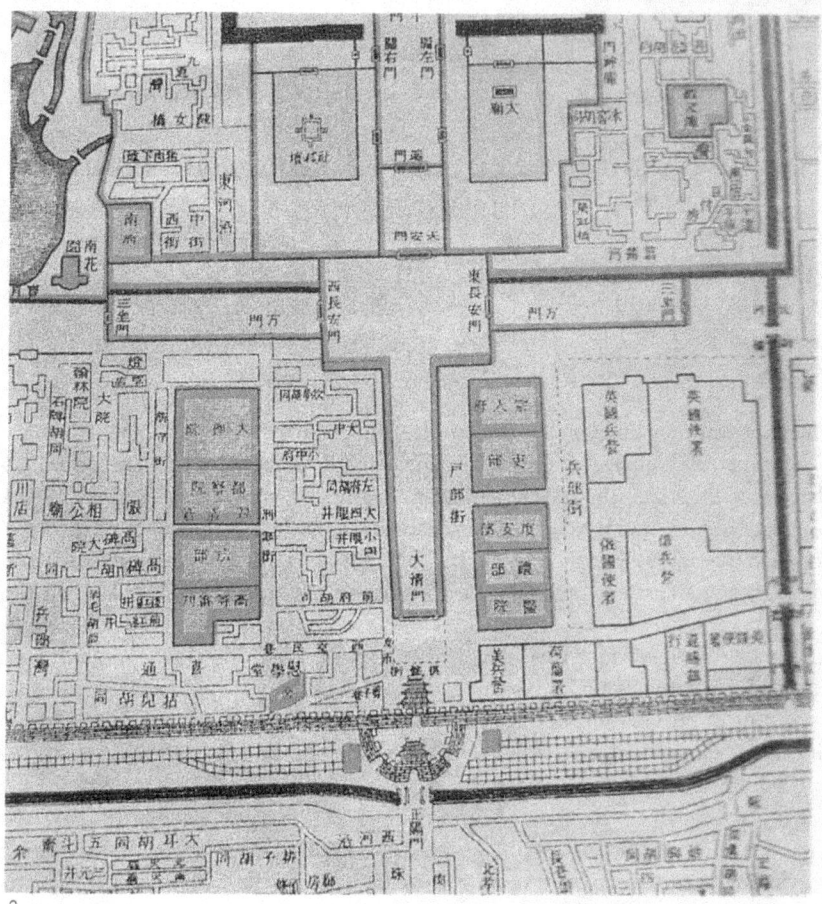

Figure 8.1 Tiananmen Square during the late Qing dynasty from a map of Beijing published in 1908. Tiananmen stands in front of the T-shaped space that still existed in 1949. Source: Wu Hung.

This rapid transformation was motivated by the planned staging of a National Day parade on the PRC's tenth anniversary in 1959, to showcase the achievements of the CCP and the strength of a resurgent China. A variety of monuments and buildings were erected around the square before this event, each with a specific symbolic meaning that consecrated Mao, Maoist thought, the revolutionary history of the Chinese people, and foundational CCP doctrines. The new structures that, along with Tiananmen, surrounded the square included: the Great Hall of the People (the Congress), the Museum of Chinese History, and the Monument to the People's Heroes, which stands near the center of the plaza (see Figure 8.2).

Shortly after Mao died in 1976, the CCP put 700,000 "volunteers" to work around the clock to construct a Memorial Hall honoring him (Schell 1994: 26). Mao's body

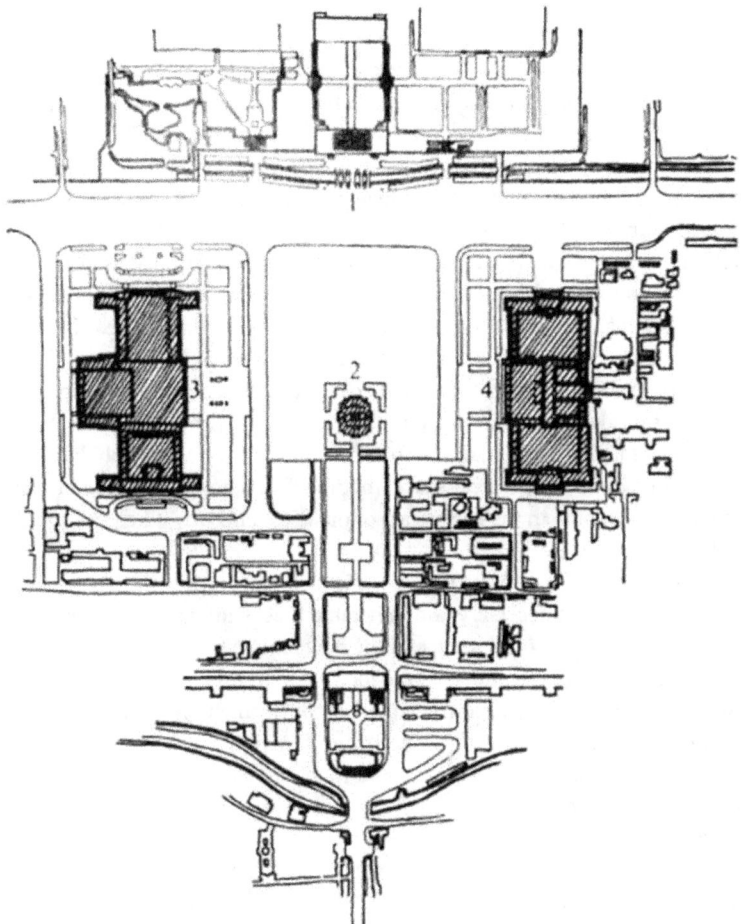

Figure 8.2 Tiananmen Square in 1959: 1. Tiananmen; 2. Monument to the People's Heroes; 3. Great Hall of the People; 4. Museum of Chinese History. Mao's Mausoleum now stands south of the Monument to the People's Heroes. Source: Wu Hung.

was embalmed and it has been kept in the Memorial Hall (or Mausoleum), situated at the southern end of the plaza, ever since. This building represents, according to Ellen Laing, a "repository of political symbolism signifying a closed chapter in the history of the [CCP] and the [PRC]" because it literally closes off Tiananmen Square (Laing quoted in Hung 2005: 130).

Laing contends that Tiananmen Square, with the construction of its surrounding buildings and monuments, became a symbolic political space. Each part of Tiananmen Square and its environs—in place by 1959—represented something about the CCP, the PRC, and its leader: Mao's portrait was at the front and center of Tiananmen, an obvious symbol of the new leader's dominance; the Congress and the Chinese History Museum, which flanked the square's sides, displayed the strength of the ruling government and China's long history; and the Monument to the People's Heroes reflected China's recent past (known as the *bainian chiru*, the "century of humiliation," 1839–1949, from the First Opium War to the founding of the PRC), its liberation, and the main architect and supposed beneficiary of its future: "the people," through its bas-relief representations of key historical revolutionary episodes, seen as "prototypes of 'people's revolution'" (Schell 1994: 25).[1]

Nelson Lee argues that it was the May 4, 1919, demonstration at Tiananmen, which was provoked by anger over the Treaty of Versailles, that converted this "empty space in front of [Tiananmen] into a public space of political significance" (Lee 2009: 32). Tiananmen and its surrounding area had long before this been regarded more as a central point in the Chinese national and cosmological perception, and in connection to a range of fundamental Chinese philosophical and cosmological concepts (Meyer 1991).[2] It was for these two main reasons, its long history as a symbolic site, and its new function as a public political space, that the CCP chose Tiananmen to remain as the center of the capital in the early years of the PRC, and why it became a focal point, around which the CCP rebuilt the city.[3]

To Mao, who had the firm ideological belief that "revolution meant destruction and transformation," it was necessary and inevitable that Beijing should be greatly altered and remade in the image of himself, and the new regime (Hung 2005: 8). Mao Zedong and Tiananmen Square remain closely associated, and this connection was reinforced by music as well as visual symbolism. For example, during the Cultural Revolution, the song "I Love Beijing Tiananmen" (*wo ai Beijing Tiananmen*) by Jin Yueling (composed in 1970), with its lyrics "I love Beijing Tiananmen, The sun rises above Tiananmen, The great leader Chairman Mao, Leads all of us forward," was sung daily by schoolchildren, all across China.

The connections between Mao and Tiananmen Square and the connections between state and society were also influenced by the sonic aspects of significant public events at the plaza, as well as pieces of music, and the site's visual symbolism, which has been analyzed by Wu Hung (2005) and Chang-tai Hung (2007) among others. These sonic aspects of public events at Tiananmen Square, including chanting and singing, have not received as much scholarly attention as the visual aspects of events and rituals held there. However, for those who attended parades or rallies at Tiananmen Square, and have given accounts of them, the sonic aspects of such events clearly formed a significant part of their experiences, and subsequent recollections.

In this chapter I will analyze written accounts, such as memoirs and British Foreign office records, to consider the implications of the rebuilding of Tiananmen Square on the sonic aspects of important events in this space, and how the sonic politics of this especially symbolic site resonated across China, owing to technological mediation. According to my research, two elements of the Tiananmen Square soundscape dominate accounts of significant public events there post 1949: the voice of the people and the voice of the party. Both of these key soundscape elements reflected and inspired sonic environments across China and, when broadcast throughout the nation, influenced how Chinese citizens identified with the new CCP regime and how individuals related to the masses. These two notable aspects of the soundscape developed significantly during the Mao years (the period which is this chapter's primary focus), in events at this huge public political space imbued with deep symbolism. Since the death of Mao, the tension between these two voices has required careful management by the party, which raises the question of whether or not the political symbolism of Tiananmen Square truly became a "closed chapter," as Ellen Laing stated (Laing quoted in Hung 2005: 120), with the construction of Mao's mausoleum.

Why Focus on Sound?

Studies of public events at Tiananmen Square, like most cultural historical studies generally, have tended to privilege the visual over the aural.[4] A result of this bias toward the visual is that, where the state and society relationship is concerned, we are usually left with a clearer understanding of what messages the state was attempting to convey, rather than how these messages were received by society. For example, we can see the architecture of Tiananmen Square, the design of particular monuments there, and the placards that were used in parades, but we do not know if the symbolism explicated by an author really registered with those that saw these things firsthand—or if audiences could even see them. Sound would have been impactful on people regardless of where they were standing during any event in Tiananmen Square, however, and it would have been inescapable in many other moments when the visual would not have registered. This suggests that a focus on sound could complement our apprehension of the real effectiveness of CCP propaganda and political work at Tiananmen Square and beyond.

Another reason why sound during the Mao years should be studied more is simply because amplified sound technologies and sound-based political work were clearly of importance to the CCP. An analysis of the extensive sound-based political work of the CCP, to which this chapter is contributing, could reveal much about the relative importance and effectiveness of sound in the role of propaganda work. The CCP stated in a 1950 *People's Daily* editorial that "radio broadcasting is the single most powerful educational and propaganda tool for the masses," with "outstanding potential… especially… in places where transportation and communication are inconvenient; for the large number of illiterate people; and in cases where newspaper circulation is difficult to achieve" (Kielman 2017: 221). As the CCP knew, the two main reasons why amplified sound had more power than printed media were the low literacy rate and the poor infrastructure that existed when the PRC was established. These facts are attested to elsewhere. According to the Chinese Ministry of Education the literacy rate in the PRC in 1950 was 20 percent,[5] and at this time China was considered to be "less well provided with transport facilities than any other large country in the world" (Comtois 1990: 784).

In the first few decades of the PRC era, the party dramatically increased amplified sound sources across the nation: in 1949 there were 500 loudspeakers in China. In 1957 there were 993,200 and this increased significantly to 2,987,500 in 1958. By 1964 there was said to be 6,000,000. In the same period (1949–64) the number of radio stations in China grew from just 8 to 1,975 (Liu 1975: 120). These figures tell us something about the emphasis that the CCP placed on new media, as well as increased output and improved technical expertise at places such as the East German-designed North China Wireless Electronics Materials Factory (*Huabei wuxiandian qicai lianhechang*), which enabled the production of transistorized sound equipment by 1957 (Jones 2014: 50). The loudspeaker statistics also correlate with significant mass campaigns (increased proliferation of amplified sound technologies usually coincided with the implementation of new mass movements), such as the shift to communal farming and the Great Leap Forward (*da yue jin*), and give an idea of the massive increase in amplified sound that would have been apparent in people's daily lives over the first few decades of the PRC.

Amplified sound politicized people's existences by circulating and intensifying Maoist discourse, which was intended to transform the minds of the people. Mao, unlike Stalin in this respect, truly believed that the minds of the peasants could be politically transformed (Gray 2006), and so the methods of mass persuasion and mass mobilization were especially targeted towards the preliterate, who made up the vast majority of the population. Sound was integral to this process. Mao was inspired by the seizures of power he witnessed in Hunan province in 1927, when poor peasants organized themselves into associations, revolted against their landlords, and aggressively humiliated them. Mao praised the peasant associations, noting how they eliminated old ties that the masses had to other authorities, such as clans, and political and religious leaders. He also commended the peasant associations' usage of simple repetitive slogans that "penetrated into [the peasants] minds and [were] on their lips" to the extent that even local children would parrot them, even though they did not understand their meanings.[6]

As Walter Ong, the literary scholar and priest known for his work on orality and literacy and their connection with human consciousness, states, "oral peoples" (the non-literate) consider words and sound to have great power (Ong 2013: 32). Ong explains that "all sound, and especially oral utterance, which comes from inside living organisms, is 'dynamic'" (Ong 2013: 32). Ong contrasts the way in which oral peoples think about words with the way in which literate people do, saying, "deeply typographic folk forget to think of words as primarily oral, as events, and hence as necessarily powered: for them, words tend rather to be assimilated to things, 'out there' on a flat surface" (Ong 2013). Oral peoples, according to Ong, can also more easily retain and deploy phrases that are repetitive, rhythmic, and formulaic (Ong 2013: 34).

Mao also understood the power of words in a society where the majority of people were preliterate. He learned from the Hunan rebellions the power of rhetoric, that words and slogans could "grow wings,"[7] and he believed that the peoples' minds could be changed so that CCP propaganda could be inculcated everywhere. Mao's thoughts on the power and hold of slogans chime with Ong's descriptions of "proverbs which are constantly heard by everyone so that they come to mind readily and which themselves are patterned for retention and ready recall" and the way in which oral peoples do their thinking in "mnemonic patterns, shaped for ready oral recurrence" (Ong 2013). When we consider Mao's views on the importance of slogans, alongside Ong's theories on the power of "mnemonic patterns," we can gain a better understanding of the thinking behind CCP propaganda work and its success in influencing the discourse of a mostly preliterate nation. We can also gain a better understanding of what the legacies of this propaganda work were and why the sonic politics of the Mao era still lingered decades after his death.

In CCP propaganda work, sound and the physical process of "speaking out" were just as important as the actual content of the slogans. As Anagnost has argued, in the early PRC years the masses were mobilized into legitimating new Maoist ideas in a way that involved the "physical body itself [becoming] the medium for registering the collision of material forces in history" (Anagnost 1997: 19). Anagnost (1997), Liu (2010), Perry (2002), and Hershatter (1997) have all described how the CCP encouraged people to emotionally "speak bitterness" about repression before 1949 by various forces, such as the Nationalists (Guomindang, the ruling party until 1949) and foreign powers. As Anagnost states, people released "bodily anguish" by using (simple and repetitive) narratives about past repression that were encouraged by the CCP, and it was this "circulation of violence between writing, the spoken word and the body" that is "central to understanding how class subjects were constructed in revolutionary China" (Anagnost 1997: 19). The writing aspect of this circulation did not involve the majority of people though. Most used the spoken word and the body to circulate narratives imposed upon them by the party and formerly promulgated by intellectuals. This type of speaking out usually happened in small groups that were organized by the state for political thought work and discussion (Whyte 1974).

Speaking out, chanting, bodily anguish, and a different type of circulation of sound occurred at Tiananmen Square, however, during large political events such as National Day parades and rallies. From an analysis of some of the sounds that were being received and produced at Tiananmen Square, I believe that we can ascertain more about the connections between state and society, and individuals and the masses in Mao's China. In considering how these sounds were mediated by new broadcasting technology, we can also glean more about national identity in China, in this period. In the following analysis of sounds at Tiananmen Square, I will draw somewhat from the "historical soundscape" concept of R. Murray Schafer (1993). A soundscape is a broad term, meaning an "acoustic field of study," and it could be a musical composition, a radio program, or an acoustic environment. An "acoustic environment" can be studied "just as we can study the characteristics of a given landscape," according to Schafer, and a "historical soundscape" could be reconstructed using "earwitness" accounts, writings by those who have "directly experienced and intimately known" sounds and can produce an accurate description of them (Schafer 1993: 8, 9). Earwitness accounts can be found in novels, interviews, memoirs, and newspapers. I will be using "earwitness" accounts in my work, in order to analyze and understand the Tiananmen Square soundscape. Many of the "earwitness" accounts I will be using in the following section come from memoirs. There are more of these particular sources for the Cultural Revolution era, because of the large amount of "scar literature" (*shanghen wenxue*) describing the tragedies that ordinary Chinese people experienced during this period. For the earlier period of my study, I will mainly use some British Foreign Office records, and earwitness accounts within other academic literature.

The Tiananmen Square Soundscape during the Mao Years: Voices of the Party and the People

As stated earlier the two elements that dominated the soundscape of Tiananmen Square during the Mao era (1949–76) were the voice of the people, who mainly chanted slogans, and the voice of the party,[8] represented primarily by amplified sound from loudspeakers.[9] These two elements of the soundscape developed in significance in relation to both the changes in the built environment of Tiananmen Square and in connection with party policies, and they resonated beyond Tiananmen Square and beyond the Mao years, owing to the symbolic importance of the site, and the images and sounds from events at Tiananmen Square being broadcast elsewhere in China and abroad.

Amplified sound at Tiananmen Square was of importance right from the beginning of the PRC's founding, as Mao's first speech had to be heard by the people assembled in front of Tiananmen. As the plaza was expanded stage by stage, there was a clear need for further amplification, so that sound could be broadcast to all areas during parades and other events. The North China Wireless Electronics Materials Factory "designed, produced and installed the loudspeaker systems for Beijing's Chang'an Avenue and the wired sound columns" in time for the tenth anniversary (Jones 2014: 50). The loudspeakers and wired sound columns allowed the voice of Mao and others to be carried all across the square. Slogans and speeches could be broadcast from the loudspeakers so that acclamations would be returned, and a feedback loop would be achieved, which incorporated the voice of the people and reinforced Mao and the CCP's preeminence and the people's connection to Mao, the party, and the country.

The "voice of the people" was technologically mediated in this feedback loop. Loudspeakers were used in order to make more efficient the call and response system used by parade organizers and parade-goers. According to a British Foreign Office report from May 2, 1952, the May Day parade of the day before featured a range of slogans being summoned by "cheer leaders" over the loudspeakers. For example, the "masses" were "continuously called upon to cheer for the Chairman [Mao Zedong] to the practical exclusion of everyone else."[10] The slogans were not printed out and dropped from the air (as they might have been at other parades) but were instead only shouted across the loudspeakers and in response toward Tiananmen and Mao.[11]

Amplified sound was, therefore, needed to help the sonic aspect of the parades run smoothly. It ensured that parade attendees were brought into the event and understood what was occurring and what was expected of them. As Wu Hung makes clear in his account of witnessing a Tiananmen Square National Day parade in 1955, the movements and sounds that he was expected to make from his place on the plaza were "not triggered by sight," as he was then a child and could not see any of the festivities, so his actions were instead triggered by other senses: by sound and by being part of a large crowd. He was "moved by a nameless collectivity of which [he] had become a part," and along with the rest of the crowd, he waved and shouted slogans (Hung 2005: 22).

This endless chanting of simple repetitive slogans still resonates with many parade attendees roughly fifty years later, as demonstrated by Chang-tai Hung's interviews with them. They all "expressed… reverence for [Mao]," and one in particular recalled having to repeat "Long live Chairman Mao!" many times over (Hung 2007: 419). The repetition of this particular slogan, directed up toward Mao on Tiananmen by huge crowds of people on Tiananmen Square, captured in photographs and on film and radio, traveled far beyond Beijing. It reflected and fostered the deification of Mao, as C.T. Hung explains, and the sacred nature of the space in which Mao and the people were situated only exacerbated the growth of the Mao cult.

The slogans that emanated from the loudspeakers were to be repeated by parade attendees and were often broadcast live on radio and filmed for later broadcast.[12] They were carefully choreographed so as to transmit certain political ideas across mainland China and abroad. The slogans were a way of communicating to people in China, but they were also transmissions to other nations, to countries that China was opposed to, and countries it had friendly relations with. The slogans to be chanted were, like every aspect of the parades, ultimately determined by the Propaganda Department of the CCP Central Committee (Hung 2007: 424). Nothing could be chanted that did not have official approval. British Foreign Office workers in Beijing analyzed the content of the slogans each year in order to ascertain what the party was attempting to convey about policy and direction.[13] The content of the yearly slogans, as Hung (2007) and Ye and Barmé have explained,[14] can be analyzed in order to retrospectively chart CCP policy and the growth of the Mao cult. The chanting of the slogans can also be considered in relation to questions of performativity and who exactly the audience and performers were at the parades: Mao or the parade attendees? Another important question is, how did the chanting of slogans at public events, and the energetic bodily way in which they were voiced, referred to in this chapter as the "voice of the people," influence the connection that the people had with Mao, the party, and their nation? In the following section I will analyze some earwitness accounts of chanting in public events at Tiananmen Square, in order to consider this question.

Chanting, Crowds, and the Sonorous Envelope

Slogans and chanting intensely with vast crowds were key aspects of the "voice of the people," which grew in intensity during the Mao years, and especially during the Cultural Revolution, so as to become a problematic issue for the party after the death of Mao. By considering the sonic and bodily aspect of the chants, as described in various Mao-era memoirs, I intend to explain how the "voice of the people" developed even though the people were essentially being coerced into voicing particular sentiments chosen by the party, at events that were directed by the party. The act of chanting loudly as part of a large crowd conferred a certain sense of power on the audience and upon individuals within the crowd, according to many accounts of people who attended events at Tiananmen Square, and this could perhaps be explained in part by the psychoanalyst Didier Anzieu's theory (1976) of the "sonorous envelope."

Anzieu posited that the sonorous envelope "originates in the womb as the prenate experiences two senses as if they were a single sense ... touch and sound" (Goodale 2013: 220; originally from Anzieu 1976). After birth, when we notice the loss of the original sonorous envelope of the womb, we feel exposed to a range of tactile and sonic sensations, and so we develop another sonorous envelope, which can act as a "protective cocoon." Goodale explains that "as we age we incorporate new sounds into our sonorous envelope. Thus the baby adopts the sound of the father's voice and the voices of siblings into his or her envelope" (Goodale 2013: 220). Sonorous envelopes have the potential to make people feel protected in certain moments, such as when "the sound of voices combined into one... lends individuals the courage to face violent threats" (Goodale 2013: 220). Many protests against an ostensibly more powerful status quo have benefited from protestors experiencing the "protective cocoon" of sound. The sonorous envelope can also give those who chant in parades a feeling of belonging and power, derived from a similar sense of protection.

A sonorous envelope can prevent political deliberation too. In Goodale's article he provides a number of examples regarding politics in the United States and how the sonorous envelope can be used to drown out others and prohibit any form of real dialogue or agonism. This form of "protective cocoon" is often nonviolent, Goodale asserts, and it could have positive consequences in a society like the United States, in which there is often great divergence between political parties and their supporters, as it can help people who have significant points of disagreement to avoid conflict. The prevention of political deliberation in an authoritarian country, such as the PRC, is a different matter, however, and this has implications for the specific nature of sonorous envelopes there. As mentioned above, the Party chose the slogans for the parades on Tiananmen Square in advance, and the specific wording of the slogans was often published in the press or distributed on printed slips around the city before the parade took place.[15] Tiananmen Square was a vast public space, with enough room for more than half a million people. The sonorous envelope of this huge crowd, with its carefully calibrated slogans showing unambiguous support and opposition for certain things, would have intimidated those who did not subscribe to the values of the Party.

This dual nature of the sonorous envelope, its capacity to engender a feeling of protection as well as project aggression, is mentioned in Goodale's essay but is perhaps more apparent in the Chinese and Maoist context, where there was a set of fixed slogans, a huge crowd of people, and an officially sanctioned event watched over by the autocratic leadership of Mao and the Party, which was recorded for broadcast elsewhere. All of these things ensured that the sonorous envelope of Tiananmen Square made those who felt positively toward the Party feel a sense of belonging, whereas those who opposed the Party (on or away from Tiananmen Square) would have felt intimidated and coerced into either relinquishing opposition in the face of an overwhelming mass voice or simply conforming. The warmth of the sonorous envelope and connectiveness that people would have felt as part of a large crowd could also have converted many to the causes that they chanted about or made them feel a sense of belonging. The sonorous envelope encompassing the masses in China might also have been an even more powerful protective force and could have provoked greater "courage" than it would elsewhere, because of the more relational construction of personhood in Chinese culture, where identity is not given to be intrinsic and fixed but is instead constantly being created, altered, and dismantled according to particular social relationships (Yang 1994: 192).

Official political events at Tiananmen Square broadcast political discourse and methods of behavior that were legitimated across the nation, because they were permitted and organized by the Party. Anyone who did not consider themselves to be a part of the masses was vulnerable to the anger of the crowd whose noise and violence were made permissible and actively encouraged by Mao and the Party, particularly during the less strictly organized Cultural Revolution era rallies.

A number of scholars have written on the subject of the crowd and how people within a group can behave in irrational and destructive ways that they would not consider if alone. Le Bon has claimed that crowds are characterized by "impulsiveness, irritability, incapacity to reason, the absence of judgment and of the critical spirit [and] the exaggeration of the sentiments" (Le Bon 1897: 16), and Aldous Huxley has termed such behavior "herd intoxication" (Huxley 2005: 365–72). Crowds can be powerful, and from many Cultural Revolution era memoirs we can see that while the chanting of simple, repetitive slogans at rallies gave some a feeling of pride and strength, others could feel pressure to conform or fear at feeling themselves to be outside of the crowd, or sonorous envelope. What is often striking about many of these accounts is the intensity of the physical act of speaking out at Tiananmen Square rallies, and the more unrestrained nature of the events, especially when compared with the parades.

To give some examples: in Nanchu's *Red Sorrow* the author describes how her elder brother, Ming, joined the Red Guards at a Tiananmen Square rally and "jumped until his legs cramped, shouted until his throat bled, and cried until he had no tears to shed" (Nanchu 2001: 5). Whether or not this is an exaggeration, it is evident from this description that many people in this era, particularly young people, wanted to use their body and voice in order to prove their revolutionary zeal. Similarly, in Shen's *Gang of One* the author describes how when Mao Zedong appeared at a Tiananmen Square rally, there was a sense of elation and repeated "deafening shouting" of "long live Chairman Mao," as some people around fainted from excitement. Fan Shen shouted as loudly as possible too in an attempt to generate a sense of excitement that he did not truly feel about the revolution, and he was eventually carried from the Square after pretending to faint (Shen 2004: 59). Fan Shen believed his friends to be genuinely excited and emotional, and he could not quite understand why. He felt guilty and uneasy about feeling "nothing" at the sight of the Great Leader (Shen 2004: 59). From both Fan Shen and Nanchu's accounts we can get a sense of the "bodily anguish" (Anagnost 1997) that people strived for at Tiananmen Square. The voice, used for chanting for long periods of time, seems to have been a key part of establishing one's commitment to the nation and Mao's revolution, and Tiananmen Square was the perfect symbolic site in which to experience the bodily anguish that would affirm these things.

People who were unable to establish this connection, like Fan Shen, could have felt vulnerable in such a place. The concept of the "fungibility" of people (meaning the replaceability of people) within a crowd explains something of how individuals can feel vulnerable when among many other people who seem homogenous. Felstiner (2012) examines how the fungibility of a crowd can work against the interest of the individuals within that crowd, and how such people can be exploited as a resource, in his article "The Weakness of Crowds." The context of Felstiner's article is the technological industries of Silicon Valley, the "exploitable labor pool" that the crowd constitutes, and the "futurist crowd-driven utopia" that sees only potential and "wisdom" in these new forms of crowds. The concept of fungibility connects to Maoist China as well, even though much of Felstiner's focus is on a particular geographic location and societal stratum of the modern-day United States. Fungibility pertains to people being interchangeable within a crowd. As Felstiner explains:

> Dissatisfied crowd members… are faced with the choice of discontinuing their participation or attempting to improve the crowd… [when] everyone is fungible, and the numbers are so large, why would a crowd member choose voice over exit? The truly discontented… will look at the sheer size of the available pool, and the interchangeability of its constituents, and recognize the futility of becoming a squeaky wheel. Instead, they will just leave.
>
> (Felstiner 2012)

We can surmise that at Mao's parades any discontented individuals would have experienced the same realization. The fungibility of the individuals within Tiananmen Square rendered any possible form of opposition irrelevant. "The people" were deemed to be what was important in the PRC, as evidenced by various monuments around Tiananmen Square, but the nature of the crowd ensured that each individual was easily replaceable. Furthermore, if an individual chose to opt out at Tiananmen Square, then owing to the symbolism of the public political space they were in, its centrality and obvious significance for national life, they would in effect be opting out of the public political sphere and the new vision of their country.[16]

The sights and sounds of events at Tiananmen Square, when circulated via print, radio, and film recordings,[17] also ensured that people clearly recognized both their own fungibility and the passion and fervor of the "voice of the people." Some people developed an acute fear of crowds, the sounds that they made at rallies, and the latent sense of violence that they projected. Yang Rae, a former Red Guard, writes in her memoir, *Spider Eaters* (2013), of her frequent nightmares concerning crowds. The sound of the voice of the people is a recurring theme in these nightmares:

> Around me the frenzied revolutionary masses were yelling at the top of their voices. Everybody hated me. I was a tiny boat sinking in a vast raging ocean. I wanted to speak up, to debate with others and defend myself, but no one was

willing to listen to me. They were all convinced that I was guilty. So they sentenced me to death. The sentence was to be carried out immediately.

(Yang 2013: 36)

Yang relates another nightmare in which "the revolutionary masses were in a great rage. Their voices, 'Down with so and so!' overwhelmed the sound of thunder" (Yang 2013: 120). Yang describes again how in this nightmare she wanted to speak but the masses would not listen. Instead they just chanted slogans and then attacked her physically. She was being denounced in this (nightmare) situation because the group she is perceived to be a part of, which used to be venerated, is now the object of virulent scorn, as encouraged by the Party. In this sense even whole crowds could be fungible: easily replaceable by other crowds that were now deemed to be ideologically correct.

The dual aspect of the crowd and the sonorous envelope is evidenced in these accounts. These things gave individuals a sense of power or a sense of fear, depending on how much one aligned with their values. Sound, and the intense bodily way in which people received and produced it during the events at Tiananmen Square, was a significant element in reinforcing both of these aspects, and if we take into account the concepts of the sonorous envelope and fungibility, along with Ong's understanding of the power of sound and simple slogans among nonliterate people, and Anagnost's explanation of how the spoken word and the body were central to how class subjects were constructed in the PRC, we can understand something of how the sonic events at Tiananmen Square were deeply affective to the people who experienced them, and influential nationwide.

To briefly summarize the developments in the two key aspects of the Tiananmen Square soundscape during the Mao years: the voice of the Party was extended across Tiananmen Square before the tenth-year anniversary of the PRC's founding and remained somewhat stable, whereas the voice of the people became more intense and unrestrained during the Cultural Revolution years.[18] While the political public square was speaking out in an area that had been carefully designed to evoke specific Party approved symbolism, and the Party and Mao decided the content of political speech at Tiananmen Square, the intense bodily way in which the people spoke out there generated a fervent sonic politicization that the Party had some difficulty constraining in the years following Mao's death, as I shall now explain.

The Sonic Legacies of the Mao Years

As Doreen Massey states, "places do not have single, unique 'identities'; they are full of internal conflicts" and "the specificity of a place is continually reproduced" and is not "a specificity which results from some long, internalized history" (2010: 8). In some respects, Mao and the CCP attempted to create a single unique identity for Tiananmen Square. It was a public political space that was meant to attest to the glory of Mao and the PRC and support the idea that "the people" were central to the new regime. The Party has made further architectural alterations at Tiananmen Square in the years following Mao's death (Yu 2006: 78), but what has not changed is the Square's position as the national center. It is the supreme public political site in China, despite developments in its physical environment and the CCP's policy since the late 1970s of depoliticizing public spaces (Hung 2005: 244).

Significant protest movements at Tiananmen Square occurred in 1976 and 1989. These events underline the challenges to CCP depoliticization and the extent to which the sights and sounds of significant events at Tiananmen Square are still ingrained within the psyche of the populace. From the 1976 and 1989 protests we can see evidence of the existing tension between the two key aspects of the Tiananmen Square soundscape mentioned in this chapter. Though it is beyond the scope of this chapter to fully delineate the political and social contexts informing these events, I will briefly describe some selected details from them and the interactions and confrontations of the two main aspects of the soundscape.

The first and lesser-known Tiananmen Incident occurred on April 5, 1976, when people assembled to show disapproval at the mourning for recently deceased Premier Zhou Enlai, which was perceived to be curtailed and inadequate. More than 1 million people gathered at Tiananmen Square in a protest that included "verbal declarations and outbursts" as well as wreaths, poems, and handbills that honored Zhou Enlai and also contained criticisms and comments related to the contemporaneous political situation (Teiwes and Sun 2004: 218). The government moved to suppress the protests, and even though a police van broadcasting messages through its loudspeaker was overturned, the police and militia were "restrained" in doing this. The main strategy employed by the government was to repeatedly play an amplified speech by the mayor of Beijing, Wu De, which stated that "bad elements" had caused the unrest and called for everyone to leave the plaza (Teiwes and Sun 2004: 219).

This first incident at Tiananmen Square, which erupted just as the Mao years were coming to a close, was in some respects a precursor of the larger event in 1989, in which the same two aspects of the soundscape were present and the death of a popular politician was also a catalyst, but the outcome of this later event was far more violent and tragic. The 1989 protests at Tiananmen Square were part of a broader democracy movement that saw similar large-scale demonstrations in a number of cities in mainland China and Hong Kong. Tiananmen Square was once again the symbolic site to which national and international attention was directed. International attention was in fact particularly significant by 1989 as foreign television crews now had direct access to the protests as they unfolded, a result of the "Reform and Opening up" (*gaige kaifang*) of the PRC in the late 1970s.

Music played a significant role in the 1989 protests at Tiananmen, Beethoven's "Ode to Joy" was played over the protestors' loudspeaker at the Monument to the People's Heroes (Schell 1994: 127), and on a number of occasions the protestors held each other's hands and sung the "Internationale"—the anthem of Socialism (Schell 1994: 63, 149, 151).[19] Sound, considered more broadly, in relation to the two main elements of the soundscape discussed above, is also a significant detail in accounts of what took place at that time. The collective chanting that had been in evidence during the parades and Cultural Revolution rallies was also made use of during the protests as activists shouted short slogans in unison to bring attention to particular viewpoints such as (on May 5th) "Freedom of the press is good for stability" (Pan 2011: 334). Also, on May 13 "student activists adapted Mao's words from 'The Great Union of the Popular Masses' to show their firm stand to sacrifice for the mission of national salvation" (Pan 2011: 346). The protestors were attempting to use the power of the mass voice for revolutionary aims, in the same way that the mass voice had been used during the Cultural Revolution. The rhetorical content of their chants was also important and also harkened back to the revolutionary years of Mao.

The chanting of slogans and singing were accompanied by many other sounds. During the protest movements there was a "cacophony," a "din of chanted political slogans, songs, drums, and raucous orations delivered through handheld bullhorns," as well as a "wail of sirens as ambulances manned by Red Cross volunteers ferried unconscious fasters off to nearby hospitals" (Schell 1994: 87). In Orville Schell's descriptions we see again the connection between the voice, bodily anguish, and revolutionary political experience at Tiananmen Square, one of the major legacies of CCP sound-based political work during the Mao years.

One constant theme among the complexity of this soundscape was the obvious confrontation between the voices of the Party and the voices of the people. Some observers described this sonic tension as a kind of "air war" (Berman and Lee 1991: 94). Protestors had loudspeakers mounted on the Monument to the People's Heroes. From these they addressed the assembled crowds as well as the Party and the world's media with a mixture of "exhortation, oratory, invective, [and] ridicule" (Berman and Lee 1991: 96). The Party had their own loudspeakers, of course, and as with the 1976 protests, they frequently broadcast messages encouraging and warning people to leave the plaza. The "mature" and "mellifluous" voice emanating from the government loudspeakers contrasted sharply with the sometimes "trebly" and unamplified voices of protesters (Berman and Lee 1991: 96).[20]

Such was the constancy and reach of the amplified voice of the Party at Tiananmen Square that during one secretive meeting at the Monument to the People's Heroes, protestors needed to speak very softly into a portable loudspeaker in order to be heard by those around them, but not be audible to spies from the police, military, or Party who were likely nearby (Chiu 1991: 338). In this moment we can ascertain one significant difference between the voice of the people and the voice of the Party: the extent to which on certain occasions, or when voicing certain content, it was desirable or safe to be heard. There were still definite limitations, therefore, to the power of the voice of the people, and these limitations remain.

Conclusion

Since 1989 the "image of Tiananmen Square [has become] politically sensitive, and it [has been] less frequently and more carefully mentioned than before" (Zhao 2005: 263). Parades are more tightly regulated and orchestrated now, and they are primarily produced for the TV audience. In recent celebrations, such as the fiftieth anniversary of the founding of the PRC, in 1999, "Beijing residents were told to stay home and enjoy the week-long festivities on television" (Lee 2011: 419). Tiananmen Square remains a central and charismatic public political space, but it now also has a more widely known history, domestically and internationally, as a site of protest.

Control over the sound and music heard at Tiananmen Square is of great importance for the Party today. The sounds, as much as the images, from parades and rallies in the Mao years inspired many aspects of the later protest movements and led to the need for much more careful negotiation between the two key elements of the soundscape. The Party's need to reconfigure its usage and promotion of Tiananmen Square as a charismatic public political space post-1989 and the continued usage of this space by the public as a place of protest perhaps indicate that at least in terms of the sonic aspects of Tiananmen Square's political symbolism, the death of Mao in 1976 and the construction of his mausoleum did not truly constitute a "closed chapter" in the history of this vitally important site.

Notes

1   The significance of the "people" was also apparent in the numerous expansions to the square before 1959. In 1949 the site had only enough space to hold 70,000 people; within ten years it could hold 600,000, though Mao had optimistically ordered it to be built "big enough to hold an assembly of one billion" (Hung 2005: 23).
2   For example, the *yin-yang* and five-phase worldviews. According to Meyer, Beijing was "an idea long before it was a city" and this idea "gave shape and shape substance to the city and its surroundings, to the province in which it was located, to the whole of what we call China, and ultimately to the world," which was conceptualized according to Beijing, "the center to the circumference" (Meyer 1991: 1).
3   Orville Schell, in *Mandate of Heaven*, points out the "shadow identity" of Tiananmen, which existed long before the fall of the Qing dynasty in 1911. Schell describes the two marble *huabiao* (pillars) "topped with stylized wings and mythical animals, one facing the palace and the other the city, reminders to the emperor of the indissoluble connection between ruler and ruled." In ancient times these *huabiao* were said to be made of wood, so that the subjects could carve criticisms and complaints on them. Schell claims that even after the *huabiao* were remade in marble, "their presence served as reminders that at the same time that the Square served as the seat of state power it was also a place where citizens were entitled to remonstrate" (Schell 1994: 22).
4   Haiyan Lee's (2011) "The Charisma of Power and the Military Sublime in Tiananmen Square," Chang-tai Hung's (2007) "Mao's Parades: State Spectacles in China in the 1950s," and Wu Hung's (2005) *Remaking Beijing: Tiananmen Square and the Creation of a Political Space* are good examples of scholarly works that analyze the visual symbolism of public events at Tiananmen Square.
5   https://www.nytimes.com/2001/02/12/news/chinas-long-but-uneven-march-to-literacy.html, accessed June 1, 2018.
6   https://www.marxists.org/reference/archive/mao/selected-works/volume-1/mswv1_2.htm, accessed July 18, 2018.

7   https://www.marxists.org/reference/archive/mao/selected-works/volume-1/mswv1_2. htm, accessed July 18, 2018.
8   These are my terms created for my soundscape analysis, rather than terms used in China at the time. I refer to the "voice of the people" in the singular form, as this was meant to be a unified voice that would articulate what the party demanded from it.
9   Other sounds that were heard during events at Tiananmen Square, such as National Day parades, included artillery salvoes and the noise of aircraft flyovers. These also formed part of what I have described as the "voice of the party."
10 British Foreign Office. Foreign Office Files for China, 1949–56. Shanghai celebrations of Third Anniversary of founding of the People's Democratic Republic, October 1, 1952; May Day 1953 celebrations in Beijing. FO 371–105351, 2.
11 Ibid.
12 The content of some of these radio broadcasts, beyond the scope of this chapter to detail, is related in several sources. A Foreign Broadcast Information Daily Service Report entitled, "700,000 in Peking National Day Parade" (FBIS-FRB-64-192, Readex), relates the live radio broadcast of the 1964 National Day parade. Another record on "Listener Reactions to the 1956 National Day Special Program" (B92-1-209-79, Shanghai Municipal Archives), summarizes the responses of listeners, and provides a taste of what would have been heard on the radio during the National Day festivities in the 1950s. Yu Hua also describes his experience of watching National Day newsreels and documentaries during the Cultural Revolution, which always came to his "little" hometown "well into winter," and would be played in the cinema (Hua 2012: 32).
13 For example, from a Foreign Office report regarding the 1959 May Day parade in Beijing, A.D. Wilson analyzes the meaning behind the appearance of new slogans concerning Tibet and Taiwan and the absence of slogans used in previous years related to culture and the economy. British Foreign Office. Foreign Office Files for China, 1957–66. Celebrations and Anniversaries of China, May 6, 1959; May Day Parade in Peking. FO 371–141357, 3.
14 http://www.chinaheritagequarterly.org/features.php?searchterm=017_nationaldays. inc&issue=017, accessed July 18, 2018.
15 British Foreign Office. Foreign Office Files for China, 1949–56. Shanghai celebrations of Third Anniversary of founding of the People's Democratic Republic, October 1, 1952; May Day 1953 celebrations in Beijing. FO 371–105351, 2.
16 Some were very anxious about being rejected by crowds/the masses. As Li Nanyang states in *Morning Sun*, a 2003 documentary on the Cultural Revolution (4:24 in Barmé et al. 2003), "The motherland, the party, and the revolution came first, and yourself, you were nothing unless you were part of the great cause. To be excluded was to be without a purpose in life. That was very, very painful."
17 Nien Cheng describes seeing a large photograph of Mao Zedong reviewing the Red Guards at Tiananmen Square on the front page of a newspaper. She was struck by the sound of this scene, even though she was only viewing a photograph; as she states, Mao "smiled and waved as he received a thunderous ovation from the youngsters gathered below" (Cheng 2010: 58). Wei, in *A River Forever Flowing*, states, "the movie theaters showed only documentaries of Chairman Mao receiving the Red Guards in Tiananmen Square in Beijing" at the beginning of the Cultural Revolution (Wei quoted in He 2003: 33).

18 This intense drawing in of people to the soundscape was evident across China throughout the Cultural Revolution with the broadcasting and performances of Quotation songs (Jones 2014) and Model Operas. As Barbara Mittler states, "the soundscapes of the Cultural Revolution… opened up new avenues of experience for those living in the countryside, on one hand, and in the cities, on the other," because the Model Operas "gave people, both in the countryside and in the cities, regular opportunities to take part in large-scale cultural performances, both actively or as audiences—providing more opportunities than ever before (or after) to experience music in very immediate fashion" (Mittler 2016: 253).
19 Beethoven had the reputation of being a "revolutionary" in China, as explained in Jindong Cai and Sheila Melvin's *Beethoven in China* (2015).
20 Another contrast between the "voice of the party" and the "voice of the people" at the 1989 protests was that the "voice of the party" was more in unison than the "voice of the people," which could in this instance be considered more in the plural form "voices of the people." Orville Schell describes how walking through the Square was like "roaming a huge bazaar filled not with merchants selling goods but with people trading ideas, giving speeches, debating, and arguing politics with one another" (Schell 1994: 87).

Bibliography

Anagnost, Ann. 1997. *National Past-times: Narrative, Representation, and Power in Modern China*. Durham, NC: Duke University Press.

Anzieu, Didier. 1976. "L'enveloppe Sonore du Soi." *Nouvelle Revue de Psychanalyse* 13: 173–9.

Berman, Mitch, and Susanne Wah Lee. 1991. "Orwell's Bells." *Conjunctions* 16: 94–101.

Cai, Jindong, and Sheila Melvin. 2015. *Beethoven in China: How the Great Composer Became an Icon in the People's Republic*. Melbourne, Australia: Penguin Specials. Penguin eBooks.

Cheng, Nien. 2010. *Life and Death in Shanghai*. New York: Grove Press.

Chiu, Fred Y. L. 1991. "The Specificity of the Political on Tiananmen Square, or a Poetics of the Popular Resistance in Beijing." *Dialectical Anthropology* 16 (3/4): 333–47.

Comtois, Claude. 1990. "Transport and Territorial Development in China 1949–1985." *Modern Asian Studies* 24 (4): 777–818.

Felstiner, Alek. 2012. "The Weakness of Crowds." Available online: https://limn.it/articles/the-weakness-of-crowds/, accessed May 28, 2020.

Goodale, Greg. 2013. "The Sonorous Envelope and Political Deliberation." *Quarterly Journal of Speech* 99 (2): 218–24.

Gray, Jack. 2006. "Mao in Perspective." *The China Quarterly* 187: 659–79.

He, Ming Fang. 2003. *A River Forever Flowing: Crosscultural Lives and Identities in the Multicultural Landscape*. Greenwich, CT: IAP.

Hershatter, Gail. 1997. *Dangerous Pleasures: Prostitution and Modernity in Twentieth-century Shanghai*. Berkeley, CA: University of California Press.

Hua, Yu. 2012. *China in Ten Words*. New York: Anchor Books.

Hung, Chang-tai. 2007. "Mao's Parades: State Spectacles in China in the 1950s." *The China Quarterly* 190: 411–31.

Hung, Wu. 2005. *Remaking Beijing: Tiananmen Square and the Creation of a Political Space*. London: Reaktion Books.
Huxley, Aldous. 2005. *The Devils of Loudun*. London: Vintage Books.
Jones, Andrew F. 2014. "Quotation Songs: Portable Media and the Maoist Pop Song." In *Mao's Little Red Book: A Global History*, edited by Alexander C. Cook, 43–60. Cambridge: Cambridge University Press.
Kielman, Adam. 2017. "Zou Qilai!: Musical Subjectivity, Mobility, and Sonic Infrastructures in Postsocialist China." PhD thesis, Columbia University.
Le Bon, Gustave. 1897. *The Crowd: A Study of the Popular Mind*. New York: Macmillan.
Lee, Haiyan. 2011. "The Charisma of Power and the Military Sublime in Tiananmen Square." *The Journal of Asian Studies* 70 (2): 397–424.
Lee, Nelson K. 2009. "How Is a Political Public Space Made?—The Birth of Tiananmen Square and the May Fourth Movement." *Political Geography* 28: 32–43.
Liu, Alan P.L. 1975. *Communications and National Integration in Communist China*. Berkeley, CA: University of California Press.
Liu, Yu. 2010. "Maoist Discourse and the Mobilization of Emotions in Revolutionary China." *Modern China* 36 (3): 329–62.
Massey, Doreen. 2010. "A Global Sense of Place." Available online: http://www.aughty.org/pdf/global_sense_place.pdf, accessed May 28, 2020.
Meyer, Jeffrey F. 1991. *The Dragons of Tiananmen: Beijing as a Sacred City*. Columbia, SC: University of South Carolina Press.
Mittler, Barbara. 2016. "Just Beat It! Popular Legacies of Cultural Revolution Music." In *Listening to China's Cultural Revolution: Music, Politics, and Cultural Continuities*, edited by Paul Clark, Laikwan Pang, and Tsan-Huang Tsai, 239–68. New York: Palgrave Macmillan.
Nanchu. 2001. *Red Sorrow: A Memoir*. New York: Arcade Publishing.
Ong, Walter J. 2013. *Orality and Literacy*. New York: Routledge.
Pan, Tsung Yi. 2011. "Constructing Tiananmen as a Realm of Memory: National Salvation, Revolutionary Tradition, and Political Modernity in Twentieth-Century China." PhD thesis, University of Minnesota.
Perry, Elizabeth. 2002. "Moving the Masses: Emotion Work in the Chinese Revolution." *Mobilization: An International Quarterly* 7 (2): 111–28.
Schafer, R. Murray. 1993. *The Soundscape: Our Sonic Environment and the Tuning of the World*. Rochester, VT: Destiny Books.
Schell, Orville. 1994. *Mandate of Heaven: The Legacy of Tiananmen Square and the Next Generation of China's Leaders*. New York: Simon and Schuster.
Shen, Fan. 2004. *Gang of One: Memoirs of a Red Guard*. Lincoln: University of Nebraska Press.
Teiwes, Frederick C., and Warren Sun. 2004. "The First Tiananmen Incident Revisited: Elite Politics and Crisis Management at the End of the Maoist Era." *Pacific Affairs* 77 (2): 211–35.
Whyte, Martin King. 1974. *Small Groups and Political Rituals in China*. Berkeley, CA: University of California Press.
Yang, Mayfair Mei-hui. 1994. *Gifts, Favors, and Banquets: The Art of Social Relationships in China*. Ithaca, NY: Cornell University Press.
Yang, Rae. 2013. *Spider Eaters: A Memoir*. Berkeley, CA: University of California Press.

Yu, Shuishan. 2006. "To Achieve the Unachievable: Beijing's Chang'an Avenue and Chinese Architectural Modernization during the PRC Era." PhD thesis, University of Washington.

Zhao, Liang. 2005. "Modernizing Beijing: Moments of Political and Spatial Centrality." PhD thesis, Harvard University.

Filmography

Barmé, Geremie, Richard Gordon, and Carma Hinton, directors. 2003. *Morning Sun [Documentary]*. USA: Long Bow Group, DVD.

9

Broadcasting Infrastructures and Electromagnetic Fatality: Listening to Enemy Radio in Socialist China

Hang Wu

For socialist China, regulating the distribution of sounds and sound infrastructures was part of the nation-building project. During this era, building nationwide broadcasting networks was an important agenda for the Chinese Communist Party (CCP) to mobilize the labor force for agricultural and industrial modernization and to connect the individual with the collective and the national. To achieve an ideal distribution of national radio broadcasts, the Chinese socialist state not only controlled the content production and broadcasting infrastructures but also banned listening to so-called enemy radio (*ditai*)—Mandarin-based foreign radio stations that often targeted Chinese audiences with anti-Communist propaganda. Most enemy radio stations were those managed and controlled by Taiwan, the United States, the UK, and Australia, such as Voice of Free China (Taiwan), Voice of America (VOA), the British Broadcasting Corporation (BBC), and ABC Radio (Australia), among others. This chapter will hence focus on the state's attempts to control illicit listening in the historical context of Chinese socialism and its nation-building project in the 1960s and 1970s.

In the international context, the 1960s and 1970s were also a time period when the politics of the Cold War generated the "airy curtains" of broadcasting warfare (Badenoch, Fickers, and Henrich-Franke 2013). The curtains of electromagnetic waves functioned as an airy break between the Eastern and Western Blocs, but it also paradoxically put them in communication through a process of mutual contamination. One of the most important defining features of high-quality broadcasting signals was that it enabled radio broadcasting to go across national borders. These borders are often demarcated by boundary lines, mountains and rivers, military units, immigration offices, and other institutional and material regimes—anything imagined to be "solid." This ethereal quality of signals led to a celebration of radio broadcasting's deterritorializing capacity that problematizes the totalized imagination of nation, nationhood, and other kinds of supranational formations. However, recent studies on the materiality of media remind us that sounds and electromagnetic signals also have their infrastructural bases—radio stations, state institutions, antennas, wires, transmitters, receivers—that are no less solid or less material. Media scholars and historians contend that these infrastructures not only facilitate or necessitate flows of information, goods, and capital but also organize unneutral spaces and assemble spatial and political history with their different material orientations (Starosielski 2015; Yang 2009). With this, we have already identified two tendencies of radio broadcasting: its deterritorializing drive and its powers of reterritorialization and stabilization aimed at achieving a fixed arrangement and distribution of sounds, usually within one nation. That is why radio broadcasting feels at once "airy" and "solid."

This chapter, therefore, begins with an analysis of these two polarized tendencies: the deterritorializing tendency grounded in the technology of broadcasting and the reterritorializing tendency of the nation-state. To be sure, these issues remain unthinkable without taking into account traffic, movement, flow, and transmission, as we cannot simply talk about radio technologies without considering how broadcasting signals were transmitted within a given historical situation. Therefore, the issue of distribution emerges. Ideally, transmission is equal and all-encompassing. However, as Benedict Anderson (2006) points out, a smooth and flattened distribution that unifies all human communities proves impossible due to the inevitable diversity of vernacular languages, a linguistic heterogeneity that he refers to as the fatality of languages (2006: 43).

It is in his discussion of the origins of national consciousness that Anderson introduces the term "fatality." He first identifies three factors and their interactions that gave rise to national consciousness and the embryo of the modern nation-state: print technologies as a new mode of communication, capitalist production and a set of capitalist production relations, and the fatal diversity of human languages. He then speaks of the vernacularizing thrust of print capitalism, which assembles varied idiolects into languages for the print, much fewer in number and capable of being reproduced and circulated, although still within a limited territory. Gradually, these languages became the languages of power, which were later standardized as national languages. This "fatality of human linguistic diversity" inherently limits the notion of the nation-state: "For whatever superhuman feats capitalism was capable of, it found in death and languages two tenacious adversaries. Particular languages can die or be wiped out, but there was and is no possibility of humankind's general linguistic unification" (2006: 43). The fatality of language, in other words, pertinaciously cuts the flow of capital, generating uneven distribution.

Building on Anderson's notion of the fatality of vernacular languages, Thomas Lamarre (2017) developed the idea of the "electromagnetic fatality" of the broadcasting system. Lamarre argues that broadcasting, like vernacular languages, also functions as a limit. He shows that with national broadcasting infrastructures, while the ideal is to achieve even distributions, the signals nonetheless "invariably fall short or go too far" (Lamarre 2017: 298), and areas covered by signals do not completely coincide with national territory: "Thus the technical problems of vernacular language identified by Anderson (standardization of speech and of scripts) become entangled with technical problems associated with electromagnetic signals (frequency allocation and relays)" (2017: 298). The fatality of electromagnetic signals, therefore, generates uneven distributions and technological differentials.

I will, therefore, focus on how the uneven distribution of broadcasting signals introduced technical difficulties to China's nation-building project in the socialist era. Through a discussion of how the electromagnetic fatality facilitated illicit listening to enemy radio stations in socialist China, I argue that while radio broadcasting functioned as one of the favorite tools of the Chinese socialist state to call forth ideal socialist citizens, it also created technological and infrastructural problems for the formation of a well-delineated national community and its exercise of power. The first part of my discussion will focus on the construction of the national network of radio broadcasting in socialist China in order to form an "imagined listening community" (Birdsall 2012). It considers how different power apparatuses subjected radio listeners to their operation to produce the ideal national citizen. The second part draws on memoirs of the sent-down youth[1] (*zhiqing*) and historical archives to address the illicit listening to enemy radio stations at the border of China, showing how the national initiative to promote broadcasting technologies helped to introduce multiple ways of organizing listening experiences. Looking at radio broadcasting from the angle of its uneven distribution within and beyond the Chinese national territory will contribute to a historicized and materialist understanding of the broadcast medium. It will also offer an opportunity to resituate socialist China, which is often considered as isolated from the global circuits of media production during the Cold War, into transnational networks by calling attention to the cross-border circulation of broadcasting signals.

Nation-Building and the Listening Socialist Subject

Radio broadcasting has played a crucial role in the nation-building project in the twentieth century by facilitating the feeling of temporal simultaneity and the experience of the nation as an "imagined listening community," a term coined by Carolyn Birdsall (2012) in her elaboration of Anderson's concept of the "imagined community." As Birdsall shows, in radio broadcasting, the one-to-many mode of communication takes precedence over one-to-one interpersonal communication, thus allowing for interactions at a longer distance that emphasize

> the experience of carnival as an acoustic event, with broadcasts publicizing the event and dispersing its sounds to a regional and national listening audience. This shift enabled the festival to be expanded beyond the face-to-face interaction of the urban marketplaces, as radio increasingly stretched the time-space coordinates of the festival and allowed for participation at a distance.
>
> (Birdsall 2012: 101)

During the Chinese socialist era, radio broadcasting, regarded as an important tool for China's nation-building project, was directly controlled by the state. In the early 1950s, the Chinese socialist state began to construct nationwide radio reception networks with which the everyday hearing of the masses could be controlled to form an imagined listening community (Wang 2019). The Chinese socialist state's effort to achieve a stabilized distribution of broadcasting signals was driven by the desire for a fixed listening point and an ideal listening subject. The smooth flow of signals and sounds without any flaw or glitch was imagined as capable of permeating every corner of the vast territory of China, from domestic spaces to border areas. Looking at how signal transmission and radio listeners were regulated in this peculiar historical context reveals how different power techniques worked together to evoke the feeling of an imagined listening community inhabited by ideal listening subjects—the citizens of the Chinese socialist state. For my concept of power techniques, I draw on Michel Foucault's (2007) discussion of three power mechanisms in his lecture "Security, Territory, Population," which include the power of the security apparatus, state power, and disciplinary power.

The Building of National Broadcasting Networks

The construction of national broadcasting infrastructures in socialist China was largely about the regulation of the environment, or what Foucault calls the milieu, which refers to "a certain number of combined, overall effects bearing on all who live in it" (2007: 21). The environment consists of "a set of natural givens—rivers, marshes, hills—and a set of artificial givens—an agglomeration of individuals, of houses, etcetera" (2007: 21). For Foucault, the security apparatus is a form of power that specifically takes the environment as its object in order to attain more efficiency and productivity. To control the environment means to control the circulation of material goods, populations, natural resources, infrastructures, and often ideas. The goals of controlling the milieu through broadcasting networks in socialist China were, on the one hand, to achieve better allocations of agricultural and industrial resources to modernize the country and, on the other hand, to better disseminate ideas on a national scale. Although the focus of this chapter is to examine radio as a means of distributing broadcast sounds rather than how techniques revolving around radio were designed and implemented to benefit agricultural and industrial production, it is still important to recognize that the control of the milieu can be both material and immaterial.

Radio was only one among many other media, including film, television, the novel, and *lianhuanhua* (picture books), that were adopted by the state to circulate ideas in socialist China. During the 1960s and 1970s, in remote and rural areas where the public viewing of officially endorsed films was restrained by the limited accessibility to screening infrastructures, radio became an important supplement for shaping the new socialist subject known as the *shehui zhuyi xinren* ("Socialist New Man"). Nicole Huang's study on the Chinese communal culture of the mid-1970s notes that the auditory practice of *ting dianying* ("listening to films") was intertwined with the collective film viewing of that period of time. She observes that films were edited specially as soundtracks for radio broadcasting:

> The popularity of feature films in the mid-1970s relied to a great extent on the omnipresence of Central People's Radio… For those who lived in remote areas

and who had limited access to film venues, radio broadcasts equipped them with relevant expertise in a socialist visual culture in which everyone was encouraged to be an active participant.

(Huang 2003: 175)

When there was a technological problem of film distribution and techniques of viewing in the socialist nation-building project, techniques of sound were introduced to solve it. The medium of radio provided a solution to shore up deficiencies in other media infrastructures that were also designed for the nation-building project, such as cinema. Radio broadcasting's capacity for long-distance transmission meant that it could act as a substitute for audiovisual media in remote rural areas. But in order for radio to function properly for the nation-building project, it had to be supplemented by other techniques and practices. For example, to make socialist firms and broadcasts accessible to people in remote areas, technicians had to carry screening equipment, radio sets, and often dynamos to remote rural areas where electric power transmissions or broadcasting infrastructure were unavailable.

In the late 1950s, the Chinese state announced that it had successfully built its national broadcasting networks, with more than 1,700 main radio broadcast stations and more than 7,200 stations in the nationwide people's communes (Zhou 1959). The construction was connected not only with the creation of the feeling of simultaneity and homogeneity within this one nation-state but also with the state's ideals of international socialism and the progress of human achievement on a global scale. The broadcasting infrastructure was seen by the socialist state as a technology that served, on the one hand, to "connect the central and the local and the Chinese Communist Party and the massive working class," and, on the other hand, to promote "socialist revolutions and constructions... as well as world peace and human progress" (Zhou 1959: 5).[2]

Another government document regarding the regulation of radio broadcasting epitomizes the socialist ideal of how state control of broadcasting might contribute to the nation-building project and the dissemination of international socialism. This document, entitled "Radio Broadcasting Technology Maintenance and Management," was drafted by the Zhongyang guangbo shiwuju (State Central Broadcasting Service General Office) and published in 1977 in *Guangbo yu dianshi jishu* (Radio and TV broadcast engineering), the official journal of the state administration of radio. It states clearly the essential role of radio broadcasting in the political agenda of the Communist state:

Radio broadcasting is an important tool of the dictatorship of the proletariat; it undertakes the glorious task of disseminating Marxism-Leninism, as well as Mao Zedong's thoughts and his proletarian revolutionary route, and of publicizing the policies of the party. To ensure uninterrupted broadcasting, we must establish strict rules and regulations in order to complete the party's publicity works, to achieve secured broadcasting, and to spread the voice of the Central Committee of the Party all over China and the whole world in a timely and accurate manner.

(Zhongyang guangbo shiwuju 1977: 5)

The goal of connecting the central and the local as well as the proletariat and the leaders of the party recalls what Lamarre describes as the ideal for national broadcast infrastructures, namely, a flat sovereignty: "The emitted signal is supposed to radiate to the edges of the bounded national territory, thus erasing distinctions between the centre and the periphery, between urban and rural, by folding everyone into the centralizing forces of national broadcast" (2017: 298). However, we can also identify a deterritorializing drive here that strove to make the sound of the socialist state audible to audiences outside the country, indicative of a desire for a supranational formation that could potentially unite all proletarians. This supranational formation can be seen in the cultural practices and politics of other socialist states as well. For instance, as Lonán Ó Briain shows, video broadcasts in late-colonial Hanoi developed a "Sino-Soviet-influenced musical cosmopolitanism" that took musical and political inspirations from the Soviet Union and China (2018: 265).

Ideal versus Illicit Listening

To achieve these goals, the socialist state believed that radio broadcasting, in terms of not only its content production but also its infrastructure and social impact, had to be controlled strictly to ensure an ideal way of listening. There were good reasons for this. The nationwide broadcasting networks have proven to be of central importance in promoting political and cultural mobilization, not to mention issues of national security. For instance, the banning of Voice of America was a national security measure taken as a direct response to the outbreak of the Korean War. In Kuisong Yang's study (2010) of how socialist China attempted to eliminate the influence of VOA in China, he notes that the CCP started to interfere with broadcast signals of the Mandarin VOA right after the establishment of the People's Republic of China in 1949 (2010: 28). In November 1950, immediately after China's intervention in the Korean War, a series of editorials appeared in major official newspapers, including the official newspaper of the CCP, *People's Daily*, advocating the banning of VOA in support of North Korea and China. One of these essays, for instance, deems VOA a weapon that is "even more vicious than the atomic bomb" (Yang 2010: 29). With the state promotion of banning VOA and the escalation of the Korean War, the number of VOA listeners in China soon diminished (Yang 2010: 29). The term *"guangbo zhan"* ("broadcasting war"), used by the Chinese socialist state to refer to the broadcasting intrusions of Taiwan in the 1960s and 1970s, also exemplifies the intricate relation between radio broadcasting, warfare, and national security.

The Chinese socialist state's regulations of radio broadcast involved control not only over content but also over the means of distribution through the management of signal transmission and reception. The "Radio Broadcasting Technology Maintenance and Management" document designated specific regulations regarding how to avoid signal interferences from enemy stations in order to control the signal transmission:

No. 22: Working staff should increase their political responsibility during the process of signal transmission; they should also know well the activities of near-frequency enemy radio stations. If signal cross talk is detected, staff should immediately transfer to other frequencies in order to prevent wrong transfers and report it to their leaders as soon as possible.

(Zhongyang guangbo shiwuju 1977: 15)

Broadcast accidents include... radio broadcast being forced to stop due to signal interference from enemy radio.

(Zhongyang guangbo shiwuju 1977: 27)

In addition, as some radio stations in China have mistakenly retransmitted unsanctioned broadcasting programs from foreign stations, this document also required that "in the operational process, there should be measures to avoid mistakenly transmitting enemy radio broadcast to the public" (Zhongyang guangbo shiwuju 1977: 40). However, complete control over the broadcasting signal was still impossible, as listeners were able to use shortwave radio receivers, especially those living in the border regions, to receive signals from what the state referred to as enemy stations. Therefore, the state also intervened to regulate listeners and ways of listening. One of their techniques was to directly ban enemy broadcasts and punish illicit listening. In the 1970s, the state severely criminalized the practice of listening to enemy radio broadcasts. Moreover, some listeners faced charges of espionage (*jiandie zui*) for sending letters to these radio stations that contained "confidential information concerning politics, military, diplomacy, public security, and economics in China" (Shanxi sheng zhengfa ganbu xuexiao ziliaoshi 1983: 86).

Why did people send letters to enemy stations when this practice was considered a crime? And how did they get caught? Besides the possibility of interpersonal surveillance and reporting, Yu Wang's study of radio broadcasting and enemy radio in Mao's China offers another possible explanation. He notes that the Taiwanese station Voice of Free China deliberately used provocative messages in different languages to approach these listeners and encourage them to send letters; the station also set up overseas mailboxes to decrease the risk of letter interception (Wang 2019: 151–8). These measures proved effective for preventing letter correspondence across the Taiwan Strait, as Voice of Free China received 509 letters in 1962, over 90 percent of which were politically sensitive. Wang contends that this transnational communication was tacitly allowed by the socialist state due to the "economics of shortage," since money sent from overseas Chinese to their relatives in mainland China served as a vital source of foreign currency, which was critically deficient in the 1950s and 1960s (2019: 156). As Wang argues, other than undermining state power, illicit listening to enemy stations and transgressive correspondence were considered by the state as ways of identifying internal enemies.

The identification of enemies within the state is an exercise of the power of the sovereign state, which Foucault sees as an archaic form of power. Its operation is hinged upon a juridical, legislative separation between citizens and enemies and what is permitted and prohibited. It submits individuals to the domination of the sovereign through a process of objectivizing or, in other words, of identifying individuals as the enemy in order to rationalize violence against them. The appearance of new forms of power, the disciplinary and the security apparatus, does not cancel the old (Foucault 2007: 7). Rather, they function alongside each other. While the juridical form of power subjects illicit listeners to prison sentences, the disciplinary power permits listeners to transform themselves, bodies and souls, into the ideal subject without their self-determination being fully undermined. Through the process of internalizing principles and rules, they subjugate their bodies to a state of docility.

From the perspective of sound studies, Foucault's discussion of the disciplinary mechanism and state power echoes nicely with how Attali speaks of music, or any organization of sounds: "what links a power center to its subjects, and thus, more generally… is an attribute of power in all of its forms" (1985: 6). Attali points out three uses of sounds—ritual, representative, and bureaucratic—which correspond to different forms of power. The use of music in ritual is to "make people *forget* the general violence," representative is to "make people *believe* in the harmony of the world," and bureaucratic is to "*silence*" and censor "all other human noise" (1985: 19). While state power functioned to silence the noise of enemy radio broadcasts, disciplinary power worked to make people believe in the ideal of the socialist imagination.

Several posters demonstrated these socialist visions with regard to radio and the ideal listener. For example, one poster published in 1954 shows how families were channeled into the newly established socialist country through radio sets (Figure 9.1). It depicts a spacious room with a young couple and three kids enjoying their abundant food. A radio set, a portrait of Chairman Mao, a calendar, and a clock are set in the background. Given that China only has a single time zone, the calendar and the clock here are meaningfully indicative of what Anderson describes as the homogenous and empty time of the imagined community (2006: 24). In border areas, especially where ethnic minorities resided, radio infrastructure functioned as an essential extension of the central government in Beijing.[3] A poster titled "The Grasslands Are Connected with Beijing" (*Caoyuan lian Beijing*, 1977) stages several Mongolian children sitting around a radio receiver in the grasslands (Figure 9.2). Three of them are looking at the receiver with curiosity and enthusiasm, and the girl to the left appears to have stopped reading her book to listen to the broadcast carefully. It can, therefore, be seen how radio broadcasting is essential to connecting the Mongolian minority at the border of China with the capital of the socialist state, Beijing. A network of signals and sounds connects the center of the socialist state with residents at the border, engulfing the latter into the synchronous temporality of the nation and transforming them into national citizens. Most interestingly, this poster also foregrounds domesticated sheep as if they are also listening to radio broadcasts with these Mongolian children, evoking the popular imagination of Mao Zedong as the shepherd of socialist China.[4] If the illicit listeners to enemy radio are subject to juridical penalty and the power of domination, these ideal listeners—parents, children, and sheep—suggest a disciplinary control that aims at transforming human bodies and souls. Disciplinary power, therefore, contrasts sharply

Figure 9.1 "Chairman Mao Gives Us a Happy Life." Xin Liliang, March 1954; IISH collection, BG E16/269. Source: chineseposters.net.

Figure 9.2 "The Grasslands Are Connected with Beijing." Wang Zhiping and Guo Chongguang, October 1977; Landsberger collection, BG E13/334. Source: chineseposters.net.

with the objectivizing power of domination. Instead, it is subjectivizing, attuning bodies and sensory organs to the controlled media environment. Nonetheless, once the sound of harmony fails to transform one's mind and body into the ideal type, the door to the prison cell opens.

Illicit Listening at the Border

As scholars in sound studies have noted, a fixed and ideal point of listening is hardly possible (Attali 1985; Szendy 2016). Peter Szendy contends that hearings are "floating points or lines of flotation that compose, in the space of a few measures, a possible listening in the form of control or reciprocal overhearing" (2016: 36). For Szendy, it is overhearing and espionage that exemplify polyphonies and multiple points of listening:

> Overhearing, then, appears to name or evoke a certain proliferating polyphony of listening: multiple lines of listening—in the sense of telephone lines—that are connected, redouble themselves, interfere with each other, and sometimes get blurred. The English word overhearing does share this technical or technological connotation: In the field of telecommunication, it designates what in French is called *diaphonie*, namely a defect in transmission caused by the transfer of a signal, channel, or a line onto another. A superposition of voices, the interference of another, secondary line with the primary one. When we hear strange voices

from another conversation over the phone or when some alien music interferes with a recording.

(Szendy 2016: 14–5)

Here, Szendy notes that overhearing has always been associated with the often flawed distribution of signals as well as the limit of signal infrastructures or, to use his own words, "a defect in transmission." It was through the infrastructural defect in signal transmissions that listening to enemy radio broadcasting in socialist China was facilitated. The electromagnetic fatality introduced another kind of infrastructural problem in socialist China that led to multiple ways of structuring the listening experience, which in turn problematized the notion of the Chinese socialist nation-state.

The Sent-Down Youth

In one of his most well-known essays, the Chinese author and scriptwriter Ah Cheng recalls his memory of listening to enemy radio during the Chinese Cultural Revolution when he was sent to the Yunnan countryside, the far southwest border area of China. He writes of the difficulties of receiving signals from the Zhongyang renmin guangbo diantai (China National Radio), the official centralized broadcasting station in socialist China, and how he and other sent-down educated youth turned to foreign radio stations:

> I don't know whether it was popular among all educated youths in China to listen to foreign radio stations—so-called enemy stations—in the 1970s, but in Yunnan, they all did. Yunnan was a special place. It was so remote that signals from the China National Radio were hardly audible and it took days for newspapers to be delivered to the mountains. Once they arrived, they'd be stored in the party secretary's house. We'd ask him to shred a piece of newspaper when we needed to roll our cigarettes. For enemy radio fans, the national radio station and newspapers were no more than references. Listening to enemy radio was not solely for the purpose of staying politically informed, but, more important, for entertainment.
>
> (Ah 2017)

It was not rare among educated young people to listen to enemy radio in the Chinese border areas. Ah Cheng was among millions of *zhiqing*, the urban educated youth who were mobilized by the Chinese Communist Party to vacate cities for remote rural areas in the late 1960s and 1970s in a mass political campaign known as *Shangshan xiaxiang yundong* ("Down to the Countryside Movement"). The sent-down youths helped to distribute broadcasting equipment from the urban centers to the rural border areas (Honig and Zhao 2015). For example, Shanghai officials provided broadcasting cables to Xishuangbanna, Yunnan Province, for sent-down youth to install fifty stations and perform tasks related to broadcasting, and these officials were eager to do it because broadcasting served as one of the primary means by which people living in remote areas could follow national and regional news (Honig and Zhao: 510). The CCP expected these youth to remold their pro-bourgeois ways of thinking by toiling with peasants in the countryside, learning from the proletarians, and, ultimately, transforming themselves into the Socialist New Man. While to be the ideal human being implies that one should take an ideal listening point, the illicit listening of these educated youth in the remote areas exemplifies a different kind of listening practice facilitated by a technological difference with respect to signal transmissions.

In the border areas, as the above quotation shows, broadcasts of the China National Radio (Zhongyang renmin guangbo diantai) were almost inaudible—a technological problem of their centralized distribution. Broadcasts from enemy radio stations could, however, be heard in these places, depending on the location of reception. In southern China, Taiwanese, Hong Kong, and Vietnamese radio broadcasts were relatively easy to access; in the northern area, it was the Soviet Union stations. The proximity of geographical locations could indeed enhance the distribution of broadcasting in nearby regions. Other memoirs also recall how these educated youth listened to enemy radio in the mountainous area of the northeast border:

> There were more than a dozen educated youth in my "collective institutional household." Our political opinions were basically the same. Therefore, no one would betray us. It was not very dangerous to listen to "enemy radio" as we were in the remote mountainous areas. At that time, national broadcasts and magazines were full of clichés like "The enemy is rotten day by day, whereas we are getting better every day." Who believes that? Only by listening to "enemy radio" were we able to know what was going on for real. It was the transistor radio on the market that made possible our listening: it was small and compact, able to receive shortwaves (unlike those in North Korea), and highly sensitive… I was allocated to the Changbai Mountain area during the Down to the Countryside Movement. This area is near North Korea and the Soviet Union. I could hardly hear broadcasting from Taiwan, while signals from the Soviet Union station and the North Korean station were strong. Sometimes we could also listen to VOA and the BBC. VOA and the BBC were undoubtedly enemy radio stations. The awkward accents of their broadcasters seemed quite strange to us because we were used to listening to the China National Radio.
>
> (Xiejia yi shusheng 2018)

While the transmission of national broadcasting and therefore the regulation of listeners by a centralized power fell short of reaching Chinese border areas like Yunnan and the Changbai Mountain, the state promotion of radio technology as the tool for modernizing the country further facilitated illicit listening to enemy radio. For example, high schools included radio technology as part of their curriculum. In a report from the Shanghai No. 3 Girls High School, the author shows how teachers and students actively participated in assembling radio receivers and doing experiments with other wireless devices: "Teachers realized that guiding students in scientific and technological activities was not only a war against the bourgeoisie but also one of the essential ways of cultivating talents for developing science in

China to catch up with and go beyond international levels" (Shanghai shi disan nvzi zhongxue 1966).

Assembling radio sets was quite common among radio fans in the 1970s. During this period, science and engineering journals published a large number of essays offering instructions for both specialists and amateurs on how to assemble transistor radio receivers. In an essay titled "How to Build Simple Transistor Radio Receivers," published in *Kexue dazong* (Popular Science) in 1963, the author introduces the diagram to readers and offers instructions on avoiding technological mistakes (Wu 1963). The essay also shows that assembling a radio receiver was not only economically affordable but also technologically viable in the 1960s: "If you can buy all these components from the electronics shop nearby, you can try to build a transistor radio receiver… It is not difficult for experienced radio fans to follow the diagram and build the radio receiver… and it only costs ten yuan or maybe a little bit more" (Wu 1963: 27). In this diagram, a bifurcation between headphones and loudspeaker and between individual and public listening appears, which already implies multiple ways of listening in socialist China that complicated the univocal way of engineering sounds (Figure 9.3).

Memoirs from sent-down youths in Sichuan and Fujian Provinces record how assembling radios facilitated listening to enemy radio in remote areas. As radio receivers were considered to be "luxuries" that most individuals or families in the 1970s could not afford to buy, some sent-down youths in Leshan, Sichuan Province, organized an amateur radio group and collected money from all the group members to buy components and build a transistor radio receiver. With this receiver, they were able to receive signals of enemy radio from Taiwan and the United States (Cao 2017: 201). In Fujian, assembling valve radio sets helped sent-down youths to listen to Hokkien-based programs from NHK (Japan Broadcasting Corporation) (Wei 2009: 46).

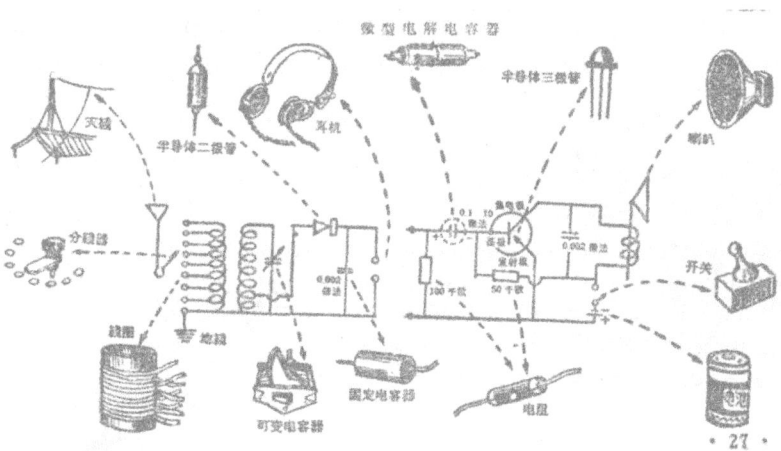

Figure 9.3 Diagram illustrating how to build a radio receiver. Source: Ai Wu.

Teresa Teng and the Broadcasting War over the Taiwan Strait

There were mainly two kinds of programs the illicit listeners chose to listen to: political news and entertainment programs. News from enemy stations offered another way for these educated youths to know what was happening in China and other parts of the world because news reports and information were strictly controlled and censored in China. That is to say, listening to enemy radio might have fulfilled listeners' desires to access news from different sources, especially those beyond the control of the state. There might also be pleasures in the transgression involved in illicit listening. Besides political news, what also attracted these illicit listeners were entertainment programs. One example is the popular music genre, which was deemed by leftist critics *mimi zhi yin* ("sounds of decadence") and *huangse gequ* ("yellow music"), whose style stands in contrast to the aesthetics of revolutionary romanticism and realism in socialist China. The origins of "yellow music" can be traced back to the phonographic culture in colonized Shanghai during the 1930s. In Andrew Jones' study of gramophone recordings and jazz music in China, he shows that although yellow music should be seen as part of the Chinese nation-building project in the republican era, it was usually condemned by nationalist and leftist critics "as a 'decadent sound' capable of seducing citizens away from the pressing tasks of nation-building and anti-imperialist resistance" (2001: 8).

These retrospective writings often mention Teresa Teng, one of the most well-known Taiwanese singers of yellow music, and their collective experience of listening to her songs. Ah Cheng, recalling how the sent-down youths at the southern border listened to Teng's song together, describes her voice as "to die for" (2017). The radio station Voice of Free China in Taiwan often broadcast Teng's songs in the 1970s, and their audience included soldiers, editors, and even government officers in mainland China: "When fans of Teresa Teng listened to her beautiful voice, their bodies trembled with excitement and, possibly, fear" (Ma 2013: 49).

And it was not without reason that Teng's songs were so prominent. During the Cold War, the Republic of China (ROC, Taiwan) turned Teng's songs into auditory weapons through radio broadcasting via loudspeakers over the Taiwan Strait, from the Kinmen Islands in particular. The Kinmen Islands were and still are controlled by the ROC government. They are only about two kilometers away from the Chinese mainland city Xiamen (Fujian Province). Both sides established radio stations in Xiamen and Kinmen and, beginning in the 1950s, launched their so-called broadcasting war. Powerful loudspeakers were used to broadcast front-line indoctrinations to the "enemy" across the strait. With loudspeakers, each side could hear the other without a radio receiver. As Shubin He (2018) writes, "The broadcasting team in Xiamen used the same loudspeakers as the US Navy (Figure 9.4a). The power of one audio amplifier was 250 watts, and nine audio amplifiers made up one extremely powerful loudspeaker. The sound could cover a radius of ten kilometers." One black-and-white photo (Figure 9.4b) shows a broadcasting announcer, Wu Shizi, holding this loudspeaker, which the broadcasting team members jokingly referred to as "the nine-headed bird."

As Wu Shizi himself recalls, "The broadcasting team initially broadcast with loudspeakers. The speed of speaking with loudspeakers was generally lower, around 100 words per minute, while the speaking rate for wireless broadcasting was 160 to 180 words per minute. Because announcers were shouting to audiences across the strait, they sometimes even lost their voices" (Wu quoted in Yan 2016: 161–2). The use of loudspeakers that could not simply be turned off demonstrates the peculiar pervasiveness of Chinese socialist broadcasting. As Li's study (2020) of the soundscape of socialist China shows, the assemblage of radio, loudspeaker, and human agents demonstrates a "uniquely 'Maoist' way of using radios and loudspeakers" that contributed to a "more pervasive" and "more ephemeral and subliminal" sensory experience of Chinese listeners (2020: 27).

As Wu Shizi spoke fluent Hokkien, he was among the earliest announcers who used this vernacular language, instead of Mandarin, in the broadcasting war against Taiwan. During this time, the Xiamen radio station was already often broadcasting traditional Hokkien opera to call forth nostalgic feelings among Taiwanese soldiers on the Kinmen Islands, since many of those soldiers were native speakers of Hokkien and had close connections with Fujian Province, only being forced to leave due to the defeat of Kuomintang in the civil war of the 1940s. Kinmen radio used Teng's love songs, including the famous "Tian mimi" (Sweet Honey Honey) and "Yueliang daibiao wo de xin" (The Moon Represents My Heart), as a weapon in response to Xiamen's broadcasts to attack red China through loudspeakers bought from Japan (He 2018). Listening to her songs in Xiamen through loudspeakers was no longer clandestine—even for the illicit listening to these enemy radio stations, there still existed multiple ways of listening. While these sent-down youths were secretly choosing their favorite programs to listen to, loudspeaker listeners across the Taiwan Strait were involuntarily caught up in acoustic warfare.

Jones notes that only after the late 1970s did the legacy of yellow music begin to reclaim audiences in the mainland through the songs of Teng. However, this process has taken a long time. Even in the 1980s, after China's economic reform, Teng's songs were still strongly criticized in the mainland. The book *Zenyang jianbie huangse gequ* (How to Identify the Yellow Music), published in 1982, refers to one of Teng's most well-known cover songs, "Heri jun zai lai" (When Will You Return?), as yellow music, contending that its love theme hides the "social reality of blood and tears" (1982: 44). Despite these criticisms, with the end of the Cold War and the triumph of the Western Bloc, Teng soon became one of the most favorite pop icons of post-socialist China who not only "conquered the audience in mainland China" but also "transformed the soundscape dominated by the 'clanging sound of bronzes and stones' of revolutionary model opera" (Liu 2019: 80). Teng's tremendous popularity in mainland China should, at the very least, be attributed to the broadcasting war over the Taiwan Strait and the militarized use of radio technologies. In the period of hostility between the two sides on China's southeast border, the simultaneous existence of Teng's voice and of the broadcast Hokkien operas, as signals and acoustic vibrations, reveals a profound relation between Taiwan and the mainland China prior to their geopolitical separation.

Figure 9.4a Screenshot of film made during the Battle of Iwo Jima between the US Navy and the Imperial Japanese Army in 1945, showing the US soldiers using a similar loudspeaker. Source: Archive Films Editorial 1945.

Figure 9.4b Wu Shize holding "the nine-headed bird" loudspeaker. Source: Yan Lifeng.

Conclusion

As I have shown in this chapter, radio broadcasting is at once airy and solid because of the two tendencies associated with it: the deterritorializing tendency to flow across borders and the reterritorializing tendency to achieve a fixed listening point within one nation-state or one region. While electromagnetic signals can easily go across what have been delineated as national and regional borders, their distribution and reception are also often harnessed by different power apparatuses, state power in particular. I discussed three forms of power and how they work together to ensure an ideal distribution of sound infrastructures and ideas: the apparatus of security as the control of national broadcasting networks, the disciplinary power that aims to cultivate the ideal listening subject, and the power of the state to ban listening to enemy radio broadcast. The importance of radio broadcasting as a means of communication makes this medium especially susceptible to state interventions to secure improved circulation. Banning the practice of listening to enemy radio stations can, therefore, be seen as controlling a means of communication and attempting to produce even and smooth distributions. However, the electromagnetic fatality introduced uneven distributions of infrastructures, sounds, and power, making an imagined listening community inherently limited and heterogeneous.

Acknowledgments

This chapter grew out of my participation in the graduate seminar "Sound, Technology, and Power" at McGill University, and I must thank Jonathan Sterne and my classmates for inspiring me to embark on this project and for giving me feedback in an early draft. I must also thank the two editors of this volume, Lonán Ó Briain and Min Yen Ong, for their constructive comments and rigorous work. I presented this project at a few occasions, and I want to thank the conference and panel organizers and participants, especially Ling Kang, Andy Stuhl, and Yu Wang, for engaging intellectually in my project. Above all, I am thankful to Joel Jordon for doing extraordinary editing work for my many versions of this chapter.

Notes

1. During the 1960s and the 1970s, the Chinese socialist state launched the *shangshan xiaxiang yundong* ("Down to the Countryside Movement") and mobilized millions of educated youths to leave the city and work in the remote rural areas, with the intention of reeducating them in the countryside. Those educated youth are referred to as *zhiqing*, or the "sent-down youth."
2. The author Xinwu Zhou published this manifesto-like essay under the name of the deputy director of the Chinese State Central Broadcasting Service.

3   In the 1950s, *Zhongyang renmin guangbo diantai* (China National Radio) used five languages (Mongolian, Tibetan, Korean, Uyghur, and Zhuang) to broadcast for audiences considered ethnic minorities in China. See Zhou 1959.
4   Du (2016) discusses the representation of sheep and shepherds in the animated film *Heroic Little Sisters of the Grassland* (1965) and the role ethnicity plays in China's socialist imagination. She argues that the Mongolian sisters in this film are turned into docile lambs under the guidance of Chairman Mao.

Bibliography

Ah, Cheng. 2017. "On Listening to Enemy Radio." Translated by Yurou Zhong. The MCLC Resource Center. Available online: http://u.osu.edu/mclc/2017/07/03/on-listening-to-enemy-radio/, accessed May 28, 2020.

Anderson, Benedict. 2006. *Imagined Communities: Reflections on the Origin and Spread of Nationalism*. London and New York: Verso.

Attali, Jacques. 1985. *Noise: The Political Economy of Music*. Translated by Brian Massumi. Minneapolis, MN: University of Minnesota Press.

Badenoch, Alexander, Andreas Fickers, and Christian Henrich-Franke, eds. 2013. *Airy Curtains in the European Ether: Broadcasting and the Cold War*. Baden-Baden, Germany: Nomos Verlagsgesellschaft.

Birdsall, Carolyn. 2012. *Nazi Soundscapes: Sound, Technology and Urban Space in Germany, 1933–1945*. Amsterdam: Amsterdam University Press.

Cao, Guimin. 2017. "*Wo jiyi zhong de sanxian suiyue*." In *Sanxian fengyun: zhongguo sanxian jianshe wenxuan*, edited by Hongchun Zhang, 190–202. Chengdu: Sichuan renmin chubanshe.

Du, Daisy Yan. 2016. "The Dis/Appearance of Animals in Animated Film during the Chinese Cultural Revolution, 1966–76." *Positions* 24 (2): 435–79.

Foucault, Michel. 2007. *Security, Territory, Population: Lectures at the Collège de France 1977–1978*. Translated by Burchell Graham. New York: Palgrave Macmillan.

He, Shubin. 2018. "Dui tai xi: haixia shangkong de guangbo zhan." China Studies, Chinese University of Hong Kong. Available online: http://www.mjlsh.org/book.aspx?cid=7&tid=11&pid=1035&aid=1036, accessed May 28, 2020.

Honig, Emily, and Xiaojian Zhao. 2015. "Sent-Down Youth and Rural Economic Development in Maoist China." *The China Quarterly* 222: 499–521.

Huang, Nicole. 2003. "Sun-Facing Courtyards: Urban Communal Culture in Mid-1970s' Shanghai." *East Asian History* 25 (26): 161–82.

Jones, Andrew F. 2001. *Yellow Music: Media Culture and Colonial Modernity in the Chinese Jazz Age*. Durham, NC: Duke University Press.

Lamarre, Thomas. 2017. "Platformativity: Media Studies, Area Studies." *Asiascape: Digital Asia* 4 (3): 285–305.

Li, Jie. 2020. "Revolutionary Echoes: Radios and Loudspeakers in the Mao Era." *Twentieth-Century China* 45 (1): 25–45.

Liu, Xiao. 2019. *Information Fantasies: Precarious Mediation in Postsocialist China*. Minneapolis, MN: University of Minnesota Press.

Ma, Duosi. 2013. "Touting denglijun de rizi." *Wenshi bolan* 11: 48–9.

Ó Briain, Lonán. 2018. "Musical Cosmopolitanism in Late-Colonial Hanoi." *Ethnomusicology Forum* 27 (3): 265–85.
Shanghai shi di san nvzi zhongxue. 1966. "Tantan woxiao wuxiandian kewai huodong de bianhua." *Wuli tongbao* 7: 321–2.
Shanxi sheng zhengfa ganbu xuexiao ziliaoshi, ed. 1983. *Sifa shijian guwen xuanbian*. Shanxi: Shanxi sheng zhengfa ganbu xuexiao ziliaoshi.
Starosielski, Nicole. 2015. *The Undersea Network*. Durham, NC: Duke University Press.
Szendy, Peter. 2016. *All Ears: The Aesthetics of Espionage*. Translated by Roland Végső. New York, NY: Fordham University Press.
Wang, Yu. 2019. "Listening to the State: Radio and the Technopolitics of Sound in Mao's China." PhD thesis, University of Toronto.
Wei, Yongle. 2009. "Na suanku zhong daidian tian de rizi." In *Shanghang zhiqing wangshi*, edited by Wenbiao Wen, Chunchi Xie, and Weiguang Li, 44–8. Fujian: Shanghang xian zhengxie wenshi yu xuexi xuanchuan meiyuanhui.
Wu, Ai. 1963. "Zuo yitai jiandan de bandaoti shouyin ji." *Kexue dazong* 9: 27.
Xiejia yi shusheng. 2018. "Wenge zhong liangci qinli touting ditai shijian." China Studies, Chinese University of Hong Kong. Available online: http://www.mjlsh.org/Book.aspx?cid=4&tid=2144, accessed May 28, 2020.
Yan, Lifeng. 2016. *Taiwan chuanmei yu taiwan wenhua yanjiu*. Beijing: Jiuzhou chubanshe.
Yang, Daqing. 2009. "Submarine Cables and the Two Japanese Empires." In *Communications under the Seas: The Evolving Cable Network and Its Implications*, edited by Bernard Finn and Daqing Yang, 227–54. Cambridge, MA: MIT Press.
Yang, Kuisong. 2010. "Xin zhongguo chengli chuqi qingchu meiguo wenhua yingxiang de jingguo." *Zhonggong dangshi yanjiu* 10: 23–33.
Zenyang jianbei huangse gequ. 1982. *Zenyang jianbei huangse gequ*. Beijing: Renmin yinyue chubanshe.
Zhongyang guangbo shiwuju. 1977. "Wuxiandian guangbo jishu weihu zhidu he guanli banfa cao'an." *Guangbo yu dianshi jishu* 4: 4–56.
Zhou, Xinwu. 1959. "Yuejin zhong de zhongguo guangbo shiye." *Xinwen zhanxian* 18: 5–6.

Part Four

Performing Activism

10

"Change the World Gently with Singing": Queer Audibility and Soft Activism in China

Hongwei Bao

On June 9, 2018, the first national queer choir concert, *The Journey of Light*, was held in the concert hall at the Shanghai Conservatory of Music. For the first time, seven LGBTQ (Lesbian, Gay, Bisexual, Transgender, and Queer) choirs from across the country were brought together to perform on the same stage.[1] The event was publicized on Chinese social media (primarily WeChat, also known as Weixin, and Weibo) and livestreamed on Chinese-language music and video-streaming websites (including Netease cloud music, Douban, Bilibili, and TikTok), Chinese-language lesbian and gay dating apps (including Blued, Aloha, Rela, Lespark, and Lesdo), and international social media (including Facebook, YouTube, and Instagram). Although the offline event publicity in China was relatively low key and the organizers were careful not to brand the event as a "China's first national queer choir concert," possibly to avoid attracting unnecessary attention from the Chinese authorities, the concert was still celebrated in mainland China's LGBTQ communities as a landmark event.

This concert also marked part of the tenth anniversary celebration of the Shanghai Pride, which consisted of a film festival, a choir concert, a photography and art exhibition, and other public events. What was missing from the annual Shanghai Pride was a parade where queer people march along the streets, as is commonly seen in LGBTQ prides in other parts of the world. This is hardly surprising. Although homosexuality was decriminalized in the People's Republic of China (PRC; hereafter China) in 1997 and removed from China's *Classification of Mental Disorders* in 2001, homosexuality is still largely a taboo subject in Chinese society. This coincides with the Chinese government's highly unpredictable media censorship as well as its constant ban of unsanctioned public events. To hold a pride event consisting merely of cultural activities was already a considerable risk to take, let alone to hold a pride parade with people marching along the streets. In this context, having a pride week without a pride parade—and more precisely in this case, with a choir concert—serves as a culturally sensitive form of queer activism in the China, but how then do we interpret this type of activism?

This chapter focuses on LGBTQ choirs in China, using the Beijing Queer Chorus (*Beijing ku'er hechangtuan*; hereafter BQC) as a case study. I attended some of the choir's rehearsals when I lived in Beijing several years ago. Since leaving Beijing, I have primarily followed their websites and social media accounts. For this chapter, I have also interviewed some choir members by email and on social media. By examining how LGBTQ choirs such as BQC construct queer identities and communities and how they engage in political and social activism through live performances and online streaming, I highlight the importance of using music, sound, and digital media to communicate identity, community, and social movements. Developing the critical framework of "queer audibility" (Bao 2015), I interrogate the cultural specificity of queer activism in the Chinese context and argue for a "soft" type of activism through performing arts, culture, and media. This type of queer activism departs from a sole emphasis on visibility, confrontation, and direct intervention into politics that characterizes LGBTQ pride parades in many parts of the world. I also consider the role of the internet and social media in disseminating queer voices to the LGBTQ communities and the public across China and the Chinese diaspora. In doing so, I examine how the production and circulation of musical cultures function as a "soft," culturally sensitive, and context-specific form of political and social activism that can potentially empower socially marginalized groups in the Asia Pacific.

Queer Activism in Contemporary China

Although China has a long history of homoeroticism, the public emergence of homosexuality—and furthermore, gay identity—is a recent phenomenon. Homosexuality was introduced to China as a medical and psychiatric category at the beginning of the twentieth century (Chiang 2010; Kang 2009; Sang 2003). Gay identity, as a product of the global LGBTQ movement, emerged in urban areas as part of postsocialist China's "opening-up" drive in the late twentieth century. As Howard Chiang points out, the rise of urban queer communities in China can be attributed to three factors: the pursuit of civil rights, the claiming of cultural citizenship, and the political maneuvering of social space (2019: 187). All of these factors are situated in the context of globalization.

"Global gays" (Altman 1997), that is, the globalization of LGBTQ identity and politics worldwide, marks an important feature in queer cultures from many parts of the world. In the context of China, scholars have suggested that sexual identities and queer activism in China today were neither entirely "borrowed" from the West nor purely derived from local historical and cultural traditions; rather, we are witnessing a new hybrid form of queer identity (Bao 2018a; Engebretsen 2014; Engebretsen and Schroeder 2015; Ho 2010; Kam 2013; Kong 2010; Martin et al. 2008; Rofel 2007). Most queer activists in China dismiss the possibility of a confrontational type of queer politics modeled on Stonewall—that is, a type of political activism primarily based on open confrontation with the authorities and the general public—and represented by pride parades on city streets.[2] They instead advocate a culturally sensitive style of "soft" activism using media, culture, and "nomadic activism" (Rofel 2013) to construct identities and build communities (Bao 2011; Liu 2019). Elisabeth Engebretsen (2015) juxtaposes three landmark queer activist events in China: a Stonewall anniversary celebration in the form of a birthday party in Beijing in 1996, the Shanghai Pride in 2009, and a pride parade in Changsha in 2013. It is tempting to see these three events in a linear, progressive, and teleological manner and thus imagine that the Western type of pride parade might be the future for China. After all, China is becoming more accepting of homosexuality, and younger generations of LGBTQ people are becoming more confident and conscious of their own sexuality and rights. However, Engebretsen observes, on closer examination, that even the 2013 pride parade in Changsha did not simply emulate the Western model. The organizers took careful consideration of the local contexts and devised many temporal, spatial, and publicity tactics to reduce risks. It is thus more appropriate to see the three events as contingent and the organizers as experienced enough to understand and make strategic use of the contingent social contexts in open, flexible, and creative ways. As Engebretsen argues:

> Activists use nuanced modes of articulation and develop meaningful ways to further their political agendas while minimising the risk of censorship and violence. The communicative strategies convey messages of sameness and difference, or of transgression and compliance, depending on the perspectives of the audiences. In this way, they contribute toward creating powerful, and complex, and yet paradoxical discourses of what it means to be Chinese *and* queer, in a comparative, geopolitical perspective.
>
> (2015: 106, original emphasis)

Indeed, Chinese queer activism is characterized by its contingency, as it is dependent upon multiple factors, including state policy, geographical location, and interactions between organizers and participants. It is, therefore, difficult to come up with a generic statement of what type of activism suits China or will take place in China in the future. However, with the strengthening of political control under the rule of the current Chinese president Xi Jinping, the pride parade type of activism has become increasingly difficult in China. Based on these circumstances, I suggest that the following three types may become dominant forms of queer activism in the years to come.

The first lies within the area of litigation. Although homosexuality is not legally protected in China, an increasing number of queer individuals have taken respective public institutions and government ministries to court for their discriminatory policies and practices against gender and sexual minorities. This has been exemplified by queer filmmaker Fan Popo's 2013 case against the State Administration of Radio, Film and Television over the online censorship of his film *Mama Rainbow*, queer activist Peng Yanhui's 2014 case against the Xinyu Piaoxiang Psychiatric Clinic over gay conversion therapy, and Qiu Bai's 2016 case against the Ministry of Education over the negative depiction of homosexuality in university textbooks (Parkin 2018).

Although most of these court cases did not achieve the results the plaintiffs had hoped for, the fact that government ministries and public institutions can be potentially held to account for their wrongdoing serves as an inspiration for sexual minorities and other marginalized social groups in China.

The second dominant form of queer activism engages with the internet and social media. With the rapid development of the internet and social media in China, along with its widespread use among sexual minorities, online and social media activism have become an indispensable means of queer activism in China today. Such examples include the community response online to Lü Liping and Sun Haiying's homophobic remarks in 2011 and Sina Weibo's reversal of the ban on gay content in 2018 (Bao 2018b). It is crucial to note that online activism often works in tandem with offline activism and is usually facilitated by LGBTQ organizations, media companies, public celebrities, and the Chinese government. Online activism alone without necessary offline support and community mobilization is often insufficient in achieving a sustainable social impact.

The third type of queer activism is associated with organized cultural activities and events. This can take various forms, including film festivals, art and photography exhibitions, cultural festivals, and sporting events. Examples include the Beijing Queer Film Festival, Shanghai Queer Film Festival, PFLAG (Parents, Family and Friends of Lesbians and Gays) meetings, and the Shanghai Pride. The choir concert described at the beginning of this chapter falls under this category too. These cultural activities also include dinners, karaoke, sports, and what William Schroeder (2015) describes as, the "affective forms of having fun." These activities may not look political, but they play a significant role in constructing identities and communities and raising awareness of minority rights—as works on community music therapy in other contexts demonstrate (Stige, Ansdell, and Pavlicevic 2010). More importantly, these cultural events and activities can effectively circumvent government censorship and are therefore more likely to be effective in community building.

These three types of queer activism coexist in contemporary China, and they play different roles. Activists usually combine them for rights advocacy and community building, while selecting the most appropriate form according to their needs and specific contexts. It is difficult to predict whether the confrontational type of queer politics represented by pride parades will take place in China. As litigation can only be used in a few selected cases, the "soft" activism represented by organized cultural events, including film screenings and choir rehearsals, may dominate China's queer activism for a long time to come, given the consistency of a rigid government policy of "no support, no opposition, and no advocacy" (Wang 2015: 174) with regard to homosexuality. By combining offline public musical performance and active online engagement with the community and the general public, queer choirs in China epitomize such a "soft" activist approach. In the following section, I shall conduct a case study of how the Beijing Queer Chorus engages with community building and cultural activism before I go on to discuss its wider implications for understanding the role of music and digital media for queer activism in China today.

"Sing for a Better World": Beijing Queer Chorus

Founded in 2008 and originally named Shining Jazzy Chorus (*Sanlengjianyi hechangtuan*), BQC was the first major LGBTQ choir that performed publicly in China. It is a member of the Asian LGBT Choir Network and is also one of the first Asian members of the Gay and Lesbian Association of Choruses. The choir has around 170 members in total; however, a smaller group of about fifty people meet regularly every weekend for rehearsals (WeChat interview with Laurence on September 13, 2019). Most choir members are in their twenties and thirties, and most self-identify as LGBTQ, but there are straight and queer-friendly people as well. BQC has a presence on WeChat, Weibo, Douban, TikTok, Bilibili, YouTube, Facebook, and other social media and video-streaming sites (Figure 10.1).

BQC's English slogan is "sing for a better world," but its Chinese slogan sounds more interesting: "change the world gently with singing" ("*Yong gesheng wenrou gaibian shijie*"). If to "change the world" conveys an activist ambition—that is, the choir is not simply there for fun or to achieve musical excellence; it has a social purpose as well—"gently with singing" conveys an approach different from the commonly perceived "hard" and "direct" approach to queer political activism mentioned earlier. After sending a straight-identified male journalist to a BQC rehearsal, global news media outlet *Vice* observed: "They do not seem eager to work hard to fight for equal rights or push boundaries. They just want to dress beautifully and sing nice songs elegantly" (Vice 2018). BQC has its own way of engaging politically. As choir member Ling Yu put it: "Chorus is a gentle form of expression. In this community, when dozens of people stand on the same stage and sing the same song, it is the softest way for rights advocacy. Its power cannot be underestimated" (The Paper 2019).

While BQC's supposedly apolitical nature may be a survival strategy in China, where politicized groups are often more prone to state intervention, there is ample

Figure 10.1 Screenshot of the Beijing Queer Chorus on Weibo (accessed February 10, 2019).

evidence that the choir members are thinking of activist strategies differently. Although there is no strong political or religious opposition to homosexuality in China, sexual minorities nevertheless face enormous pressure from traditional ideas of family and posterity, as well as the public's general lack of knowledge regarding homosexuality. In this context, building queer communities and raising public awareness about LGBTQ issues become paramount. Visibility and positive representations have their own problems, but they can act as viable starting points. As the choir states on its Weibo account (a microblogging social media platform): "We are doing our best to contribute to China's queer movement, by presenting positive images of queer communities, by combating prejudice with beautiful tunes, and by performing in public to showcase diversity" (Lei 2013). Choir member Laurence remarked: "We need people to stand in front of the public and let them know that LGBTQ are ordinary people and are not different from others" (WeChat interview, September 13, 2019). Another choir member nicknamed Bamboo agreed: "We adopt a gentle approach to the world, and we hope that the world can also treat gay people gently" (Vice 2018).

Being part of an inclusive community reflects a lot of choir members' experiences in the choir. In my interview, choir member Simon reflected:

> The critical things which made me feel really involved in the BQC are the people here, and what they do, or what we do... In BQC, people just gently sing here, and do what they can to make the community better. The singers, the non-singing volunteers, everyone creates a place like home where nobody needs to hide or to pretend anymore. Thus, I'm willing to stay here, not only to enjoy this place, but also to make this place better and benefit more people.
>
> (Email interview, September 13, 2019)

Indeed, for its members, the choir has become a "heterotopia" (Foucault 1986), or an "other space" different from the mainstream society, in which queer identities are imagined, communities are formed, and solidarity is forged. Choir members are experimenting with new forms of social relations and queer kinship that are not possible elsewhere in a heteronormative society.

On December 22, 2018, BQC held a concert titled *Sing, and the Hills Will Echo* (*Qunshan huixiang*) to mark its tenth anniversary. The concert program contained three parts and included a wide repertoire of music: Part One consisted of eight classic songs, including Franz Schubert's "Ave Maria" and Wang Luobin's "The Crescent Moon Rises" (*Ban'ge yueliang pa shanglai*); Part Two presented a suite of eight songs from Hayao Miyazaki's films, sung in Japanese; Part Three showcased five original songs or adaptions with queer themes, including "Li Lei and Han Meimei Are Thirty Years Old" (*Li Lei he Han Meimei sanshi sui le*), which satirizes gender stereotypes in society, and "The End of the Chou Year and Beginning of the Yin Year" (*Choumo yinchu*), a piece adapted from the traditional musical form of storytelling in Beijing dialect with drum accompaniment (*jingyun dagu*). One of the choir's favorite songs is "I Am What I Am (*Wo*)," a piece inspired by the late Hong Kong queer singer Leslie Cheung's performance. The choir have specially composed new lyrics for the song while maintaining the existing musical score. These lyrics serve as a tribute to the Hong Kong queer icon Leslie Cheung, who committed suicide in 2003; they also demonstrate the choir members' confidence in their own sexualities:

> Without hiding, live the life I love.
> Without a mask, stand right in the light.
> I am what I am.
> I am a firework of my own color.
>
> (BQC 2018, their translation)

To contribute to queer community building in China, BQC also actively engages with popular issues in the LGBTQ communities. The relationship between parents and their queer children becomes particularly pronounced in the lead-up to the Chinese New Year, when young people working or studying away from home have to return to their families to spend the festive season. For many queer people, this is a difficult time of the year, as they have to confront generation gaps and deal with pressures from parents and relatives to get into heterosexual marriages. In January 2018, BQC held a concert before the Chinese New Year (Figure 10.2). The concert was titled *So Far, So Long* in English; the Chinese title *Yuanxing yu Guxiang* literally means "Traveling and Homecoming." Conductor Yuan Ye explained the rationale for the title as follows: "Hometown has a particular meaning to queers… it is an embarrassing and even heavy topic for sexual minorities during the Chinese New Year" (Vice 2018).

Figure 10.2 Beijing Queer Chorus at the *So Far So Long* concert, Beijing, January 2018. Source: Beijing Queer Chorus.

Branded as a "music salon," *So Far, So Long* was a combination of performance art and a traditional choir concert. A female singer stood in the middle of the platform, wearing a face mask, symbolizing the masked life one leads as a closeted queer person. Video footage was shown between songs, showing a gay man making a Skype call to his mother, telling her that he missed home but could not go home because of his own sexuality. This conversation spoke to many queer people's experiences and thus created a touching effect among the queer audience. By addressing issues specific to queer people, BQC constructs an affective community through the sharing of choral music and performance.

Starting as a small choir, with only a few members and no audience at all, BQC has become an increasingly successful choir in recent years. Although very few big concert halls accept them because of their amateur status and their queer identity, they have managed to perform in smaller venues in Beijing, including independent theaters, music salons, art spaces, and community centers. While a few venues are queer-friendly, often BQC has to conceal its queer identity when hiring venues and making event publicity. As Simon explained:

> We face a lot of pressure from society. For example, when we look for a concert venue, we may be refused simply because of our queer identity. Also, we need to avoid using some key words denoting sexuality when posting on social media due to China's media censorship. But our identity can also be a strength to some degree, just like a point of differentiation. It's easier for us to get support from those who support gender and sexual equality.
>
> (Email interview, September 13, 2019)

Despite continuing discrimination, queer identity can also bring the choir some performance opportunities. For example, the choir was invited to sing the song "Season of Love," a song from the Broadway musical *Rent*, on stage when the musical toured Beijing in 2018. It has also been invited to attend music festivals in different parts of the world, including Various Voices Dublin 2014, the GALA Choruses Festival held in Denver in 2016, and the Hand in Hand Asian Queer Choral Festival in Seoul in 2017. Choir member Liu Xiao was fully aware of the pros and cons of using the queer "label": "Starting with the 'label' and ending with nice vocal music: that's the nature of the choir" (Vice 2018). As choir members are brought together by their shared gender and sexual identities and have benefited from the empowering experience of sharing their music and performance in the communal expression of these identities, they also have to work very hard to improve their singing and performance skills. For BQC, the queer identity, therefore, functions as both an obstacle to and an opportunity for its sustainable development.

Online Streaming and Social Media Communication

To publicize themselves and their events, queer community groups, including BQC, constantly have to navigate China's opaque censorship system and complex media landscape and learn to work with different types of media. LGBTQ cultures are sensitive issues on Chinese media. Queer content has been persistently banned on China's state media and frequently censored in cyberspace. Despite the continuing existence of media censorship in China, the degree of censorship varies for different types of media. Overall, state media institutions, such as the *People's Daily* and China Central Television, enforce stricter censorship rules than commercial media or media companies run at provincial and municipal levels; online and social media platforms usually enjoy more freedom than print media (Yang 2011); English-language media, including China Global Television Network, often has more press freedom than their Chinese counterparts as a result of the Chinese government's "media going out" strategy, in which English-language media play a key role in the Chinese government's public diplomacy (Thussu, de Burgh, and Shi 2018). In recent years, an increasing number of LGBTQ-friendly media content have emerged, demonstrated by the increasing number of nominations and prize winners at the annual Rainbow Media Awards, organized by Beijing Gender Health Education Institute, a Beijing-based LGBTQ nongovernmental organization and media watchdog.

Although queer issues cannot be covered by the Chinese-language state media because of censorship, BQC has been working with Chinese-language commercial and English-language international media to promote themselves and publicize their events. Simon, who is in charge of the choir's international publicity, introduces his publicity strategy:

> Each platform may have its unique style, so we need to think about the most suitable words, and how to interact with the audience. WeChat and Weibo are two major platforms, and we need to think carefully about the contents and the time to post, quite like a marketing department of a real company. For the social media platforms overseas, things are easier because BQC's main audience are within China. The followers of our overseas social media are mainly friends that we met from previous international events, such as Portland Gay Men's Chorus, GALA Choruses Festival, Hand in Hand Asian LGBT Choral Festival. These social media platforms are places to maintain old friendships. But being easy to maintain doesn't mean we can treat these platforms like a deserted place. Keeping overseas accounts up to date is very important. These platforms are usually the first windows for some potential audience to get to know us, and then some collaboration opportunities may arise.
>
> (Email interview, September 13, 2019)

Most BQC members are "born digital natives," meaning they are social media savvy. They not only use a wide range of social media platforms but have devised platform-specific publicity strategies, including inventing bespoke taglines to target specific user groups. Some of these taglines include:

Bilibili: "Take Control of the Bullet Screen"
Douban: "Tailor-Made for the Art-Loving Youth"
Facebook: "We are with the World"

Instagram: "Smiling Faces under the Rainbow"
Netease Cloud Music: "Hear the Harmonious Voice from the Sky"
TikTok: "Unruly Singers"
Weibo: "Tease These Cute Queers"
YouTube: "Gentle Voices from the Orient"

These context-specific taglines demonstrate a nuanced understanding of the technological and cultural specificity of each social media platform; they also showcase sophisticated skills in niche marketing and "narrow-casting" (Naficy 1993), a communication strategy often used by, in, and for minority groups. For example, the Bilibili blurb ("Take Control of the Bullet Screen") highlights the interactive feature of the video-streaming website (where the audience can leave superimposed textual comments on screen, a phenomenon known as *danmu*); the TikTok blurb ("Unruly Singers") targets rebellious youth who often use the short video-streaming website for self-expression, identity performance, and fun; and the Douban blurb ("Tailor-Made for the Art-Loving Youth") attracts a predominantly young, well-educated, and middle-class user group. Although international social media platforms, such as Facebook, Twitter, and YouTube, are officially banned in China and require the use of Virtual Private Networks for access, BQC loses no opportunity to engage with its international audience. Its Facebook blurb ("We Are with the World") emphasizes the cosmopolitan disposition of Facebook and the choir, whereas its YouTube blurb ("Gentle Voices from the Orient") deliberately conjures up a sense of Orientalized cultural alterity to attract an international audience who are interested in China and Chinese culture.

Publicity on each social media site requires specific strategies for audience engagement and the recognition of key features, major user groups, and various technological affordances. For video-streaming websites, such as Bilibili, TikTok, and YouTube, uploading video clips of rehearsals and performances usually suffices, often with English or bilingual subtitles to facilitate international social media users. For microblogging sites, such as Weibo and Facebook, news updates and contextual information about the videos are frequently added because of the interactive nature of these social media sites. To give visitors a better sense of the choir's social purpose, BQC often includes China's queer community news in their Weibo news update.

BQC's most labor-intensive social media engagements take place on WeChat, the biggest social media platform in the Chinese-speaking world (Wang 2016). BQC's 2019 tour to Japan showcases their sustained and strategic engagement with audiences and fans through WeChat. BQC attended the Hand in Hand Queer Choral Festival in Tokyo on April 12–15, 2019 (Figure 10.3). The choir's online publicity on WeChat started on March 19, nearly a month prior to the festival. Besides announcing the news of BQC's plan to attend the choral festival, the choir also advertised a "Friend of BQC" position, inviting a BQC fan to travel with the group to Tokyo to experience the festival, although the chosen fan would have to cover their own expenses for the trip. The article posted on WeChat on April 10 announced that a young woman had been selected by the group as the "Friend of BQC" for this trip: this young woman identifies herself as straight but queer-friendly; she loves music and has a vlog (video blog)

Figure 10.3 Beijing Queer Chorus in Japan, April 2019. Source: Beijing Queer Chorus.

account with a decent number of followers, thus making her a perfect fit to help the group with video-recording and online publicity. In the same article, BQC also invited audience members and fans to post in the comments section questions that they hoped to ask queer people in Japan and promised that BQC would ask their Japanese friends these questions on their behalf during the festival. This interactive strategy worked: a few fans posted their questions online about queer life in Japan. During the festival, pictures were posted online showing the choir members' activities in Japan, including participating in the festival and visiting different parts of the country. Immediately after the festival, interviews with choir members and Japanese queers were published on WeChat, together with an announcement that there would soon be an "experience sharing session" ("*fenxiang hui*"). The session took place at Destination, a LGBTQ club and cultural center in Beijing, on April 27, where choir members met their audience and fans and shared stories about their trip to Japan.

From the above example, we can see that throughout the process—before, during, and after the trip—BQC members were fully aware of their celebrity status and they strategically kept their audience and fans engaged: from online (e.g., posting questions) to offline participation (e.g., recruiting a fan to join the group on tour and holding a debriefing meeting to share with fans about their experiences in Japan). Recruiting a straight-identified but queer-friendly fan showcases the choir's deliberate efforts to engage with people outside the queer communities, and this conveys a positive message of inclusivity to the public. Their regular debriefing meetings also act as good opportunities to publicize the group's upcoming concerts and to recruit new choir members. Regular events like these contribute to queer community building by bringing together LGBTQ people in a local queer venue.

The publicity strategy adopted by BQC—making effective use of social media and interacting frequently with audience members and fans offline and online—is not new and is by no means unique. However, we should bear in mind that BQC is a self-organized and not-for-profit grassroots organization where every member works for the choir for free and in their spare time; income from performances is primarily used for the logistics of renting rehearsal and performance venues, as well as touring and attending music festivals. All of their social media activities are carried out by choir members and volunteers out of their love for the choir and the community. The creative, affective, and digital labor involved in these social media engagements showcases enthusiasm and creative energies in China's urban queer communities, as well as collective efforts of queer community building at the grassroots level.

Queer Audibility and Soft Activism

BQC's ways of engaging with music and social media may seem ordinary and mundane. They rehearse, perform, and regularly engage with audiences and fans online and offline. Choir members easily become friends and often hang out together, forming a close-knit community and support network for each other. They seldom feel that they are engaging in political or social activism. A sense of activism is often felt as an afterthought when they meet journalists and researchers for interviews. It is the sense of finding a community that they feel a part of, making friends, and having fun that binds the choir members together. Yet all this takes place in an environment where homosexuality is not widely accepted in society and LGBTQ rights are far from being guaranteed by law. The choir members are predominantly young, urban, cosmopolitan, and middle class, and they sometimes manifest a sense of "homonormativity"—that is, following the scripts and norms of a heterosexual society (Duggan 2004), but they have nonetheless empowered many people living at the margins of society who are troubled by their sexualities.

BQC's soft approach to activism is exemplary of most queer activist strategies in China today, ranging from reading clubs to film festivals, and from sports clubs to dinner groups. Most of these strategies involve bringing people together and doing things as a collective. These collectives do not look political from the outside, and many are not motivated by political and activist ambitions, but their activities are crucial to the formation of queer communities and identities. Many queer people feel isolated due to the lack of support from their families and friends. Encouraging them to leave the online space and private homes to meet other queer people is often the first step to identity construction and community building. Only when queer people feel more comfortable with and among themselves can they stand up to pressures from family and society and demand more rights, respect, and recognition. At critical moments, such energies can even be galvanized for political action and rights advocacy. For example, in March 2018, as soon as Weibo banned gay content on its social media platform, many individuals and groups began using the hashtag #Iamgay to protest the ban. This eventually led to a reversal of the ban (Bao 2018b). In discussing everyday queer politics in China, Schroeder writes: "In *tongzhi* [queer] China, this politics of the everyday is frequently characterized by an emphasis on fun and does not seek to effect immediate structural change. Rather, it opens up an affective space in which change is potentiated or felt" (2015: 76).

BQC's queer activism points to the importance of sound and voice in grassroots politics and social movements. Queer activism has long emphasized the importance of sight and visibility: "Coming out," after all, is a strategy primarily based on visuality, with the assumption that visibility underpins truth and authenticity, and therefore sexual minorities exist and deserve recognition. This activist strategy is widely acknowledged and practiced in many parts of the world. But sights and visibility do not have to be the only means of political engagement; sound and audibility can be equally potent but have so far been undertheorized in queer studies and media politics. Nick Couldry (2010) argues for the importance of voice, understood as the effective opportunity for people to speak and be heard on what affects their lives in contemporary politics. In discussing queer filmmaker Cui Zi'en's queer politics, I highlighted Cui's activist strategy of "making sounds" to disrupt the silence about sexual minorities in China by coming up with a critical term "queer audibility" (Bao 2015). As Cui puts it poetically and metaphorically vis-a-vis queer filmmaking in China:

This is called "making sounds" (*fasheng*). Echoes (*huixiang*) always follow sounds. The effects of sounds differ on walls. Walls in China are particularly good at absorbing sounds. However, there are still echoes and there are still people who can hear the echoes. Sounds act like sparks of fire. They make burning flames as they accumulate. Sounds do not disappear completely as if they were in a complete vacuum.

(Cui quoted in Bao 2015: 50)

The phrase "making sounds" or "making oneself heard" has also been frequently used by BQC members to describe the purpose of their musical performances and media activities, succinctly captured by the title of a song they sing, "Can You Hear Me?" BQC member Ruan Ruan made her point by using the metaphor of "voice":

Whatever your sexual orientation, your role in society is a kind of voice. It is reasonable for any kind of voice to exist in society. It should not be abandoned. The real harmony and tolerance should be that each person can play a role. We shouldn't just accept a single voice... If we don't do anything, if we don't voice our support for sexual minorities to get equal rights, they will never be recognized. Every one of us needs to take one more step forward to speak out and take action to support them.

(Quoted in CGTN 2018)

Ruan's words are informed by a more direct mode of political engagement: she encourages people to stand up to support LGBTQ rights. However, in this context, she was not talking about gay pride parades or Stonewall types of direct confrontation with the police and the public. Her proposed action points seem rather mundane: coming to queer public events to support queer people and speaking against gender and sexuality-based discriminations. As Charlie Liu, organizer of the Shanghai Pride, remarked:

> In China, there are no parades. Perhaps we don't really need it. That's why we have different cultural events such as film festivals and theatre. Sports events like the bike ride and the run are the closest we can get to a parade. You know, obstacles are not there to help you stumble; they are there to help you overcome them.
>
> (2019)

Liu's optimism points to the multiple and flexible forms of queer activism, as well as creative ways of political engagement in contemporary China. This type of activism can take place offline or online, including leaving encouraging comments on social media platforms and condemning homophobic remarks online. Engebretsen characterizes this form of activism as "mobile, transformative, multilingual and based on a multimedia platform," which "feeds off the most unlimited speech and reach of new media technologies" (2015: 105). Engebretsen also highlights the significance of recognizing this type of soft activism as a de-Westernizing and de-colonial strategy in queer studies, which tends to be Euro-American centric:

> A "queer China" perspective complicates simplistic theories and politics of queer pride and liberation more generally. In turn, the emergent catalogue of queer activist world-making—the fractions, instances, *ad hoc* organising alongside digital archiving and story-telling of transnational reach—are likely to be better situated to organize meaningfully for justice and equality in lasting ways.
>
> (Engebretsen 2015: 106)

Indeed, it is important to think along with, away from, and even outside of the queer politics of pride, visibility, and "coming out" in transnational queer activism. It is also necessary to attend to the cultural specificity of each social and cultural context and devise appropriate activist strategies. Thinking creatively about sound and audibility is an alternative way to conceptualize queer politics out of the Western context.

Conclusion

The growing number and increasing popularity of queer choirs in China, along with many other forms of cultural activism, remind us of the importance of voice, sound, and queer audibility in the Global South. These groups help us understand how the production and dissemination of musical cultures can be used politically to empower minority groups and marginalized people in the Asia Pacific. As musical cultures make audible the voices of gender and sexual minorities, they also help us rethink queer subjectivities and activist strategies outside the more dominant European and American frameworks. As the BQC slogan suggests, these musical cultures can help to "change the world gently with singing."

Notes

1 I would like to thank members of Beijing Queer Chorus for accepting my interviews, and they include: Simon, Claire, Laurence, and Teal. I have used pseudonyms for these interviewees to protect their identity. The pictures used in this chapter are courtesy of the Beijing Queer Chorus.
2 The Stonewall Riots, also known as the Stonewall Uprising or the Stonewall Rebellion, refers to a series of spontaneous and violent demonstrations by LGBTQ communities against a police raid that began in the early morning of June 28, 1969, at the Stonewall Inn in New York. The event was often celebrated as the beginning of the modern LGBTQ movement.

Bibliography

Altman, Dennis. 1997. "Global Gaze/Global Gays." *GLQ: A Journal of Lesbian and Gay Studies* 3: 417–36.

Bao, Hongwei. 2011. "People's Park: The Politics of Naming and the Right to the City." In *Queer Paradigm II: Interrogating Agendas*, edited by Matthew Ball and Burkhard Scherer, 115–32. Oxford: Peter Lang Publishers.

Bao, Hongwei. 2015. "Digital Video Activism: Narrating History and Memory in Queer China, 'Comrade' China." In *Queer/Tongzhi China: New Perspectives on Research, Activism and Media Cultures*, edited by Elisabeth L. Engebretsen and William F. Schroeder, 35–56. Copenhagen: NIAS Press.

Bao, Hongwei. 2018a. *Queer Comrades: Gay Identity and Tongzhi Activism in Postsocialist China*. Copenhagen: NIAS Press.

Bao, Hongwei. 2018b. "Homosexuality, Social Media Activism and the Future of a Queer China." *Asia Dialogue*. Available online: http://theasiadialogue.com/2018/04/27/homosexuality-social-media-activism-and-the-future-of-a-queer-china/, accessed April 22, 2019.

BQC. 2018. "I Am What I Am." Available online: https://www.youtube.com/watch?v=73c4tjGUwU4, accessed April 22, 2019.

BQC. 2019. "Beijing Queer Chorus: About Us." Available online: https://site.douban.com/beijing-queer-chorus/, accessed April 22, 2019.

CGTN. 2018. "Rainbow Rights." Available online: https://www.bilibili.com/video/av32208392/, accessed April 22, 2019.

Chiang, Howard. 2010. "Epistemic Modernity and the Emergence of Homosexuality in China." *Gender and History* 22 (3): 629–57.

Chiang, Howard. 2019. "Gay and Lesbian Communities in Urban China." In *Handbook on Urban Development in China*, edited by Ray Yep, June Wang, and Thomas Johnson, 187–201. Cheltenham: Edward Edgar Publishing.

Couldry, Nick. 2010. *Why Voice Matters: Culture and Politics After Neoliberalism*. London: Sage.
Duggan, Lisa. 2004. *The Twilight of Equality: Neoliberalism, Cultural Politics, and the Attack on Democracy*. Boston, MA: Beacon Press.
Engebretsen, Elisabeth L. 2014. *Queer Women in Urban China*. London: Routledge.
Engebretsen, Elisabeth L. 2015. "Of Pride and Visibility: The Contingent Politics of Queer Grassroots Activism in China." In *Queer/Tongzhi China: New Perspectives on Research, Activism and Media Cultures*, edited by Elisabeth L. Engebretsen and William F. Schroeder, 89–110. Copenhagen: NIAS Press.
Engebretsen, Elisabeth L., and William F. Schroeder, eds. 2015. *Queer/Tongzhi China: New Perspectives on Research, Activism and Media Cultures*. Copenhagen: NIAS Press.
Foucault, Michel. 1986. "Of Other Spaces." *Diacritics* 16: 22–7.
Ho, Loretta Wing Wah. 2010. *Gay and Lesbian Subculture in Urban China*. London and New York: Routledge.
Kam, Lucetta Yip Lo. 2013. *Shanghai Lalas: Female Tongzhi Communities and Politics in Urban China*. Hong Kong: Hong Kong University Press.
Kang, Wenqing. 2009. *Obsession: Male Same-Sex Relations in China, 1900–1950*. Hong Kong: Hong Kong University Press.
Kong, Travis. 2010. *Chinese Male Homosexualities: Memba, Tongzhi and Golden Boy*. New York: Routledge.
Lei, Ma. 2013. "Sanleng jianyi hechang tuan: yong yinyue yu pingquan." Available online: https://helanonline.cn/archive/article/4391, accessed April 22, 2019.
Liu, Charlene. 2019. "Maybe We Don't Really Need Pride Parade in China." *ChinaLGBT*. Available online: https://www.chinalgbt.org/charlene-liu, accessed April 22, 2019.
Martin, Fran et al., eds. 2008. *AsiaPacifiQueer: Rethinking Genders and Sexualities*. Urbana, IL: University of Illinois Press.
Naficy, Hamid. 1993. "From Broadcasting to Narrowcasting: Middle Eastern Diaspora in Los Angeles." *Middle East Report* 180: 31–4.
Parkin, Siodhbhra. 2018. "LGBT Rights-Focused Legal Advocacy in China: The Promise, and Limits, of Litigation." *Fordham International Law Journal* 41 (5): 1243–62.
Rofel, Lisa. 2007. *Desiring China: Experiments in Neoliberalism, Sexuality, and Public Culture*. Durham, NC: Duke University Press.
Rofel, Lisa. 2013. "Grassroots Activism: Non-Normative Sexual Politics in Postsocialist China." In *Unequal China: The Political Economy and Cultural Politics of Inequality*, edited by Wanning Sun and Yingjie Guo, 154–67. Abingdon: Routledge.
Sang, Tze-Ian D. 2003. *The Emerging Lesbian: Female Same-Sex Desire in Modern China*. Chicago, IL: The University of Chicago Press.
Schroeder, William F. 2015. "Research, Activism, and Activist Research in Tongzhi China." In *Queer/Tongzhi China: New Perspectives on Research, Activism and Media Cultures*, edited by Elisabeth L. Engebretsen and William F. Schroeder, 89–110. Copenhagen: NIAS Press.
Stige, Brynjulf, Gary Ansdell, and Mercédès Pavlicevic, eds. 2010. *Where Music Helps: Community Music Therapy in Action and Reflection*. London: Routledge.
The Paper. 2019. "Beijing ku'er hechang tuan: yong gesheng wenrou gaibian shijie." Available online: https://www.thepaper.cn/newsDetail_forward_3006492, accessed April 22, 2019.
Thussu, Daya Kishan, Hugo de Burgh, and Anbin Shi, eds. 2018. *China's Media Go Global*. London: Routledge.

Vice. 2018. "Ku'er hechang tuan." Available online: http://www.vice.cn/read/the-vice-was-here-queer-chorus, accessed April 22, 2019.

Wang, Qian. 2015. "Queerness, Entertainment, and Politics: Queer Performance and Performativity in Chinese Pop." In *Queer/Tongzhi China: New Perspectives on Research, Activism and Media Cultures*, edited by Elisaebth L. Engebretsen and William F. Schroeder, 153–78. Copenhagen: NIAS Press.

Wang, Xinruan. 2016. *Social Media in Industrial China*. London: UCL Press.

Yang, Guobin. 2011. *The Power of the Internet in China*. New York: Columbia University Press.

11

Sounds of Political Reform: Indie Rock in Late New Order Indonesia

M. Rizky Sasono

On April 23, 1998, amid widespread student protests demanding political reform toward the end of the authoritarian regime of President Suharto, a group of buskers calling themselves Indonesian Buskers Union (SPI) decided to perform at a protest in Universitas Gadjah Mada (UGM), the oldest university in Yogyakarta. Using battered guitars that were slightly out of tune, these members of SPI performed four songs. One of their songs used the melody of an Indonesian popular song from 1994, entitled "*Semua Ada Disini*" (Everything Is Here), a song popularized by child singer Enno Lerian, whose music videos were frequently broadcast by local television stations in the 1990s. SPI changed the words of the song into a critique of Suharto's so-called New Order (*Orde Baru or Orba*)[1] policies, focusing in particular on widespread corruption, collusion, and nepotism associated with his regime: "We plant rice, it grows (into a) factory; We plant corn, it grows buildings; We plant capital, it grows corruption."

For protesters familiar with provocative speeches from political activists, they found the musical performance especially inspirational for two reasons: First, the theme of corruption presented by SPI brought into view a first-person perspective on this issue, with the lines "Corruption, we can just enjoy it" and "Hey, Indonesia" evoking the sense of irony for an imagined society (Anderson 1983). The call-and-response chorus performed what could be seen as an act of unity based on the reimagining of what it means to unite. SPI, who lived an itinerant life in urban city slums, were considered to be the true representation of the oppressed in an often-mediated political forum. Hence, the overwhelming crowd response. Second, the performance of SPI also demonstrated that music could play a significant role in energizing this community of dissent. SPI was able to engage the crowd through the shared sonic experience of a familiar pop song. The crowd was already accustomed to the melody of the song, especially the interactive chorus popularized during the golden age of Indonesian popular music in the 1990s, and so a sing-a-long began.

Later, while waiting for the next speaker, the appointed master of ceremonies Mochamad "Operasi" Rachman—an activist and student of the Indonesia Institute of the Arts of Yogyakarta—sang a spontaneous ditty with improvised lyrics in front of thousands of protesters. In parts of the song, his melodic line, singing style, and vocal timbre resembled that of Shannon Hoon from the US band Blind Melon, whose

1993 hit song "No Rain" was popular among alternative rock fans in Indonesia. In drawing on international popular hits from indie and alternative rock, these student protesters built up a nationwide community of dissent, eventually contributing to ousting Suharto on May 21, 1998.

Against the backdrop of these student-led political protests and performances under the late New Order regime, this chapter presents an ethnographic and archival account of the students' politically inflected musical lives.[2] The research focuses in particular on Yogyakarta, a city with the largest concentration of higher education institutions in Indonesia (Firman 2010) and the most fervent anti-New Order activities (Human Rights Watch 1998; Lane 2008). Using the method of "playback and feedback" (Feld and Brenneis 2004: 267), this investigation draws on interviews with former student protesters and musicians, some of whom I knew from the period under study. During the push for political reform in 1998—a period known as *Reformasi,* which culminated in the fall of Suharto—I was an undergraduate student at UGM. Although I did not consider myself an activist, I participated in the occasional campus protests as was the case for many college students at that time who did not view themselves as radical activists but wished to show their support for the democratization process. Thanks to the rich sound recording and print archives of my collaborators, this research is also an oral history of campus musical and activist life. In seeking to understand the underlying meaning of indie rock for these musicians and fans, this chapter examines the politics of the music as it was experienced, practiced, and embodied by students of the 1998 protests.

Popular Music, Media, and Politics in Late New Order Indonesia

The 1990s was a momentous decade for popular music in Indonesia, when television provided a wide range of options from international popular music to an unprecedented number of viewers. Private television stations such as RCTI and SCTV started to operate in 1989 and 1990. These stations started to incorporate appealing music programs airing contemporary pop performances and videos from Indonesian and foreign artists. Satellite dishes, already perched on rooftops across the archipelago, were officially permitted to pick up foreign-run, international channels in the early 1990s too (Luvaas 2009: 253). In 1993, MTV began broadcasting in Indonesia as part of the newly established private network Global TV. This station played a much more diverse mix of music from international pop stars of the time, as well as niche performers on shows like "Alternative Nation" showcasing lesser-known bands. Less frequently, other international programs, such as "The Chart Show" from the UK, were also broadcast (Luvaas 2009; Resmadi 2019). Access to televised music encouraged fans who already benefited from the booming production of popular cassette tapes and radio airplays.

Radio had a substantial influence on the musical life of college campuses. Various music programs guided listeners—both musicians and nonmusicians—and shaped their musical preferences. Campus listeners often tuned in to evening rock programs and submitted song requests to local radio DJs. Some of the requesters were so regular that they became well known too. For instance, listeners in Yogyakarta became accustomed to the name Hari Untarto, a biology student at UGM who regularly called the local radio station with song requests (Purwantini 2017). Commercial radio stations also succeeded in molding the taste of young people who were involved in student activism. Even in politically troubled times, commercial radio tried to convince students that their frequency offered the best sounds. Multiple radio advertisements could be found on the pages of UGM's student press, Balairung, which was closely associated with student movement activities (Juliastuti 2006). Throughout the decade, there were multiple ads of radio stations published as partnership with Balairung. The outreach of radio management into student-based organizations such as Balairung also benefited students as they could gain spots for events.

Several campus radio stations were established in the early 1990s. Three examples are Swaragama FM, based at UGM, which received funding for equipment from that institution; Saraswati, a community radio station run by students and community members at the Indonesia Institute of the Arts; and Masdha, which received funding and training from Universitas Sanatha Dharma (Jurriëns 2009). For students, these stations provided the cheapest form of entertainment and the primary source for them to engage with the latest local and international popular music. Radio broadcasters often spoke directly to listeners by naming them in phrases such as "young friends" (*Kanca Muda*) and "young academics" (*Akademia muda*). This was not only for the local stations. Many of the crew and announcers of commercial stations such as Geronimo FM and Yasika FM were either college students or former college students, which illustrates how students engaged in popular music off-campus too.

Student musicians were influenced by late-night rock programs on radio stations in Yogyakarta that played songs from hair metal bands of the 1980s and 1990s and were tape-recorded by fans. Home taping from original cassettes was a common practice for students of the period too. Often students practiced home taping to compile a mixtape that they dedicated to special people in their lives or for personal collections of songs they did not have. These mixtapes were treated as compilation albums with customized do-it-yourself (DIY) cover sleeves. For aspiring musicians, it was common to circulate original cassettes to colleagues in order to have it copied for personal use.

The 1990s supplied young people with an ever-growing repertoire of identity typologies, a resource bank of genres, sounds, and ideas ripe for appropriation (Luvaas 2009). These musical styles being channeled through various media and broadcasting technologies intersected with another powerful mindset of youths at that time: *Reformasi*. *Reformasi* represented the culmination of a succession of political controversies in the 1990s, which led to an escalation in political dissent throughout the nation. Student protests were mainly directed toward capitalist development policies (*Pembangunan*) that benefited the elites, and the military's dual function (*Dwifungsi*), which legalized their intrusion into the social life of Indonesians while simultaneously serving as guardians of the political elite (Elson 2001; Hill 1994; Kingsbury 2003). In 1994, two prominent media outlets, Tempo and Detik, were banned. Two years later, the Suharto government intervened in the party congress of the opposition Indonesian Democratic Party (*Partai Demokrasi Indonesia*; henceforth PDI) and attempted to disempower their popular leader, Megawati Soekarnoputri. According to one respondent, many believed the takeover of the PDI headquarters—known as the July 27, 1996, Kudatuli incident—was executed by the capital district military command (Pebriyanto 2018). The riot that followed was blamed on the People's Democratic Party (Partai Rakyat Demokratik; henceforth PRD), an erstwhile underground radical group formed mainly by student activists. Following Kudatuli, a number of activists were captured, tortured, and imprisoned. Amid the economic crisis that hit Southeast Asia from mid-1997 coupled with a series of political incidents throughout the 1990s in Indonesia, more and more students began to take to the streets to stage protests.

Student Cover Bands

Many students engaged with new forms of popular music via television and radio, or via cassettes that were shared through home taping and mixtapes. Influenced by UK indie rock, US alternative rock, and the global underground scene since the early 1990s, these new sounds began to gain ground on college campuses and impact students' political perspectives. Drawing on musical influences heard on the broadcast media, campus bands tended to mimic international bands that were popular at the time. Some campus bands were especially known for their cover songs. Kehutanan Band (originally named Sylvia Death), a band founded mainly by students from the Department of Forestry, principally performed songs by Metallica. Another crowd favorite was Traxtor, led by law student and bassist Agung Saptono, who was skilled at performing songs from Brazilian heavy metal outfit Sepultura. Fahrenheit, comprised students from several universities, and they were renowned for their Bon Jovi covers. These bands' popularity was consistent with most of young Indonesians' preference for rock and heavy metal at the time, and this potential market was also what drew Sepultura, Metallica, and Bon Jovi to perform in Indonesia in the 1990s.

In imitating international rock bands, these groups were mostly concerned with instrumental technique and sounding aesthetically similar to the original recording. One of the highlights of the 1992 Gama Fair, an annual campus festival at UGM, was a band that consisted of students from the Department of Engineering, FNT Band, whose vocalist Misbach Fuady Sitompul was known for his mastery in imitating the vocal timbre of C.J. Snare of Firehouse and Axl Rose of Guns "n" Roses. In their performances, FNT band's staple songs were "When I Look into Your Eyes" (Firehouse) and "Estranged" (Guns n' Roses).

Covering rock and heavy metal songs was considered trendy and cool as it demanded skill, especially for guitar solos. For most musicians, this was achieved through hours of identifying the exact chords, chord progression, and sound by ear through multiple rewinds and forwards of album cassette tapes; most were copied versions from the original cassettes. Arya Panjalu, an art student and guitarist of punk band Blackboots, explains the multiple times cassette tapes were tangled due to excessive playing. Panjalu also states that it was common for student musicians to record songs from the radio, and he says, "If we're lucky they will air songs that we requested. Even so it might not be the complete song as the broadcaster often speaks before the song ends" (Panjalu, interview, January 30, 2019). For aspiring musicians, it was common to circulate original cassettes among friends. Mixtape exchanges didn't just turn bands on to particular songs; they often were integral to the larger stylistic education that formed musical identity (Drew 2019: 142).

Indie Rock in Yogyakarta

In the mid-1990s, hair metal was still popular, but genres such as grunge, alternative-rock, brit-pop, and indie-pop were also emerging as new trends (Resmadi 2019). These new sounds began to gain ground on college campuses, where several bands would often play the same songs in a single student-organized concert. Hearing the same song performed by different performers was not an issue because, for some, performances were only considered as leisurely activities or hobbies. More serious musicians usually had original material to perform on their set-list alongside the cover songs. Most of these original songs were recorded on demo-tapes as campus bands strove to be the next indie-rock act to be signed by a major record label. The period also saw major US labels successfully sign previously hard-headed underground bands, such as Nirvana, Rage Against the Machine, and Green Day. Major Indonesian distributors also supported alternative sounds at this time, with Aquarius Musikindo releasing albums by Dewa 19 and Nugie in 1995, and Musica releasing a compilation album of alternative party hits in 1996.[3]

In line with the expectation for major label music productions, bands sent demo-tapes to radio stations. With the help of radio workers who were largely students, some of the demo-tapes were aired in radio programs. Radio stations started to support local musicians by establishing indie-specific radio programs. Geronimo FM started a program called G-Indie in 1996 to have local music heard by larger number of audiences. The radio program presented weekly indie chart "*Ajang Musikal*" (Musical Event) and began accepting song requests from listeners. Their indie chart was broadcast every Sunday evening based on requests from radio listeners, who were mostly students, including music organizers for campus events.

A G-Indie exponent, Sheila on 7, was signed by Sony Music Indonesia in 1999 and became the label's prominent pop act for more than fifteen years. Despite differences in subgenres of music, these guitar-driven music expressions were considered indie for their unsigned status. This notion of indie corresponds to what David Hesmondhalgh refers to as "pseudo-indie," where bands put effort in getting public attention in the indie sector, before crossing over into the pop mainstream (Hesmondhalgh 1999: 55). While some of the band's aesthetics were geared toward the mainstream tendencies, most of G-Indie bands were considered what David Ensminger considers as "serving as an antidote to the aural sheen of soulless pop that tends to inhabit radio frequencies" (Ensminger 2014: 100).

G-Indie also launched the magazine *Jurnal G-Indie* in 1996, and they invited music enthusiasts and students to write music-related articles. This loosely framed indie journal covered a wide range of topics. In one edition (see Figure 11.1) they featured a biography of Billy Corgan (Smashing Pumpkins), an article on Maxi Priest and Nina Hagen, a profile of unsigned band Pisang from East Java, and a report on

Figure 11.1 Cover of *Jurnal G-Indie* issue from August/September 1997. Source: Mohamad Aman Ridhlo.

the recording process of Emha Ainun Najib, a poet, essayist and humanist renowned for his avant-garde gamelan ensemble, Kiai Kanjeng. While some articles were related to music in the form of biographies or concert reviews, others revealed the students' intellectual mentality and included attacks on conservatives. In one edition, a student writer articulated his interpretation of Friedrich Nietzsche's philosophical thoughts of nihilism. This controversial article in an indie media publication highlighted the close relations between students, activism, and the notion of indie culture. The author of the article was Mohamad Aman Ridhlo, a vocalist with Kehutanan Band, the Metallica cover band mentioned earlier. In 1997 he began to actively engage in protest with several outfits: in a protest, he often took the vigilant role of informing protesters on surveillance operations conducted by police intelligence, and during the evening, he ran an amateur small-scale community radio station playing songs from his cassette collection.

Ridhlo did not limit his social interaction with indie-rock institutions such as G-Indie. As a musician playing metal, his interactions were within the louder side of the indie spectrum. These sound communities did not exist primarily on the broadcast media. In fact, indie and underground musicians often socialized at rehearsal studios, which flourished in the 1990s among aspiring high-school and college students. Some studios were sites of particular social communities that were recognized by specific sound styles. Moore (2013) observed that this indie sound world can be traced to the underground, and the diversity of so-called non-mainstream genres from blues to death metal and punk to rockabilly and electronica fall under the indie umbrella because they are acceptably antithetical to the dominant popular aesthetic.

Alamanda Studio, for example, was renowned for its members being musicians who were influenced by indie rock or alternative rock similar to that found on MTV. The bands at this studio pursued indie aesthetics (see Hibbert 2005). Meanwhile, some of their louder counterparts were based at Lex Rost and Latagha, two studios that regularly recorded metal, punk, reggae, and hardcore. Most of these musicians were active students in colleges throughout Yogyakarta. Their activities were celebrated in the 1998 DIY compilation album *United Underground*, which was a collective production (Figure 11.2). The album furthered the understanding of indie not being restricted to a genre of music with a particular sound and style but also a type of community-based musical production with a distinctive mode of independent distribution (Fonarow 2006: 26), having artistic freedom, and the possibility for bands to work autonomously (Den Drijver and Hitters 2017). Despite the apparent musical differences and orientations of the two studio communities, the terms "indie" and "underground" can be used interchangeably to describe their recordings (Moore 2013: 140).

Another way that indie society from this period encouraged a sense of community was through band stickers. For promotional objectives many bands produced and disseminated stickers to fans during their performances. Oftentimes, these stickers were stuck to rehearsal studio walls, a legacy of indie community membership that lives on in todays' music scene in Indonesia. Thus, a sticker would indicate that the band was a member of the indie community. For indie or underground enthusiasts,

Figure 11.2 Cassette cover for the compilation album *United Underground* (1998). Source: Athonk Sapto Raharjo.

these stickers were commonly applied to their motorcycles or helmets—motorcycles are popular means of transportation for citizens of Yogyakarta. The phenomenon of using band stickers on helmets reflects a particular visual feature of indie culture that was associated with the music; indie participants used this appearance and style as a primary indicator of the subculture (see Hebdige 1979). Fans of this music scene could be identified from the multiple band stickers attached to their helmets regardless of the genre the band carries.

Students Connect with "the People"

Students considered themselves as collaborators with "the people" (*rakyat*) or the "little people" (*wong cilik*)—these terms refer to common people, non-elites, and the illiterate (Anderson 1990: 61), or those who occupy the lower strata of the political and economic structures, the poverty-stricken, marginalized, and those who have been pushed aside (Weintraub 2006: 412). Following the trend of political activism in the late New Order, students "descended" (*turun ke bawah*) to become members of this lower class of society and advocated on their behalf. One of the earliest examples of this kind of activism was when students advocated against the development of the World Bank-supported Kedung Ombo water reservoir in Central Java, which flooded thirty-seven villages and displaced approximately 22,000 people (Cleary 1995). These protests often highlight a sense of oppression in the word "people." The radical PRD, the ad-hoc People's Movement for Justice (GARDA), and the People's Struggle for Change (KPRP), among others, claimed to represent the marginalized by inserting the word "people" into their organizations' names and then taking on specific causes. For instance, on November 1, 1997, a group identifying as the Anti-Suharto Regime People's Movement (*Gerakan Rakyat Anti Soeharto*) staged a protest at UGM advocating issues of human rights abuses, such as the Santa Cruz massacre in East Timor (now Timor Leste), as well as championing the cause of economically marginalized people in Papua New Guinea.

Besides frequent street protests held on campuses, this notion of "the people" has long been incorporated into university teaching. In the final year of undergraduate studies, students were required to take part in community service internships (*Kuliah Kerja Nyata*; see Reuter 2002). Students were dispatched to selected villages for two months to carry out programs that would benefit the local communities. Some of the most common programs were the upgrading of infrastructure, such as building bridges and water tanks, erecting village signage, or establishing small-scale businesses. Associations with "the people" were also present in the vernacular. UGM was described as "Universitas Ndeso"—a name that could be interpreted either as mockery or as a source of dignity (Ambarita 2012: 20). *Ndeso*—a Javanese adjective depicting rural attributes and implying locality, provinciality, and even backwardness—is a term used for the university's academic orientation as a means of describing how this process cares for the rural and "little people" in society. The actions of one-time UGM rector, Koesnadi Hardjasumantri, illustrate how university administrators got involved too. He granted access to street vendors to serve students within the campus ground and considered giving space to street vendors in the university master plan in 1987 (Dumairy 2018: 84). This approach is consistent with the need to support "the people" who were subjected to restrictive orders and barred from being independent by the New Order government. UGM cultivated a campus-wide philosophy as a place "of the people" and "for the people," which provided space for sharing in the struggle.

Late New Order student activism was characterized by outreach programs focusing on "the people" (Heryanto 1997: 117; see also Lee 2016). In order to develop and spread ideas, activists had to go beyond seeing subjugated people as victims. New activist organizations emerged in the late 1980s on university campuses, and they engaged with non-student sectors forming ad-hoc groups. But the New Order's campus policy (Normalization of Campus Life/Student Coordination Board) prohibited students from being involved in political activities (Boudreau 2004), and these student activities were restricted. Other forms of activities considered relatively apolitical were ones in which students could indulge in their personal interests or hobbies, such as photography, hiking, literature, and music. These activities and religious activities were free from military surveillance. Over time, student activists moved into these other spaces and began to create activist music performances.

Sonic Activism on Campus

Performing arts, such as music and theater, were not considered political compared to reading groups or ideological studies, which could be deemed a threat to the state.

Protests were a popular activity for students, even for relatively apolitical students, like myself. Music was one of the main activities that brought our community of student protesters together. I was in one of the many student bands that hovered around campuses in search of a stage at this time. My band, DRS.HIM, was also part of the musical network that orbited around colleges, performing what we referred to as "indie." In retrospect, these sounds remind us of the countless protests and of students' anxiety prior to clashing with the police. The sound archive from this period also informs a genealogy of musical life, which reminds us of how campuses were viewed as a gathering place for the expression of political dissent and production of creative output.

Organizations such as the Student Executive Body (*Badan Eksekutif Mahasiswa*), which operated in every department at UGM, organized a music performance at least once a year. There was a high frequency in the number of music performances staged considering the number of student organizations, and certain times of the year were busier than others. For instance, every year, the welcoming party for new students organized by seniors always included a music stage with performances by local bands. According to a former student music organizer, Widi Asmara, organizing music was the simplest form of activity. Sound systems could be hired from nearby music studios, and numerous student musicians or campus-based bands were willing to perform (Widi Asmara, interview, August 5, 2018). The program committees usually had connections with local music studios that offered discounted sound systems. In this way, with the many groups staging performances, university campuses became vibrant places for live music.

This constellation of politics mixed with the aesthetics of liberation became a melting pot for activities around campus and elevated the notion of "the people." The emphasis on campuses as promoting a shared locus of political activities and new sounding aesthetics can be exemplified through the events that occurred at UGM in the mid-1990s. For example, on November 7, 1996, a group of students from LPM Sintesa, a student film club at the Department of Political Science, delivered a statement regarding the police intervention on a student protest in solidarity of a detained journalist in Jakarta. The issue of journalism and freedom of expression became a hot topic especially in the months following the murder of a Bernas journalist who was responsible for exposing corruption in the regency of Bantul, southern Yogyakarta (Sen and Hill 2000: 69). Many students came to the protests before a violent police raid, which forced the gathering to end earlier than originally planned. One month later, an annual festival took place at the same site, which encouraged students to experience and embrace the spirit of struggle and change.

In December 1996, UGM held an annual anniversary celebration of the institution in the form of a festival called Gama Fair. Held on the UGM campus, which crosses a busy main city street in Yogyakarta, this annual festivity took place in a strategic location and sought to offer something for everyone. The festival embraced different communities by selling foods, crafts, and traditional medicines; traders showcased goods produced by local small entrepreneurs and marginalized communities, including tattoo artists. The tattoo stand was particularly controversial because this was not long after tattooed bodies were seen as an index for alleged gangsters who were targeted for execution by Suhartos' security forces (see Bourchier 1990). Organized by students and lecturers, this celebratory occasion nurtured the perception of the campus as belonging to "the people." The weekend event attracted not only students but also many other members of society from the city of Yogyakarta, including working-class families and their children. Just as the idea of protest brought elements of "the people" onto campus, the idea of campus belonging to "the people" was an attempt to rid the site and institution of the elite, which reinforced the label *Universitas Ndeso*. The Gama Fair took on the Bhaktinian insight of carnival, which subverts and liberates the postulation of a dominant style or atmosphere through humor and chaos. This space encouraged humor, performance, and chaos as a means to subvert previously established hierarchies of the oppressed (Bhaktin 1968). The annual event subverted both New Order developmental policies favoring middle-class society and the traditional capitalist stance of university campuses. Unsurprisingly, this event managed to attract diverse members of society.

For music enthusiasts, Gama Fair served as an opportunity to see exciting new bands from across the city. Gama Fair's music performances were loosely curated by a collective of students. They followed the local trend of inviting bands that were popular among students. A number of G-Indie acts performed in the 1996 and 1997 Gama Fairs along with their louder counterparts. Punk band Blackboots debuted their performance at Gama Fair 1996 at a tattoo stand, simply from the merit that one of tattoo contest organizers of the event was the lead singer of the band (Athonk Sapto Raharjo, interview, September 15, 2019). This opened the doors for more obscure sounds of the underground to reach a plural audience. Blackboots, mostly made up of students from the Indonesia Institute of the Arts of Yogyakarta, later featured at an event organized by a student group from the Department of Law at UGM in 1997. Just as with many other small gigs organized by student organizations, Gama Fair raised the underground to the surface of the popular at an event attended by a diverse audience (Figure 11.3).

My inquiry into music performances at Gama Fair and other campus events around this period provides a close-up view of the wider scene. These performances provide just one example of a revolutionary shift in musical and cultural style. Around this time—the mid-1990s—a significant number of well-known indie bands and underground musicians began to play at campuses and their music was experienced by more pluralistic audiences. The meaning of these events rests on the elevation of diverse sounds reverberating within the space of liberation. Indie was interpreted loosely against the backdrop of a festival for "the people."

In aligning these differences at the festival, former activist Titok Hariyanto described to me how various interests in political reform from different student groups were "similar but not the same." He elaborated: "we all walked in the same direction, but it wasn't like a military march where each stride had to be timed and precise. Some walked fast, some in stride. Others walked more casually, or in zig-zag mode, but also in the same direction" (Titok Hariyanto, interview, March 24, 2018). Writing of the nationwide context at this time, Brent Luvaas also acknowledged "the nation's youth

Figure 11.3 Blackboots performing at UGM in 1997. Source: Athonk Sapto Raharjo.

were perched on the edge of a precipice they could barely see over. They had a sense that something new and better was waiting for them on the other side, but couldn't say exactly what it was" (Luvaas 2009: 9). Considering these politically turbulent times as a "gap" between the lived experience of the New Order regime and an imagined life in a liberated world, the period reflects a peculiar feature between "liminality" and "speculation." Victor Turner describes liminal period as the quality of ambiguity and disorientation that occurs in the middle stage of a rite of passage (Turner 1969). The gap can also resemble speculative aspects during an uncanny present: "befuddled search for direction experienced by people in times of crisis" but at the same time it offers spaces of creativity (Bryant and Knight 2019: 78).

The forming of these sound communities operated similarly to that of other forms of activism where student organizations were central to the political struggle. In the political setting of the late New Order Indonesia, communication between students sustained the struggle for *reformasi*. For example, in response to the banning of the Tempo and Detik magazines in 1994, an underground activist group named Indonesian Students in Solidarity for Democracy (SMID) released a critical statement, signed by their secretary general, Andi Munadjal on June 23, 1994. On the printed statement he claimed to represent a collective of ad-hoc student groups from different cities. The mode of students as active political agents of change culminated at the turn of 1998. On January 22, 1998, through a network of students across the nation, a statement created by student senate leaders at the University of Indonesia for political reform was declared (*Indonesia Daily News Online*, January 23, 1998). This marked the start of intensive all-out protests that the student group GARDA referred to as "the year of the struggle," continuing the previous "year of awakening" in 1997.

Conclusion

At the welcome week concert for new UGM students in 1996 the campus rock collective Sande Monink—which was also a hub for radical students—performed a concert of highly politicized rock songs. Their performance was confirmed just hours after their vocalist was released by the police following several days in captivity for his involvement in political activism. In emphasizing the urgency of political education to new students, he described the physical ordeal he went through during police interrogation to the audience (Yul Amrozi, interview, August 1, 2018). During his performance, the audience could see the physical marks from police beatings that were still visible on his face. After *reformasi* Sande Monink continued their musical activism by organizing weekly Sunday morning performances in front of the Department of Philosophy at UGM and conducted a series of large-scale corporate-sponsored indie rock concerts involving notable acts in the late 1990s and early 2000s (Arya Kresna Maheswara, interview, August 2, 2018). Sande Monink provides an example of the transformation of indie music from its entanglement with the political turmoil of the late New Order to a more casual understanding of indie afterwards. In this way, the Indonesian indie scene goes beyond the widely circulated definition of indie as a musical production affiliated with small independent record labels with a distinctive mode of independent distribution or a genre of music that has a particular sound or stylistic conventions.

In his study of the underground scene in Indonesia during the political turmoil of 1998, Jeremy Wallach demonstrated an adherence to independence in these genres. He observed how many underground rock enthusiasts were also activists (Wallach 2003). With many of these students regarded as political activists, they were also cultural activists who contributed to the creation of a radical new music scene in Yogyakarta and elsewhere in Indonesia. Similarly, this chapter illustrates how activism gave way to the students' own interpretation of liberation and change within the realm of indie culture.

While their activities might adhere to definitions of indie culture elsewhere in the world, the meaning of indie in Indonesia during the late New Order has a distinct connotation: indie culture was seen as a means of liberation that was in tune with students' aspirations for the future and struggle for political change. Although many references to indie music in other parts of the world associate the culture with students (Garland 2014; Hibbert 2005; Shank 1994), indie in late New Order Indonesia is unique due to its close association with politics. The birth of the indie scene in Yogyakarta was entangled with and fed by student activism in the late New Order. The resulting disposition was not limited to musical tastes informed by global influences but also shaped by the embodiment of local politics. The mental attitude of students as mediators of "the people" was manifested in their political and cultural activism. Through networks of students and their imagined collective liberation, campus music traditions shifted from mastery of mimicry (rock covers) to performances of self-expression (original compositions). This approach to indie and underground music is best summarized in the phrase the "year of struggle," in which students, indie musicians, and political activists united under one cause, *reformasi*.

Notes

1 The term "late New Order" is often used to refer to the last decade of Suharto's thirty-two years of rule from 1966 to 1998; here I am principally using the term in reference to the 1990s.
2 In exploring the intersection of protest and indie music during the 1990s, this chapter contributes to wider debates on indie culture, underground music, and DIY aesthetics in Indonesia (see Baulch 2007; Kieran and Walsh 2015, 2019; Luvaas 2009, 2013a, 2013b; Martin-Iversen 2014; Moore 2013; Wallach 2003, 2008).
3 The complete compilation album is available at https://www.youtube.com/watch?v=zwj6kR3XLt0, accessed July 20, 2020.

Bibliography

Ambarita, Domu D. 2012. *Jokowi: Spirit Bantaran Kali Anyar*. Jakarta: Elex Media Komputindo.
Anderson, Benedict. 1983. *Imagined Communities: Reflections on the Origin and Spread of Nationalism*. London and New York: Verso
Anderson, Benedict. 1990. *Language and Power: Exploring Political Cultures in Indonesia*. Ithaca, NY: Cornell University Press.
Azerrad, Michael. 2001. *Our Band Could Be Your Life: Scenes from the American Indie Underground, 1981–1991*. New York: Little, Brown and Company.
Baulch, Emma. 2007. *Making Scenes: Reggae, Punk, and Death Metal in 1990s Bali*. Durham and London: Duke University Press.
Bhaktin, Mikhail. 1968. *Rabelais and His World*. Translated by Hélène Iswolsky. Cambridge, MA: MIT Press.
Bordieu, Pierre. 1977. *Outline of a Theory of Practice*. Cambridge: Cambridge University Press.
Boudreau, Vincent. 2004. *Resisting Dictatorship: Repression and Protest in Southeast Asia*. Cambridge: Cambridge University Press.
Bourchier, David. 1990. "Law, Crime and State Authority in Indonesia." In *State and Civil Society in Indonesia*, edited by Arief Budiman, 177–212. Clayton, Victoria: Centre for Southeast Asian Studies, Monash University.
Bryant, Rebecca, and Daniel M. Knight. 2019. *The Anthropology of the Future*. Cambridge: Cambridge University Press.
Cleary, Seamus. 1995. "In Whose Interest? NGO Advocacy Campaigns and the Poorest: An Exploration of Two Indonesian Examples." *International Relations* 12 (5): 9–35.
Den Drijver, Robin, and Erik Hitters. 2017. "The Business of DIY: Characteristics, Motives and Ideologies of Micro-Independent Record Labels." *Cadernos de Arte e Antropologia* 6 (1): 17–35.

Drew, Rob. 2019. "The Cassette in 1980s Indie Music Scenes." *Rock Music Studies* 6 (2): 138–52.
Dumairy, Tarli Nugroho. 2018. *Ekonomi Pancasila Warisan Pemikiran Mubyarto*. Yogyakarta: Gadjah Mada University Press.
Elson, R. E. 2001. *Suharto: A Political Biography*. Cambridge: Cambridge University Press.
Ensminger, David A. 2014. *Mavericks of Sound: Conversations with Artists who Shaped Indie and Roots Music*. Lanham, MD: Rowman and Littlefield.
Feld, Steven, and Donald Brenneis. 2004. "Doing Anthropology in Sound." *American Ethnologist* 31 (4): 461–74.
Firman, Tommy. 2010. "Multi Local-Government under Indonesia's Decentralization Reform: The Case of Kartamantul (The Greater Yogyakarta)." *Habitat International* 34 (4): 400–5.
Fonarow, Wendy. 2006. *Empire of Dirt: The Aesthetics and Rituals of British Indie Music*. Middletown, CT: Wesleyan University Press.
Garland, Shannon. 2014. "Music, Affect, Labor, and Value: Late Capitalism and the (Mis) Production of Indie Music in Chile and Brazil." PhD thesis, Columbia University.
Hebdige, Dick. 1979. *Subculture: The Meaning of Style*. London and New York: Routledge.
Heryanto, Ariel. 1997. "Indonesia: Towards the Final Countdown?" *Southeast Asian Affairs* 1997: 107–26.
Hesmondhalgh, David. 1999. "Indie: The Institutional Politics and Aesthetics of a Popular Music Genre." *Cultural Studies* 13 (1): 34–61.
Hibbert, Ryan. 2005. "What Is Indie Rock?" *Popular Music and Society* 28 (1): 55–77.
Hill, Hal. 1994. *Indonesia's New Order: The Dynamics of Socio-Economic Transformation*. Honolulu: University of Hawai'i Press.
Human Rights Watch. 1998. *Academic Freedom in Indonesia: Dismantling Soeharto-Era Barriers*. New York: Human Rights Watch.
James, Kieran, and Rex Walsh. 2015. "Bandung Rocks, Cibinong Shakes: Economics and Applied Ethics within the Indonesian Death-Metal Community." *Musicology Australia* 37 (1): 28–46.
James, Kieran, and Rex Walsh. 2019. "Religion and Heavy Metal Music in Indonesia." *Popular Music* 38 (2): 276–297.
Juliastuti, Nuraini. 2006. "Whatever I Want: Media and Youth in Indonesia before and after 1998." Translated by Camelia Lestari. *Inter-Asia Cultural Studies* 7 (1): 139–43.
Jurriëns, Edwin. 2009. *From Monologue to Dialogue: Radio and Reform in Indonesia*. Leiden: Brill.
Kingsbury, Damien. 2003. *Power Politics and the Indonesian Military*. London and New York: Routledge.
Kruse, Holly. 2003. *Site and Sound: Understanding Independent Music Scenes*. New York: Peter Lang.
Lane, Max. 2008. *Unfinished Nation: Indonesia Before and After Suharto*. London: Verso.
Lee, Doreen. 2016. *Activist Archives: Youth Culture and the Political Past in Indonesia*. Durham and London: Duke University Press.
Luvaas, Brent. 2009. "Generation DIY: Youth, Class, and the Culture of Indie Production in Digital-Age Indonesia." PhD thesis, University of California, Los Angeles.
Luvaas, Brent. 2013a. *DIY Style: Fashion, Music and Global Digital Cultures*. London and New York: Bloomsbury.
Luvaas, Brent. 2013b. "Exemplary Centers and Musical Elsewheres: On Authenticity and Autonomy in Indonesian Indie Music." *Asian Music* 44 (2): 95–114.

Martin-Iversen, Sean. 2014. "*Bandung Lautan Hardcore*: Territorialisation and Deterritorialisation in an Indonesian Hardcore Punk Scene." *Inter-Asia Cultural Studies* 15 (4): 532–52.

Moore, Rebekah E. 2013. "Elevating the Underground: Claiming a Space for Indie Music among Bali's Many Soundworlds." *Asian Music* 44 (2): 135–59.

Pebriyanto, Fajar. 2018. "Sekjen PDIP minta SBY ungkap kasus 27 Juli." Available online: https://nasional.tempo.co/read/1110896/sekjen-pdip-minta-sby-ungkap-kasus-27-juli-1996/full&view=ok, accessed April 23, 2019.

Purwantini, Agustina. 2017. "Jogja Itu Candu yang Kontradiktif." Available online: https://www.kompasiana.com/agustinapurwantini/5910b4ddf17e61a4038b4568/jogja-itu-candu-yang-kontradiktif?page=all, accessed October 1, 2019.

Resmadi, Idhar. 2019. *Based on a True Story: Pure Saturday*. Jakarta: Kepustakaan Populer Gramedia.

Reuter, Thomas. 2002. *Inequality, Crisis and Social Change in Indonesia: The Muted Worlds of Bali*. London and New York: Routledge.

Sen, Krisna, and David T. Hill. 2000. *Media, Culture and Politics in Indonesia*. South Melbourne, Victoria: Oxford University Press.

Shank, Barry. 1994. *Dissonant Identities: The Rock 'n' Roll Scene in Austin, Texas*. Hannover, NH: Wesleyan University Press.

Turner, Victor. 1969. *The Ritual Process: Structure and Anti-Structure*. New York: Aldine De Gruyter.

Wallach, Jeremy. 2003. "'Goodbye My Blind Majesty': Music, Language, and Politics in the Indonesian Underground." In *Global Pop, Local Languages*, edited by Harris M. Berger and Michael T. Carrol, 53–86. Jackson, MS: University Press of Mississippi.

Wallach, Jeremy. 2008. *Modern Noise, Fluid Genres: Popular Music in Indonesia, 1997–2001*. Madison, WI: University of Wisconsin Press.

Weintraub, Andrew N. 2006. "Dangdut Soul: Who Are 'the People' in Indonesian Popular Music?" *Asian Journal of Communication* 16 (4): 411–31.

12

Finding Agency in Hawaiian Online Collaborative Music Videos: Reclaiming "*Kaulana Nā Pua*" in a Contemporary Context

Min Bee and Jordan Anthony Kapono Bee

Kaulana nā pua a'o Hawai'i
Kūpa'a ma hope o ka 'āina

Famous are the children of Hawai'i
Ever loyal to the land

"*Kaulana Nā Pua*" (Famous Are the Children/Flowers) is a famous Hawaiian protest song. It was written by Ellen Keko'aohiwaikalani Wright Prendergast[1] in 1893, shortly after the last reigning monarch of Hawai'i, Queen Lili'uokalani, was deposed, when members of the Hawaiian Kingdom's Royal Hawaiian Band,[2] then known as the Royal Hawaiian Military Band, arrived at her home appealing to her to compose a song. They were protesting the forced signing of an oath of allegiance to the new Provisional Government of Hawai'i (which comprised mainly Hawaiian subjects of American descent and US citizens and foreign residents, whose intentions were to seek more power and control for themselves, through voting rights and the privileging of white American plantation owners' interests, and ultimately for the future annexation of Hawai'i to the United States). One of Prendergast's daughters gives an account of what happened that day:

> "We will not follow this new government," they asserted. "We will be loyal to Liliu [Queen Lili'uokalani]. We will not sign the *haole's*[3] paper, but will be satisfied with all that is left to us, the stones, the mystic food of our native land." So they begged her to compose their song of rebellion.
>
> (Extracted from Damon 1957: 317)

Originally titled, "*Mele 'Ai Pōhaku*" (Stone-Eating Song), the song "*Kaulana Nā Pua*" became a powerful anthem protesting the overthrow of the Queen which eventually led to the annexation of the Hawaiian Kingdom. The song, "*Kaulana Nā Pua*," is still very much alive today in the hearts of Native Hawaiian activists. Sung in the Hawaiian language, it is a song of strength and resistance and is mobilized as a call for Hawaiian sovereignty (Silva 2004: 135). It is also known as "*Mele Aloha 'Āina*" (Patriot's Song).

In June 2013, Project *Kuleana*, a Hawaiian grassroots initiative, released an online collaborative music video of "*Kaulana Nā Pua*,"[4] which featured many well-known Native Hawaiian musicians, such as Palani Vaughan, Keali'i Reichel, Ernie Cruz Jr, Brother Noland, Manu Boyd, and Sonny Lim. Established in 2011 by three Native Hawaiian men, Sean Nāleimaile, Kīhei Nāhale-a, and Kamakoa Lindsey-Asing, who were inspired by multimedia music movement Playing for Change,[5] Project *Kuleana* filmed a number of Hawaiian musicians performing in iconic locations on the islands—places that were meaningful to the artists. It was marketed as an inter-island *kani ka pila* (to play music), as the artists themselves came from Hawai'i's different islands, to promote *lōkahi* (unity), *kuleana* (responsibility, right or privilege), and *aloha 'āina* (love for the land, love for the nation, patriotism). Project *Kuleana* describe themselves as "a movement to utilize music as a vehicle to educate our community and to develop layers of understanding to strengthen our *lāhui* Hawai'i [Hawaiian community or rather nation]."[6]

Using Project *Kuleana*'s video of "*Kaulana Nā Pua*" as a case study, this chapter will examine the diverse ways in which Hawaiian activists have used online collaborative music video projects to reclaim and reinforce a sense of place and to raise political consciousness and social justice ideals via subliminal messages, which are exclusively targeted toward *Kānaka Maoli* (Native Hawaiians).[7] These videos—with their high-quality recordings, soothing vocal melodies, and beautiful scenic shots capturing meaningful places in Hawai'i—have gone viral owing to their popularity on social networking sites, such as Facebook, Instagram, and YouTube. These initiatives have helped to build solidarity between *Kānaka Maoli* and foster agency as these video projects utilize music and iconic places to empower *Kānaka* by connecting with their language and culture, as well as raising awareness of native histories for viewers. In this chapter—through a close viewing—we will exemplify the semiotic strategies and political drivers of Project *Kuleana*'s music video of "*Kaulana Nā Pua*," through both the visual narrative and the messages that lie encoded within the lyrical content. Through the use of place (Cresswell 2015; Massey 1994) and strategic choice of song, we will demonstrate how online collaborative music videos as mobilizing structures use *aloha* to reclaim places and educate future generations. This study will explore the complexities at work and the hermeneutical strategies (Dibben 2009; Przybylski 2018) that are at play in the production of these videos. In doing so, we will argue that online collaborative music videos form an agentic part of a growing grassroots platform for Hawaiian cultural-political expression.

Music and Protest in Hawai'i

Mele (meaning "song," "chant," or "poetry") has always been a fundamental medium of Hawaiian communication—whether to convey knowledge (e.g., history, genealogy, creation stories), express feelings, honor a place or individual, or tell a story. Hawaiian musicians have used songs to protest native sovereign rights since the nineteenth century (known as *mele kūʻē* "songs of resistance"), and this was noticeably revisited during the 1960s and 1970s. Beginning in 1966, local radio station KCCN began to broadcast Hawaiian music exclusively. This included the music of Genoa Keawe, Mahi Beamer, Gabby Pahinui, and Sons of Hawaiʻi, all of whom performed in the "old styles" and kept "alive a tenuous and fragile musical tradition," which had been mainly supported by rural working-class Hawaiians (Lewis 1991: 58). The station soon became popular with "urban-oriented, socially conscious, dissatisfied Hawaiians" (Lewis 1991: 58), who were in search of their cultural roots. KCCN became key in the dissemination of music of the Hawaiian renaissance.[8] This music was in opposition to the kind found in the Hawaiʻi tourist industry, which comprised the Tin Pan Alley style from the US continent (with composers even deriving from the US continent making up "Hawaiian" tunes) and *hapa haole* (half-white)[9] tunes, both of which largely catered to the tourist imagination of exoticism and seduction.[10]

Following Hawaiʻi's statehood in 1959 and the boom in tourism and urban development, Native Hawaiians feared they were being squeezed out of their own land. In response, Hawaiian bands began to adopt names associated with places in Hawaiʻi, such as Sunday Manoa and Mākaha Sons of Niʻihau (Lewis 1985: 192). Some musicians ceased performing in tourist-filled Waikiki, disassociating themselves from *hapa haole* music. To carry out their *kuleana*, they chose to position themselves in accordance to the concerns of the Hawaiian people, current issues, and events. Themes of songs shifted from romantic paradise ideals to serious pertinent issues such as land ownership, urban development (resorts, hotels, condominiums), homesteads, hostility toward tourists, the bastardization of Hawaiian culture and history (such as the illegal overthrow of the Hawaiian monarchy in 1893), and the fight for the preservation of the Hawaiian culture, race, and language. There was a reemergence of Hawaiian pride (*haʻaheo*) in the 1970s and onwards, bringing more people to learn about ancient voyaging techniques, traditional ways of living (cultivating taro, restoring fishponds), Hawaiian music and language, crafts, and Hawaiian history. It was a grassroots movement. Awareness of the illegal overthrow of the Hawaiian monarchy in 1893 was widely publicized, as was the past history of the silencing of Hawaiian people through their language and culture.[11]

Music became a key force in spreading the awareness of the injustices felt by *Kānaka Maoli*. In the 1970s, numerous protest songs (or sovereignty songs) were written. Protests surrounding the continued naval bombardment of the island of Kahoʻolawe produced a number of protest songs, such as Harry Kunihi Mitchell's "*Mele O Kahoʻolawe*." Mitchell's son, Kimo, and George Helm, both activists, disappeared at sea while attempting to make contact with two other activists who were occupying Kahoʻolawe. George Helm, who was also a musician, saw the power in music and stated, "What we needed was to get Hawaii active and off their ass. Music is the easiest way I know, because people tune into music... that's what I use music for" (quoted in Lewis 1991: 54). Musicians venting their anger toward the US government and disputes on land ownership triggered songs like "Broken Promise" by Henry Kapono;

songs opposing urban development include "Concrete Castles," by Leon Siu; "Hawaii 78," written by Mickey Ioane and made famous by Israel Kamakawiwoʻole[12]; "Nanakuli Blues," also known as "Waimanalo Blues" (by Thor Wald); and "All Hawaii Stand Together," by Liko Martin.[13]

Music plays an important role in defining ideologies, disseminating information, and in mobilizing people to rise up. It gives cultural legitimacy and emotional urgency, and its expression gives opportunities for artists and people to articulate and experience resistance. Music is both reflective and generative. It unifies and propels people to think collectively. It facilitates a "collective sense of identity and feeling of community" and has the ability to spiritually transport them to a common place—an imagined "spiritual homeland" (Whiteley, Bennett and Hawkins 2005) and an imagined future. It sets boundaries and also creates a sense of place for those who identify. It gives people the power to assert agency over their collective experiences. For leading *Kanaka Maoli* activist and musician, Leon Siu, performing music is revolutionary and instant. He says,

> Music is the easiest way to transmit ideas and new insight. The arts is revolutionary, it brings about changes, inspired by thought. Music is immediate. Every movement has been driven by music… It is the responsibility [or *kuleana*] of the artist. How do we write something with the idea to improve something or bless the people who listen?… The role of the artist in society is as a revolutionary tool. It is the making of art that forms society not government.
>
> (Interview, August 7, 2016)

More recently, in the Protect Mauna Kea movement,[14] music, chant, and *hula* have played a central role in the resistance to the building of the Thirty Meter Telescope. They have been used as a platform to disseminate traditional knowledge and awareness of the building of the Thirty Meter Telescope, mobilizing people into action to stop its construction. The command to unite and rise up is a common theme in songs for Mauna Kea. Songs such as "Rise up," by Ryan Hiraoka and featuring Keʻala Kawaʻauhau (a pivotal member of the seminal Hawaiian rap activist group Sudden Rush); "Stand up and Rise," by One Rhythm; "Warrior Rising," by Hawane Rios; and "We Are Mauna Kea," by Sudden Rush, are such examples.

"*Kaulana Nā Pua*": The Song, a Protest Music Video, and Expanding Social Networks

Project *Kuleana*'s online collaborative music video version of "*Kaulana Nā Pua*" is effective and iconic in a number of ways. First, the song itself triggers an act of "sonic-social remembrance" (Liew 2014: 508) to *Kānaka Maoli* and their supporters. Second, it plays a significant role in the decolonization process, and third, with the added dimension of being a collaborative video (with a visual dimension) embedded in online posts on social network platforms, it works as a powerful vehicle to advocate for change and deepen the viewer's understanding of *Kānaka Maoli* issues.

The choice of the song "*Kaulana Nā Pua*" is significant. As Rosenthal and Flacks write, "we understand meaning in music as part of a tradition we're taught" (2011: 53). In other words, we appropriate the music we hear as we relate it to our own cultural and social experiences. "*Kaulana Nā Pua*" triggers an act of "sonic-social remembrance" (Liew 2014: 508), as testified by the streams of comments from viewers on social media[15] that hark back to the injustices suffered by *Kānaka Maoli* from the overthrow of the monarchy to the forced annexation of the islands to the United States and the countless land struggles. It reminds *Kānaka Maoli* of their feelings of dispossession incurred through the loss of self-determination and it renews their current fight for sovereignty. The song serves as a collective cultural memory where *Kānaka Maoli* can return to their dormant memories of the past. It acts as a form of "reflective nostalgia" (Boym 2001) in which *Kānaka Maoli* long for the old times and places lost. "*Kaulana Nā Pua*" and other *mele kūʻē* gained a renewed significance during the Hawaiian Renaissance. George Helm deliberately performed songs mainly from the early nineteenth century by Native Hawaiians, as these songs "in their fragile, rural voices, spoke out against the destruction of Hawaiian culture" (Lewis 1991: 61). Helm calls these "Hawaiian Soul" (Lewis 1991: 61). Eyerman and Jamison coined the importance of the "mobilization of tradition" (Eyerman and Jamison 1998) in which music and other cultural traditions are created and re-created during social movements, but as the movement fades, the musical memories remain, only to resurface in another event. The mobilization of tradition helps to "link protests to previous political struggles" and place "the social movement in the history of contentious politics" (Ruhlig 2016: 60). In the same way, the contemporary performance of "*Kaulana Nā Pua*" can also be viewed as a way of commemorating and connecting *Kānaka Maoli* to past generations, and standing on the shoulders of the Hawaiian activists who chose to speak, as well as linking and contextualizing current *Kanaka Maoli* struggles with Hawaiʻi's embittered histories, thus propelling and asserting a sense of agency.

"*Kaulana Nā Pua*," as with many of the other song choices of Project *Kuleana*'s and Mana Maoli's[16] collaborative music video projects, plays a central role in the decolonization process. The Tin Pan Alley style and *hapa haole* tunes that flooded (what became perceived as) Hawaiian music from the late nineteenth century up to the Hawaiian Renaissance became a colonizing force, a force, which, coupled with "exotic" *aloha*,[17] enabled the state to capitalize on the marketing and branding of the islands to tourists for economic purposes. Denning argues that decolonization is as much of a musical event as a political event. In fact, he goes so far as to say that

> [the] decolonization of the ear preceded and made possible the subsequent decolonization of legislatures and literatures, schools and armies. The global soundscape was decolonized by the guerrilla insurgency of these new musics before the global statescape was reshaped... to argue that decolonization is a musical event, that a musical decolonization and prefigured political decolonization, suggests that empire and colonialism was itself a musical event.
>
> (Denning 2015: 80–1)

"*Kaulana Nā Pua*" and other protest songs of that era, together with the "new" Hawaiian music from the 1970s and 1980s, stood in opposition to the exotic, fun, happy-go-lucky music that dominated outsider perceptions of Hawaiian music—the music that many *Kānaka Maoli* felt had destroyed their cultural identity. The regular performance of this anticolonial music became an act of sonic resistance, served in part to decolonize the ear as well as to decolonize Hawaiian culture and society.

Sound technology itself also plays a central role in shaping sonic resistance and power. This has been witnessed in past global histories, for instance: the involvement of elements of manipulation and perception in the process of recording on the phonograph during 1900–20 by fieldworkers (Kursell 2011); the use of radio, which was originally seen as a symbol of the French colonizer in Algeria, which later took on a different meaning and became associated with anticolonial struggles and was intrinsic in the making of the revolution (Fanon 1965); vernacular gramophone music, which became fundamental to decolonization for example in India, Indonesia, Hawai'i, Brazil (Denning 2015, 2016); and how it was not radio but sound systems that led to votes for Jamaican independence (Bronfman 2016). In the case of Project *Kuleana*'s production of "*Kaulana Nā Pua*," it is the twin combination of the visual in the audiovisual (collaborative music video) and new media that has generated agency in Hawai'i's decolonization process. Music video together with new media and its social networks have provided many marginalized communities with a new lease of life (see Ambikaipaker 2016; McCosker 2015; Warner 2013) by creating not just a (resistant) space and expanding visibility and reach within national borders but a global connectivity. Where music videos were once the reserve of record companies and the elite, as evident from the 1980s with the creation of MTV, now music videos are spread across a diverse network of platforms where there is much less vetting of clips (Vernallis 2013: 208) and the absence of these gatekeepers. In contrast to MTV viewers, where the only options were to watch and listen, viewers on online platforms (such as YouTube and Facebook) are able to watch, listen, read, blog, or interact (Burns and Hawkins 2019: 2), thus sustaining a deeper connectivity and sense of connection. They are able to construct virtual communities and connect individuals and collectives to other likeminded stories, blogs, vlogs, forums, and groups, thus widening the network of communication and exchange while building on social consciousness and awareness, and fostering a sense of belonging and identity (see also Bao's chapter in this volume). In the case of "*Kaulana Nā Pua*," the video was posted and shared on Project *Kuleana*'s and their supporters' social media platforms, news websites, blogs, radio and television websites, activist community websites and social media pages, profile pages of individuals, and more. Watching "*Kaulana Nā Pua*" has enabled *Kānaka Maoli* to frame their own experiences, connect, and turn their shared experience into collective action. Kraidy writes that music videos draw viewers together "into publics and counter-publics, however temporary" and that they "are best understood as instruments of visibility in a symbolic economy that suffers from attention scarcity" (Kraidy 2012: 272).

Online platforms such as YouTube and Facebook have afforded "a contemporary way through which the past may be recalled in a new techno-memory economy"

(Liew 2014: 513), and in this case for decolonizing ends, thus providing an impetus for change, especially within marginalized communities, where previously change was not possible due to suppression and the lack of awareness and/or means (financial sources, structural powers in place, censorship, and limited outlets to voice discontent). These platforms have enabled a reclamation of oppression, political status, and a "relegitimization of [an]… egalitarian existence" (Tan 2017: 33).

Signs, Intertextuality, and the Reclamation of Place in Project *Kuleana*'s "*Kaulana Nā Pua*" Music Video

The added dimension of the visual image gives new meaning and "different connotations and contextual associations" (Taylor 2007: 235) to the music and lyrics. It can also help to clarify and analyze the music (Cook 1998: 74). However, this is not always a straightforward process. What makes this production of "*Kaulana Nā Pua*" unique are the many signs displayed within the visuals that accompany the lyrics, which are interpreted through the viewer's personal context, identity, and knowledge, as we will illustrate in this section; these understandings elicit reactions and responses. Turino writes, "Identity is grounded in multiple ways of knowing with affective and direct experiential knowledge often being paramount. The crucial link between identity formation and arts like music lies in the specific semiotic character of these activities which make them particularly affective and direct ways of knowing" (1999: 221). Basing our thoughts on Peircean semiotics, when "*Kaulana Nā Pua*" is heard by *Kānaka Maoli*, its aural familiarity indexically associates it within a patriotic context. It is an indexical legisign of the overthrow of the Hawaiian Kingdom, and because of this, it functions for *Kānaka Maoli* as a dicent sign.[18] The signs within "*Kaulana Nā Pua*" elicit powerful emotional responses throughout the music and the visual images, thus creating an intensely meaning-rich video.

Direct intertextuality is prevalent in the music video of "*Kaulana Nā Pua*." There are intra-musical, numerous extra-musical features, and "metaphor driven intertextual signals" (De Paor-Evans 2018: 4). In the video, the places chosen for each location of the filming of the visual content are significant sites of resistance and contestation, or reminders of grassroots native revival and sustainability projects (such as fishpond and taro farm restorations). Vernallis writes that "music video has always been self-reflexive, as well as intertextual with nearby forms and genres… music videos frequently remediate material" (Vernallis 2013: 227–8), and this is particularly the case with many *Kanaka Maoli* collaborative online music videos, with their intertextual links to past embittered histories and contested sites. Intertextuality is used here as a way of embedding knowledge and confining information to only those in the know and who understand the various references aggravating dicent signs for *Kānaka Maoli* activists. In Project *Kuleana*'s "*Kaulana Nā Pua*" video, there are references to past exploitations and reminders of the Hawaiian Kingdom's past royalty and chiefs, as well as prompts and provocations of contentious issues for *Kānaka Maoli* in contemporary times.

A Close Viewing of Project *Kuleana*'s "*Kaulana Nā Pua*" Video

The video formally begins with a chant, "*Ke Au Hawai'i*," from students of Ke Kula 'O Samuel M. Kamakau, which is a public charter school. The contemporary chant was written by Lale Kimura with the aim of instilling pride in young Hawaiians, that one day these descendants of the ancestors will rise up, become proud of their identity as Hawaiians, and, in the (spiritual) presence of their ancestral chiefs, build upon the work of their ancestors. The song then begins with a *pueo* strum (double strum) on the 'ukulele played by Kamakoa Lindsey-Asing, which sets the tone for the rest of the song. The *pueo* strum, a stylistic technique that became prominent from the mid-twentieth century onwards, signifies a rallying call and invokes a sense of pride to the *Kānaka Maoli*.

Palani Vaughan, a beloved musician, historian, and activist in the Native Hawaiian community, is the first named singer in the video and he is seen singing the lyrics "famous are the children of Hawai'i ever loyal to the land."[19] The visuals capture him singing at the Royal Mausoleum, which is where the Hawaiian monarchs are buried. It was the final resting place for the Kamehameha and Kalākaua dynasties.[20] To the viewer in the know, this is a reminder of who the *Kānaka Maoli* are, and it instils a sense of lineage and belonging. It is also worth noting that the frequently used English name "Royal Mausoleum" is not used in the captions, and instead the original Hawaiian name, *Mauna 'Ala* (Fragrant Hills), is used. This renaming can be interpreted as a way of reclaiming ownership and belonging to the land—especially places of important significance to *Kānaka Maoli*—as well as reasserting the authority and guardianship of the ancestors and the authority and authentic use of the Hawaiian language.[21]

Viewers in the know are reminded not only of whom their real leaders were but also of their ancestors. Hawaiians were voyagers (like their Polynesian cousins) and Kekuhi Keali'ikanaka'oleohaililani sings in Palekai on Hawai'i island—a place where in recent times, revival crafting processes of sailing vessels, such as the Hōkūle'a and Hikianalia, set sail for their voyages. The chant in the beginning of the song also harks back to the chiefs of the land.

Reminders of past historical exploitations are featured in multiple scenes. Much of Hawai'i's past wealth was associated with whalers and the greed of sugar barons who built up their empires. The Reciprocity Treaty with the United States, which eliminated taxes and tariffs on sugar exports, came into effect in 1875, attracting many American businessmen. Keali'i Reichel sings the lyrics "when the evil-hearted messenger comes with his greedy document of extortion"; he sings this in Pā'ia in Maui. Pā'ia was a plantation village that originated in the latter half of the nineteenth century. It was known for its sugar mill and the first of its kind powered by electricity in Hawai'i. Hawaiian royalty came to witness and marvel at this new technology, built by Claus Spreckels, a sugar baron from San Francisco. Spreckels acquired land in and around central Maui as he established good relations with King Kālākaua and he built extensive ditches in order to facilitate massive amounts of water for sugar production—a controversial subject today, as instances such as these have led to Hawaiians being left with limited amounts of water, depriving them of the ability to farm their staple food, taro, efficiently.[22]

"When the evil-hearted messenger comes with his greedy document of extortion" is repeated and this time it is sung by Ernie Cruz, who was a member of the prominent musical duo the Kaʻau Crater Boys. He sings in front of ʻIolani Palace, which was the royal residence of King Kalākaua and Queen Liliʻuokalani. ʻIolani Palace maintains a strong emotional significance for *Kānaka Maoli* as it was the place in which the last reigning monarch, Queen Liliʻuokalani, was tried and imprisoned for nine months. Another reminder of Hawaiian royalty occurs when Brother Noland sings "no one will fix a signature to the paper of the enemy." The location he sings in is Kaniakapūpū, which was once King Kamehameha III and Queen Kalama's summer palace. What remains are the ruins, as seen from the shot, and that remains a sacred space for many Hawaiians.

A contentious issue for *Kānaka Maoli* is the US military, a hostility that stems from the summoning of US Marines for the overthrow of the Queen Liliʻuokalani. Suspicions about the US military presence have especially arisen over the use of land for military activities, which is interpreted by *Kānaka Maoli* activists as a bombardment of sacred property. Guitarist Glen Smith sings "with its sin of annexation and sale of native civil rights" in Puʻuloa (the old Hawaiian name for what is now known as Pearl Harbor; note the renaming of places again). The visual clip shows in the background, dark dirty ocean water, Pearl Harbour, and a battleship, all juxtaposed with a beautiful rainbow (see Figure 12.1).

Another concern for *Kānaka Maoli* lies in the domain of tourism. Despite generating the highest revenue for Hawaiʻi, for *Kānaka Maoli* activists, tourism is associated with

Figure 12.1 YouTube screenshot of Glen Smith in Puʻuloa singing "*Kaulana Nā Pua*" (accessed June 9, 2020).

land struggles and "cultural prostitution" (Trask 1993:140). This hostile sentiment can be gleaned in the writing of Robert and Anne Mast:

> Tourists are momentarily awed by the natural splendor of Hawai'i... But it would be rare indeed to come across a briefing by a tour guide that described how the land and other resources of Hawai'i were transformed from an earlier pristine splendor into a gaudy, rich/poor tourist haven. Similarly, you never come across a sign in Waikīkī that says, "The land upon which this hotel sits was stolen from the Kanaka Maoli."
>
> (Mast and Mast 1996: 56)

In a similar vein, Haunani K Trask associates tourism with "cultural prostitution" (Trask 1993: 140) and theft. She writes:

> The cheapening of Hawaiian culture (for example, the traditional value of *aloha* as reciprocal love and generosity now used to sell everything from cars and plumbing to securities and air conditioning) is so complete that non-Hawaiians, at the urging of the tourist industry and the politicians, are transformed into "Hawaiians at heart," a phrase that speaks worlds about how grotesque the theft of things Hawaiian has become.
>
> (Trask 1993: 3)

The "*Kaulana Nā Pua*" video features a couple of scenes filmed in Waikīkī, the main tourist strip in the island of O'ahu. Manu Boyd echoes the words "with its sin of annexation and sale of native civil rights," and the captions list him as singing in Helumoa, Waikīkī. The Sheraton Waikīkī hotel stands in the background. Once again, we see the reclaiming of language, and the place name, Helumoa (meaning "chicken scratch"), is used, which harks back to a story of a supernatural rooster. Instead of featuring Waikīkī as a tourist hot spot, the historical Helumoa is recalled. Helumoa was once the favorite retreat and home to the chiefs and kings. It was also the place in which King Kamehameha camped to begin the takeover of O'ahu. Today, Helumoa comprises the Sheraton Waikīkī, Royal Hawaiian Hotel, and the Royal Hawaiian Shopping Center—it is the heart of hotels, tourists, and entertainment.

In another frame, Līhau Hannahs-Paik sings "we do not value the government's sums of money" against a blurred distant backdrop of hotels and condominiums in Waikīkī. This is a stark reminder that Waikīkī was far from what we see today. Although Waikīkī today is rich with tourists and urban development, in the 1400s Waikīkī had a wealth of other resources. Waikīkī, which means "spouting water," had rivers and springs flowing in the area. It had irrigation systems constructed, resulting in fishponds built and taro fields planted since the 1400s, and in the 1450s, Waikīkī was the government center of O'ahu. To the *Kanaka Maoli* activist, "we do not value the government's sums of money" is a stark reminder that taro—once the main staple food source for Hawaiians and which is also viewed as an ancestor in the Hawaiian worldview—had been replaced with the development of hotels, luxury condominiums, and commercial entertainment. Money or capitalism does not represent a Hawaiian worldview of wealth, but health and sustainability, and good stewardship of the land, are what matters. (This harks back to the original title of the song, *Mele 'Ai Pōhaku*, that they would rather eat rocks than take money.) The backdrop of hotels and condominiums demonstrates a clash of worldviews—of which, most modern Hawaiians live amongst but have not benefited from.

A reminder of, and a provocation to, *Kānaka Maoli* about what was lost is evoked as Keao Costa sings "we do not value the government's sums of money." He sings outside the Supreme Court, and again we note that the Hawaiian name is used in the caption, Ali'iolani Hale. This phrase is highlighted musically with the use of *ka leo ki'e ki'e* (Hawaiian-style falsetto), seen in older forms of Hawaiian music. Its use here strategically emphasizes the significance of the lyrics. Ali'iolani Hale is seen again as Mike Ka'awa sings "tell the story of the people who love their land." These words are echoed by Palani Vaughan once again at the Royal Mausoleum as a final reminder of the Hawaiian Kingdom, with its past chiefs and royalty.

The song closes with Palani Vaughan saying, "*aloha 'āina*" and Leina'ala Kalama-Heine saying, "We back Lili'ulani" and a final parting shot of a wandering tourist in a cheesy pink *aloha* shirt at the end of the song walking past 'Iolani palace, completely oblivious to the filming session going on (Figure 12.2).

The significant places featured in the video are used as markers of resistance as demonstrated through the renaming of places and the reminders of past histories. Watson writes that "geographic places are not merely a *setting* for a music video, but also a defining element and even an *active participant* in complex narratives about

Figure 12.2 YouTube screenshot of a tourist walking in front of 'Iolani Palace while Ernie Cruz sings "*Kaulana Nā Pua*" (accessed June 9, 2020).

a region's community, traditions, practices, and culture" (Watson 2019: 280). Project *Kuleana*'s video of *"Kaulana Nā Pua"* demonstrates that places are bound up in contested meanings and personal and collective experiences. What we see here is a demarcating of boundaries, the renewal of cultural meaning and memory, and the reclaiming of space.

To take it a step further, the video does not simply educate the viewer on place; it also provides a lens into indigenous land education. Land education places "Indigenous epistemological and ontological accounts of land at the center, including Indigenous understandings of land, Indigenous language in relation to land and Indigenous critiques of settler colonialism" (Tuck, Mackenzie, and McCoy 2014: 13).

Aloha and the *"Kaulana Nā Pua"* Music Video

The focus of this chapter thus far has been on the diverse agentic strategies used to strengthen *Kanaka Maoli* identity and awareness. This section will examine how the notion of *aloha* is used across all platforms to invite listeners to understand and to empathize with *Kanaka Maoli* values and issues, as well as to demonstrate how *aloha* has also been used as a form of resistance. Collaborative music videos on social platforms provide a voice to a broader audience, a global audience, as they display aesthetically pleasing, welcoming, and beautiful shots of Hawaii, where the viewer is able to capture and experience a sense of Hawai'i. We suspect that there is a subliminal agenda to these videos: *Aloha* is conveyed to draw the viewer (or tourist) in, to instill a sense of intrigue and curiosity, and to attract people to become invested in Hawaiian issues. Where *aloha* was once "hijacked" and used as a state apparatus (see Teves 2015, 2018), *Kānaka Maoli* are now using *aloha* to fight for their purposes, to *protect* their interests, their culture, their land, instead of a state-operated *aloha*, which is focused on the tourist gaze and other capitalist objectives.

To the outsider, each of these videos presents a beautiful Hawaiian landscape accompanied by soothing melodies. These videos appeal to the gaze, or in this case, voyeuristic gaze of any individual less acquainted with topical Native Hawaiian issues. Lena (2008) discusses the voyeuristic gaze in relation to black rap music videos. She describes the voyeuristic gaze as

> [a] learned mode of apperception that draws upon stereotypic notions of the "other"... Voyeurs mobilize preconceptions of experience, landscape, and people to see "exotic" others. They draw upon expectations of what "typical black behaviour" or "the inner city" will look like, when encountered. The presumption is that members of the dominant group utilize the voyeuristic gaze to consume, understand, or authenticate images.
>
> (Lena 2008: 266)

She also states that "the racial voyeuristic gaze draws upon the most pernicious stereotypes." In the same way, these videos afford the viewer the ability to engage with Hawaiian ways of living, such as in Mana Maoli's production of "Island Style, 'Ōiwi Ē,"[23] which depicts a (somewhat imaginary) relaxed lifestyle of what Hawaiian families do, which is "we eat and drink and sing all day." The "*Kaulana Nā Pua*" video—with its beautiful backdrops of scenic Hawai'i, sounds and visuals of the slide guitar, and lull of the sung Hawaiian language—has succeeded in attracting the imagination of viewers, and this is revealed in some of the YouTube comments:[24]

"I am from Iceland and this makes me want to move to Hawaii."

(slatsdeploy)

"I love this, I too am not Hawaiian, but my heart was opened to the Aloha spirit and i am uplifted still by the beautiful language and music of the people. At this time of great suffering in the world I look to Hawaii and photos posted every day from a friend and it gives me peace."

(Jean G)

"How beautiful, cannot wait until we visit this beautiful paradise again."

(Margaret Anderson)

"Absolutely beautiful music... I didn't understand a word but it made me cry. Thank you for sharing. :)"

(Delphine Geia)

"Lovely. I don't understand any word but I was moved. Great job my Austronesian brothers. Mabuhay! from the Philippines."

(Lester Andes)

What we see here reveals the successful use of the Hawaiian concept *kaona* (hidden or inner meaning). This is almost akin to a hidden transcript (Scott 1990), and is also seen in other cultures, such as the Tibetan concept called *nang don* (inner meaning). *Kaona* is defined in Puku'i and Elbert's Hawaiian Dictionary as "hidden meaning, as in Hawaiian poetry; concealed reference, as to a person, thing, or place; words with double meanings that might bring good or bad fortune" (Puku'i and Elbert 1986). In the case of "*Kaulana Nā Pua*" and other Hawaiian collaborative music videos, the Hawaiian aesthetic of *kaona*[25] is skillfully embedded in the video, disguising the true meaning of the text, which may take some deciphering or can sometimes remain unbeknownst to the viewer. The lyrics sung in the Hawaiian language and the visual dimension reveal to the insider the true intentions of the video, as the places that are strategically chosen resonate deeply within the *Kānaka Maoli*, who are aware of the complex and contentious issues.

One of the underlying foundations of "*Kaulana Nā Pua*" lies in the concept of *aloha 'āina* (love of the land)—a concept reinstalled and harnessed during the Hawaiian nationalist movement, and its politicized use can be seen in the naming of the political group Hui Hawai'i Aloha 'Āina, which was formed in 1893, to protest the overthrow of the Hawaiian government (Silva 2004: 11, 130–131). *Aloha* is a term that has taken on many different meanings through Hawaiian history: from love, affection, kindness within a familial setting highlighting an understanding of mutual care and benefit (Puku'i, Haertig and Lee 2002:3), to a customary salutation (see Chun 2011:32–4), to a Christian missionary representation of unconditional love (regardless of reciprocity) (see Kanahele 1986: 197–207; Teves 2015: 707), to a commercialized and state-exploited *aloha* for the benefits of tourism and disciplining of Native Hawaiians (Marusek 2017; Ohnuma 2008; Teves 2015, 2018; Trask 1993). Ohnuma proposes that the reciprocal duty of *aloha* was finally restored but this time for patriotic means—to serve and honor the ancestors on the land. She writes that "aloha 'āina works to 'take back' aloha from collusion with capitalist exploitation and alienation" and this became "a decolonized *aloha*" (Ohnuma 2008: 379–80).

Fostering Agency

Today, *Kānaka Maoli* activists are reclaiming the term *aloha* and using it as a form of resistance and agency. They endeavor to protect their culture, their identity, their land, and their future generations. Project *Kuleana*'s "*Kaulana Nā Pua*" collaborative music video conveys *aloha* as it welcomes in *all* viewers (*Kānaka Maoli* and non-native Hawaiians), exhibiting warmth through its soothing melody and beautiful scenic backdrops of the islands, while at the same time demonstrating *aloha 'āina* through the Hawaiian lyrics and through the use of signs, intertextuality, and the reclaiming and renaming of places. The choice of the song "*Kaulana Nā Pua*" triggers a collective sonic-social remembrance for *Kānaka Maoli* as past injustices such as the overthrow of the Hawaiian monarchy and illegal annexation are immediately recalled to mind. The music video invites the individual to join in the cause and not stand alone. As a collaborative music video, the collective of famous Hawaiian musicians demonstrates a sign of unity for the cause and a sense of togetherness within the Hawaiian community. Through demonstrating a shared past in the visual dimension of the video by featuring places of resistance, cultural lineage, old ways of living, and engaging well-known Hawaiian musicians, activists, and schoolchildren from Hawaiian charter schools, these collaborative music videos are a powerful method for empowering *Kānaka Maoli* and fostering individual and collective agency. It instills hope and helps affirm native identity, especially in the face of structural adversity. Hawaiian music has and still is used as a vehicle to mobilize people (and structures) and engender change. With the added visual dimension of a music video and an expanding network of online communities through different social media platforms, online collaborative music videos form an agentic part of a growing grassroots platform for Hawaiian cultural-political expression, protecting and promoting indigenous rights, and restoring the sovereignty of the Hawaiian Kingdom.

Acknowlegdments

We would like to thank Danielle Espiritu for her expertise, time and invaluable feedback on an earlier version of this chapter.

Notes

1. Ellen Kekoʻaohiwaikalani Wright Prendergast, who was a close friend of the Queen, is attributed as the author of the song's lyrics, but research by Stillman has shown, through an 1895 copy of the sheet music (the earliest copy that has been discovered) and a close review of copyright trends, that Royal Hawaiian band member J.S. Lisbornio might well be the composer of the melody "*Kaulana Nā Pua*" or at least the arranger. For more information on this, refer to Stillman (1999).
2. The Royal Hawaiian Band was established in 1836 under King Kamehameha III. They performed for state occasions and accompanied Hawaiian monarchs on their trips.
3. A Caucasian person.
4. For a version of this video, see https://www.youtube.com/watch?v=bhibLQFebpQ, accessed June 9, 2020.
5. Playing for Change began in 2002 as an initiative to use music to break down barriers and overcome distances between people. Its producers travel around the world with a mobile recording studio and cameras recording local artists, whose performances would be presented in an immaculately edited collaborative music video. For more information, see https://playingforchange.com/, accessed May 4, 2020.
6. https://www.facebook.com/pg/ProjectKULEANA/about/?ref=page_internal, accessed May 4, 2020.
7. The author uses the terms Kānaka Maoli, Kānaka, Native Hawaiian, and Hawaiian interchangeably throughout this chapter. In all instances reference is made to the original human inhabitants of Hawaiʻi.
8. The Hawaiian Renaissance of the late 1960s and 1970s was a cultural revitalization movement during which *Kānaka Maoli* turned introspectively to question their Hawaiian indigenous identity and this triggered a revival to relearn traditional ways of living. There was also a revival in the arts, music, dance, and chant. Its effects are still felt today.
9. *Hapa haole* music generally refers to songs sung mostly in English with a smattering of Hawaiian words or pidgin English words. It became prevalent in the first few decades of the twentieth century and incorporated the styles trending at the time (ragtime, Dixieland, jazz, etc.).
10. It is worth noting that Aunty Genoa and other Hawaiian musicians also wrote music for the *hapa haole* tradition as well.
11. The Hawaiian language as a medium of instruction was banned in 1896 with Hawaiian strongly discouraged in public places. *Hula* was also banned in the nineteenth century.
12. Ricardo Trimillos (2019) has also written about the politics within "Somewhere over the Rainbow."

13 More examples of Hawaiian protest music can be gleaned from the writings of Akindes (2001), Franklin and Lyons (2004), Kalyan (2006), Kanahele (2012), and Ong (2017).
14 The issue on Mauna Kea lay with the continuous development and building of telescopes from the late 1960s from different institutions from around the world in order to further astronomy research (see http://kahea.org/issues/sacred-summits/timeline-of-events, ,accessed September 11, 2020, for more information). More importantly, the Hawaiians see this as a desecration to their ʻāina, their land. For many Native Hawaiians and their supporters, they do not take issue with astronomy or science, but the offense lies with the fact that they see Mauna Kea or Mauna a Wākea not just a mountain but the most sacred place on the islands, an ancestor, and the mountain is home to many deities, and is a graveyard for the bones of the dead, with temples and *heiaus* (places of worship or sacred stone platforms). The protestors see themselves not as protestors but as protectors of Mauna a Wākea. For them, Mauna a Wākea is not just a mountain but a temple itself, a place of spiritual significance. In addition, there are also issues of land ownership: the sacred summit is part of the Hawaiian Kingdom and Crown and Government lands—lands that were illegally seized from the Hawaiian Kingdom in 1893, when the sugar plantation owners with US military backing overthrew the monarchy. They feel that the United States and State of Hawaii have no rightful jurisdiction over it and so feel empowered to challenge the construction projects (Noelani Goodyear-Kaʻōpua 2017). There are also added physical concerns, such as sewage waste, the preservation of endangered plant and bird species, and water pollution.
15 For example https://www.youtube.com/watch?v=bhibLQFebpQ, accessed May 28, 2020.
16 Another grass-roots cultural initiative with similar aims as Project *Kuleana*. They also support Hawaiian cultural education through their work in Hawaiian charter schools. For more information, see https://www.manamaoli.org/, accessed June 9, 2020.
17 In this context, we use *aloha* to mean "love," "kindness," and "affection."
18 Refer to Turino (1999) for more information on Peircean semiotic theory for music. Here, we interpret an "index" to refer to a sign that relates to the object evoked by direct relation (such as a puddle, which symbolizes that it has rained or is raining) and a legisign to represent its belonging. A dicent sign refers to signs that are in the receiver's subconscious, such as body language.
19 Kindly note that all lyrics in this section have been translated into English. The song is sung in Hawaiian.
20 This is with the exception of Kamehameha the Great.
21 This can also be seen in the renaming of streets, such as Dole Street, which up to the 1950s was called Kapaʻakea Street (meaning "coral bedrock" or "limestone").
22 There are also concerns of drinking water contamination caused by leaked fuel from the US Navy Red Hill Bulk Fuel Storage Facility located in Kapūkaki (now known as Red Hill), which sits 100 feet above the Southern Oʻahu Basal Aquifer, which is one of the primary sources for drinking water for the island. For more information, see https://sierraclubhawaii.org/redhill, accessed July 25, 2020.
23 To view the video, visit: https://www.manamele.org/islandstyleoiwie, accessed May 4, 2020.

24 The following quotes are available online from https://www.youtube.com/watch?v=bhibLQFebpQ, accessed June 9, 2020.
25 *Kaona* was commonly used in *mele* and in the Hawaiian language, so the importance of tone and context was key to understanding the true meaning of what was being expressed.

Bibliography

Akindes, Fay. 2001. "Sudden Rush: *Na Mele Paleoleo* (Hawaiian Rap) as Liberatory Discourse." *Discourse* 23 (1): 82–98.

Ambikaipaker, Mohan. 2016. "Music Videos and the 'War on Terror' in Britain: Benjamin Zephaniah's Infrapolitical Blackness in Rong Radio." *Communication, Culture & Critique* 9: 341–61.

Boym, Svetlana. 2001. *The Future of Nostalgia*. New York: Basic Books.

Bronfman, Alejandra M. 2016. *Isles of Noise: Sonic Media in the Caribbean*. Chapel Hill, NC: University of North Carolina Press.

Burns, Lori, and Stan Hawkins. 2019. "Introduction: Undertaking Music Video Analysis." In *The Bloomsbury Handbook of Popular Music Video Analysis*, edited by Lori Burns, 1–12. New York: Bloomsbury Academic.

Chun, Malcolm Naea. 2011. *No Na Mamo*: Traditional and Contemporary Hawaiian Beliefs and Practices. Honolulu: University of Hawai'i Press.

Cook, Nicholas. 1998. *Analysing Musical Multimedia*. Oxford: Oxford University Press.

Cresswell, Tim. 2015. *Place: An Introduction*. Chichester: Wiley Blackwell.

Damon, Ethel M. 1957. *Sanford Ballard Dole and His Hawaii*. Palo Alto, CA: Pacific Books.

Denning, Michael. 2015. *Noise Uprising: The Audiopolitics of a World Musical Revolution*. London: Verso.

Denning, Michael. 2016. "Decolonizing the Ear: The Transcolonial Reverberations of Vernacular Phonograph Music." In *Audible Empire: Music, Global Politics, Critique*, edited by Ronald Radano and Tejumola Olaniyan, 25–44. Durham, NC: Duke University Press.

De Paor-Evans, Adam. 2018. "The Intertextuality and Translations of Fine Art and Class in Hip-Hop Culture." *Arts* 7 (4): 80.

Dibben, Nicola. 2009. "Nature and Nation: National Identity and Environmentalism in Icelandic Popular Music Video and Music Documentary." *Ethnomusicology Forum* 18 (1): 131–51.

Eyerman, Ron, and Andrew Jamison. 1998. *Music and Social Movements: Mobilizing Traditions in the Twentieth Century*. Cambridge: Cambridge University Press.

Fanon, Frantz. 1965. *A Dying Colonialism*. New York: Grove Press.

Franklin, Cynthia, and Laura Lyons. 2004. "Land, Leadership, and Nation: Haunani-Kay Trask on the Testimonial Uses of Life Writing in Hawai'i." *Biography* 27: 222–49.

Goodyear-Ka'ōpua, Noelani. 2017. "Protectors of the Future, Not Protestors of the Past: Indigenous Pacific Activism and Mauna a Wākea." *South Atlantic Quarterly* 116 (1): 184–94.

Kalyan, Rohan. 2006. "Hip-hop Imaginaries: A Genealogy of the Present." *Journal for Cultural Research* 10 (3): 237–57.

Kanahele, George S. 2002. "The Dynamics of Aloha." In *Pacific Diasporas*, edited by Paul Spickard, Joanne L. Rondilla and Debbie Hippolite Wright, 195–210. Honolulu: University of Hawai'i Press.

Kanahele, George S. 1986. *Ku Kanaka Stand Tall: A Search for Hawaiian Values*. Honolulu: University of Hawai'i Press.

Kanahele, George S. 2012. *Hawaiian Music and Musicians*. Honolulu: Mutual Publishing.

Kraidy, Marwan M. 2013. "Contention and Circulation in the Digital Middle East: Music Video As Catalyst." *Television & New Media* 14 (4): 271–85.

Kursell, Julia. 2011. "A Gray Box: the Phonograph in Laboratory Experiments and Fieldwork, 1900–1920." In *The Oxford Handbook of Sound Studies*, edited by Trevor Pinch and Karin Bijsterveld, 176–97. New York: Oxford University Press.

Lena, Jennifer C. 2008. "Voyeurism and Resistance in Rap Music Videos." *Communication and Critical/Cultural Studies* 5 (3): 264–79.

Lewis, George. 1985. "Beyond the Reef: Role Conflict and the Professional Musician in Hawaii." *Popular Music* 5: 189–98.

Lewis, George. 1991. "Storm Blowing from Paradise: Social Protest and Oppositional Ideology in Popular Hawaiian Music. Popular Music." *Popular Music* 10 (1): 53–67.

Liew, Kai Khiun. 2014. "Rewind and Recollect: Activating Dormant Memories and Politics in Teresa Teng's Music Videos Uploaded on YouTube." *International Journal of Cultural Studies* 17 (5): 503–15.

Marusek, Sarah. 2017. "The Aloha Paradox: Law, Language, and Culture in Hawai'i." *Space and Polity* 21 (1): 108–122.

Massey, Doreen. 1994. *Space, Place, and Gender*. Minneapolis, MN: University of Minnesota Press.

Mast, Robert H., and Anne B. Mast. 1996. *Autobiography of Protest in Hawai'i*. Honolulu: University of Hawai'i Press.

McCosker, Anthony. 2015. "Social Media Activism at the Margins: Managing Visibility, Voice and Vitality Affects." *Social Media + Society* 1 (2): 1–11.

Ohnuma, Keiko. 2008. "'Aloha Spirit' and the Cultural Politics of Sentiment as National Belonging." *The Contemporary Pacific* 20 (2): 365–94.

Ong, Min Yen. 2017. "Navigating *Kuleana* in Hawaiian Protest Music." Paper presented at *The European Society for Oceanists*, Munich, Germany, June 29–July 2.

Przybylski, Liz. 2018. "Customs and Duty: Indigenous Hip Hop and the US-Canada Border." *Journal of Borderlands Studies* 33 (3): 487–506.

Puku'i, Mary Kawena, and Samuel H. Elbert. 1986. *Hawaiian Dictionary*. Honolulu: University of Hawai'i Press.

Puku'i, Mary Kawena, E.W. Haertig, and Catherine A. Lee. 2002. Nānā I Ke Kumu (Look to the Source) Volume I. Honolulu: Hui Hānai.

Rosenthal, Rob, and Richard Flacks. 2011. *Playing for Change: Music and Musicians in the Service of Social Movements*. Boulder, CO: Paradigm Publishers.

Ruhlig, Tim. 2016. "'Do You Hear the People Sing' 'Lift Your Umbrella'? Understanding Hong Kong's Pro-Democratic Umbrella Movement through YouTube Music Videos." *China Perspectives* 4 (108): 59–68.

Scott, James C. 1990. *Domination and the Arts of Resistance: Hidden Transcripts*. New Haven, CT: Yale University Press.

Silva, Noenoe K. 2004. *Aloha Betrayed: Native Hawaiian Resistance to American Colonialism*. Durham, NC: Duke University Press.

Stillman, Amy Kuʻuleialoha. 1999. "ʻAloha ʻĀina:' New Perspectives on 'Kaulana Nā Pua.'" *Hawaiian Journal of History* 33: 83–100.

Tan, Shzr Ee. 2017. "Taiwan's Aboriginal Music on The Internet." In *Music, Indigeneity, Digital Media*, edited by Thomas R. Hilder, Henry Stobart, and Shzr Ee Tan, 28–52. Rochester: University of Rochester Press.

Taylor, Pamela G. 2007. "Press Pause: Critically Contextualizing Music Video in Visual Culture and Art Education." *Studies in Art Education* 48 (3): 230–46.

Teves, Stephani Nohelani. 2015. "Aloha State Apparatuses." *American Quarterly* 67 (3): 705–26.

Teves, Stephanie Nohelani. 2018. *Defiant Indigeneity: The Politics of Hawaiian Performance*. Chapel Hill, NC: The University of North Carolina Press.

Trask, Haunani-Kay. 1993. *From a Native Daughter*. Honolulu: University of Hawaiʻi Press.

Trimillos, Ricardo. 2019. "Hawaiian and American Pasts Confronting a Native Hawaiian and a Globalized Present: Reworking Harold Arlen's 'Over the Rainbow' by Israel Kamakawiwoʻole." In *Making Waves: Traveling Musics in Hawaiʻi, Asia, and the Pacific*, edited by Frederick Lau and Christine R. Yano, 187–203. Honolulu: University of Hawaiʻi Press.

Tuck, Eve, Marcia McKenzie, and Kate McCoy. 2014. "Land Education: Indigenous, Post-colonial, and Decolonizing Perspectives on Place and Environmental Education Research." *Environmental Education Research* 20 (1): 1–23.

Turino, Thomas. 1999. "Signs of Imagination, Identity, and Experience: A Peircian Semiotic Theory for Music." *Ethnomusicology* 43 (2): 221–55.

Vernallis, Carol. 2013. *Unruly Media: YouTube, Music Video, and the New Digital Cinema*. Oxford: Oxford University Press.

Warner, Cameron David. 2013. "Hope and Sorrow: Uncivil Religion, Tibetan Music Videos, and YouTube." *Ethnos* 78 (4): 543–68.

Watson, Jada. 2019. "Rural-Urban Imagery in Country Music Videos: Identity, Space and Place." In *The Bloomsbury Handbook of Popular Music Video Analysis*, edited by Lori Burns, 277–97. New York: Bloomsbury.

Whiteley, Sheila, Andrew Bennett, and Stan Hawkins. 2005. *Music, Space and Place: Popular Music and Cultural Identity*. Abingdon: Routledge.

Index

Achang language 38, 46 n.17
acoustic environment 157
activism
    queer 9, 193–6, 204–6
    soft 9, 195, 196, 204–6
    sonic 219–23
Adlington, Robert 132
Adorno, Theodor W. 22, 29 n.7
advocacy 196, 197, 205
agency
    collective 8, 240
    individual 34
Ah, Cheng 181, 184
Ahdi Mark 38–40, 44
airwave 133–4
Aisyah, Aznur 114
Alamanda Studio 217
Algeria 232
aloha 228, 231, 236, 237–40, 242 n.17
    aloha 'aina 10, 228, 237, 239–40
Althusser, Louis 131
alyir nissat be alzi nima (brothers and sisters) 36
American Forces Network (AFN) 134
American Forces Radio and Television Service (AFRTS) 134
Ammann, Raymond 22
Anderson, Benedict 172, 173, 178
anthropology 16, 34
Anzieu, Didier 160
appropriation 75, 113, 213
Apsara dance 93
Aquarius Musikindo 215
Arana, Miranda 74
archive 19, 20, 34, 52, 58, 66, 83, 173, 212, 220
Arnado, Janet M. 66
Art Kalja (Art Culture) 26
Arts Council Korea (ARKO) 116
Asia Christian Services (ACS) 4, 34–7

Asia Christian Services and Gospel Broadcasting Mission (ACS-GBM) 34
Asia Pacific 1–5, 10, 111, 194, 206
Association of Southeast Asian Nations (ASEAN) 3
Attali, Jacques 131, 178
audience/audiences
    concerts 6, 24, 41, 42, 56, 112, 115
    local 106
    media 91–107
    radio 93
    television 91–107
aural 61, 62, 131–4, 155, 215, 233
Australian Broadcasting Corporation 29 n.10
Australian Aid (AUSAID) 25
authenticity 29 n.11, 205
authoritarian 3, 10, 75, 85, 160, 211
authority 3, 7–8, 10, 45, 131, 135, 234
avant-garde 217

Bahasa Indonesia 52, 66
Bali 96, 97
Bandar, Meikhan Sri 53, 54
Banks Islands 15, 26
Barendregt, Bart 1
Barmé, Geremie 159
Bayon TV 92, 94, 95, 98, 101
Beijing 141, 151, 152, 154, 158, 159, 164, 166, 166 n.2, 178, 193–5, 198, 200, 203
Beijing Queer Chorus (BQC) 8, 9, 193–4, 196–205, 207, 207 n.1
Beijing Queer Film Festival 196
belonging 8, 16, 19, 24, 160, 161, 221, 232, 234, 242 n.18
Benjamin, Walter 7, 22, 29 n.7, 138
Bilibili 193, 197, 201, 202
Billboard 114
Birdsall, Carolyn 173

Bithell, Caroline 92
Blackboots 214, 221, 222
Blind Melon 211
blog 84, 85, 232
Bolter, Jay David 34
Bolton, Lissant 17, 20, 22
border
    national 8, 171–8, 181–4, 187, 232
    regional 173, 181, 187
Boyd, Manu 228, 236
British Broadcasting Corporation (BBC) 171, 182
broadcasting. *see also* media; radio broadcasting
    commercial 4, 6, 20, 22, 23, 39, 50, 85, 91, 103–5, 140, 201, 213, 237, 240
    community 3–5, 7, 9, 10, 19, 20, 23, 34–6, 39, 40, 42–4, 52, 53, 55, 56, 58, 65, 66, 106, 173, 174, 178, 187, 194, 196–200, 202, 204, 211, 213, 217, 219, 220, 228, 230, 232, 234, 238, 240
    history 1, 2, 4, 8–10, 15, 17, 18, 21, 34–6, 45, 66, 73, 86, 93, 106, 131, 133, 138–42, 151–5, 157, 163, 166, 171–4, 194, 212, 228, 229, 231–4, 236, 237, 240
    mobile 4, 10, 15, 33, 50, 51, 59–65, 241 n.5
    network 8, 35, 38, 135, 140–2, 171, 174–6, 187
    policy 26
    public service 15, 26, 84
    war 176, 184–6
Brother Noland 228, 235
BTS 114, 126
Buchanan, Donna A. 86
bullhorns 165
Bull, Michael 61
Burma. *see* Myanmar

ca Huế 76, 77, 79
cải lương 76, 77, 91
Cakau, Moses 20, 25, 26
call to prayer *(adhan)* 61–5
Cambodia 5, 6, 91–7, 100, 102, 103, 105–7
Cambodian Living Arts (CLA) 92–4, 103–5

campaigns 135, 140, 156, 181
    mass 156
campus radio 9, 213
camriəŋ yiike (*yiike* singing) 97, 100–3, 108 n.10
capitalism 106, 172, 237
Carter, Jason 132
cassette tape. *see* tape
Cát Vận 86
censorship
    media 193, 200, 201
    state 9, 131
Changsha 195
chant 4, 49, 55, 57, 62, 107 n.5, 151, 154, 157–65, 228, 230, 234
Charpentier, Jean-Michel 20
Cha, Victor 136
Cheng, Nien 167 n.17
chèo 76, 77, 80, 85, 86
Chiang Mai 4, 33–5, 38, 40, 46 n.19, 46 n.20
China 4, 7, 8, 10 n.1, 33, 35–7, 41, 42, 45 n.1, 46 n.17, 51, 74, 132, 134, 137, 141–3, 144 n.12, 145 n.21, 151, 152, 154–9, 161, 162, 164, 166 n.2, 167 n.8, 168 n.19, 171–3, 188 n.4, 193–4, 206–7
    Beijing Queer Chorus 197–200
    LGBTQ community 8–9, 193–9, 201, 203, 204, 206, 207 n.2
    nation-building 173–6
    online streaming and social media communication 200–4
    queer activism in 194–6
    queer audibility and soft activism 204–6
    Teng and Taiwan Strait 184–6
    youths in 181–3
China Central Television 201
China Global Television Network 201
Chinese Communist Party (CCP) 8, 151–9, 163–5, 171, 175, 176, 181–2
Chinese New Year 199
Cho Hŭisŏn 116
choir(s) 8, 39, 102, 193, 194, 196–206
"*Chŏkpyŏk*" (Red Cliff) 117–19
Chŏng, Noshik 113

Chorn-pond, Arn 93, 106
Christianity 33, 37
ch'uimsae 111, 112, 122–4
clandestine 8, 185
classical music 44, 79, 92, 93, 103, 105, 113, 115, 137
Cohen, Matthew Isaac 106
Cold War 5, 171, 173, 184, 185
collaborative music videos 10, 228, 230–2, 238–40, 241 n.5
colonialism/colonization 10, 139, 231, 238. *see also* decolonization
    settler 238
commercialism 4, 6, 20, 22, 23, 29 n.5, 29 n.8, 39, 50, 85, 91, 103–5, 140, 201, 213, 237, 240
Communist Party of Vietnam 73
community
    consumption 3, 6, 51, 105, 112, 115, 121, 122, 135, 142
    imagined 2, 5, 7, 173, 178, 198, 224
    imagined listening 4, 8, 49, 53, 173, 174, 187
    minority 2, 44, 74, 84, 85, 87, 178, 196, 202, 206
    radio 16–20, 22–8, 33–41, 44, 45, 171–8, 181–5, 187
    sound 1–2, 217, 222
compact disc (CD) 23, 24, 38, 92, 94, 103–5
consumer 66, 103, 114, 115
consumption 3, 6, 51, 105, 112, 115, 121, 122, 135, 142
control 6–8, 19, 28, 44, 50, 62–4, 74, 80–2, 86, 94, 131–8, 143, 166, 171, 174–8, 180, 184, 187, 195, 227
convergence culture 61
copyright 23, 241 n.1
cosmological
    concept 154
    perception 154
cosmopolitanism 51
Costa, Keao 237
Couldry, Nick 205
cover 9, 18, 41, 184, 185, 202, 213, 215–18
    student cover band 214–15
creativity 26, 74, 85, 101, 106, 138, 222

Crowe, Peter 20, 21, 26
Cruz, Ernie Jr. 228, 235, 237
Cui, Zi'en 205
cultural policy 25–7
cultural prostitution 236
Cultural Revolution 8, 151, 154, 157, 159, 161, 163–5, 167 n.12, 167 n.16, 167 n.17, 168 n.18, 181
culture/cultural
    activism 196, 206, 223
    bearer 75
    broker 6, 74–6, 84–6, 88 n.3
    capital 20, 24, 25, 112
    change 92
    event 116, 196, 206
    production 7, 131–3, 135, 136, 142, 144 n.8
    prostitution 236
    revival/revitalization 9, 17, 85, 91, 93, 142, 233, 234, 241 n.8
    revolution (*see* Cultural Revolution)
    sustainability 6, 75, 103
Cumbo, Georges 24

dance 17, 19, 21, 41, 42, 68, 91–3, 102, 103, 114, 118, 138
dangdut 53, 62
decolonization 230–2
democracy 16, 19
    movement 151, 164
Democratic People's Republic of Korea 7, 139
Denning, Michael 231
deterritorialization 171, 172, 176, 187
    reterritorialization 172
Dewa 19 215
diaphonie 180
digital recording 1, 6, 20, 24, 29 n.4, 39, 43, 65, 83, 112, 114, 194, 196, 204, 206
digital video disc (DVD) 33, 39, 103, 105, 144 n.11
Discipline and Punish (Foucault) 138
do-It-Yourself (DIY) 51, 213, 217
domestic worker 4, 49, 50, 52, 55, 62, 64, 65, 67
Douban 193, 197, 201, 202

East Asia 2, 10, 35
Eastern Bloc 171
    Western Bloc 171, 185
East Timor (Timor Leste) 219
echo chamber principle 115, 123
editing 39, 44, 81
electricity 15, 37, 234
electromagnetic signals 171–3, 181, 187
Engebretsen, Elisabeth L. 195, 206
Ensminger, David A. 215
entrepreneurialism 5, 106, 220
environmentalism 5, 8, 40, 106, 121, 141, 155, 157, 158, 164, 174, 180, 204
espionage 177, 180
ethnic minority 4, 33, 87, 178, 188 n.3
ethnomusicology 46 n.14, 67
experimentation 75
Eyerman, Ron 231

Facebook 24, 29 n.11, 49–58, 61–3, 66–8, 78, 84, 92, 102, 105, 116–20, 193, 197, 201, 202, 228, 232
    Facebook Messenger 50, 67
fan 126, 202, 203
Far East Broadcasting Company (FEBC) 33, 35, 38, 46 n.8
fatality 172, 173, 181, 187
Felstiner, Alek 162
festival 19, 24, 42, 43, 83, 95, 107, 138, 173, 193, 196, 200, 202–4, 206, 214, 220, 221
film 7, 39, 40, 68, 93, 105, 111, 112, 137, 138, 141, 159, 162, 174, 175, 186, 188 n.4, 193, 195, 196, 198, 204–6, 220, 228, 233, 236, 237
Finchum-Sung, Hilary 113, 120
Finnegan, Ruth 1
Flacks, Richard 231
folk opera 91, 132, 185
folk song 75, 117
Foucault, Michel 7, 16, 19, 28, 138, 174, 177, 178
fourth curtain 138
François, Alexandre 21–2
Freemuse 132
free radio broadcasting 27

Fujian 183–5
    Xiamen 184, 185
fungibility 162, 163

Gama Fair (1992) 214, 220, 221
Gang of One (Shen) 161
gaqchit 43
Gardissat, Paul 18–20, 22
gay dating app (Blued, Aloha, Rela, Lespark, and Lesdo) 193
gaze 238–9
    voyeuristic 238–9
Geertz, Clifford 75
geming guqu 139
genre gap 107
Geronimo FM 9, 213, 215
G-Indie 9, 215–17, 221
globalization 194
Global TV 212
Goodale, Greg 160
Gospel Broadcasting Mission (GBM) 4, 38, 39, 44, 46 n.6
gospel singers 42, 43
gramophone 184, 232
Grant, Catherine 106
Great Leap Forward 156
Green Day 215
Group 109 133
Grusin, Richard 34
GugakFM 116–18, 120, 124, 127 n.7
guitar 22, 37–9, 42, 43, 100, 105, 132, 140, 211, 214, 215, 239
Guomindang 157

hallyu. see Korean Wave
Hamidun, Hafiz 58–62
Hannahs-Paik Lihau 236
Hanoi 5, 73, 76, 87, 176
Han, Sŭngho 142
Haom Rooŋ (The Sacred Pavilion) 92, 100–1, 104
hapa haole (half-white) 229, 231, 241 n.9
hapa haoli music 229, 231, 241 n.9, 241 n.10
Harkness, Nicholas 126 n.3
Harrison, Simon 16, 27
hát bài chòi 76

hát chèo 76
hát văn 81
Hawai'i 1, 227–8
  aloha 238–40
  Kānaka Maoli and foster agency 228–40
  "Kaulana Nā Pua" 230–40
  music and protest 228–30
Hawaiian Renaissance 229, 231, 241 n.8
Helm, George 229, 231
Helumoa 236
"Here Comes Nolbo" *(Nolbo ka onda)* 116, 120
heritage
  cultural 1, 6, 75–6, 86, 102, 107, 111, 112
  heritagization 1, 6, 75–6, 85, 86, 93, 102, 104, 106, 107, 111, 112
  musical 93
Herman, Francis 26
Hershatter, Gail 157
He, Shubin 184
Hesmondhalgh, David 215
Hikianalia 234
Hill, Juniper 92
Ho Chi Minh 76
Hokkien 61, 183, 185
Hōkūle'a 234
Hồng Ngát 76, 77, 81, 82
Huang, Nicole 174–5
Hua, Yu 167 n.12
Hui Hawai'i Aloha 'Āina 240
hula 230, 241 n.11
human rights 219
Hung, Chang-tai 154, 159
Hung, Wu 154, 158
Huxley, Aldous 161
Hwa hwa (How are you?) 36
Hyŏn, Songwŏl 143

identity
  alternative 36, 41, 45, 49, 50, 78, 117, 121, 206, 212, 215, 217
  ethnic 4, 5, 33, 35, 37, 38, 41–3, 45 n.1, 74, 178, 188 n.4
  musical 4, 44, 50, 215
  national 7, 17–19, 91, 106, 111, 157
  political 2, 6, 86, 159
  postcolonial 4, 34, 44
  social 34
ideology 6, 7, 34, 73, 131–8, 141
indie
  culture 217, 218, 223, 224 n.2
  festival 19, 24, 42, 43, 83, 107, 138, 173, 193, 196, 200, 202–4, 206, 214, 220, 221
  labels 133, 140, 142, 215, 223
  music 223, 224 n.2
  rock 9, 212, 214–18, 223
  scene 9, 223
indigenous/indigeneity 1, 2, 4, 10, 17, 21, 33–45, 46 n.14, 52, 238, 240, 241 n.8
Indonesia 4, 9, 211–12, 223–4, 232. *see also* Singapore, Indonesian workers
  activism 219–23
  bands 214–15
  indie rock 215–18
  popular music, media, and politics 212–14
  student and people 218–19
Indonesia Institute of the Arts of Yogyakarta 211, 213, 221
Indonesian Buskers Union (SPI) 211
Indonesian Democratic Party *(Partai Demokrasi Indonesia)* 213
Indonesian domestic worker 4, 49, 52, 55, 64, 65
Indonesian People's Democratic Party *(Partai Rakyat Demokratik)* 214
Indonesian Students in Solidarity for Democracy (SMID) 222
infrastructure 8, 15, 155, 171, 172, 174–6, 178, 181, 187, 219
  sound 171, 187
Instagram 6, 112, 114, 120, 127 n.6, 193, 202, 228
intangible cultural heritage (ICH) 1, 5, 6, 75–6, 83, 86, 107, 112
intellectual property 84, 86
internet 2, 4, 26, 33, 84, 105, 112, 118, 121, 133, 194, 196
  Singapore's Indonesian worker (*see* Singapore, Indonesian workers)
intertextuality 10, 233, 240

'Iolani Palace 235, 237
Islam 4, 44, 49, 50, 55, 56, 62, 63

Jamison, Andrew 231
Japan 133, 136, 139, 140, 183, 185, 202, 203
jazz 82, 87, 184
Jeongdong Theatre *(Chŏngdong kŭkchang)* 117–21
Jones, Andrew F. 184, 185
Jorgenson, John 136
juche 132, 134–7, 139, 140, 143

Kachin 34, 42, 45 n.1, 46 n.15
kaeryang 137
Kalākaua, David, King of Hawai'i 234, 235
Kalama-Heine, Leina'ala 237
Kalinoe, Lawrence 21
Kamakawiwo'ole, Israel 230
Kamehameha, Kings of Hawai'i 234–6, 241 n.2
Kānaka Maoli 228–40, 241 n.7, 241 n.8
Kaniakapūpū 235
kaona 239, 243 n.25
Kapono, Henry 229
kastom 3, 15, 17, 19–28, 29 n.8, 29 n.11
"*Kaulana Nā Pua*" 230–40
KCCN 229
Keali'ikanaka'oleohaililani, Kekuhi 234
Keawe, Genoa 229
Kedung Ombo water reservoir 218
Kerkvliet, Benedict J. 73, 85
Khmer 6, 91–2, 105–7, 107 n.5, 108 n.8
  lkhaon bassac 95–100
  traditional dance, music, and theater 92–5, 103–5
  wedding songs *(phleng kar)* and Yiike songs *(Camriəŋ Yiike)* 100–3
Khmer Cultural Heritage 92, 97–8, 100–1
Kim, Chŏngchŏl 141
Kim, Chŏngnam 141
Kim, Chŏngwŏn 115
Kim, Hoeil 135
Kim, Il Sung 131, 135, 136, 138–41, 145 n.24
Kim, Jong Il 131–3, 136, 138–41, 143 n.1
Kim, Jong Un 138, 141, 142

Kim, Sumin 142
Kimura, Lale 234
Kim, Wŏn'gyun 139
Korea 2, 5, 7, 112–14, 116, 125, 131–43, 144 n.12, 176, 182
Korean Central News Agency 133
Korean Literature and Arts Union 133
Korean War 134, 135, 140, 142, 176
Korean Wave 6, 111–26
Korean Workers' Party 133, 145 n.20
Ko Yŏnghŭi 141
K-pop 6, 62, 111–15. see also *p'ansori*
Kraidy, Marwan M. 232
kugak 111–26
Kunreuther, Laura 36
Kwangmyŏngsŏng 134
kwimyŏngch'ang 111

Laing, Ellen 153–5
Lamarre, Thomas 172, 176
land 10, 18, 21, 104, 228, 229, 231, 234–40, 242 n.14
language 6, 15, 18, 19, 23, 29 n.8, 33, 35, 37–9, 41, 43, 46 n.17, 66, 95, 108 n.10, 132, 134, 172, 177, 185, 188 n.3, 193, 201, 227–9, 234, 236, 238, 239, 241 n.11, 242 n.18, 243 n.24
  accent 182
Larkin, Brian 37
LaVerne Morse 33, 35–7
Layard, John 19
Lazarus Fish 40–5, 47 n.23
Le Bon, Gustave 161
Lee, Eungchel 123
Lee, Nelson K. 154
Lena, Jennifer C. 238–9
Lenin, Vladimir 79, 131, 138
Lerian, Enno 211
Lesbian, Gay, Bisexual, Transgender, and Queer (LGBTQ) 8–9, 193–9, 201, 203, 204, 206, 207 n.2
lianhuanhua 174
Ligo, Godwin 18, 19
Li, Jie 185
Lili'uokalani, Queen of Hawai'i 227
Lindsey-Asing, Kamakoa 228, 234
Lindstrom, Lamont 16, 21, 27, 28 n.1

linguistics 15, 132, 144 n.5, 172
lip-sync 83
listening
    ideal 8, 174, 176–80, 182, 187
    illicit 8, 171, 173, 176–86
    mobile 10
Lisu 4, 33–5, 37–41, 43–5, 45 n.1,
      46 n.20
    Ahdi Mark-GBM 38–40
    Christian radio 33–45
    directness, liveness, and shortwave
      radio 36–8
    Lazarus Fish-MACM 40–4
Liu, Charlie 206
Liu, Xiao 200
Liu, Yu 157
live broadcasting 40
liveness 36, 65
livestreaming 6, 111, 114–17, 120, 121
lkhaon bassac 6, 91, 93–100, 107 n.6
lkhaon yiike 6, 91, 93–5, 97–8, 101–3,
    108 n.10
loudspeaker 7, 37, 63, 105, 134, 155, 156,
    158, 159, 164, 165, 183–6
    hidden speaker 7, 132, 134

madangnori 116, 120
Mai Văn Lạng 75–6, 81, 84–6, 88 n.8
Malaysia 91
Maliangkay, Roald 134
Malinowski, Bronisław 16
malmit jiasu (preachers) 37
malpha dama 36
Mana Maoli 231, 239
Manchuria 139
Mandarin 8, 61, 171, 176, 185
Mandate of Heaven (Schell) 166 n.3
man Vanuatu 25
Mao Zedong 151, 152, 154–61, 163–6,
    166 n.1, 167 n.17, 175, 178
Martin, Liko 230
Marxism 175
Marx, Karl 79, 136, 175
Massey, Doreen 163
massovaya persnya 139
Mast, Anne B. 236
Mast, Robert H. 236
Maui 234

meaning
    hidden 239
    inner 239
Meari (Echo) 133
media. *see also* censorship; social media
    evangelism 41
    mediatization 34
    new 2, 4, 6, 34, 45, 92, 93, 112, 156,
      206, 232
    old 24, 43, 61, 62, 76, 80, 83
Melanesia 3, 15, 16, 21, 28
Melanesian Festival of Arts 29 n.11
mele
    mele aloha 'āina 228
    mele kū'ē 229, 231
memory 22, 181, 231, 232, 238
metal 214, 217
    hair 215
Metallica 214, 217
Meyer, Jeffrey F. 166 n.2
migrant worker 49, 52, 58, 65–8
"*Mileix matdda a'ma Mulashiddei*"
    (Unforgettable Mulashidi) 37
Milstein, Denise 93
minority 2, 4, 33, 44, 74, 84, 85, 87, 178,
    195, 196, 198, 200, 202, 206, 207
missionary 4, 33, 34, 37, 40, 44, 240
Mittler, Barbara 132, 168 n.18
mnemonic 157
mobile phones 4, 15, 50, 51, 60–5
Mongolia 178
Moranbong 142, 143
Morse family 35, 37
Morse, J. Russel 40
Moscow Conservatoire 137
Mota Lava 15, 22
movie. *see* film
MP3 37, 39, 55, 57, 59, 61, 62, 84
MTV 212, 217, 232
muezzin 65
music industry 4–6, 10, 17, 23, 44, 86, 87 n.1
    economy 74, 142, 232
music-making
    collaborative 10, 228–32, 238–40
    participatory 7, 138
music/musical
    arrangement 8, 79, 80, 86, 87, 137, 143,
      172

composition 5, 6, 21, 77, 83, 86, 100–3, 137, 138, 157, 224
entertainment 42
on internet 53–61
and place (*see* place)
scenes (*see* scenes)
score 199
sonic envelopes and call to prayer 61–5
sonic selfies and life-journaling 50–3, 65
traditional 5, 16, 21, 38, 73–85, 87, 91–4, 100, 103–7, 112, 116, 120, 122, 126, 198
Music of Vanuatu: Celebrations and Mysteries 22
music video 8–10, 39, 53, 58, 67, 83, 84, 114, 115, 211, 228, 230–3, 237–40
collaborative 10, 228, 230–2, 238–40, 241 n.5
Myanmar 4, 33, 35, 37–43, 49
Myanmar Agape Christian Mission (MACM) 4, 34, 40

Nāhale-a, Kīhei 228
Nāleimaile, Sean 228
Nambawan FM 98 20, 25
Nam, Yun Jin 114
Nanchu 161
nang don 239
narrowcasting 4, 50–3, 61, 65–8
nasa 43
national identity 17–19
nationalism 74, 86
nation-building 171, 173–80, 184
Ndeso 219, 221
Neng 54, 56–8, 60, 67–8
Netease Cloud Music 193
newēt song 18
New Hebrides Cultural Centre 19–20
New Order *(Orde Baru)* 9, 211–14, 218, 219, 221–3, 224 n.1
Ngọc Phan 77
Nguyễn Thế Kỷ 86
NHK (Japan Broadcasting Corporation) 183
Nirvana 215

noise 10, 62, 80, 131, 161, 167 n.9, 178
North Burma Christian Mission (NBCM) 33, 40
North China Wireless Electronics Materials Factory 156, 158
North Korea 2, 7, 131, 143, 145 n.25, 176, 182
  broadcasting news 140–2
  juche ideology 134–7
  Pyongyang 131–4
  songs 137–40
nostalgia 131, 231
Nugie 215
Nujiang Lisu 33, 36, 37, 41–3, 47 n.24
Nur Assyifa 56–8

Ohnuma, Keiko 240
Ol Samang's *Lkhaon Bassac* (OSLB) 94–7, 100, 102, 105, 107
Ong, Walter J. 156–7, 163
online 4–6, 7, 9, 20, 29 n.11, 37, 49, 51, 53, 55, 56, 58, 63, 66, 67, 84, 85, 112, 114–16, 120–2, 126, 133, 142, 194–6, 200–4, 206, 228, 230–3, 240. *see also* Internet
ownership 3, 4, 17, 19, 21, 22, 27, 86, 229, 234, 242 n.14

Pacific Ocean 1, 2, 4
Pacific War 135, 136
Pahinui, Gabby 229
Pak, Pŏmhun 122
Palin, Michael 132
p'ansori 6, 111–12, 126, 126 n.1, 126 n.2, 137
  ch'uimsae 122–4
  in K-Pop 113–14
  kugak 120–2
  SNS 116–20
  spreading of awareness 125–6
  V Live 114–16
Papua New Guinea 21, 219
parade
  May Day 151, 158, 167 n.13
  National Day 152, 157, 158, 167 n.9, 167 n.12
Park, Chan E. 120, 122

Park Chung Hee 134
Pearl Harbor 235
People's Daily 155, 156, 176, 201
People's Liberation Army 151
People's Republic of China (PRC) 7, 33, 151, 176, 193
Perris, Arnold 131
Perry, Elizabeth 157
PFLAG (Parents, Family and Friends of Lesbians and Gays) 196
phlae pkaa 94
phleng kar (wedding) 100–5, 108 n.8
Phnom Penh 93, 94, 103, 105
phonograph 184, 232
place 2, 8, 16, 17, 25, 42, 49, 56, 61, 81–3, 104, 106, 116, 124, 140, 143, 153, 158, 160, 162–4, 166, 181, 195, 196, 198, 201–4, 206, 219, 220, 228, 230, 231, 233, 234, 236, 238, 239, 242 n.14
Plato 136
Playing for Change 228, 241 n.5
Pochonbo Electronic Ensemble (Pochŏnbo chŏnja aktan) 133, 140, 142
poetry 86, 228, 239
politics/political
    change 9, 223
    music 3, 5, 7–9, 73–87, 151, 154, 157, 160, 168 n.20, 171, 176, 177, 194, 196, 205, 206, 212–14, 220, 223
popular
    culture 9, 35, 42, 111, 138
    music 3, 15, 19, 23, 103, 106, 116, 134, 184, 211–14
    singer 42
portable/portability 7, 37, 60, 61, 137, 142, 165
Port Vila 15, 20, 22
postcolonialism 10
power 7, 8, 16, 18, 21, 26, 28, 34, 43, 73, 81, 85, 87, 123, 131, 151, 155–7, 160, 163, 165, 172–5, 177, 178, 180, 182, 184, 187, 197, 227, 229, 230, 232
Preah Puthy Ciy Komar (The Understanding of a Child's Victory) 95, 97
Prendergast, Ellen Keko'aohiwaikalani Wright 227, 241 n.1

pride 42, 53, 161, 193–6, 206, 229, 234
    Shanghai Pride 193, 195, 196, 206
Project *Kuleana* 9–10, 228–38, 240, 242 n.16
proletarian 136, 175, 176, 182
propaganda 10, 84, 86, 134, 155–7, 159, 171
Protect Kaho'olawe 229
Protect Mauna Kea 230, 242 n.14
protest
    protestors 8, 160, 164, 165, 242 n.14
    student 9, 211–13, 220
Protestantism 8, 9, 151, 160, 164–6, 205, 211–14, 217–21, 223, 227–33, 240, 242 n.13
psychological operations 25, 94, 142, 173, 177–8, 217
public broadcasting and private secrets 19–22
public technology 37
pueo strum 234
punk
    post-punk 214, 217, 221
    scene 214, 217, 218, 221
Pyongyang 7, 131–41, 143, 144 n.11, 144 n.12

qasidah 55, 56, 58, 60, 61, 65
qibbe 38
Qiu, Bai 195
qotbaiq (friends) 36
quan họ singing 77
queer 8, 9, 193–207. *see also* activism
    audibility 8, 9, 194, 204–6
Quốc Anh 76

radio. *see also* broadcasting
    broadcasting (*see* radio broadcasting)
    campus 9, 212–13
    channel 4, 24, 33, 178
    commercial 213
    enemy 8, 171, 173, 177–8, 181–5, 187
    independent 9, 16, 18, 24, 33, 35, 87, 217, 219, 223
    national 8, 15, 17, 20, 22, 23, 25, 26, 73, 75, 84, 171, 181, 182
    pirate 10, 39, 47 n.25

religious mediation 38–40
shortwave 35–8, 177, 182
radio broadcasting 8, 17, 19, 22–5, 34, 41, 44, 116, 134, 155, 171–3, 187
   ideal listening 176–80
   nation-building 173–6
   sent-down youth 181–3
   Teng and Taiwan Strait 184–6
Radio Vanuatu 20, 23, 25
Rage Against the Machine 215
rally/rallies 7, 151, 154, 157, 161, 162, 164, 166
rap 42, 230, 238
recording
   equipment 39, 42, 43, 45
   facility 35
   industry 5, 22–5
   mobile 241 n.5
   process 217
   studio 4, 22, 23, 35, 40, 41, 43, 73, 74, 80–3, 85, 241 n.5
   technology 1, 5, 7, 17, 23, 24, 27, 34, 37, 50, 51, 58–9, 61, 81–2, 112, 114, 117, 122, 126, 134, 141, 157, 172, 175, 176, 182, 232, 234
record label 215, 223
"Red Book" *(Redŭbuk)* 116
Red Guard 151, 161, 162, 167 n.17
red music 74, 77, 83, 85
Red Sorrow (Nanchu) 161
reformasi 212, 213, 222–4
Reichel, Keali'i 228, 234
religion 34
resistance 64, 85, 184, 227, 229, 230, 232, 233, 237, 238, 240
restoration
   fishpond 229, 233, 236
   taro farm 233
revolution 7, 8, 136, 154, 157, 161, 162, 232. *see also* song
Ricoeur, Paul 106
Ridhlo, Mohamad Aman 217
rock 9, 39, 212–18, 223, 224
Roland 142
Romania 136
Rosenthal, Puku 231
Royal Hawaiian Band 227, 241 n.2

Royal Mausoleum 234, 237
Royal University of Fine Arts 95, 104
rɔbam yiike 91, 102, 103
Russia 74, 134, 145 n.21

Salemink, Oscar 75
SaMoeYi 33, 38, 39
Sande Monink 223
Saraswati (radio station) 213
satellite 134, 135, 142, 212
Saunders, Frances Stonor 134
saxophone 140
scenes 9, 93, 94, 97–9, 104, 107 n.5. 116, 118, 122, 126, 214, 217, 218, 221, 223, 234, 236
Schafer, R. Murray 157
Schell, Orville 165, 166 n.3, 168 n.20
Schroeder, William F. 196, 205
Schultz, Carsten D. 114–16, 124
score 78, 199
Second Indochina War 88 n.7
Second World War 22
secrecy 4, 16, 21, 27
security apparatus 174, 178
seed theory 137–8
selfie 4, 49–53, 55, 57, 58, 65, 66, 78
semiotics 228, 233
   Peircean 233, 242 n.18
sent-down youth 181–3
Sepultura 214
Shanghai 167 n.15, 181–4, 193, 195, 196, 206
Shanghai Conservatory of Music 193
Shanghai Queer Film Festival 196
shangshan xiaxiang yundong ("Down to the Countryside Movement") 181, 187 n.1
Shelemay, Kay Kaufman 3
Shen, Fan 161, 162
shōka 139
sholuwat 55, 58, 60, 62
Shostakovich, Dmitri 131, 132
Sichuan 183
sign 215, 227, 233, 236, 242 n.18
   dicent 233, 242 n.18
silence 4, 50, 81, 86, 178, 205
Siljje 37–8

Singapore, Indonesian workers 49–50, 68 n.2, 69 n.7
   narrowcasting 50–3, 65–8
   Smule to WhatsApp 53–61
   sonic envelopes and call to prayer 61–5
singing 8, 34, 37, 39–45, 51, 53, 58, 97, 101, 113, 138, 151, 154, 165, 200, 234–6
Siu, Leon 230
skɔɔ bassac 98–100, 107 n.6
skɔɔ yiike 91, 102
Skype 55, 200
slogan 8, 102, 156–61, 163, 165, 167 n.13, 197, 207
smartphone 61, 133
Smith, Glen 235
Smule 49, 53–5, 68 n.3
social activism 10, 194, 204
socialism 8, 133, 135, 164, 171, 175
Socialist New Man 174, 182
social media 5, 8–10, 24, 28, 33, 49–51, 53, 55, 60, 63, 65, 67, 68 n.3, 105, 112, 114, 115, 120, 122, 193, 194, 196–8, 200–6, 231, 232, 240. *see also* Facebook; Instagram; Twitter; WeChat; WhatsApp
social media communication 200–4
social network 2, 78, 228, 230–3
social networking services (SNS) 6, 111, 112, 114–16, 123–6
   kugak 120–2
   video material on 116–20
social platform 238
solidarity 9, 53, 66, 198, 220, 222, 228
song
   ballad 37, 38, 68
   culture 1, 5, 9, 16, 20, 25, 35, 42, 73–6, 84–6, 92, 111–13, 117, 138, 161, 174, 175, 184, 202, 217, 218, 223, 228, 229, 232, 236–8, 240
   healthy 134
   political 211–24
   protest 9, 227, 229, 232
   revolutionary 8, 77, 133, 136, 139, 151, 152, 154, 157, 161–3, 165, 175, 184, 185, 221, 230
   social commentary on 51, 53, 85
   sovereignty 229–30

Song, Hyerim 141
Songlines 132
sonic envelopes 61–5
sonic-social remembrance 230, 231, 240
sonic warfare 171, 176, 185
sonorous envelope 8, 159–63
Sony Walkman effect 61
sorikkun 6, 111–13, 120, 121, 126, 126 n.1
sound. *see also* community
   engineer 80, 81, 83
   and space 7
   studies 67, 155, 178, 180
soundscape 154, 155, 157–9, 163–6, 167 n.8, 168 n.18, 185, 231
   historical 157
South China Sea 85
Southeast Asia 1–4, 10, 33–5, 44, 49, 67, 214
South East Asia Evangelizing Mission. *see* Asia Christian Services (ACS)
South Korea 5, 134, 140, 141, 143, 144 n.8, 144 n.12
South Pacific Commission 20
sovereignty 9, 10, 176, 228, 229, 231, 240. *see also* song
Soviet Union 8, 131, 132, 136–8, 141, 144 n.9, 145 n.21, 176, 182
space 7, 9, 10, 19, 24, 39, 50–2, 56, 61–5, 82, 95, 112, 126 n.1, 138, 151–5, 159, 160, 162, 163, 166, 166 n.1, 173, 180, 194, 204, 205, 219, 221, 232, 235, 238
speaker 7, 8, 18, 37, 61–3, 65, 105, 132–4, 155, 156, 158, 159, 164, 165, 183–6, 211
   hidden 7, 132, 134
Spider Eaters (Yang) 162–3
Spotify 62
Spreckels, Claus 234
Stalin, Joseph 131, 132, 135, 136, 138, 145 n.18, 156
Stillman, Amy Kuʻuleialoha 241 n.1
Stonewall 194, 195, 206, 207 n.2
string band music 15, 19, 22, 23
student 9, 42, 43, 105, 125, 132, 134, 138, 165, 182, 234
   activism 219–23
   bands 214–15
   and people 218–19

Index 257

protests 211–14, 217–21, 223
  UGM 211–14, 219–23
Student Executive Body *(Badan Eksekutif Mahasiswa)* 220
studio 4–6, 22–4, 35, 36, 38–44, 73, 74, 76, 80–7, 95, 105, 217, 220
  engineer 80–3, 86, 135
style
  political 94, 107 n.3, 211–14, 218–23
  punk 214, 217, 221
  subcultural 218
  traditional 74, 77, 83, 116
  youth 181–3
Sudden Rush 230
Suharto 9, 211–13, 219, 221, 224 n.1
sustainability 6, 75, 84, 85, 103, 233, 237
Swaragama FM (radio station) 213
symbol 93, 132, 151, 153–5, 162, 163, 166, 200, 232, 242 n.18
Szendy, Peter 180–1

Taiwan 8, 52, 167 n.13, 171, 176, 177, 182–6
Tank Man 151
tape 5, 18, 23, 33, 37, 41, 212–15
Taruskin, Richard 132, 133
technologically-mediated voice 34
technology 1, 5, 7, 17, 23, 24, 27, 34, 37, 50, 51, 61, 112, 114, 117, 122, 126, 134, 141, 144 n.12, 157, 172, 175, 182, 232, 234
television
  channel 133
  national 6, 91
theater 6, 7, 76, 91–5, 97, 98, 100–7, 107 n.5, 112, 117, 138, 219
Thompson, Ambong 23, 25
Tiananmen Square 7, 8, 151–5
  Great Hall of the People 152, 153
  Mao and *(see* Mao Zedong)
  Memorial Hall 152, 153
  Monument to the People's Heroes 152–4, 164, 165
  Museum of Chinese History 152, 153
  slogans and chanting 159–63
  sonorous envelope 8, 159–63
  and sound 155–8
  soundscape 154–5, 157–9, 163–6, 167 n.8, 168 n.18

Tibet 167 n.13, 239
TikTok 193, 197, 202
time-lapsed iterative approach 58
Tin Pan Alley 229, 231
Titnit Titwa (One Mind, Same Root) 42
Titon, Jeff Todd 75
topoi 7, 137, 145 n.22
totalitarianism 131, 144 n.9
tourism 93, 94, 102, 229, 235, 236, 240
tradition 2–6, 10, 15–17, 19–23, 26, 28, 29 n.5, 34, 35, 38–40, 44, 45, 68, 73–8, 81–7, 88 n.7, 91–107, 108 n.8, 111–14, 116, 117, 120–2, 126, 126 n.1, 136, 194, 198, 200, 220, 221, 224, 229–31, 236, 238
  mobilization of 231
transient worker 4, 49–52, 65–7
transnationalism 10
Trask, Haunani Kay 236
Treaty of Versailles 154
Trimillos, Ricardo 241 n.12
Turner, Victor 222
Twitter 6, 112, 114, 116, 202

'ukulele 234
United Nations (UN) 2
United Nations Educational, Scientific and Cultural Organization (UNESCO) 20, 83
United States of America (USA) 35
United Underground (1998) 217, 218
Universitas Gadjah Mada (UGM) 9, 211–14, 219–23
Uriminzokkiri 7, 133

Vanuatu 2–4, 15–17, 27–8, 28 n.1, 29 n.11
  kastom 17–19, 25–7
  national identity 17–19
  public broadcasting and private secrets 19–22
  recording industry and broadcasting 22–5
Vanuatu Broadcasting and Television Corporation (VBTC) 3–4, 20, 25
Vanuatu Cultural Centre (*Vanuatu Kaljoral Senta;* VKS) 19–28
Vaughan, Palani 228, 234, 237
Venkatraman, Shriram 51

video 4, 7, 9, 10, 39, 41, 49, 51–3, 55–8,
   61, 112, 114–23, 125, 126, 137, 142,
   176, 193, 197, 200, 202, 203, 228,
   230–40. *see also* music video
video compact disc (VCD) 33
Vietnam 5, 8, 29 n.8, 46 n.8, 73–5, 88 n.3,
   88 n.4, 91
   intangible cultural heritage 75–6
   reform era 85–7
   traditional music 76–83
Vietnamese New Year 199
Vimeo 24, 52
vinyl 134
violence 39, 133, 143, 157, 161, 162, 178,
   195
V Live 6, 112, 114–16, 123, 126 n.4. *see
   also p'ansori*
vlog 51, 202, 232
vocalization 125, 137
voice 8, 10, 15, 16, 19, 25, 27, 28, 34–8,
   40–5, 58, 65, 66, 79, 87, 137, 143,
   154, 155, 158–63, 165, 167 n.8, 168
   n.20, 175, 180, 184, 185, 194, 205–7,
   231, 233, 238
Voice of America (VOA) 171, 176, 182
Voice of Free China 171, 177, 184
"voice of the party" 154, 158, 163, 165, 167
   n.9, 168 n.20
"voice of the people" 8, 154, 158, 159, 162,
   163, 165, 167 n.8, 168 n.20
Voice of the United Nations' Command
   (VUNC) 134
Voice of Vietnam Radio (VOV) 5, 73–8,
   80, 81, 83–7, 88 n.8, 88 n.12
Vois Blong Provins 26
Vois blong Torba project 26
Vois Blong Yumi 25
voyeuristic gaze 238

Waikīkī 229, 236
Wangjaesan Light Music Band
   (Wangjaesan kyŏng ŭmaktan) 133,
   140, 142
Wang, Xinyuan 50–1
Wang, Yu 177

water 19, 22, 78, 81, 218, 219, 234–6, 242
   n.22
   tanks 219
WeChat 193, 197, 198, 201, 203
wedding 6, 91, 92, 94, 97, 100–5, 107, 107
   n.5, 108 n.8
Weibo 193, 196–8, 201, 202, 205
Weixin 193
Western art music. *see* classical music
WhatsApp 4, 50, 52–61, 63
Woleg, Edgar Howard 15, 26–7
Wu, De 164

Xi, Jinping 195
Xu, Huixin 41

Yamaha 142
Yang, Chinha 115
Yang, Kuisong 176
Yangon 4, 33, 34, 40, 42
Yangon Christian College and Seminary
   (YCCS) 41–3
Yang, Rae 162–3
yellow music 184, 185
Yiike songs *(Camriəŋ Yiike)* 100–3, 108
   n.10
Yogyakarta 9, 211–13, 215–18, 220, 221,
   223
Youku 134
youth 26, 39, 42, 44, 45, 173, 181–5, 187
   n.1, 202, 213, 221
YouTube 24, 26, 51–3, 58, 59, 62, 66, 84,
   86, 88 n.8, 88 n.10, 92, 104, 105,
   114–16, 125, 126, 134, 193, 197,
   202, 228, 232, 235, 237, 239

Zain, Maher 58, 61, 62
Zhongyang guangbo shiwuju (State Central
   Broadcasting Service General
   Office) 175, 177, 187 n.2
Zhongyang renmin guangbo diantai
   (China National Radio) 181, 182,
   188 n.3
Zhou, Enlai 164
zikir 55, 56, 58

www.ingramcontent.com/pod-product-compliance
Lightning Source LLC
Chambersburg PA
CBHW072132290426
44111CB00012B/1862